Unique

The ^ Inside Guide To Washington State

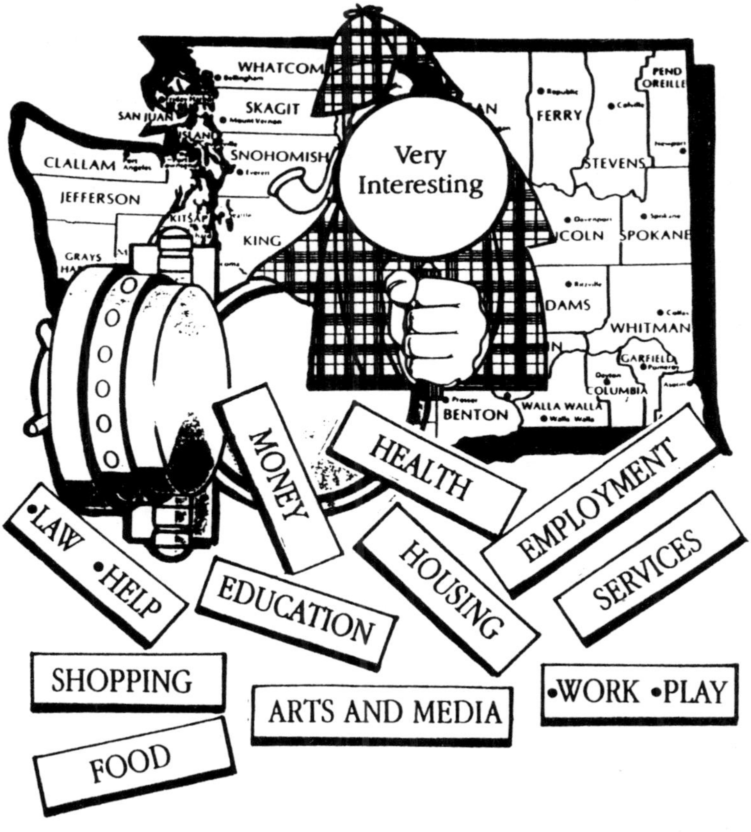

Very Interesting

LAW •HELP

MONEY

HEALTH

EMPLOYMENT

SERVICES

EDUCATION

HOUSING

SHOPPING

ARTS AND MEDIA

•WORK •PLAY

FOOD

THE EVERGREEN PRESS
"WE THRIVE ON QUALITY AND CREATIVITY"
POST OFFICE BOX 83
ELLENSBURG, WA 98926-0083
(509) 962-3078

Publisher's Cataloging in Publication
(Prepared by Quality Books Inc.)

Lewis, Charles L., 1952-
   The unique inside guide to Washington state / Charles L. Lewis. --
1st ed. --
   p. cm.
   Includes index.
   ISBN 0-9625990-2-6

   1. Washington (State)   I. Title.

F891   917.97

                                    QBI91-511

DEDICATION

This is for my colleagues, and the students of Central
Washington University.

TABLE OF CONTENTS

OVERVIEW

Symbols of Statehood...1
Environment and Livability..................................2
Geography and Climate.......................................3
Housing...4
Sports..4
Age...4
Education...5
Performing Arts...5
Other Activities..5
Washington's Economy..7
Recent Developments...8
The Future..8
Population..8
Cost of Living..9
Retirement..9
Taxes..10
Elected Officials..11
Political Parties..16
Selected Indicators by County..............................17

PART ONE

Housing.(Landlord Tenant Rights)...........................21
Employment...35
Home Business..51
Holistic Medicine..57
Education..65
Worship..75
The Media (Television, Radio, Newspapers, Movies)..........77
Legal.(Small Claims Court, Marriage).......................91
Crime..97
Consuming...101
    Washington Public Auctions............................105
    Washington's Unclaimed Property.......................106
Wine..107
Travel..111
Bed and Breakfasts..115
Museums...123
Parks...131
Washington Indians..133
Military..137
Social Service..139
1-800 Toll-Free Phone Numbers.............................147
Washington State Agricultural Facts.......................149
Washington's Counties and Seats (Map).....................150

PART TWO

SOUTHEAST REGION 153

    Adams County 158
    Asotin County 162
    Benton County 165
    Columbia County 169
    Franklin County 172
    Garfield County 176
    Whitman County 179
    Walla Walla County 182

NORTHEAST REGION 187

    Ferry County 192
    Lincoln County 195
    Pend Oreille County 198
    Spokane County 210
    Stevens County 213

NORTH CENTRAL REGION 217

    Chelan County 222
    Douglas County 227
    Grant County 231
    Okanogan County 236

SOUTH CENTRAL REGION 241

    Kittitas County 245
    Klickitat County 248
    Yakima County 252

NORTHWEST REGION 259

    Island County 265
    San Juan County 268
    Skagit County 271
    Snohomish County 275
    Whatcom County 282

SEATTLE KING REGION 287

    King 295

SOUTH PUGET SOUND REGION 323

    Pierce County 327
    Thurston County 341

SOUTHWEST REGION 347

    Clark County 353
    Cowlitz County 357

Lewis County..361
Skamania County..370
Wahkiakum County.......................................373

OLYMPIA PENINSULA.......................................377

Clallam County...383
Grays Harbor County....................................387
Jefferson County.......................................392
Kitsap County..395
Mason County...399

City-County Reference List.............................403
Books About Washington.................................407
Area Codes and Three Digit Zip Codes...................411
Airports...412
Highway Distances......................................413
Washington Ferry System................................414
Ski and Snow Reports...................................415

INDEX..416

ABOUT THIS BOOK

This book was written for Washingtonians as well as outsiders who are interested in visiting or relocating to The Evergreen State. There are many informative books that tell about Washington's colorful past; its breathtaking geography; wonderful restaurants, lodging, and things to do. Infact, many of these fine publications are listed in the Books About Washington Section of this book. This book, however, is a bit different than other books available on the Evergreen State. Some of the things listed above, are covered here, but not to the point of boring you to tears.

Unlike many other insider books, it offers the Washingtonian as much as it offers visitors to the state. Part one of this book tells about housing, employment; including how to start your own home business, education, worship, legal assistance, the media, crime statistics, public auctions, unclaimed property, social services, travel, small claims court, marriage, divorce, landlord and tenant rights, among many other informative and useful subjects.

Part two breaks the state down into nine regional sections and covers each of Washington's thirty-nine counties individually. You'll find such things as: the major cities, fairs and festivals, populations, climate, assessed value, total area, ethnic breakdowns, public school districts, hospitals, courts, crisis help services, multiple service centers, counseling and mental health services, employment and training services, family planning, food/clothing/housing assistance, health services, veterans services and a whole lot more.

There is something in this book for every individual, family, business and organization in the state of Washington, and for visitors wanting to learn more about this most "liveable" and endearing of states. I'm certain it will be of great benefit to all who reads it. Actually, it should have been subtitled:

"THE HELP BOOK."

Overview

Washington State is located in the northwest corner of the
contiguous forty-eight states between 49 degrees and 46
degrees N Latitude. It is bordered on the north by Canada,
on the south by Oregon, on the west by the Pacific Ocean,
and on the east by Idaho.

Washington has a milder climate than any other state on the
latitude due to the unique moderating influence of the
Pacific Ocean.

STATE SEAL

ENTERED THE UNION	11 November 1889, as the 42nd state
NICKNAME	The Evergreen State
MOTTO	Alki, a Chinook Indian word meaning bye and bye
CAPITOL	Olympia
AREA	Land: 66,570 square miles Water: 1,622 square miles Total: 68,192 square miles
RANK BY AREA	20th of the 50 states
POPULATION, 1990	4,761,000
RANK BY POPULATION	18th of the 50 states
POPULATION DENSITY	71.6 persons per square mile

SYMBOLS OF STATEHOOD

BIRD	Willow Goldfinch
COLORS	Green and Gold
DANCE	Square Dance
FISH	Steelhead Trout
FLOWER	Coast Rhododendron

FOLK SONG	Roll On Columbia, Roll On by Woodie Guthrie (adopted 1987)
FRUIT	Apple
GEM	Petrified Wood
GRASS	Bluebunch Wheatgrass
SHIP	President Washington
SONG	Washington My Home by Helen Davis (adopted 1959)
TREE	Western Hemlock

ENVIRONMENT AND LIVABILITY

Washington is one of America's most livable states. A variety of climates and terrains create unending recreational possibilities. In 1986, Rand McNally rated Washington State as the number one vacation spot in the United States. The state's cities and towns offer a wide range of cultural and entertaining activities, everything from sports to symphonies, along with fine dinning. Hundreds of community events dot the states calendar, including parades, rodeos, salmon derbies, festivals, and fairs. Daily living is made comfortable with numerous attractive shopping centers, modern housing, fresh air, clean water, and safe neighborhoods.

GEOGRAPHY AND CLIMATE

Washington contains seven geographic regions that have
distinct topographies, climates, natural resources and
habitation patterns. The Cascade Mountain Range bisecting
the state represents one region. The area west of the
Cascades to the Pacific Ocean is characterized by evergreen
forests, volcanic mountains, broad valleys, and natural
water formations of all types. Three geographic regions
comprise western Washington: The Puget Lowlands, the Olympic
Peninsula and Southwest Washington. Inland across the
Cascades lies level farmlands, orchards and vineyards.
Eastern Washington contains the Columbia Basin, the Okanogan
Highlands and the Blue Mountains.

The states geography features two major mountain ranges,
12.7 million square acres of forest land, and 15.8 million
square acres of farm and range land. Water covers 1,622
square miles, accounts for 2.4 percent of Washington's total
area, and includes 3,000 miles of saltwater shoreline,
hundreds of lakes as well as one of the nation's largest
river systems.

Elevations within the state range from sea level along the
shores of its many ocean beaches to 14,410 feet at the top
of Mount Rainier, one of the grandest peaks in all of North
American. Mean elevation in Washington is 1,700 feet.

Washington's overall climate is milder than any other state
at the same latitude because of the moderating influence of
the Pacific Ocean. The states weather is generally dictated
by warm, moist air masses from the Pacific Ocean moving
eastward across the state. Each time this moisture-laden air
rises over mountains, precipitation occurs and the air
becomes dryer. This process results in two general patterns
for the state.

The region west of the Cascade Mountain Range is broadly
characterized by mild winters with moderate precipitation
and warm summers with slight precipitation. East of the
Cascades, the climate generally is semi-arid characterized
by cold winters with slight precipitation and summers that
are very hot and dry.

HOUSING

Washington has experienced a substantial growth in residential construction over the last two decades. As a result, more than half of the homes in the state are less than 20 years old. Homes of this era are characterized by large, more open designs incorporating modern technology in heating, plumbing and kitchen appliances as well as energy saving construction. Since power costs have been substantially lower in Washington than in any other part of the country, over half the homes in Washington have clean electric heat and electric appliances. Many have spectacular views of snowcapped mountains, picturesque shorelines or other unique scenic vistas.

SPORTS

Washington has a full menu of major league sports with Seahawks football, Supersonics basketball, and Mariners baseball located in Seattle. College fans have numerous schools to root for. Tacoma has a team in AAA baseball while four others have Class A teams. Four cities have regular horse racing. For those who prefer to participate rather than watch, there are local baseball, softball, soccer, and bowling leagues for all ages. Swimming, tennis, raquetball, and golf (with 123 golf courses) are also popular.

AGE

Washington's population is younger than the national average. In the late 1980s the median age of Washington residents was 31.7 years. The fraction of residents under age 45 was 2.7 percent above the national average.

EDUCATION

Washington residents are among the nation's most educated.
In the late 1980s, nine out of ten Washington adults between
the ages of 25 and 64 years had completed at least 12 years
of schooling. This compares to eight out of ten for the nation
as a whole. Only one state has a higher ratio. Almost 60
percent of Washington's residents over 25 years had attended
at least one year of college, ranking Washington fifth in
the nation. Almost one in five (19 percent), had four or
more years of college eduction compared to 16 percent nation
wide.
(see sections on Eduction and Counties for addition
information)

**THE MUSEUM OF NATIVE
AMERICAN CULTURES...**
Is a five story museum
which houses the
largest collection of
Indian arts and
artifacts in the
Northwest.

PERFORMING ARTS

Washington has invested in some of the finest performing
arts facilities available anywhere. Both Seattle and Spokane
have legacies of World Fairs in 1962 and 1974 respectively,
as well as other theaters. Other cities with good facilities
include: Longview, Olympia, Tacoma, and Yakima.

Many top-caliber performing arts groups are located in
Washington. Foremost among these are the Seattle Symphony
Orchestra, which has performed in Europe; The Seattle Opera,
which features internationally famous performers; The
Northwest Chamber Orchestra, and The Pacific Northwest
Ballet. Bremerton, Bellevue, Olympia, Spokane, Tacoma,
Vancouver, Wenatchee, and Yakima also have symphony
orchestras. Port Angeles has a symphony and a light opera
group. Bellevue, Bellingham, Olympia, Spokane, and Tacoma
have chorale groups.

OTHER ACTIVITIES

Not surprisingly, residents enjoy a wide variety of water
oriented activities from boating and fishing to wind
surfing. Washington has more boats per capita than any other
state. Marinas dot the shoreline of Puget Sound.

Numerous events provide entertainment for tourist and residents alike. Many communities have annual festivals, rodeos, numerous arts and crafts fairs, etc. For details on these see a copy of **"Statewide Calendar of Events."** For kids, there is Fantasy Land in Federal Way, Never Never Land in Tacoma, zoos in Seattle, Spokane, and Tacoma, an aquarium in Seattle, and Northwest Trek. Waterslide parks have been installed in Spokane, Kennewick, Lake Chelan, Blaine, Everett, Issaquah, Federal Way, Puyallup, Tacoma, and Vancouver.

WASHINGTON'S ECONOMY

Washington's economy has become increasingly diversified in the last two decades. The major industries are aerospace with $14 billion gross income in 1986, forest products with $7 billion, food processing with $4.8 billion, and primary metals production with $2.2 billion. Agriculture is also a major contributor with $3 billion. Growth in the service and trade sectors has been so great, that non-manufacturing jobs now out-number manufacturing jobs by five to one.

Personal income in the state totalled $66.3 billion in 1986, resulting from a Gross State Product of $77.7 billion.

Unemployment rates have traditionally remained above the national average due in part to the state's strong rate of economic expansion. Im-migration occurs more rapidly during cyclical upswings in Washington than does out-migration during downswings. Large seasonal employment in major industries such as construction, forest products, fishing, agriculture, food processing, and tourist related trades also contributes to higher average unemployment levels.

HISTORICAL DEVELOPMENT

- In 1880 population of Washington was only 75,000. A number of events have taken place since then that propelled Washington into its current prominence as one of the major crossroads on the Pacific Rim. They include:

- Establishment of the state's first transcontinental railroad link in 1883.

- Gaining of statehood in 1889.

- Discovery of gold in the Klondike in 1893 resulting in Seattle becoming the primary staging and departure point for all Alaskan and Yukon shipping.

- Inauguration of Trans-Pacific steamship service to Asia in 1896.

- Construction of a series of multi-purpose dams along the Columbia/Snake River system starting in the 1930's and continuing into the 1960's. This brought irrigation to more than one million acres of desert land in eastern Washington and large-scale power generation giving Washington the lowest power rates in the nation.

- World WarII brought on the establishment of a major aluminum industry, expanded aircraft production and shipbuilding, and establishment of the nuclear industry at the Hanford facilities in eastern Washington.

As you can see a wide variety of Washington's industries were established or vastly expanded during the 1940's. Combined with the state's timber production, fisheries and dry farming, these industries created a strong diversified industrial base founded upon abundant natural resources and a skilled labor force. Combined with a strategic location and excellent deep-water harbors, Washington has become a major hub for the Pacific Rim. Two-way trade through Washington ports has mushroomed to over $33 billion annually.

RECENT DEVELOPMENTS

The economies of the United States and other industrialized nations have experienced major structural changes since the 1970's. Washington has not been immune to these changes. Employment has declined in traditional industries like agriculture, forest products, and primary metals. At the same time, sharp increases in employment have occurred in instruments, electrical and non-electrical machinery, wholesale and retail trades, and many service sector businesses.

THE FUTURE

Washington's economy will continue to diversify and expand through the end of the century. Statewide employment will grow at an average annual rate 25 percent greater than that for the nation as a whole. Recently the U.S. Department of Commerce forecasted that Washington's total employment would rise by over 30 percent in the next 15 years. During the same period, per capita personal income in the state is expected to return to levels slightly higher than the national average.

The Commerce Department also projects that Washington's industrial base will expand faster than the country as a whole. Strong growth is forecasted in durable goods manufacturing, primary metals, fabricated metals, machinery, and instruments.

The state will continue to have abundant, low-cost electric power to supply its newly emerging industries. A large pool of highly skilled workers, first class universities and research institutions, and pleasant living environments will contribute to the rapid expansion of Washington's advanced technology sectors. Industry will also benefit from the important and growing role of the state's coastal cities as transportation and distribution centers. The state's position as a center for international investment and trade reflects its strategic geographic location as well as a concerted public and private effort to serve the rapidly growing markets of Pacific Rim countries.

POPULATION

Washington's population is over 4.7 million, making it the 18th most populous state in the nation. From 1980 to 1986 the state's population increased by 7.0 percent, which was 17 percent greater than the nation as a whole. By the 2000, Washington's population is expected to exceed 5.2 million; most of this growth will occur in metropolitan areas.

COST OF LIVING

To provide a useful and reasonably accurate measure of the differences in cost of living between various cites, the American Chamber of Commerce has developed an index comparing local prices in six categories. All categories are rated against an overall national index of 100. Comparisons for selected cities are shown for the late 1980s:

	Composite Items	Grocery	Housing	Utilities	Trans-portation	Health Care	Misc. Goods & Service
Seattle	109	110	105	90	116	133	111
Spokane	104	105	101	86	98	130	108
Tacoma	102	99	110	53	97	137	110
Tri-Cities	95	100	80	76	94	133	100
Vancouver	104	115	99	69	116	129	102
Wenatchee	99	104	93	60	110	107	108
Yakima	101	100	94	92	114	127	99
Denver	109	105	137	75	110	111	102
New York	137	106	179	175	115	159	115
Phoenix	106	97	114	101	111	115	102
Salt Lake	102	101	98	95	102	103	107
San Francisco	135	108	222	56	120	151	119
St. Paul	104	92	118	95	117	109	97

RETIREMENT

Retired senior citizens living in Washington are given special benefits:

Retired persons over 61 years of age with total disposable incomes under $12,000 per year may claim exemption from all regular property tax levies on the first $28,000 valuation or 50 percent of the total valuation on their home. Those with income between $12,000 and $14,000 per year may claim exemption from all regular property tax levies on the first $24,000 valuation or 30 percent of the total valuation (up to $40,000) on their home. In addition anyone over 61, with disposable income under $18,000 per year may claim exemption from all excess property tax levies above the regular levy.

In addition to the exemption above, anyone eligible for those may elect to defer all property tax levies and assessments on their home. These will not become delinquent until the tax liens equal 80 percent of the owner equity in the property.

Persons over 70, who have lived here at least 10 years, or honorably discharged veterans over 65, who lived here 5 years, may obtain free hunting and fishing licenses. Eligible veterans also receive free salmon punch cards. Any resident over 65 may also obtain a free razor clam license.

Persons over 62, with local disposable incomes under $18,000, may apply for a yearly pass which entitles them to free admission to any state park and a 50 percent reduction in the campsite rental fee. Persons over 65 are also exempt from fees for collection of wood debris in parks for personal use.

TAXES

Washington has an uncomplicated tax system that has been in place for more than 50 years without significant change. In 1986 the total state and local tax burden ranked 17th in the nation and just slightly over the national average with $115.91 per $1,000 personal income. **There is no tax on personal income, interest, dividends, or capital gains.**

Three taxes provide most state and local revenues: the retail sales and use tax generates 45 percent; the property tax 30 percent; and the business and occupation tax 11 percent. Due to constitutional prohibition on net income taxes, non-tax revenue sources are relied on to fund many public services.

Washington's 6.5 percent state sales and use tax is levied on most retail purchases and some services. Local government add another 0.5 to 1.0 percent. In some areas local transit systems are supported with another 0.6 percent. **Groceries and medicines are exempt from sales tax.** Totals in selected cities include:

Bellevue	8.2	Bellingham	7.8	Everett	7.9
Olympia	7.9	Seattle	8.2	Spokane	7.9
Tacoma	7.8	Tri-Cities	7.8	Vancouver	7.6

Businesses and self-employed persons pay the business and occupation tax on gross income based on their activity. Rates vary from 0.484 percent for retailers and manufacturers to 1.5 percent for service occupations.

Washington's property tax is primarily a local tax collected by the counties for distribution to local school districts, county, city, and town governments, and other locally created taxing districts. The total of all regular levies is limited by the state constitution to one percent of true and fair property value. In addition, state law limits annual increases in a taxing district's regular levies to six percent. Voters may authorize special levies, which are not subject to constitutional and statutory limitations, with a 60 percent majority. Household goods and personal effects are exempt.
(see Selected indicators for property tax levies)

ELECTED OFFICIALS

		TERMS EXPIRE
GOVERNOR	Booth Gardner (D)	1/93
LT GOVERNOR	Joel Pritchard (R)	1/93
SECRETARY OF STATE	Ralph Munro (R)	1/93
STATE TREASURE	Daniel K. Grimm (D)	1/93
STATE AUDITOR	Robert V. Graham (D)	1/93
ATTORNEY GENERAL	Ken Eikenberry (D)	1/93
SUPERINTENDENT OF PUBLIC INSTRUCTION	Dr. Judith Billings (NP)	1/93
INSURANCE COMMISSIONER	Dick Marquardt (R)	1/93
COMMISSIONER OF PUBLIC LANDS	Brian Boyle (R)	1/93

STATE SUPREME COURT

ACTING CHIEF JUSTICE	James A. Anderson	1/95
JUSTICE	Robert F. Brachtenbach	1/95
JUSTICE	James M. Dolliver	1/93
JUSTICE	Barbara Durham	1/97
JUSTICE	Richard P. Guy	1/95
JUSTICE	Charles Z. Smith	1/97
JUSTICE	Robert F. Utter	1/93
JUSTICE	Fred H. Dore	1/93
JUSTICE	Charles W. Johnson	1/97

U.S. SENATORS

SENATOR BROCK ADAMS (D)
513 Hart Senate Office Bldg.
Washington, DC 20510 (202)224-2621

Washington State Office:
2988 Jackson Federal Bldg, 915 Second Ave,
Seattle 98174 (206)442-5545

Eastern Washington Office:
770 US Courthouse, W 920 Riverside,
Spokane 99201 (509)456-6816

Southern Washington Office:
702 East Evergreen Blvd, Suite 823-B,
Vancouver 98661 (206)696-7797

SENATOR **BROCK ADAMS**

·**SENATOR SLADE GORTON (R)**
730 Hart Senate Office Bldg.
Washington, DC 20510 (202)224-3441

Washington State Office:
3206 Jackson Federal Bldg, 915 Second Ave,
Seattle 98174 (206)442-0350

Southwest Washington Office:
Federal Office Bldg, 500 W. 12th St,
Vancouver 98660 (206)696-7838

Eastern Washington Office:
697 U.S. Courthouse, W. 920 Riverside,
Spokane 99201 (509)353-2507

SENATOR **SLADE GORTON**

U.S. REPRESENTATIVES

1ST CONGRESSIONAL DISTRICT

CONGRESSMAN JOHN MILLER (R)
1406 Longworth HOB, Washington, DC 20515
(202)225-6311

Washington State Office
145 Third Ave. South, Edmonds 98020

(206)672-4224

1st CONGRESSIONAL DISTRICT
JOHN MILLER

2ND CONGRESSIONAL DISTRICT

CONGRESMAN AL SWIFT (D)
1502 Longworth HOB, Washington, DC 20515
(202)225-2605

District Office: Bellingham
308 Federal Building 98225,(206)733-4500

District Office: Everett
201 Federal Building, 98201 (206)252-3188

2nd CONGRESSIONAL DISTRICT
AL SWIFT

3RD CONGRESSIONAL DISTIRCT

CONGRESSWOMAN JOLENE UNSOELD (D)
1508 Longworth HOB, Washington, DC 20515
(202)225-3536

District Office: Olympia
207 Federal Buidling, 98501 (206)753-9528

District Office: Vancouver
700 E. Evergreen Blvd, 98663 (206)696-7942

3rd CONGRESSIONAL DISTRICT
JOLENE UNSOELD

4TH CONGRESSIONAL DISTRICT

CONGRESSMAN SID MORRISON (R)
1434 Longworth HOB, Washington, DC 20515
(202)225-5816

District Office: Yakima
212 East "E" St, 98902, (509)575-9891

District Office: Tri-Cities
3311 W. Clearwater, Suite 105
Kennewick 99336 (509)376-9702

District Office: Wenatchee
23 South Wenatchee Ave, Suite 210
98801 (509)662-4294

5TH CONGRESSIONAL DISTRICT

CONGRESSMAN THOMAS J. FOLEY (D)
1201 Longworth HOB, Washington, DC 20515
(202)225-2006

District Office: Spokane, Downtown
W 601 First Ave, 2W, 99204 (509)353-2155

District Office: Spokane Valley
W. 601 First Ave, 2W, 99216 (509)926-4434

District Office: Walla Walla
28 West Main, 99362 (509)522-6370

6TH CONGRESSIONAL DISTRICT

CONGRESSMAN NORMAN D. DICKS (D)
2429 Rayburn HOB, Washington, DC 20515
(202)225-5916

District Office: Tacoma
1019 Pacific Ave, Suite 916, 98402
(206)593-6536

District Office: Bremerton
301 Great Northwest Building
500 Pacific Ave, 98310 (206)479-4011

7TH CONGRESSIONAL DISTRICT

CONGRESSMAN JIM McDERMOTT (D)
1107 Longworth HOB, Washington, DC 20515
(202)225-3106

District Office: Seattle
1809 7th Avenue, 98101 (206)442-7170

8TH CONGRESSIONAL DISTRICT

CONGRESSMAN ROD CHANDLER (R)
233 Cannon HOB, Washington, DC 20515
(202)225-7761

District Office: Bellevue
33526 160th Avenue SE, Suite 105
98008 (206)442-0116

CONGRESSIONAL DISTRICT 1: Parts of King, Kitsap and Snohomish counties.

CONGRESSIONAL DISTRICT 2: Clallam, Jefferson, Island, Mason, San Juan, Skagit and Whatcom counties. Also includes parts of Grays Harbor and Snohomish counties.

CONGRESSIONAL DISTRICT 3: Cowlitz, Lewis, Pacific, Thurston, and Wahkiakum counties. Also includes parts of Clark, Grays Harbor and Pierce Counties.

CONGRESSIONAL DISTRICT 4: Benton, Chelan, Douglas, Franklin, Grant, Kittitas, Klickitat, Okanogan, Skamania and Yakima counties. Also includes parts of Clark and Walla Walla counties.

CONGRESSIONAL DISTRICT 5: Adams, Asotin, Columbia, Ferry, Garfield, Lincoln, Pend Oreille, Spokane, Stevens and Whitman Counties. Also includes parts of Walla Walla County.

CONGRESSIONAL DISTRICT 6: Parts of King, Kitsap and Pierce counties.

CONGRESSIONAL DISTRICT 7: Part of King County.

CONGRESSIONAL DISTRICT 8: Parts of King and Pierce counties.

POLITICAL PARTIES

Communist Party
1408 18th, Seattle 98122
(206)329-9171

Democratic Party Washington State
1701 Smith Tower,
Seattle 98104
(206)583-0664

Libertarian Party of Washington
507 Third Ave #1
Seattle 98104 (206)329-5669

Republican Party Washington State
Nine Bellevue Dr #203
Bellevue 98005 (206)451-1988

Socialist Party
POB 3102, Seattle 98103
(206)632-5098

Socialist Workers Party
5517 Rainier Ave S.
Seattle 98118
(206)723-5330

SELECTED INDICATORS BY COUNTY

RANK	UNEMPLOYMENT PERCENT 1989			PERSONAL INCOME PER CAPITA (IN DOLLARS 1988)	
1	Skamania	18.8	1	Lincoln	$21,324
2	Columbia	13.4	2	King	$20,624
3	Klickitat	13.3	3	Garfield	$19,555
4	Adams	12.0	4	San Juan	$17,482
5	Okanogan	12.0	5	Snohomish	$16,568
6	Yakima	11.9	6	Columbia	$15,927
7	Franklin	11.8	7	Chelan	$15,680
8	Ferry	11.6	8	Adams	$15,413
9	Chelan	10.5	9	Walla Walla	$15,108
10	Grays Harbor	10.3	10	Kitsap	$15,067
11	Pend Oreille	10.2	11	Whitman	$15,027
12	Grant	10.0	12	Benton	$14,810
13	Pacific	9.7	13	Skagit	$14,783
14	Stevens	9.3	14	Thurston	$14,710
15	Kittitas	8.9	15	Pierce	$14,661
16	Lewis	8.9	16	Clark	$14,391
17	Douglas	8.8	17	Spokane	$14,373
18	Clallam	8.5	18	Jefferson	$14,330
19	Skagit	8.4	19	Douglas	$14,289
20	Cowlitz	8.2	20	Island	$14,276
21	Benton	7.7	21	Cowlitz	$14,192
22	Mason	7.6	22	Clallam	$14,142
23	Wahkiakum	7.5	23	Pacific	$14,120
24	Walla Walla	7.1	24	Whatcom	$13,950
25	Whatcom	6.6	25	Franklin	$13,901
26	Spokane	6.5	26	Grays Harbor	$13,852
27	Pierce	6.3	27	Asotin	$13,732
28	Thurston	6.3	28	Grant	$13,615
29	Clark	5.9	29	Wahkiakum	$13,567
30	Jefferson	5.7	30	Klickitat	$13,393
31	Kitap	5.4	31	Okanogan	$13,240
32	Asotin	5.1	32	Yakima	$13,063
33	Snohomish	4.9	33	Kittitas	$13,008
34	Lincoln	4.8	34	Lewis	$12,782
35	Garfield	4.6	35	Skamania	$12,687
36	Island	4.6	36	Mason	$12,427
37	King	4.5	37	Stevens	$11,573
38	San Juan	4.0	38	Pend Oreille	$10,656
39	Whitman	2.7	39	Ferry	$10,117
State Average		**6.2**	**State Average**		**$16,468**

NET EARNINGS PER WORKER (IN DOLLARS 1988)

1	Skamania	$32,740
2	Garfield	27,105
3	King	27,034
4	Lincoln	25,878
5	Island	25,584
6	Snohomish	25,487
7	Kitsap	25,400
8	Wahkiakum	25,049
9	Benton	24,299
10	Pierce	23,958
11	Franklin	23,273
12	Cowlitz	22,798
13	Columbia	22,759
14	Adams	22,759
15	Grays Harbor	22,277
16	Stevens	21,735
17	Thurston	21,081
18	Grant	21,058
19	Spokane	20,708
20	Clark	20,665
21	Mason	20,536
22	Lewis	20,433
23	Pacific	19,785
24	Skagit	19,665
25	Walla Walla	19,561
26	Whitman	19,535
27	Douglas	19,386
28	Whatcom	18,882
29	Chelan	18,702
30	Clallam	18,690
31	Kittitas	18,513
32	Klickitat	18,499
33	Okanogan	18,073
34	Yakima	18,041
35	Jefferson	17,370
36	Asotin	16,076
37	Ferry	14,875
38	San Juan	13,964
39	Pend Oreille	12,810
State Average		**$23,821**

PERCENTAGE OF LAND IN FARMLAND 1987

1	Whitman	%100
2	Lincoln	100
3	Adams	94.9
4	Douglas	84.9
5	Walla Walla	83.7
6	Franklin	83.1
7	Garfield	74.8
8	Asotin	67.5
9	Grant	65.1
10	Yakima	58.8
11	Benton	58.7
12	Columbia	58.1
13	Klickitat	58.0
14	Spokane	54.3
15	Ferry	54.0
16	Okanogan	39.6
17	Stevens	33.3
18	Kittitas	27.3
19	Clark	23.6
20	San Juan	15.4
21	Island	13.8
22	Thurston	12.2
23	Whatcom	9.2
24	Wahkiakum	8.8
25	Skagit	8.6
26	Lewis	7.9
27	Pend Oreille	7.0
28	Chalan	6.2
29	Snohomish	6.1
30	Pacific	6.0
31	Pierce	5.5
32	Cowlitz	5.2
33	King	4.0
34	Kitsap	3.8
35	Grays Harbor	3.6
36	Clallam	2.4
37	Mason	1.9
38	Jefferson	1.0
39	Skamania	0.6
State Average		**%37.9**

REAL PROPERTY VALUE PER CAPITA 1989				PROPERTY TAXES PER CAPITA 1989		
1	San Juan	$122,937		1	San Juan	$1,082
2	Pend Oreille	55,270		2	Lincoln	804
3	King	52,654		3	Garfield	803
4	Jefferson	49,774		4	King	664
5	Lincoln	47,453		5	Adams	580
6	Island	43,395		6	Jefferson	543
7	Mason	39,839		7	Franklin	519
8	Ferry	39,813		8	Columbia	516
9	Snohomish	39,584		9	Thurston	491
10	Cowlitz	38,247		10	Snohomish	474
11	Chelan	37,975		11	Mason	474
12	Garfield	37,954		12	Cowlitz	473
13	Whatcom	37,757		13	Skagit	471
14	Adams	37,714		14	Chelan	468
15	Skagit	36,656		15	Grant	467
16	Kitsap	33,774		16	Whatcom	466
17	Clallam	33,318		17	Pacific	463
18	Pacific	33,008		18	Pierce	446
19	Colombia	32,978		19	Douglas	429
20	Clark	32,063		20	Clark	428
21	Grant	32,063		21	Benton	425
22	Thurston	30,741		22	Whitman	421
23	Klickitat	30,629		23	Lewis	408
24	Douglas	30,295		24	Kitsap	408
25	Pierce	29,364		25	Walla Walla	408
26	Kittitas	29,120		26	Spokane	405
27	Okanogan	28,661		27	Clallam	402
28	Walla Walla	28,589		28	Island	399
29	Skamania	28,114		29	Grays Harbor	392
30	Franklin	27,824		30	Klickitat	386
31	Lewis	25,987		31	Okanogan	369
32	Grays Harbor	25,978		32	Pend Oreille	367
33	Stevens	25,727		33	Kittitas	364
34	Spokane	25,553		34	Stevens	331
35	Benton	25,372		35	Ferry	328
36	Whitman	25,261		36	Skamania	326
37	Yakima	22,534		37	Yakima	318
38	Wahkiakum	21,051		38	Wahkiakum	269
39	Asotin	19,279		39	Asotin	266
State Average		**$38,345**		**State Average**		**$506**

OFFICIAL ABSTRACT OF THE RESULTS OF THE

GENERAL ELECTION OF WASHINGTON STATE

NOVEMBER 1990

County	Registered Voters	Votes Cast	Percent Turnout
Adams	5,453	3,281	60.17%
Asotin	8,040	4,698	58.43%
Benton	53,988	37,604	69.65%
Chelan	23,863	15,279	64.03%
Clallam	28,414	20,028	70.49%
Clark	96,565	66,343	68.70%
Columbia	2,332	1,556	66.72%
Cowlitz	34,709	22,737	65.51%
Douglas	11,294	7,377	65.32%
Ferry	2,612	1,861	71.25%
Franklin	13,403	8,044	60.02%
Garfield	1,473	1,064	72.23%
Grant	22,280	15,166	68.07%
Grays Harbor	28,496	17,975	63.08%
Island	25,739	16,511	64.15%
Jefferson	11,779	8,279	70.29%
King	744,029	428,843	57.64%
Kitsap	84,035	51,633	61.44%
Kittitas	12,650	7,720	61.03%
Klickitat	7,735	5,030	65.03%
Lewis	28,171	20,260	71.92%
Lincoln	5,456	4,196	76.91%
Mason	18,801	13,067	69.50%
Okanogan	15,025	10,359	68.95%
Pacific	10,057	7,127	70.87%
Pend Orielle	4,899	3,405	69.50%
Pierce	233,331	128,026	54.87%
San Juan	7,135	5,203	72.92%
Skagit	39,734	26,566	66.86%
Skamania	3,853	2,664	69.14%
Snohomish	202,251	114,894	56.81%
Spokane	166,594	110,886	66.56%
Stevens	14,702	9,899	67.33%
Thurston	80,913	53,708	66.38%
Wahkiakum	1,983	1,566	78.97%
Walla Walla	21,194	13,215	62.35%
Whatcom	61,572	39,660	64.41%
Whitman	18,623	9,848	52.88%
Yakima	71,918	47,073	65.45%
TOTAL	2,225,101	1,362,651	61.24%

NOTES

PART ONE

NOTES

Housing

STATE MONEY FOR HOUSING

Mortgage Credit Certificate Program:
Tax credits to prospective first-time home buyers purchasing
manufactured, newly-constructed or existing homes.

Single-Family Home Ownership Program:
Below-market loans to first-time home buyers with a 5%
downpayment.

Multi-Family Program:
Financing to developers of multi-family projects where at
least 20% or more units will be rented to lower-to
mid-income persons, the elderly or the handicapped.

Congregate Housing/Retirement Service Center Program:
Construction financing for developers to produce housing for
the elderly.

Insured Home Improvement Program:
Loans to make home improvements in the City of Seattle.

For information on the above programs contact:

WASHINGTON STATE HOUSING FINANCE COMMISSION
710 Second Ave, Suite 1090
Seattle, WA 98104 (206)464-7139

URBAN HOMESTEADING

The Urban Homesteading Program
provides for the transfer of
federally-owned one-to four
family residences to communities with homesteading plans
approved by HUD. Homesteading
communities, in turn, transfer these properties for a nominal
fee, to qualified families or individuals. In qualifying
homesteaders, communities take into consideration the applicant's need for housing and ability to accomplish the
necessary repairs.

Special priority is given to applicants whose income is at
or below 80% of the median for the area. Current homeowners
are excluded.

The homesteader agrees to repair, maintain and occupy the
property for a minimum of five consecutive years. The property
must meet health and safety standards within one year and must
be brought up to local standards for decent, safe, and sanitary
housing within three years. When all requirements are met,

the homesteader receives full and clear title to the property.
Homesteading communities are required to target the program to
locally designated neighborhoods and to provide needed improvements of neighborhood services and facilities.

Washington has two **Urban Homesteading Coordinator/Cities**,
they are: Spokane, Ms. Linda Storms, Northwest Regional
Foundation, E. 525 Mission, Spokane, 99202, (509)483-4663

Yakima, Ms. Dixie Kracht, Housing Supervisor, CDBG Manager
112 South 8th Street, Yakima,98901,(509)575-6101

For general information on Urban Homesteading in Washington
contact:

HUD Field Office, Arcade Plaza
Building, 1321 Second Ave,
Seattle,98101-2054,(206)442-4521

U.S. REAL PROPERTY SALES LIST

The U.S. Real Property Sales List is published by the Federal Property Resources (FPRS) of the U.S. General Services
Administration (GSA). Operating under the authority of the
Federal Property and Administrative Services Act of 1949,
FPRS is a nationwide organization engaged in selling property
no longer need by the Federal Government. FPRS is staffed by
real estate professional and markets property in all 50
states, including Washington.

Properties vary widely in value and type. A single issue
of the U.S. Real Property Sales List may describe former Federal
office buildings, small parcels of unimproved land, high-rise
building sites in large cities, major acreage for commercial or
industrial development, and warehouses. Occasionally,
former military family housing and individual residents
confiscated by law enforcement officials may also be offered.

As a representative of all taxpayers, GSA is required by
law to obtain fair market value for any property it sells.

Generally, major properties are sold at auction, and less
expensive properties are disposed of by sealed bid.   In
either case bidders are required to place a bid deposit.

Sealed bids are made on a special bidding form.   The bids
are opened on a specific date, and the property is awarded
to the highest bidder at or above fair market value.

FPRS has four regional sales offices, therefore, the U.S.
Real Property Sales List is divided into four sections,
with sales property listed by state and city or county.
A map shows the states covered by each regional office.
FPRS also has two field offices, and some of the listing
ask you to contact these offices. For additional information on property being offered or about the real property
program, write or phone:

Office of Real Estate Sales (9DRF)
U.S. General Services Administration,
GSA Center, Room 2476, Auburn, WA
98001,(206)931-7554.

To receive the next issue of the U.S. Real Property Sales
List, or notices of future sales of individual properties
write to:

U.S. General Services Administration (9KS)
525 Market St, San Francisco, CA, 94105

LANDLORD AND TENANT RIGHTS

In Washington, a landlord-tenant agreement can be
established orally or written. A written agreement is
required only when the parties intend to create an agreement
for a year or longer. However, it is always a good idea to
get a written agreement.

A rental agreement does not have to have any special
language, it can be as simple as a handwritten letter
prepared by one or both parties. It can consist of one
document or several. Many landlords use a basic rental
agreement form and enclose a separate document that includes
detailed rules and regulations regarding the use of the
rented property. Both can be binding on the tenant.

The Landlord – means the owner, lessor, or sublessor of the
dwelling unit or the property of which it is a part, and in
addition means any person designated as representative of
the landlord.

The Tenant – a tenant is any person who is entitled to
occupy a dwelling unit primarily for living or dwelling
purposes under a rental agreement.

Types of Tenancies

Basically there are three types of tenancies:
Month-to-Month or Periodic Tenancies, tenancies for a
specified "set term" of less than one year, and tenancies
for a term of more than one year. Month-to-Month or Periodic
Tenancy has no termination date, it remains in effect until
one or both parties terminate it by written notice. It is a
Month-to-Month Tenancy if the rent is paid on a monthly
basis. It is a Periodic Tenancy if the rent payment is made
on some other regular basis.

The tenancy for a term less than a year has a preset termination date and is terminated without the requirement of a written notice. The way in which rent is paid has no bearing on the length of this kind of tenancy.

The Landlord Duties

Duties are responsibilites imposed by law. The Landlord Tenant Act (LLTA) imposes many duties upon the landlord. These duties are listed in RCW 59.18.060 of the LLTA. Following is a description of some of them:

a. <u>Premises must be fit for habitation</u> - The landlord will at all times during the tenancy keep the premises fit for human habitation.

b. <u>Compliance with all applicable laws</u> - The landlord must maintain the premises to substantially comply with any applicable code, statute, ordinance, or regulation governing their maintenance or operation, which the legislative body enacting the applicable code, statute, ordinance or regulation could enforce as to the premises rented.

c. <u>Premises must be structurally sound</u> - The landlord must maintain roofs, floors, walls chimneys, fireplaces, foundations, and all other structural components in reasonably good repair so as to be usable and capable of resisting any and all normal forces and loads to which they may be subjected.

d. <u>Common areas must be clean and safe</u> - The landlord must keep any shared or common areas reasonably clean, sanitary, and safe from defects increasing the hazards of fire or accidents.

e. <u>Infestation control</u> - The landlord must provide a reasonable program for the control of infestation by insects, rodents, and other pests at initiation of the tenancy, and control infestation during tenancy except where such infestation is caused by the tenant.

f. <u>Repairs</u> - The landlord must, except where the condition is attributable to normal wear and tear, make repairs and arrangements necessary to put and keep the premises in as good condition as it by law or rental agreement should have been, at the commencement of the tenancy.

g. <u>Keeping the premises secure</u> - The landlord must provide reasonably adequate locks and furnish keys to the tenant.

h. <u>Utilities and appliances</u> - The landlord must maintain all electrical, plumbing, heating, and other facilities and appliances supplied by him in reasonably good working order.

i <u>Keeping the premises weathertight</u> - The landlord must, maintain the dwelling unit in reasonably good weathertight condition.

j. **Removal of garbage** – The landlord must, except in the case of a single family residence, provide and maintain appropriate receptacles in common areas for the removal of ashes, rubbish and garbage, incidental to the occupancy and arrange for the reasonable and regular removal of such waste.

k. **Heat and water** – The landlord must, except where the building is not equipped for the purpose, provide facilities adequate to supply heat and water and hot water as reasonably required by the tenant.

l. **Identifying the landlord** – The landlord must designate to the tenant the name and address of the person who is the landlord by a statement on the rental agreement or by a notice conspicuously posted on the premises. The tenant shall be notified immediately of any changes by certified mail or by an updated posting. If the person designated in this section does not reside in the state where the premises are located, there shall also be designated a person who resides in the county who is authorized to act as an agent for the purposes of service of notices and process, and if no designation is made of a person to act as agent, then the person to whom rental payments are to be made shall be con-sidered such agent.

m. **Limitations on the landlord's duties** – The purpose of the landlord's duties is to provide tenants with habitable premises. There are however, two specific limitations on these landlord duties.

a). If damage is caused by the tenants, their families, or their guests, landlords are not required to make repairs.

b). Landlords cannot be penalized for not making repairs if the tenant denies their landlord access to the premises.

The Tenant's Remedies

To be able to obtain a remedy to a complaint, the tenant must satisfy some requirements, and take several procedural steps. They are:

a. **Paying the rent** – The tenant shall be current in the payment of rent before exercising any of the remedies accorded him under the provisions of the LLTA. Provided, that this section shall not be construed as limiting the tenant's civil remedies for negligent or intentional damages: Provided further, that this section shall not be construed as limiting the tenant's rights in an unlawful detainer proceeding to raise the defense that there is no rent due and owing.

b. **The tenant must first give notice** – If the tenant is current in his rent and utility payments and wants to file a complaint, he must first give the landlord notice of his complaint. The notice must:

1). It must be written

2). It must include the address or location of the premises.

3). If known it should contain the name of the owner of the property.

4). It should describe and list what is required of the landlord.

5). It should be delivered to the landlord, his agent, or the person who collects the rent.

These steps must be followed closely; keep a copy of it for your records.

How long does the landlord have to reply?

Depending upon the nature of the tenant's complaint, the landlord has varying time frames for making a response. The LLTA states:

For the purpose of this chapter, a reasonable time for the landlord to commence remedial action after receipt of such notice by the tenant shall be, except where circumstances are beyond the landlord's control:

1). Not more than twenty-four hours where the defective condition deprives the tenant of water or heat or is imminently hazardous to life.

2). Not more than forty-eight hours, where the landlord fails to provide hot water or electricity.

3). Subject to the provisions of subsections (1) and (2) of this section, not more than seven days in the case of repair under RCW 59.18.100 (3).

4). Not more than thirty days in all other cases. In each instance the burden shall be on the landlord to see that remedial work under this section is completed with reasonable promptness. Where circumstances beyond the landlord's control, including the availability of financing, prevent him from complying with the time limitations set forth in this section, he shall endeavor to remedy the defective condition with all reasonable speed.

What if the landlord does not respond?

If, after waiting the above time periods and the landlord does not respond, the tenant can take possible actions:

1). He can terminate the rental contract.

2). He can make the necessary repairs himself and deduct their cost from the rent payment.

The Tenant's Duties

The Landlord-Tenant Act has two sides to it; one for the landlord of which we have already discussed, and one for the tenant, which we will cover here.

a.   __Paying rent and complying with the laws__ – The tenant's
duties are covered in RCW 59.18.130, where they are arranged
in six subsections. The section begins with the following
requirement:

Each tenant shall pay the rental amount at such times and in
such amounts as provided for in the rental agreement or as
otherwise provided by law and comply with all obligations
imposed upon tenants by applicable provisions of all
municipal, county, and state codes, statutes, ordinances,
and regulations.

b.   __Keeping the premises clean__ – Subsection (1) states, the
tenant must keep that part of the premises which he occupies
and uses as clean and sanitary as the conditions of the
premises permit.

c.   __Removing garbage and fumigating__ – Subsection (2) states,
the tenant must properly dispose from his dwelling unit all
rubbish, garbage and other organic or flammable waste, in a
clean and sanitary manner at reasonable and regular inter-
vals and assume all costs of extermination and fumigation
caused by the tenant.

d.   __Using utility fixtures and appliances properly__ –
Subsection (3) states, the tenant must properly use and
operate all electrical, gas, heating, plumbing, and other
fixtures and appliances supplied by the landlord.

e.   __Tenants must not harm the premises__ – Subsection (4)
states, the tenant must not intentionally or negligently
destroy, deface, impair, or remove any part of the structure
or dwelling with the appurtenances thereto, including the
facilities, equipment, furniture, furnishings, and
appliances, or permit any member of his family, invitee,
licensee, or any person acting under his control to do so.

f.   __Tenants must not use the premises for any improper__
__purpose__ – Subsection (5) states, the tenant must not
permit a nuisance or common waste. The term "nuisance" and
"waste" are legal words, they relate to using the premises
in an illegal manner or in a way that would be destructive
to the property. For instance, if illegal drugs were being
sold out of the premises, this would be against state and
federal law.

g. __Returning the premises in good condition__ – Subsection (6)
states, that the tenant must, upon termination and vacation,
restore the premises to their initial condition except for
reasonable wear and tear or conditions caused by failure of
the landlord to comply with his obligations under this chapter:
Provided, that the tenant shall not be charged for normal
cleaning if he has paid a nonrefundable cleaning fee.

The Landlord's remedies

If the tenant does not adhear to the above duties, the

landlord can: 1). Force the tenant to perform them or, 2). terminate the rental agreement and evict the tenant.

The landlord must give notice

As with tenants, a landlord must take certain preliminary steps to remedy his complaints. First the landlord must notify the tenant. The notice requirement must include:

1). The notice must be written.

2). The notice must be addressed to the tenant and describe in detail the landlord's complaint and the actions he wants the tenant to take to rectify it.

3). It must be delivered to the tenant within a reasonable time after the deficiency has been discovered.

4). The notice will be effective for 60 days after it has been received by the tenant.

How soon must the tenant reply?

Unlike the landlord, the tenant must not just begin the directed action(s), but must completely finish it within the allotted time. The reasonableness of the allotted time depends upon the nature of the condition. The tenant has 30 days to correct a condition that:

1). Has the possibility of causing substantial adverse health or safety hazards to the tenant or others.

2). Greatly increases the hazards of fire or accident that can be eliminated by repairs, replacement of a defective item, or cleaning.

What if the tenant does not reply?

If the tenant fails to respond as requested, the landlord can take the following actions:

1). Make the repairs himself, but at the expense of the tenant.

2). Start legal action to motivate performance or collect damages.

3). Evict the tenant from the premises.

Terminating a Month-to-Month Tenancy

Either the landlord or the tenant can terminate a month-to-month tenancy by giving notice of termination. The notice must be in writing and state the date the tenancy is to end. The termination date and the date the notice is delivered must be 20 days or more before the end of the monthly pay period.

Security and Damage Deposits

The Landlord Tenant Act recognizes two types of deposits: **Security Deposits** and **Damage Deposits**. Neither deposit can be collected by the landlord prior to two conditions being met. First, the deposit and conditions under which it is being held must be described in writing in a rental agreement. Second, the landlord must furnish the tenant with a written checklist specifying the condition and cleanliness of the housing at the beginning of the tenancy. It is required that both the landlord and the tenant sign and date this checklist, and the tenant given a copy for his/her records.

A damage deposit may only be used to repair damages to the premises that the tenant caused either negligently or intentionally.

A security deposit is used to ensure that the tenant will satisfy the obligations described in the rental agreement. The deposit may not be kept upon termination of the tenancy unless there was a written agreement between the landlord and tenant, stating under what conditions the landlord could keep the deposit.

The LLTA also requires that the landlord keep all deposits in a bank or savings and loan institution. The landlord must give the tenant a receipt for the deposits and written notification of the name and address of the institution holding the deposit.

After the tenant has vacated the premises, the landlord must send the tenant a notice that the deposit or a portion of it will be kept. This notice must be sent within 14 days after the tenant has moved and it must give a "complete and specific statement" of why the deposit was kept.

Right to enter the tenant's premises

The LLTA provides tenants a limited right of privacy. It reads as follows:

1. The tenant shall not unreasonably withhold consent to the landlord to enter the dwelling unit in order to inspect the premises, make necessary or agreed repairs, alterations, or improvements, supply necessary or agreed services, or exhibit the dwelling unit to prospective or actual purchasers, mortgagees, tenants, workmen, or contractors.

2. The landlord may enter the dwelling unit without consent of the tenant in case of emergency or abandonment.

3. The landlord shall not abuse the right of access or use it to harass the tenant. Except in the case of emergency or if it is impractical to do so, the landlord shall give the tenant at least two days notice of his intent to enter and shall enter only at reasonable times.

4. The landlord has no other right of access except by court order, arbitration, or by consent of the tenant.

State law prohibiting discrimination

In the state of Washington, it is against the law to discriminate in housing based on "race, creed, color, national origin, sex, martial status, age, or the presence of any sensory, mental or physical handicap." The state law includes the selling, renting, and advertising of real estate. Complaints must be filed with in six months after the alleged act of discrimination. The State Human Rights Commission investigates all complaints and makes preliminary findings.

APARTMENT FINDING AND RENTAL SERVICES

APARTMENTS UNLIMITED, INC.
405 W Heron, Aberdeen 98520
(206)533-1533

G & O ENTERPRISES
709½ W Market, Aberdeen
98520 (206)532-2101

STOR-MORE SELF-SERVICE
Storage, 1802 A St SE,
Auburn 98002 (206)939-8200

APARTMENT DATE CENTER
1240 118th NE, Bellevue
98004 (206)623-8670

GREATER SEATTLE GUIDE
405 114th Ave SE #204
Bellevue 98004 (206)454-4431

EBRIGHT-WIGHT INC, REAL
ESTATE, 1401 Iowa,
Bellingham 98226
(206)733-7944

FAIRHAVEN REALTY, INC
1100 11th, Bellingham 98225
(206)647-0753

GRAY MANAGEMENT COMPANY
1240 Humboldt, Bellingham
98225 (206)671-1572

KITSAP HOME RENTAL SVCS
607 High, Bremerton 98310
(206)373-1194

REAL PROPERTY MANAGEMENT
1242 NE Riddle Rd
Bremerton 98310
(206)479-2944

TALL FIRS ESTATES
1014 N Scheuber Rd
Centralia 98531
(206)736-8610

BAYVIEW APARTMENTS
1835 S 216th, Des Moines
98198 (206)824-8597

BOARDWALK APARTMENTS
22027 6th S, De Moines
98198 (206)878-1439

WHISPERING BROOK APARTMENTS
23407 16th Pl S, De
Moines 98198 (206)824-9343

APARTMENT AND HOME RENTALS
511 Valley Mall Pkwy
East Wenatchee 98802
(509)884-1018

CHEEKWOOD APARTMENTS
2222 S 234th, Kent 98032
(206)824-3228

HUNTINGTON WOOD APARTMENTS
2136 S 272nd, Kent 98032
(206)946-1000

CLEARVIEW RENTALS
1010 Douglas, Longview 98632
(206)577-0899

GPS INVESTMENTS
787 Douglas, Longview 98632
(206)425-5678

HANIO BOOKKEEPING/RENTAL
2185 35th, Longview 98632
(206)577-1430

LONGVIEW AGENCY, INC.
2119 32nd Ave, Longview
98632 (206)577-8220

PACIFIC PROPERTY SVCS
1406 Tennant Way, Longview
98632 (206)423-5759

CHURCHILL & ASSOC RLTRS
Oak Harbor 98277
(206)675-0715

CENTURY 21 OCEAN SHORES
Point Brown Ave NE
Ocean Shores 98589
(206)289-2458

APARTMENTS UNLIMITED, INC.
115 McCormick NE, Olympia
98506 (206)754-7082

BODINE SCREENING & LEASING
203 E 4th #507, Olympia
98501 (206)357-8565

HARRISON PARK APARTMENTS
2900 Limited Ln NW, Olympia
98502 (206)754-8239

APARTMENTS WEST
NE 1325 Valley Rd, Pullman
99163 (509)332-8622

ASSOCIATES BROKERS, INC.
S 405 Grand, Pullman 99183
(509)334-0562

PALOUSE EMPIRE RENTAL/REALTY
N 1045 Grand Ave, Pullman
99183 (509)334-4663

PULLMAN PROPERTY MGMT
N 130 Grand Ave, Pullman
99183 (509)334-9791

WILRU APARTMENTS
SE 1815 Bleasner Dr, Pullman
99183 (509)332-5631

ADVANCE MANAGEMENT
4131 11th NE, Seattle 98105
(206)632-9050

BALLARD REALTY, INC.
1700 NW Market, Seattle
98107 (206)784-2482

CANTERBURY COURT
2600 NE 195th, Seattle 98155

(206)367-1770

CAPITOL HILL RENTAL SVCS
918 15th E, Seattle 98112
(206)447-1705

CARLSTROM APARTMENTS
4225 11th NE, Seattle 98105
(206)632-7343

EXECUTIVE APARTMENT RENTAL
300 10th, Seattle 98122
(206)447-9138

FOREST CREEK APARTMENTS
19708 15th NE, Seattle 98155
(206)361-9198

GREENLAKE SOUTH SHORE APTS.
5520/5530 E Green Lake Way N
Seattle 98103 (206)547-7385

OLYMPIC VIEW APARTMENT
16700 31st S, Seattle 98188
(206)246-3319

R&W INVESTMENTS, INC.
2815 2nd, Seattle 98121
(206)441-6821

SANDHURST APARTMENTS
7239 Sand Point Way NE
Seattle 98115 (206)522-2604

SEAHURST APARTMENTS
1101 SW 139th, Seattle 98166
(206)242-1292

SPACE FINDERS, INC.
300 Vine #16-B, Seattle
98121 (206)728-8500

SUNPOINTE APARTMENTS
6901 Delridge Way SW
Seattle 98106 (206)762-7884

VALLEY VIEW APARTMENTS
4708 S 154th, Seattle 98188
(206)244-6567

STOR-MORE SELF-SERVICE
Storage, 14803 Pacific Ave
Spanaway 98387 (206)538-8200

COMPUTERIZED THE RENTAL
E 28 Indiana, Spokane 99207
(509)327-6684

INLAND NORTHWEST RENTALS
W 222 Mission #208, Spokane
99201 (509)325-4853

RW DICKERSON MANAGEMENT & CO
E 28 Indiana, Spokane 99207
(509)327-1228

ABODES HOME & RENTAL FINDERS
9611 Gravelly Lake Dr SW
Tacoma 98499 (206)581-1789

DOBLER MGMT COMPANY
3012 S 47th, Tacoma 98409
(206)475-2405

ERA NORTHWEST PROPERTIES
9527 Bridgeport Way SW
Tacoma 98499 (206)584-3633

MAGNUSON MANAGEMENT, INC.
908 Broadway #300, Tacoma
98402 (206)572-4900

NORTHGATE VILLAGE
3615 112th SW, Tacoma 98499
(206)582-0052

NORTHWEST AFFILATED
7320 6th Ave, Tacoma 98406
(206)564-6681

OAK TERRACE APT HOMES
42 Thunderbird Pkwy SW
Tacoma 98498 (206)588-5616

REDMOND PROPERTY MANGRS.
3815 100th SW, Tacoma 98499
(206)582-0261

REEDER MANAGEMENT, INC.
11300 Bridgeport Way SW
Tacoma 98499 (206)584-6732

UNITED HOMES
8018 Pacific Ave, Tacoma
98408 (206)475-8683

PARK REGION HOMES
3201 E 33rd, Vancouver
98681 (206)694-5485

PLACES TO LIVE
1908 Main, Vancouver 98660
(206)699-5332

COLDWELL BANKER
113 2nd, Wenatchee 98801
(509)662-3663

MILLER REALTY
213 N Mission, Wenatchee
98801 (509)663-7154

WENATCHEE MANPRHOUSE APT
801 Idaho, Wenatchee 98801
(509)662-3818

WENATCHEE QUAD APTS
1250 Central, Wenatchee
98801 (509)663-1522

RENTAL SERVICE OF YAKIMA
314 N 6th Ave, Yakima 98902
(509)452-8224

relocation services

CENTURY 21 SMITH/RING
1215 120th NE, Bellevue
98004 (206)455-9600

COMMERCIAL RELOCATION
1075 Bellevue Way NE Box 493
Bellevue 98009 (206)455-1138

PAT EGECK RELOCATION
1409 140th Pl NE, Bellevue
98005 (206)644-4540

WORLDWIDE RELOCATION, INC.
40 Lake Bellevue Dr,
Bellevue 98005 (206)451-0344

ALL POINTS PROPERTIES
1550 NE Riddell Rd,
Bremerton 98310
(206)479-6760

CENTURY 21 KELLY DAVIS
298 S Main #101, Colville
(509)684-2121

VANGUARD REALTY, INC.
29500 Pacific Hwy S
Federal Way 98003
(206)941-7770

MERIDIAN VALLEY REALTY, INC.
13306 SE 240th, Kent 98042
(206)631-1222

RELOCATION NORTHWEST
2955 Both SE #103
Mercer Island 98040
(206)236-1500

CENTURY 21 BJ & MOUNTGOMERY
1200 Sims Way, Port Townsend
98368 (206)385-3305

BAKER APARTMENTS
700 E Mercer, Seattle 98102
(206)323-5909

BETA WEST PROPERTIES
601 University #2801,
Seattle 98101 (206)623-1844

JAMES ALBRIGHT REALTY
2106 NE 65th, Seattle 98155
(206)524-4200

JAMES BLEDSOE & COMPANY
POB 99466, Seattle 98199
(206)286-9229

MAC PHERSON'S INC RLTRS
12733 Lake City Way NE
Seattle 98125 (206)367-2088

NDS RELOCATION CONSULTANTS
1001 4th Ave #3200, Seattle
98154 (206)621-9774

NORTHWEST CENTER-INFORMATION
1836 Westlake N, Seattle
98109 (206)283-2739

ANTHONY BAKER & BURNS
S 150 Stevens, Spokane 99204
(509)747-6091

COMPUTERIZED THE RENTAL CO.
E 28 Indiana, Spokane 99207
(509)327-6684

SUNSHINE BROKERS, INC.
N 1000 Argpmme Rd, Spokane
99212 (509)928-4172

BROOKSIDE REALTY, INC.
7301 NE Hwy 99, Vancouver
98665 (206)699-4835

Apartment
For
Rent

Employment

FINDING A JOB

The Washington State Employment Security Department has more job listings in more occupational categories than any other single source in the state. Job placement services are available through a statewide network of approximately 30 Job Service Centers (JSCs) and their satellite offices. The JSCs operate computerized job matching systems. At the push of a button, JobNet will match your skills to the jobs for which you're qualified. No fee is charged for their service in helping you find a job.

In addition to placement services, the JSCs have local, state and national labor market information. Career counseling and aptitude/proficiency testing are also available. They also offer services for people with special needs; such as veterans, older workers or persons with disabilities.

WANT ADS

Another course worth exploring are the employment advertisements appearing in newspapers, trade magazines and professional journals. Don't delay with want ads; check them the moment they appear. If you see a promising ad, follow up on it immediately. Follow directions. If the ad says "call", call; if it says "appear in person", appear, don't call.

CIVIL SERVICE

A civil service job means working for the city, county, state or the federal government. Check with civil service agencies in your area. They are the sources of information regarding a wide range of professional, technical, clerical, crafts or service jobs in government. Jobs are filled on a merit basis as determined by the results of examinations and ratings of experience and education. No fees are charged.

PRIVATE EMPLOYMENT AGENCIES

You may want to try using the services of a private employment agency in you job search. Agencies charge a fee to either the applicant or the employer, or both, when a job placement is made.

OTHER SOURCES

Make a list of possible employers by using the telephone book or a business or industrial directory from your chosen locality to get the names, addresses and telephone numbers of organizations you feel can use your talents. Check with the Chamber of Commerce for any employer lists they might have.

YOUR RESUME

A resume is a personal inventory of you for submittal to a prospective employer. It tells what you have to offer him or her. It is a job-hunting tool, a personal cataloging of your qualifications. It "gets you on paper," briefly and accurately for the prospective employer to see.

Its main function is to secure an interview with an employer. It tells:

WHO ARE YOU?

WHAT YOU KNOW?

WHAT YOU HAVE DONE

WHAT KIND OF WORK YOU WANT

WHY YOU SHOULD BE HIRED.

PREPARING YOUR RESUME

The first step in preparing your resume, is to list your job assets under these headings:

WORK EXPERIENCE

WORK HISTORY

EDUCATION

PERSONAL CHARACTERISTICS

RESOURCES

This list will become the basic data you will use in developing your resume, so evaluate yourself realistically, and in terms of the job you are seeking. Try to put yourself in the place of the employer. If you were in his or her place, what would you want to know?

I. WORK HISTORY

List all your employment. Ask yourself the following questions about each job:

- a. What was my job title?
- b. What were the details of my job duties?
- c. Why was I hired for the job?
- d. What did I like about the job? Why?
- e. What did I dislike about the job? Why?
- f. What part of the job did I do best? Why?
- g. What part least well? Why?
- h. What experience did I gain that I can apply to another job?
- i. What special skills or talents did I develop on the job?

j. How long did I work on the job?
k. Why did I leave the job?
l. What references can I obtain, if necessary?
m. What personality factors helped make me successful on the job?

II. EDUCTION

This should be emphasized if you have had little or no work experience.

a. Schools attended, dates.
b. Courses taken, degrees, dates.
c. Subjects liked best, and why.
d. Subjects liked least, and why.
e. Subjects excelled in, grades, honors.
f. Extracurricular activities, athletics, debating clubs, etc.
g. Scholarships, honors.
h. Special skills; typing, stenography, business machines, computers, etc.

III. PERSONAL CHARACTERISTICS

Evaluate your personal characteristics for their job significance. Be as objective as possible. Weigh both your assets and possible liabilities. An honest appraisal may help you to determine where your strongest vocational interests lie.

IDENTIFYING DATA

Name
Address
Date of birth
Marital status (including number of dependents)

PHYSICAL DATA

Height and weight
Health and physical capacities

APPEARANCE (and personal grooming)
SPEECH
  Vocabulary
  Grammar
Enunciation
Pronunciation

SOCIAL CONDUCT AND ATTITUDES
  Aggressiveness
  Adaptability
  Tact
  Cheerfulness
  Reticence
  Tolerance
  Cooperativeness
  Mannerliness

IV. RESOURCES

List all possible resources; i.e., leads, sources of information, contacts and aids, which you may want to use in planning your job seeking campaign.

> a. Firms that may have the kind of job you are seeking.
> b. Business associates.
> c. Personal friends and acquaintances.
> d. School friends and instructors
> e. Employment agencies; public, private and school.
> f. Professional organizations.
> g. Trade directories.

IMPORTANT POINTERS

Try to limit your resume to one page. Use active verbs (i.e., supervised, managed, constructed, developed).

Always use the first person.

Make the resume visually pleasing. Don't let it look crowded, and be sure it is well-organized, clear and easy to read.

Be concise. List only the vital statistics. Other information can go on the application.

Sell yourself. Your skills can help enhance the organization and solve problems. Your achievements prove it.

Type your resume on a "good" grade of letter-sized paper.

Ambition

Following is a list of **Job Service Centers** located within the state. Contact the center nearest you for assistance in finding a job.

Aberdeen	2700 Simpson Avenue
Auburn	2707 "I" Street NE
Bellevue	13133 Bel-Red Road
Bellingham	216 Grand Avenue
Bingen	114 West Steuben
Bremerton	4980 Auto Center Way
Colville	161 South Wynne Street
Cowlitz County	711 Vine Street, Kelso
Ellensburg	521 Mountain View Road
Everett	840 Broadway North
Interstate	1063 Capitol Way, Olypmia
Lakewood	4908 - 112th St. SW, Tacoma
Lewis County	2015 NE Kresky Road, Chehalis
Lynnwood	6606 - 196th Street SW
Moses Lake	506 West Broadway
Mount Vernon	320 Pacific Place
North Seattle	12550 Pacific Place
Okanogan	1234 South Second
Olympia	5000 Capitol Blvd.
Port Angeles	1601 East Front Street
Rainier	2531 Rainier Ave. S., Seattle
Renton	1000 Index Avenue NE
Spokane	South 130 Arthur
Sunnyside	800 East Custer
Tacoma	1313 Tacoma Avenue South
Tri-Cities	3900 W. Court Street, Pasco
Vancouver	603 West Evergreen Blvd.
Walla Walla	215 Bridge Street
Yakima	306 Division Street

SATELLITES

Folks	516 - 5th Avenue SW
Long Beach	601 South Oregon
Newport	418 South Scott Avenue
Port Townsend	1030 Lawrence Street
Pullman	South 405 Grand
Raymond	515 Third Street
Shelton	256 West "K" Street

Following is a list, by county, of the largest employers in each of Washington's thirty-nine counties. This would be an excellent place to start in your search for employment in the Evergreen State.

ADAMS

COMPANY	PRODUCT	1990 EMPLOYMENT
1. Carnation	Agricultural processing	556
2. McCain Foods	Agricultural processing	550
3. Harvest Fresh	Agricultural processing	110
4. Pacific Produce Inc	Agricultural processing	63
5. Seneca Foods	Apple juice concentrate	61
6. Evergreen Implé.	Farm machinery	35
7. Lind Grange Supply	Fertilizer	15
8. Berger and Company	Agricultural processing	15
9. Land 'O Lakes	Feed processing	14

ASOTIN

COMPANY	PRODUCT	1990 EMPLOYMENT
1. Clarkston Schools	Public schools	225
2. Tri State Hospital	Hospital	120
3. Guy Bennet Lumber	Lumber, pulp, chips	75-100
4. POE Asphalt	Construction	10-100
5. Albertsons	Grocery store	75
6. Duckworth Boats Inc	Aluminum jet boats	23
7. Contempo	Commercial cabinetry	17
8. Pay 'N Pak	Retail home improvement store	17
9. Western Industrial Fiberglass	Septic tanks, piping	14
10. Drug Fair	Pharmacy/variety	12

BENTON

COMPANY	PRODUCT	1990 EMPLOYMENT
1. Western Hanford (includes BCSR)	Research, nuclear waste management, computers	8,200
2. Battelle Northwest	Research	3,000
3. WPPSS (Supply Sys)	Electricity	1,500
4. Kaiser Engineers	Research	830
5. Advance Nuclear	Nuclear fuels	800+
6. Lamb-Weston	Processed potatoes	600
7. Twin City Foods	Frozen potato products	480
8. Sandvik Spe. Metals	Alloys, tubing	325

CHELAN

	COMPANY	PRODUCT	1990 EMPLOYMENT
1.	Aluminum Company of America	Aluminum smelter	850
2.	Central Washington Hospital	Health care	850
3.	Chelan County PUD	Power/water	725
4.	Wenatchee Valley Clinic	Health care	394
5.	Wenatchee Public Schools	Education	386
6.	Triple C Convalescent Center	Health care	383
7.	County of Chelan	Government	320
8.	Wenatchee Valley College	Education	300
9.	Eastmont Public Schools	Education	250
10.	Asamera Minerals	Mining	180
11.	Tree Top	Food processor	175
12.	City of Wenatchee	Government	172

CLALLAM

	COMPANY	PRODUCT	1990 EMPLOYMENT
1.	ITT Rayonier	Chemical cellulose	450
2.	Daishowa America	Paper	325
3.	Rogerson Hiller Cp	Aviation products	165
4.	K-Ply	Plywood	150
5.	Battle Marine Lab	Marine research	65
6.	Portac	Lumber	50
7.	Sea Farm Washington	Pen-reared salmon	40
8.	Northwest Technical	Explosive bond alloys	25
9.	Olympic Synthetic	Stree-engineered web slings	10

CLARK

	COMPANY	PRODUCT	1990 EMPLOYMENT
1.	James River Corp	Pulp and paper	2,000
2.	SEH America	Silicon wafers	1,060
3.	Hewlett-Packard	Computer printers	875
4.	Vanalco	Aluminum	681
5.	Frito Lay	Food products	500
6.	Columbia Machine	Machinery	500
7.	Bosie Cascade	Pulp and paper	450
8.	Kyocera Northwest	Ceramic products	400
9.	Bemis	Multi-wall bags	370
10.	Jantzen	Clothing	355

COLUMBIA

	COMPANY	PRODUCT	1990 EMPLOYMENT
1.	Dayton Gen. Hosp.	Health services	109
2.	Green Giant/ Pillsburt	Can asparagus	70
3.	Columbia Cutstock	Wood for window frames	40
4.	Amer. Line Builder	Overhead power line	25 (+120 seasonal)
5.	Columbia Gran	Market & store grain/seed	11 (+ 10 seasonal)

COWLITZ

	COMPANY	PRODUCT	1990 EMPLOYMENT
1.	Weyerhaeuser Co. (Longview)	Lumber, wood products, exports, pulp, paper, chemicals	2,426
2.	Longview Fiber Co.	Paper & allied products	2,074
3.	Reynolds Metals Co	Aluminum ingots	955
4.	NORPAC	Newsprint	400
5.	J.H. Kelley Co.	Piping installation and fabricators	370
6.	Tollycraft	Fiberglass boats	276
7.	RSG Forest Prods.	Fir lumber & cedar fencing	260
8.	Reynolds Metals Co	Electrical division	237
9.	The Daily News	Newspaper	150
10.	Shurman Machine	Machinery for forest prods.	145

DOUGLAS

	COMPANY	PRODUCT	1990 EMPLOYMENT
1.	Welch Applies	Fruit	135
2.	Silicon Metaltech	Metal alloys	108
3.	Hind-Wells, Inc.	Sportswear	32
4.	Northern Fruit Co	Fruit	22 FT/200 PT

FERRY

	COMPANY	PRODUCT	1990 EMPLOYMENT
1.	Vaagen Brothers Lumber Co	Lumber	160
2.	Hecla Mining	Gold, silver	125
3.	Echo Bay Mining	Gold	175
4.	Brauner Lumber Co	Lumber	40
5.	Pope and Talbot	Lumber reload	25
6.	Inchelium Tribal Wood Treatment Plant	Wood treating	15

FRANKLIN

COMPANY	PRODUCT	1990 EMPLOYMENT
1. Universal Frozen Foods	French fries	600
2. Burlington Northern	Transportation	350
3. Lamb-Weston	Processed potatoes	350
4. Fresh Pak Sales	Fruit	83 (+150 seasonal)
5. Douglas Fruit Co	Fruit	71 (+ 30 seasonal)
6. Columbia Basin Fruit Paking	Fruit packing	50
7. Americold	Cold storage	50
8. Transtate Asphalt	Asphalt, paving	50
9. L&N Feeders	Livestock	40
10. Wilber Ellis	Ag chemicals, fertilizers	36

GARFIELD

COMPANY	PRODUCT	1990 EMPLOYMENT
1. Robert Dye Seed Ranch, Inc	Grass, small grain seed	25
2. Pomeroy Grain Growers	Stores grain	16
3. Ferd Herres Chevrolet/Farm	Cars, machinery, parts	16
4. General Tractor and Implement	Farm equipment, sales repair	10
5. Western Farm Ser.	Chemicals, fertilizer	10
6. Pomeroy Warehouse and Feed Co	Grain storage, feed	9
7. McGregor Company	Chemical fertilizers	7
8. Pomeroy Grange Supply	Hardware, chemicals, farm supplies	

GRANT

COMPANY	PRODUCT	1990 EMPLOYMENT
1. Lamb Weston, Inc	Food processing	525
2. Carnation Co	Food processing	450-500
3. Columbia Foods	Food processing	300
4. Basic Amer. Foods	Food processing	240
5. Advanced Silicon	Polysilicon	216
6. Simplot	Frozen vegetables	200
7. Sundstrand Data	Circuit boards	83
8. Witco Chemical	Filters, pozzolan	80
9. Western Kraft	Corrugated boxes	79

GRAYS HARBOR

	COMPANY	PRODUCT	1990 EMPLOYMENT
1.	Weyerhaeuser Co.	Logs, lumber, wood chips, pulp, paper, tree growing	1,400
2.	Lamb-Grays Harbor	Forest products, processing equipment	527
3.	ITT Rayonier	Pulp, chemicals, cellulose	450
4.	Simpson Door	Doors	385
5.	Grays Harbor Paper	Pulp, paper products	325
6.	Mayr Brothers	Lumber products	185
7.	Ocean Spray	Cranberries, cranberry juice	180
8.	Hoquiam Plywood	Plywood	141
9.	Mary's River Lumb.	Plywood	120
10.	Pacific Veneer	Veneer	80

ISLAND

	COMPANY	PRODUCT	1990 EMPLOYMENT
1.	Technical Services	Printed circuit boards	127
2.	Nichols Brothers	Steel & aluminum boats, marine structures	70-130
3.	Whidbey Press, Inc	Printing & publishing	45
4.	Upchurch Scientific	Research equipment	40
5.	Interstate Label	Price marking equipment	20
6.	Waterman Mill	Timber products	15
7.	Bunker	Refrigerator magnets	14
8.	Whidbey Cabinets	Kitchen cabinets	11
9.	Norfloat	Plastic net buoys	7
10.	Teleview Corp	Alarms systems/electronics	5

JEFFERSON

	COMPANY	PRODUCT	1990 EMPLOYMENT
1.	Port Townsend Paper	Paper, pulp converted products	397
2.	Allen Log	Lumber, chips, contract logging	100
3.	Coast Oyster Co	Aquaculture, oysters	85
4.	Admiral Marine Inc	Fiberglass boat building, repair	75
5.	Gary Phillips Log.	Contract logging	54
6.	Bluewater Farms	Aquaculture/salmon	25
7.	New Day Fisheries	Fish processing	25
8.	Port Townsend Boat	Boat building, repair	24
9.	Thermionics N.W.	Scientific instruments	19
10.	Halco Fence & Sup.	Lumber	16
11.	Port Townsend Shipwright's	Boat repair	15
12.	Cadillac Meter Co.	Industrial meters	12
13.	Skookum Marine	Fiberglass boat building, repair	12

KING

COMPANY	PRODUCT	1990 EMPLOYMENT
1. Boeing Company	Aircraft and parts	103,000
2. PACCAR, Inc	Heavy equipment, trucks	4,500
3. Weyerhaeuser Co	Forest products, HQS	4,348
4. Esterline Corp	Automated equipment	3,100
5. Microsoft Corp	Microcomputer software	3,000
6. Criton Technologies	Airplane parts, building	3,000
7. Seattle Times	Daily Newspaper	2,300
8. Sunstrand Data Control	Flight systems	2,300
9. Wright Schuchart	Prefab building	1,500
10. Gai's French Baking Company	Bakery	1,500

KITSAP

COMPANY	PRODUCT	1990 EMPLOYMENT
1. Puget Sound Naval Shipyard	Ship repair	12,672
2. Pope & Talbot	Forest products	250
3. Bremerton Sun Publishing	Newspaper publishing	230
4. Kitsap Newspapers	Weekly newspapers	132
5. Aro Glass	Glass	90
6. Watson Furniture	Wood and metal furniture	70
7. Fred Hill Material	Sand, gravel, concrete	50
8. Connolly Skis	Wet suits	25

KITTITAS

COMPANY	PRODUCT	1990 EMPLOYMENT
1. Twin City Foods	Frozen food processing	100
2. Shoemakers	Vents/registers	88
3. Superior Packing	Lamb processing	(300 in season)
4. Ellensburg Cement	Cement products	(40+ seasonal)
5. Ellensburg Daily Record, Inc	Newspaper	40
6. Cle Elum Lake	Plywood veneer	38
7. Zach-lift	Towing equipment	25
8. Schaake Packing	Feed lot	20
9. Washington Beef	Beef processing	15

KLICKITAT

COMPANY	PRODUCT	1990 EMPLOYMENT
1. Columbia Aluminum	Aluminum ingots	639
2. SDS Lumber Company	Lumber	350
3. Bingen Plywood Co	Plywood	85
4. Log Processing, Inc	Logging	11
5. Natures Pine Furn.	Furniture	1

LEWIS

COMPANY	PRODUCT	1990 EMPLOYMENT
1. Centralia Mining Co	Coal	758
2. National Frozen Fds	Frozen fruits/vegetables	250-550
3. Cowlitz Stud	Wood products	250
4. Muduline	Prefabricated homes	195

LINCOLN

COMPANY	PRODUCT	1990 EMPLOYMENT
1. Lincoln County	Government	130
2. Odessa Mem. Hosp.	Medical	70
3. Wilber Schools	Education	50
4. Odessa Schools	Education	41
5. Odessa Trading Co	Farm equipment	28

MASON

COMPANY	PRODUCT	1990 EMPLOYMENT
1. Simpson Timber Co	Timber	963
2. Certified Aerospace	Aerospace parts	340
3. Douglas Fir	Christmas trees	100
4. Taylor United, Inc	Shellfish	98
5. Manke Lumber Co	Logging and hauling	93
6. Skookum Lumber Co	Lumber and sliding	85
7. Olympia Wood Prod.	Lumber	60
8. Olympia Oyster Co	Shellfish	48
9. Barnes Machine	Aerospace parts	45

OKANOGAN

COMPANY	PRODUCT	1990 EMPLOYMENT
1. Omak Wood Products	Wood products	560
2. Brewster Heights Pk	Fruit processing	290
3. Magi	Fruit packing	275
4. Spokane Lumber	Wood products	180
5. Advance Nuclear	Nuclear fuels	800+

PACIFIC

COMPANY	PRODUCT	1990 EMPLOYMENT
1. Weyerhaeuser Co	Lumber, wood chips	295
2. Jessie's Ilwaco Fish Co	Fish, crab, shrimp	200-250
3. Coast Oyster Co	Fresh and frozen oysters	100-250
4. Ea1lt Point Seafood	Oysters, shrimp, crab	195
5. Jolly Rogers	Oysters	102
6. Pacific Hardwoods	Lumber	65
7. Chinook Packing Co	Fish, crab, shrimp	60-80
8. Ocean Spray Cranberries	Cranberry cooperative	31-105

9. Nelson Crab	Oysters, crab, shrimp	25-50

PEND OREILLE

COMPANY	PRODUCT	1990 EMPLOYMENT
1. Ponderay Newsprint	Newsprint	160
2. Vaagen Brothers Lumber Co	Lumber, wood chips	115
3. Public Utility #1	Electricity	55
4. Ponderay Valley Fibre, Inc	Wood chips	12
5. Seattle City Light	Electricity	23
6. Excel Boats	Aluminum boats	10
7. Inland Power/Light	Electricity	10

PIERCE

COMPANY	PRODUCT	1990 EMPLOYMENT
1. Tribune Publishing	Newspapers	800
2. Nalley's Fine Food	Food products	700
3. Simpson Tacoma Kraft	Paper products	650
4. Peterson's Fryer	Chickens	500
5. National Semiconductors	Semiconductors	450
6. Atlas Foundry and Machine Co	Castings	395
7. Buffelen Woodworks	Wood products	377
8. Kaiser Aluminum	Aluminun	365
9. Tacoma Boat Build.	Boats	453

SAN JUAN

COMPANY	PRODUCT	1990 EMPLOYMENT
1. J.J. Theodore Co	Fish processing	120
2. Friday Harbor Sand and Gravel	Gravel pit	18

SKAGIT

COMPANY	PRODUCT	1990 EMPLOYMENT
1. Texaco, Inc	Oil & gas products	348
2. Shell Oil Co, Inc	Oil & gas products	314
3. Dakota Creek	Boats	220
4. Sedro Woolley Lumber	Dimension lumber	140
5. Specialty Seafoods	Seafoods	140
6. Custom Plywood	Plywood sheeting	130
7. Concrete N.W.	Concrete products	128
8. Sugiyo U.S.A., Inc	Analouge seafood	100+
9. Bates Abrasive	Grinding wheels	74
10. Goodyear Nelson	Dimension lumber	44

SKAMANIA

COMPANY	PRODUCT	1990 EMPLOYMENT
1. Thermal Laminates	Sailboard manufacturer	16
2. Advanced Hull Dyn.	Sailboard manufacturer	15
3. Scottco	Maine cranes	15
4. Windsurfing Hawaii	Sailboard manufacturer	3

SNOHOMISH

COMPANY	PRODUCT	1990 EMPLOYMENT
1. The Boeing Company	Aircraft assembly	25,000
2. G.T.E. Northwest	Communications	2,900
3. John Fluke Manuf.	Electronics equipment	2,850
4. ELDEC Corporation	Electronic instruments	1,500
5. Advanced Tech-nologies Lab	Medical equipment	1,400
6. Bayliner Marine	Boats	1,370
7. Scott Paper Co	Paper products	1,300

SPOKANE

COMPANY	PRODUCT	1990 EMPLOYMENT
1. Kaiser Aluminum & 2. Chemical Corp	Primary aluminum, aluminum Electronic keyboards & other optical scanning devices	2,989 1,776
3. Hewlett-Packard	Signal generator, modulation analyzers & microwave test equipment	899
4. Cowles Publishing	Daily newspapers	873
5. ISC/Bunker-Romo	Teller terminal & software	620
6. Itron, Inc.	Automatic utility meter readers	518
7. Columbia Lighting	Fluorescent light fixtures	500
8. Central Pre-Mix Concrete	Concrete, concrete products	375
9. Bayliner Marine	Boats	350
10. Sun Runner Marine	Boats	250

STEVENS

COMPANY	PRODUCT	1990 EMPLOYMENT
1. Northwest Alloys	Magnesium products	503
2. Boise Cascade Corp	Lumber	380
3. Vaagen Brothers Lumber	Lumber	200
4. Plum Creek Lumber	Lumber	175
5. Colmac Industries	Coils, dry cleaning equip.	111
6. K-L Manufacturing	Garments	85
7. Valley Wood Prod.	Studs	80
8. L-Bar Products	Refining	54
9. Aladdin Steel	Wood stoves/fireplace inserts	34

| | | 10. Chopot Lumber Co | Lumber | 30 |
| 11. Panorama Wood Prod | Wood/cutstock | 30 |

THURSTON

COMPANY	PRODUCT	1990 EMPLOYMENT
1. Pabst Brewing Co	Malt beverages	450
2. Hardel Mutual Plywood Corp	Softwood plywood	250
3. Continental Can	Cans	245
4. The Olympian	Newspapers	198
5. Hytec/Lasco	Fiberglass bathroom supplies	150
6. U.S. Intelco	Communications/software	145
7. Ostroms Mushrooms	Mushroom processing	130
8. Weyerhaeuser Co	Containers	124
9. Georgea Pacific	Shipping containers	120
10. IRECO	Explosives	120
11. Rudel Products	Bindery	120

WAHKIAKUM

COMPANY	PRODUCT	1990 EMPLOYMENT
1. Jerry DeBriae Logging Co	Logging	25
2. Cavenham Managed Forests	Forest management	12
3. Dandy Digger & Sup	Post-hole diggers	10
4. Elochoman Millwork	Kitchen cabinet doors	10
5. Wahkiakum County Eagle	Newspaper and printing	5
6. J&M Chipping and Sorting	Logging chipping	5
7. W.G. Computer Sup	Anti-Static Dust Covers	3

WALLA WALLA

COMPANY	PRODUCT	1990 EMPLOYMENT
1. Iowa Beef Process.	Meat packers	1,450
2. Amer. Fine Foods	Canned vegetables	250-700
3. D&K Frozen Foods	Frozen vegetables	200-500
4. Boise Cascade	Pulp, kraft paper, corru. boxes	512
5. Key Technology	Automated food processing eq	300
6. Strauser Manuf.	Millwork products	140
7. Nelson Irrigation	Irrigation sprinkler heads	140
8. Continental Can Co	Cans	130
9. Broetje Orchards	Cold storage/apple processing	130
10. Western Fab/Finish	Matal fab. products	125
11. Louisiana Pacific	Lumber	115
12. Martin Archery	Archery products	109

WHATCOM

	COMPANY	PRODUCT	1990 EMPLOYMENT
1.	Intalco Aluminum	Aluminum ingot	1,300
2.	Georgia-Pacific	Pulp and paper	840
3.	ARCO	Oil refinery	450
4. 5.	Bellingham Frozen Foods	Food processing	400
6.	British Petroleum	Oil refinery	300
7.	Mt. Baker Plywood	Plywood	240
8.	Heath-Tecna Aerospace	Airplane composite components	200
9.	Allsop Inc	Plastics	160

WHITMAN

	COMPANY	PRODUCT	1990 EMPLOYMENT
1.	McGregor Company	Fertilizer/chemical	188
2.	Wilber/Ellis	Fertilizer/chemical	99
3.	Schweitzer Engineering	Mfg. electrical, ag consulting	55
4.	Palouse Industries	Contract labor/assembling pack.	44
5.	Whitman Company Growers Inc	Ag marketing, storing	24
6.	Schweitzer Engr.	Electric power devices	21
7.	Colfas Gazette	Publish newspapers	20
8.	Bush Distributors	Fuel distribution	20
9.	J.E. Love Company	Ag implements;nursery equip.	18
10.	Wallace Grain Pea	Processing peas and lentils	12
11.	Segner Grain	Processing; ag consulting	11

YAKIMA

	COMPANY	PRODUCT	1990 EMPLOYMENT
1.	Stadelman Fruit	Fruit/vegetable processor	1,500
2.	Del Monte Corp	Canned fruits	550
3.	Washington Beef	Beef and beef by-products	500-600
4.	Boise Cascade	Lumber and plywood	450

Home Business

STARTING A HOME BASED BUSINESS

In these times, it's becoming increasingly difficult to get by or make ends meet with just one source of income. Thus, more and more people are investigating the possibilities of, and indeed the idea of starting their own extra-income business-es. Most of these part-time endeavors are started and operated from the comfort and privacy of these people's homes.

Most of these individuals are making the extra money they need --some have wisely and carefully built these extra income efforts into fulltime, very profitable businesses--while some are just keeping busy, having fun, and enjoying life as never before. The important thing is that they are doing something they enjoy and at the same time putting extra income into their pockets.

The fields of mail order selling, multi-level marketing, and in-home party sales have never been more popular. If any of these kinds of extra-income-producing ideas appeal to you, then for sure, you own it to yourself to check them out. But, these are not the only fields of endeavor you can start and operate from home with little or no investment and learn as you go.

If you type, you can start a home-based typing service; if you have a truck or access to a trailer, you can start a clean-up/hauling service; simply collecting old newspapers from your neighborhood can get you started in the paper re-cycling business; more than a few enterprising housewives have found success and fortune by starting home and/or apartment cleaning services; if you have a yard full of flowers, you can make good extra money by supplying fresh-cut flowers to restaurants and offices in your area on a regular basis; or perhaps turn a ceramics hobby into a lucrative personalized coffee mug business. Really, there's literally no end to the ways in which you can start and operate a profitable extra-income home-based business.

The first thing you must do is some basic market research... find out for yourself, first-hand, just how many people there are in your local area who are interested in your proposed product or service, and would be willing to stand in line and pay money for it. This is known as defining your market and pinpointing your customers. If after checking around, talking about your idea with a whole lot of people over a period of one to three months, you get the idea that these people would be paying customers, than your next step should be directed toward the "detailing" of your business plan. The more precise and detailed you write out such a plan--covering all the bases relating to how you'll do everything that needs to be done, than the easier it's going to be for you to attain success. Such a plan should show your start-up investment needs, your advertising plan, your production costs as well as procedures; your sales program, and how your time will be allocated. Too often, enthusiastic and ambitious entrepreneurs start an extra-income project and suddenly find that the costs are beyond their abilities, and the time requirements more than they can meet. It pays to lay it all out on paper before you get involved, and the more detailed you can "see" everything before you start, the better your chances of success.

Here is the most important "secret" of all, relating to starting and building a profitable home-based business. Regardless of what kind of business you start, you must have the capital and the available time to sustain your business through the first six months of operation on the basis of not taking in any money. Most importantly, you must not count on receiving or spending any money coming in from your business on yourself or for your bills during those first six months. Any and all the income from your business during the first six months should be reinvested in the business in order for it to grow and reach your planned first year goal.

Once you're by that first six-month milestone, you can set up a small monthly salary or draw for yourself, and begin enjoying the fruits of your labor--but the first six months of operation for any business is very critical, so do not plan to use any of the money your business generates for yourself.

TYPES OF BUSINESS STRUCTURES

Sole Proprietorship
This is the business structure most often chosen by home-based businesses. It is a one-owner business with less formality and fewer legal restrictions than other business forms. The proprietor is responsible for business debts that may exceed his or her total investment, and this liability extends to all the proprietor's assets.

General Partnership
A business composed of two or more persons who share in the profits, loses, and management of the business. Each partner is personally liable for partnership debts, and terms of the partnership are generally formalized in a written agreement.

Limited Partnership
A business composed of one or more general partners who share full liability and one or more limited partners who share the profits but whose liability is limited to the extent of their investment. Limited partners may take no part in running the business. Limited partnerships in Washington must file a Certificate of Limited Partnership with the Office of the Secretary of State.

Corporation
A business made up of persons who have requested and received a state charter recognizing the corporation as a separate entity with its own rights, privileges, and liabilities apart from those of the individuals. Corporations may be for profit or for non-profit (religious, social, charitable, educational, etc.) purposes. One or more persons may form a Washington corporation by filing articles of incorporation with the Office of the Secretary of State.

LEGALITIES AND TAX ADVANTAGES

If you live in an area zoned as "residential only," your proposed business could be illegal. In many areas, zoning restrictions rule out almost all home businesses that involve the coming and going of customers, clients or employees other than members of the family. Many businesses that sell or even store things for sale on the premises also fall into this category.

Be sure to check with local officials to see how the zoning ordinances in your area may affect your business plans. You may need a special permit to operate your business from your home.

Many communities grant home occupation permits for business-es that involve typing, sewing and teaching, but turn thumbs down on requests from photographers, interior decorators and those who want to run home-improvement businesses from their homes. Sometimes, even if you are permitted to use your home, there are other restrictions that complicate your hopes.

Off-street parking for customers could be a part of the re-quirements of your business permit; signs are generally for-bidden in residential districts; and if you teach, there's almost always a limited on the number of students you can have a any one time.

Obtaining zoning approval for your business could be a simple matter of filling out an application, or it could involve a public hearing. The important points the "approving officials" will think about is how your business will affect the neigh-borhood. Will it increase in noise--and how will your neigh-bors feel about your business among their homes?

Check into the zoning restrictions, and then check again, to determine if you're going to need a city license and have to collect sales taxes on your transactions.

Licensing can be an involved process, and depending on your type of proposed business, it could even involve the inspect-ion of your home to determine that it meets with the local health, building and fire codes. Should this be the case, you'll have to bring your facilities up to the local code standards.

The state of Washington offers a number of services that will assist you in understanding and meeting federal, state, and local registration and licensing requirements. One-stop business registration is now available by stopping by any one of the 50 offices of the Wasghington State Department of Re-venue, Labor and Industries, Employment Security, Licensing, or the Secretary of State, or by telephoning the Business License Center toll-free (see ASSISTANCE section). A single application form is all that is needed to satisfy the licen-sing and registration requirements of these five state agencies.

Also available through the Business License Center is a

Licensing Guide Sheet. Prepared for your unique business operation, the guide indicates all licensing requirements for your business and gives addresses and phone numbers of offices in your community that can serve you.

TAXES AND RECORDKEEPING
The IRS is going to treat the part of your home you use for business as though it were a separate piece of property. This means that you'll have to keep good records and take care not to mix business and personal matters. No specific method of recordkeeping is required, but your records must clearly justify any deductions you claim.

You can begin by calculating what percentage of the house is used for business, either by number of rooms or by area in square footage. Thus if you use one of five rooms for your business, the business portion is 20 percent. If you run your business out of a room that's 10 by 12, and the total area of your home is 1,200 square feet, the business-space factor is 10 percent. An extra computation is required if your business is a home day-care center--one of the exempted activities in which the exclusive-use rule doesn't apply. Check with your tax preparer and the IRA for an exact determination.

If you're a renter, you can deduct the part of your rent which is attributable to the business share of your house or apartment. Homeowners can take a deduction based on the depreciation of the business portion of their house.

Another very good way to trim your taxes is by setting up a Keogh plan or an Individual Retirement Account. With either of these, you can shelter some of your home business income from taxes by investing it for retirement.

In addition to outlining licensing requirements, the Washington Business License Center will send you a copy of the publication Operating a Business in Washington which provides a very useful outline of federal, state, and local taxes that relate to the particular structure and nature of your business.

ASSISTANCE

STATE OF WASHINGTON

Department of Licensing
Business License Center
405 Black Lake Blvd.
Olympia, WA 98504
1-800-562-8203

**Department of Trade and
Economic Development**
Business Assistance Center
919 Lakeridge Way, Suite A
Olympia, WA 98504
1-800-237-1233 (In state)
(206)586-3021

Office of Secretary of State
Corporations and Tradmark
Division, 500 A State Office
Bldg., MB-1, Air Industrial
Park, Olympia, WA 98504
(206)753-7115

**Department of Employment
Security,** Business Resource
Network, 212 Maple Park,
KG-11, Olympia, WA 98504
1-800-233-6267 (206)753-5211

**Community Revitalization
Team,** Department of
Community Development
Ninth & Columbia Bldg.,GH-51
Olympia, WA 98504
(206)753-4900

FEDERAL OFFICES

**U.S. Federal Information
Center,** 915 2nd Ave, Seattle
98174 (206)442-0570
For tax assistance and
information: 1-800-424-1040

**U.S. Small Business
Administration,** 915 Second
Ave., Seattle 98174
(206)442-5534

SUPPORT AND NETWORKS

**Northwest Cottage Industry
Network Association**
7512 126 St, E.
Puyallup, WA 98373
(206)841-1731

Home Business Network
POB 9358
Spokane, WA 99209
(509)326-5427

**National Alliance of
Home-Based Businesswomen**
POB 506, Midland Park, NJ
07432 (201)423-9131

SMALL BUSINESS DEVELOPMENT CENTERS

ABERDEEN

Grays Harbor College
Aberdeen, WA 98520
(206)532-9020

BELLINGHAM

Western Washington Univ.
College of Business & Econ.
417 Park Hall, Bellingham
98225 (206)676-3899

COLVILLE

165 Hawthome
Colville, WA 99114-2698
(509)684-4571

LONGVIEW

1600 Maple
Longview, WA 98632
(206)577-3402

MOSES LAKE

Big Bend Community College

28th & Chanute
Moses Lake, WA 98837-3299
(509)762-5351

MT. VERNON

Skagit Valley College
2405 College Way
Mt. Vernon, WA 98273
(206)428-1282

OLYMPIA

100 Plum, POB 1427
Olympia, WA 98507
(206)753-5616

OMAK

Wenatchee Valley College
POB 2058
Omak, WA 98841
(509)826-4901

PULLMAN

Washington State University

441 Todd Hall
Pullman, WA 99164-4740
(509)335-1576

SEATTLE

Business Enterprise Center
Seattle Community Colleges
2620 Rainier Ave. So.
Seattle, WA 98144
(206)721-2026

180 Nickerson, Suite 310
Seattle, WA 98109
(206)464-5450

Small Business Export
Finance Assistance Center
312 First Ave. No.
Seattle, WA 98109
(206)464-7123

SPOKANE

Freeway Plaza Building
Suite 150, Spokane 99204
(509)456-2781

TACOMA

300 Sea-First Financial
Center, 950 Pacific Ave.
Tacoma, WA 98402
(206)272-7232

Pierce College
9401 Farwest Dr, SW
Tacoma, WA 98498
(206)964-6646

TRI-CITIES

TRIDEC
901 N. Colorado
Kennewick, WA 99336
(509)735-6222

VANCOUVER

Columbia River EDC
100 Columbia Way
Vancouver, WA 98661
(206)693-2555

WENATCHEE

Grand Central Building
25 N. Wenatchee Ave.

Wenatchee, WA 98801
(509)664-2536

YAKIMA

303 E. D St, Suite 2
Yakima, WA 98901
(509)575-2284

© 1981 VOLK

Holistic Medicine

ACUPUNCTURE

A Chinese method of treating disease or producing anesthesia by inserting sterilized metal needles into the subcutaneous layer of the skin at any of 800 specific points. It has been used for over 5000 years to treat disease; only since the late 1950's it has been used as an anesthetic.

According to ancient Chinese belief, acupuncture works by balancing the body's negative (yin) and positive (yang) life forces, which become unbalanced sickness and pain. All the organs of the body are said to be either yin or yang and the energy of life flows between yang and yin via a number of channels, called meridians, lying between the skin. By inserting needles at specific points along these channels, the balance of yang and yin can be restored. Once in place, the needles are twirled by hand or stimulated electrically.

One theory used to explain acupuncture's pain-killing effects is that it stimulates the brain, and causes it to release endorphin, a natural body opiate.

HOMOEOPATHY

This works on the principle of "like curing like." Over 200 years ago a German doctor; Samuel Hahnemann, observed that the symptoms produced by giving quinine to a healthy human subject were similar to those of the malaria it was used to treat. This led to the discovery that minute doses of lethal substances could be used to stimulate the body's healing responses.

Experimenting on himself, he went on to discover that the smaller the dose, the more powerful the effect--and that highly diluted substances containing no molecules of the original medicine, were the most profound acting of all.

Since then over 2000 poisonous and medicinal plants, and animal substances have been taken by humans in a series of studies. Results were meticulously recorded to establish a "drug picture" which is used to match a set of symptoms present in a sick person. Homoeopathy treats the person instead of the disease. In selecting the correct remedy, a "character picture" must be drawn up, taking into account physical symptoms, mental states, habits, reactions to environmental conditions, etc. There is no set remedy that can be used in every case of a particular disease.

REFLEXOLOGY

This is based on the idea that nerve endings in the feet and hands relate directly to different organs of the body. Finger and thumb pressure, accompanied by a massaging motion, are applied to the relevant zone (see diagram) for both diagnosis and treatment. The zones and degree of pressure needed are very precise. Pressure is continued for 20 minutes per zone, and should remain the same the same whichever part of the foot it's applied to. To massage a point, rotate the finger (clockwise) without losing contact. Reflexology is claimed to be particularly successful in treating congestive disorders like sinusitis, constipation, etc.

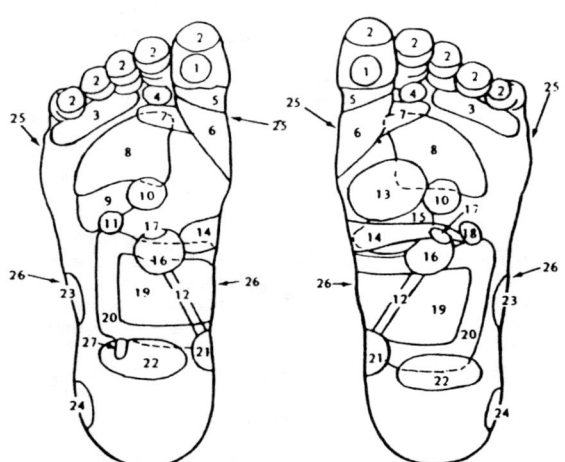

Massage Points: 1. pituitary gland 2. sinuses; top of head 3. ears 4. eyes 5. neck 6. thyroid 7. bronchial tubes 8. lungs 9. liver 10. solar plexus 11. gall bladder 12. kidney tubes 13. heart 14. pancreas 15. stomach 16. kidney 17. adrenal glands 18. spleen 19. small intestine 20. large intestine 21. bladder 22. sex glands; organs 23. hip 24. knee 25. shoulder line 26. waist line 27. appendix.

ACUPUNCTURE (ACUPUNCTURISTS)

VAN GELDER IAN
901 8th, Anacortes 98221
(206)293-4718

STEPHEN MORRISSEY
1370 116th Ave NE #106
Bellevue 98004 (206)454-9727

TIMOTHY J. LAMB
316 E McLeod Rd, Bellingham
98225 (206)647-0900

PAULA L. BROWN CERTIFIED
1903 D St, Bellingham 98225
(206)734-9500

JACK R. SHUPE
2301 Elm, Bellingham 98225
(206)647-7688

ACUPUNCTURE ACUPRESSURE CTR
1425 NE Franklin Ave
Bremerton 98310
(206)373-4991

CENTER
514 E Woodin, Chelan 98816
(509)682-5911

EAST WEST ACUPUNCTURE PAIN
127 E Inter City Ave #2
Everett 98208 (206)348-0585

NATURAL HEALING CLINICS
2613 N Stevens, Tacoma
98407 (206)752-2555

PAIN & HEADACHE MED CLINIC
7525 Custer Rd W, Tacoma
98467 (206)472-8272

K.K. LAU
301 W Lee, Tumwater 98501
(206)786-0111

ACUPUNCTURE CLINIC
1412 NE 88th, Vancouver
98665 (206)574-4074

HEROLD E. SMITH
601 E 22nd, Vancouver 98663
(206)695-1131

DIANE EGGLESTON
382 Wyatt Way NE, Winslow
98110 (206)842-0553

HOLISTIC PRACTITIONERS

CENTERINPOINT CLINIC
111 103rd NE, Bellevue 98004
(206)454-1787

BERNARD WOODROW
4156 Guide Meridian
Bellingham 98226
(206)671-4242

DR MARGOT J. POSS CLINICAL
Herald Bldg #306, Bellingham
98227 (206)678-8418

FAIR HAVEN HOLISTIC
1200 Harris Ave #412
Bellingham 98225
(206)671-4710

FOX THERAPEUTIC MASSAGE
1712 D St, Bellingham 98225
(206)734-7488

MOUNT BAKER HOLISTIC HEALTH
2301 Elm, Bellingham 98225
(206)647-7688

MARY MULLEN
119 N Commercial, Bellingham
98225 (206)671-3199

DAVID PARKE
Herald Bldg #620, Bellingham
98225 (206)671-2054

PAULA L. BROWN CERTIFIED
1903 D St, Bellingham
98225 (206)734-9500

PAM ROBERTS
1903 D St, Bellingham 98225
(206)678-8449

LAURA A. SHELTON
1321 King St, Bellingham
98226 (206)734-1580

STRESS RELEASE CENTER
1419 N State, Bellingham
98225 (206)847-2703

SARAH E. SAXTON
914 7th, Clarkston 99403
(509)758-2936

HEALING ARTS CENTER
North Beach Rd, Eastbond
98245 (206)376-4002

GERALD COSBY
Federal Way Medical Center
Federal Way 98003
(206)839-8578

SAN JUAN HOLISTIC HEALTH
42 1st St, Friday Harbor
98250 (206)378-5744

NAN K. LOPEZ
499 Rainer Blvd N
Issaquah 98027 (206)392-2201

EASTSIDE WELLNESS CENTER
143 Park Ln, Kirkland 98033
(206)827-4467

NW HOLISTIC HEALTH CENTER
4324 Martin Way E #B
Lacey 98506 (206)438-2882

RUTH ADELE
2617-B 12th Ct SW #6
Olympia 98502 (206)352-7880

RADIANCE HERBS & MASSAGE
113 E 5th, Olympia 98501
(206)357-9470

DENNIS SKLAR
1115 Black Lake SW, Olympia
98502 (206)754-8576

INNER HARMONY HOLISTIC
2516 Bethel Rd SE

Lynnwood 98037 (206)776-4888

DONALD BUTTERFIELD
1910-5 Riverside Dr
Mt Vernon 98273
(206)424-3460

MUKILTEO CHIROPRACTIC
610 5th, Mukilteo 98275
(206)355-3433

ACUPUNCTURE
113 E 5th, Olympia 98503
(206)357-9470

ACUPUNCTURE & BODYWORK
1722 Harrison Ave NW
Olympia 98502 (206)786-1195

OCEAN SHORES CLINIC
1722 Harrison Ave NW
Olympia 98502 (206)352-3435

OLYMPIA ACUPUNCTURE
406 Lilly Rd #8, Olympia
98507 (206)754-3857

CLEVE HENRIOUES
516 W Margaret, Pasco 99301
(509)547-9611

IRVIN H. MILLER
1640 Barr Rd, Port Angeles
98362 (206)457-1515

ALEX HOLLAND
210 Polk, Port Townsend
98368 (206)385-4383

ACUPUNCTURE CENTER
315 Morris S, Renton 98055
(206)255-5800

GLEN P. HUNG
4300 Talbot Rd S, Renton
98055 (206)226-4950

K. K. LAU
4361 Talbot Rd #103
Renton 98055 (206)271-0950

YANG I-YEN
1110 Goethals, Richland
99352 (509)943-1175

ACUPUNCTURE & CHINESE HERBS
2611 NE 125th, Seattle 98125
(206)364-5000

ACUPUNCTURE & FAMILY HEALTH
3110 NE 125th, Seattle 98125
(206)367-3400

ACUPUNCTURE & NEUROSCIENCE
7030 35th Ave NE, Seattle
98115 (206)527-2431

ACUPUNCTURE ASSOCIATION
1141 NW Market, Seattle
98107 (206)789-1768

ACUPUNCTURE CENTER
3304 Beacon S, Seattle
98144 (206)467-6749

ACUPUNCTURE COLLEGE
1141 NW Market, Seattle
98107 (206)789-1290

ACUPUNCTURE CTR-SEATTLE
859 S Jackson, Seattle
98104 (206)621-7501

ACUPUNCTURE OF W SEATTLE
3208 45th SW, Seattle 98116
(206)932-8762

ACUPUNCTURE/NATUROPTHIC
2705 E Madison, Seattle
98112 (206)328-7929

BASTYR COLLEGE NATURAL
HEALTH, 1408 NE 45th,
Seattle 98105 (206)632-0354

CHINESE ACUPUNCTURE CTR
1021 NE 125th, Seattle 98125
(206)367-3242

CHIOUG CHU-LAN SUZANNE
1914 N 34th #204, Seattle
98103 (206)545-7860

KIM KRULL
W 508 6th #212, Spokane
99204 (509)624-1465

GIL MILNER
W 1704 11th, Spokane 99204
(509)747-6401

HI LEE YOUNG
E 17 Empire, Spokane 99207
(509)328-3430

CHINESE ACUPUNCTURE CENTER
7905 Steilacoom SW, Tacoma
98498 (206)581-4111

A. W. IMKAMP
30620 Pacific Hwy S
Federal Way 98003
(206)839-1433

HIROYA OKAWA
700 S 320th, Federal Way
98003 (206)946-0140

NORTHERN HEALTH MASSAGE
3314 Rosedale St
Gig Harbor 98335
(206)851-7951

ACUPUNCTURE/ACUPRESSURE CTR
85 NW Alder Pl, Issaquah
98027 (206)392-7449

MARK A. IMLAY
24825 148th SE, Kent 98042
(206)630-1910

K. K. LAU
11107 Kent-Kangley Rd
Kent 98031 (206)854-8880

HIRPYA OKAWA
412 8th S, Seattle 98104
(206)682-1251

ALEX HOLLAND
2701 1st #420. Seattle 98121
(206)441-3270

STEVE MARTINEZ
1523 E Madison, Seattle
98122 (206)328-8645

MARK H. HOLTING
8540 Greenwood N, Seattle
98103 (206)783-5114

NORTHWEST CENTER FOR
HOLISTIC
4072 8th NE
Seattle 98105 (206)547-9665

SUSAN SCOTT
5312 Roosevelt Way NE
Seattle 98105 (206)525-8015

SEATTLE ACUPUNCTURE
ASSOCIATES
525 Minor, Seattle 98104
(206)622-0246

SEATTLE INS-CHINESE MEDICINE
1914 N 34th #204, Seattle
98103 (206)545-3530

MARIAN SMALL
1523 E Madison, Seattle
09122 (206)322-4416

ANN WALTZ
706½ E Denny Way, Seattle
98122 (206)328-2703

WU HSING HEALTH CENTER
416½ E Harrison, Seattle
98102 (206)323-7708

DANIEL ZIZZA
324 15th E #201, Seattle
98112 (206)329-5468

CLEARWATER MEDICAL DENTAL
CENTER
18122 State Rd 9, Snohomish
98290 (206)668-6519

LINDA & BEN HOLE MD
S 906 Cowley, Spokane 99202
(509)747-2902

EAST WEST ACUPUNCTURE
N 2302-C Argonne Rd, Spokane
99212 (509)924-6852

EASTSIDE NATUROPATHIC CLINIC
607 Market, Kirkland 98033
(206)822-3716

NATUROPATHIC PHYSICIANS
CLINIC, 11417 124th Ave NE
Kirkland 98033 (206)822-4145

AU MASSAGE
926 Commerical, Leavenworth
98826 (509)548-4420

CAROL J. CONLON
20102 Cedar Valley Rd
Lynnwood 98038 (206)776-5353

ZEN SHIN DO SHIATSU
18421 44th Ave W

Port Orchard 98388
(206)895-3229

THOMAS F. BALLARD
5312 Roosevelt Way NE
Seattle 98105 (206)525-8015

BODY-CENTERED LEARNING
1621 12th, Seattle 98122
(206)323-5621

GEORGE W. DEVER
1511 3rd, Seattle 98101
(206)624-0737

FELDENKRAUS METHOD
POB 75053, Seattle 98125
(206)362-6327

JANET E. GAGNON
753 E 35th #300, Seattle
98112 (206)632-1978

BARBARA E. GROSS
1014 15th Ave E, Seattle
98112 (206)328-8922

PAMELA HOUGHTON
6303 Phinney N, Seattle
98103 (206)789-4066

KHALSA HEALTH CENTER
1305 NE 45th #205
Seattle 98105 (206)547-2007

REFLEXOLOGISTS

B & D THERAPEUTIC MSG
Herald Bldg #310
Bellingham 98225
(206)671-3212

CAMAM REFLEXOLOGY CLINIC
524 NE 2nd, Camas 98607
(206)834-1212

NORTHERN HEALTH MASSAGE
THRPY, 3314 Rosedale St
Gig Harbor 98335
(206)851-7951

CARE INSTITUTE OF
REFLEXOLOGY
POB 191, Olympia 98507
(206)352-8168

SPORTS & THERAPEUTIC MASSAGE
750 Swift Blvd #14, Richland
99352 (509)943-4568

BETTER HEALTH-SPOKANE
W 1405 8th, Spokane 99204
(509)456-8136

FRANCELLA'S NEO-LIFE
W 3715 Elmhurst, Spokane
99208 (509)325-0159

SHIRLEY'S HOME & HEALTH
W 2024 Broadway, Spokane
99201 (509)325-5688

THE WASHINGTON STATE BASIC HEALTH PLAN

According to a 1988 estimate, there are about 785,00 uninsured persons under the age of 65 in Washington, including 450,000 who meet the income criteria of the Basic Health Plan.

Two-thirds of the uninsured population have ties to the workplace--they either work themselves, or they are spouses, children, or other dependents of working adults. Forty-one percent of the uninsured work full-time. Nearly 40 percent of the uninsured are children, and half are under age twenty-five.

What is The Basic Health Plan?

The Washington Basic Health Plan is a landmark project, designed to provide health care coverage to up to 30,000 uninsured Washington residents. Those who are eligible, pay reduced monthly premiums, based on family size and income, for health care coverage through prominent private-sector providers. The difference between their reduced premium and the cost of the health coverage is subsidized through state revenues.

The Basic Health Plan is available in selected demonstration areas to people under age 65 who do not qualify for Medicare and who have a gross family income that does not exceed 200 percent of the federal poverty level (currently $24,200 for a family of four). As stated above, according to recent studies, there are roughly 785,00 uninsured persons under the age 65 in Washington State, including 450,00 who meet the Plan's income requirements.

What benefits does the Basic Health Plan Provide?

The Plan covers doctors visits, hospital care, lab tests and x-rays, emergency care and ambulance services, and preventive care such as immunizations and routine check-ups. To keep cost down, the Plan currently does not cover such services as eyeglasses, dental care, mental health treatment, custodial care, and prescription drugs.

The Washington State Basic Health Plan is an independent state government agency, contracts with private managed health care systems to provide the Basic Health benefit package for a set monthly rate. The Basic Health Plan enrolls eligible applicants, collects their premiums, and pays the cost of the program through a mixture of participant premiums and state revenues.

The Plan is currently accepting applications for enrollment in King, Clark, Pierce, and parts of Clallam counties. Interest in participation has been high. For additional information call the toll-free information hotline at: 1-800-826-2444, or write to the Washington Basic Health Plan, 1220 Eastside St., SE.,POB 9014, Olympia, WA 98504.

Education

Washington is served by an extensive network of public and private schools that provide quality education and training from kindergarden to post-graduate level including:

- 22 four-year colleges and universities plus seven branches of out-of-state institutions. During 1986, about 109,000 students were enrolled--34,000 of these at the University of Washington, the largest single-campus university on the West Coast of the United States.

- 27 two-year community colleges. An estimated 90 percent of the state's citizens are within a half-hour's drive of a community college. About 159,000 were enrolled in 1986.

- Five vocational-technical institutes, with an additional 140,000 enrolled. Two of the institutes are located in Tacoma with others in Renton, Kirkland, and Bellingham.

- Eight regional skill development centers.

- 300 local public school districts providing primary and secondary eduction with enrollments exceeding 740,000.

- Numerous private schools generally operated by religious denominations, enroll approximately 60,000 students.

- Foreign-language based institutions, which typically operate as a supplement to regular schooling. Schools for Japanese children are available in Seattle, Moses Lake, and Portland (serving Clark County). Three other schools, located in Seattle and Tacoma teach Korean language, history and culture to junior and senior high school students.

- Some 350 private vocational schools, In the aggregate these train approximately 20,000 residents each year.

Washington has a long history of generous financial support for quality education at all levels. During the 1985-87 biennium, the state committed $1.1 billion for its four-year institutions, $520 million for its two-year colleges, and $2.4 billion for its common schools.

Among the four-year colleges and universities, 14 head-quartered in Washington as well as seven branches of out-of-state institutions are privately owned. Together these private colleges and universities enroll 27,000.

To ensure that all students in Washington have equal access to quality instruction in primary and secondary schools, the state directly funds a core curriculum of basic education. Only one other state uses this approach. Direct state funding of basic eduction accounts for about 70 percent of the total cost of public primary and secondary education.

This state support to local schools is currently $2.4 billion, the largest expenditure in the State's Biennial Budget. In the 1985-86 school year Washington schools spent $3,705 per pupil ranking it 20th in the nation ahead of such states as California, Texas, Illinois, and North Carolina. Public school students consistently score well above the national average on standardized tests.

STATE STUDENT AID & FINANCIAL ASSISTANCE

Grants, loans and work-study programs are commonly referred to as "need-based" financial aid. To qualify, you must show financial need. The amount of aid you can receive is limited by the amount of need you can document.

Your financial need is determined by the cost of your education less your family contribution. Since your family's financial situation can change from year to year, financial aid should be applied for annually. To be considered for aid, you should contact the financial aid office of the college you plan to attend as early as the fall term prior to the year you wish to receive aid. Keep in touch with the financial aid office where you are applying for aid. Problems arise when communications breakdown and deadlines are missed. The school would prefer you call too much rather than not hear from you at all.

An early application is critical because financial aid funds are limited. Ideally you should begin your financial aid application the January before the start of the fall quarter of the academic year you plan to begin attending.

FINANCIAL AID PROGRAMS OFFERED IN WASHINGTON STATE
Student financial aid available is grouped in the following categories:

Conditional Scholarship – An award given as a gift with certain condition to be met. If the conditions are not met the scholarship becomes a loan.

Scholarships, tuition exemptions or grants – These are gifts and require neither repayment nor performance of a service.

Service awards – Such awards are based on a service which the student renders for the college, as in athletics or music.

Employment – Part-time jobs are often available for students who need to earn money to apply against college costs and for those who choose to work even though they have adequate financial resources. In some colleges, cooperative work-study programs are arranged so that the student alternates periods of work with academic terms.

Loans – Loans are available from such sources as state and federal governments, education foundations, industrial organizations and private lending agencies such as banks and savings and loan organizations. Student loans are different from other types of aid in that they must be repaid, usually with interest.

WASHINGTON STATE NEED GRANT PROGRAM
Especially designed for Needy or Disadvantaged Residents.
To be eligible for the program you must show financial need,
be admitted or enrolled at a participation institution, and
may not be pursuing a degree in theology. You are considered
for the grant by the institution if you make a full financial
aid application.

THE WASHINGTON STATE WORK-STUDY PROGRAM
This program offers financial aid to needy students through
part-time employment. To participate in this program you must
be enrolled at least half-time as defined by the institution
and may not be pursuing a degree in theology. The program is
available to undergraduate, graduate, or professional students. Application for this program is automatic upon your
application for financial aid at the institution.

WASHINGTON SCHOLARS PROGRAM
The purpose of this program is to recognize and honor the
accomplishments of three high school seniors from each legislative district; encourage and facilitate privately funded
scholarship awards, and stimulate recruitment of outstanding
students to Washington public and private colleges and
universities. Eligible students representing the top one percent of the senior class are nominated by the high school
principals based upon academic accomplishments, leadership,
and community service.

CONDITIONAL SCHOLARSHIPS/LOANS PROGRAMS

Future Teachers Conditional Scholarship Program
This state scholarship was established to recruit future
teachers from students who have distinguished themselves
through outstanding academic achievements and students who
can act as role models for children including those from
targeted ethnic minorities. The $3,000 scholarships are re-
newable for up to five years and require a ten year
Washington public school teaching commitment or repayment of
the scholarship plus interest. Applications are available at
high schools and participating colleges the January prior to
the academic year for which the applicant wishes to be considered.

Nurses Conditional Scholarship
This state scholarship program is to encourage qualified individuals to serve in nursing shortage areas. Recipients
agree to nurse in a state defined shortage area for five
years or repay the scholarship plus interest. The renewable
scholarship pays the cost of attendance for the nursing program, up to $3,000 per year. Applications are available the
January prior to the academic year for which the applicant
wishes to be considered.

Teacher Incentive Loan for Mathematics and Science
This Math-Science Loan program provides need-based loans of
up to $2,500 per year to students who intend to teach math or
science at the middle or secondary level. Applicants must be
declared majors in math or science who have been accepted

into a program of teacher preparation. The loan is cancelled for recipients who teach math or science for ten years in Washington's public middle or secondary schools; otherwise it must be repaid with interest over a ten year period. In addition to a standard financial aid application, a separate application available from participating institutions, must be completed.

STATE EXCHANGE PROGRAMS

Western Interstate Commission for Higher Education (WICHE)
This program is for optometry students, providing state support to needy Washington residents enrolled in out-of-state optometry programs. Contact the HECB directly for information and applications.

Western Interstate Commission for Higher Education (WICHE) Regional Student Exchange Program. WICHE Regional Graduate programs are distinctive master's and doctoral programs in which qualified Washington residents may enroll at reduced tuition rates in out-of-state programs not offered in Washington state. Programs are primarily in the science and liberal arts rather than in the professional fields. Contact the HECB directly for information and applications.

OTHER STATE PROGRAMS

Tuition Waiver Program
Recipients of Tuition and Fee Waivers must be Washington residents, and application is automatic when you apply for financial aid from the public Washington state institution of your choice. The average waiver is $520.

For a copy of the booklet: Financial Aid Handbook: The Washington State Guide to Financial Aid for Higher Eduction write or phone: The Higher Education Coordinating Board, 917 Lakeridge Way, GV-11 Olympia, WA 98504 (206)753-3571

PUBLIC COLLEGES AND UNIVERSITIES

Central Washington University
Ellensburg, WA 98926
(509)963-1111
Enrollment: 7,109
Yearly tuition:$1,581 R&B $2,993

Eastern Washington University
Cheney, WA 99004
(509)359-6200
Enrollment: 8,200
Yearly tuition:$1,611 R&B $3,068

The Evergreen State College
Olympia, WA 98505
(206)866-6000
Enrollment: 3,237
Yearly tuition:$1,611 R&B $3,500

University of Washington
Seattle, WA 98195
(206)543-2100
Enrollment: 34,086
Yearly tuition:$1,590 R&B $3,000

Washington State University
Pullman, WA 99164
(509)335-3564
Enrollment: 17,800
Yearly tuition:$2,095 R&B $3,300

Western Washington University
Bellingham, WA 98225
(206)676-3000
Enrollment: 9,838
Yearly tuition:$1,227 R&B $2,339

PUBLIC COMMUNITY COLLEGES

Bellevue Community College
300 Landerholm Cir. SE
POB 92700, Bellevue, WA
98009 (206)641-0111
Total Enrollment: 12,974

Big Bend Community College
28th & Chanute Sts
Moses Lake, WA 98837
(509)762-5351
Total Enrollment: 2,129

Centralia College
600 W. Locust St.
Centralia, WA 98531
(206)736-9391
Total Enrollment: 3,578

Clark College
1800 E. McLoughlin Blvd.
Vancouver, WA 98663
(206)694-6521
Total Enrollment: 9,219

Columbia Basin College
2600 N. 20th
Pasco, WA 99301
(509)547-0511
Total Enrollment: 5,964

Edmonds Community College
20000 68th Ave. W.

Lynnwood, WA 98201
(206)771-1500
Total Enrollment: 7,555

Everett Community College
810 Wetmore Ave.
Everett, WA 98201
(206)259-7151
Total Enrollment: 7,054

Grays Harbor College
Aberdeen, WA 98520
(206)532-9020
Total Enrollment: 2,480

Green River Community College
12401 SE 320th St.
Auburn, WA 98002
(206)833-9111
Total Enrollment: 6,610

Highline Community College
POB 98000
Des Moines, WA 98198
(206)878-3710
Total Enrollment: 8,547

Lower Columbia College
1600 Maple St. POB 3010
Longview, WA 98632
(206)577-2300
Total Enrollment: 4,048

North Seattle Community College
9600 College Way N.
Seattle, WA 98103
(206)527-3600
Total Enrollment: 8,000

Olympia College
16th & Chester
Bremerton, WA 98310
(206)478-4506
Total Enrollment: 6,146

Peninsula College
Port Angeles, WA 98362
(206)452-9277
Total Enrollment: 2,831

Pierce College
9401 Farwest Dr. SW
Tacoma, WA 98498
(206)964-6500
Total Enrollment: 8,969

Seattle Central Community College
1701 Broadway
Seattle, WA 98122
(206)587-3800
Total Enrollment: 8,185

Shoreline Community College
16101 Greenwood Ave. N.
Seattle, WA 98133
(206)546-4101
Total Enrollment: 7,423

Skagit Valley College
2405 College Way
Mount Vernon, WA 98273
(206)428-1261
Total Enrollment: 5,636

South Puget Sound Community College
2011 Mottman Rd. SW
Olympia, WA 98502
(206)754-7711
Total Enrollment: 4,354

South Seattle Community College
6000 16th Ave. SW
Seattle, WA 98106
(206)764-5300
Total Enrollment: 6,490

Spokane Community College
N. 1810 Greene St.
Spokane, WA 99207
(509)536-7000
Total Enrollment: 6,841

Spokane Falls Community College
W. 3410 Fort Geo. Wright Dr.
Spokane, WA 99204
(509)459-3500
Total Enrollment: 15,104

Tacoma Community College
5900 S. 12th St
Tacoma, WA 98465
(206)566-5000
Total Enrollment: 5,982

Walla Walla Community College
500 Tausick Way
Walla Walla, WA 99362
(509)522-2500
Total Enrollment: 5,028

Wenatchee Valley College
Wenatchee, WA 98801
(509)662-1651
Total Enrollment: 3,410

Whatcom Community College
237 W. Kellogg Rd.
Bellingham, WA 98226
(206)676-2170
Total Enrollment: 3,085

Yakima Valley Community College
16th Ave & Nob Hill Blvd.
POB 1647, Yakima, WA 98907
(509)575-2350
Total Enrollment: 5,145

PUBLIC VOCATIONAL TECHNICAL INSTITUTES

L.H. Bates Vocational-Technical Institute
1101 S. Yakima Ave.
Tacoma, WA 98405
(206)597-7200
Total Enrollment:47,000

Bellingham Vocational – Technical Institute
3028 Lindbergh Ave.
Bellingham, WA 98225
(206)676-6490
Total Enrollment: 15,200

Clover Park Vocational – Technical Institute
4500 Stelacoom Blvd. SW
Tacoma, WA 98499
(206)584-7611
Total Enrollment: 47,969

Lake Washington Vocational Technical institute
11605 132nd NE
Kirkland, WA 98034
(206)828-5600
Total Enrollment: 25,000

Renton Vocational-Technical Institute
3000 NE 4th St.
Renton, WA 98056
Total Enrollment: 25,585

Washington Institute of Applied Technology
315 22nd Ave. S.

Seattle, WA 98144
(206)587-4220
Total Enrollment:

PROPRIETARY SCHOOLS

Art Institute of Seattle
2323 Elliott Ave.
Seattle, WA 98121
(206)448-0900
Total Enrollment:

Gene Juarez School of Beauty
10715 8th North Ave.
Seattle, WA 98125
(206)365-6900
Total Enrollment:

Glen Dow Academy of Hair Design
W 309 Riverside Ave.
Spokane, WA 99201
(509)624-3244
Total Enrollment:

Griffin Business College
1115 A Street
Tacoma, WA 98402
.(206)624-7154

Perry Technical Institute
POB 9457
Yakima, WA 98909
(509)453-0374

Resource Center for the Handicapped
20150 45th Ave NE
Seattle, WA 98155
(206)362-2273

PRIVATE COLLEGES AND UNIVERSITIES

City University
16661 Northrup Way
Bellevue, WA 98008
(206)643-2000 1-800-542-9845
Enrollment: 6,000

Cornish College of the Arts
710 E. Roy St.
Seattle, WA 98102
(206)323-1400
Enrollment: 581

Gonzaga University
E. 502 Boone Ave

Spokane, WA 99258
(509)328-4220
Enrollment: 4,155

Heritage College
Route 3, Box 3540
Toppenish, WA 98948
(509)865-2244
Enrollment: 540

Northwest College of the Assemblies of God (815)
POB 579, 11102 NE 53rd St.
Kirkland, WA 98083
(206)822-8266
Enrollment: 695

Pacific Lutheran University
Tacoma, WA 98447
(206)531-6900
Enrollment: 4,000

Saint Martin's College
Lacey, WA 98503
(206)491-4700
Enrollment: 1,000

Seattle Pacific University
Third W & W Bertona St.
Seattle, WA 98119
(206)281-2000
Enrollment: 3,400

Seattle University
Seattle, WA 98122
(206)296-6000
Enrollment: 4,514

University of Puget Sound
1500 N. Warner
Tacoma, WA 98416
(206)756-3100
Enrollment: 2,771

Walla Walla College
College Place, WA 99362
(509)527-2615
Enrollment: 1,500

Whitman College
Walla Walla, WA 99362
(509)527-5111
Enrollment: 1,200

Whitworth College
Spokane, WA 99251
(509)466-1000
Enrollment: 1,800

PRIVATE TUTORING

EASTSIDE ACADEMIC INST.
12503 Blvu-Redmond Rd,
Bellevue 98005 (206)455-2778

EASTSIDE LITERACY CLINIC
13401 Bellevue Redmond,
Bellevue 98005 (206)643-2547

HOPE CLINIC
325 118th SE #225, Bellevue
98005 (206)482-7800

SILVAN LEARNING CENTER
4140 128th SE #2A
Bellevue 98006 (206)641-7809

TEST PLUS NORTHWEST
10255 NE 20th Pl, Bellevue
98004 (206)646-9353

CHUCKANUT SCHOOL
524 32nd, Bellingham 98225
(206)733-0678

MATH ADVENTURE
1316 King, Bellingham 98228
(206)733-3033

MAHAN'S TUTORING & TESTING
801 11th, Bremerton 98310
(206)377-1810

CENTRALIA MONTESSORI
1716 W Mellen, Centralia
98531 (206)736-0572

THE LEARNING CONNECTION
93 Eastmond Ave #112
East Wenatchee 98802
(509)884-0934

CHILD EDUCATIONAL SVCS
180 W Dayton #105
Edmonds 98020 (206)774-9127

ENRICH LEARNING CENTER
250 4th Ave S, Edmonds
98020 (206)672-1850

SYLVAN LEARNING CENTER
7500 212th St SW #110
Edmonds 98020 (206)774-3922

TELETUTOR
POB 207, Edmonds 98020
(206)778-4300

UNCLE RAY'S
Ellensburg 98926
(509)962-5676

SYLVAN LEARNING CENTER
32717 1st Ave S, Federal Way
98003 (206)838-0507

EXCELL LEARNING CENTER
2810 W Clearwater Ave #102
Kennewick 99366
(509)735-0523

SYLVAN LEARNING CENTER
25028 104th SE #201, Kent
98031 (206)854-7111

LF BAUM & ASSOCIATES
7840 126th Ave NE
Kirkland 98033 (206)822-2345

SYLVAN LEARNING CENTER
12545 Totem Lake Blvd
Kirkland 98034 (206)823-8727

BASIC SKILLS INSTITUTE
1605 15th Ave, Longview
98832 (206)638-4582

SYLVAN LEARNING CENTER
829 11th Ave, Longview 98632
(206)577-3939

EDUCATIONAL TUTORING
3236 78th SE #101
Mercer Island 98040
(206)238-1095

MATH TUTORING & SAT PREP.
8817 SE 61st, Mercer Island
98040 (206)232-6284

NORTHWEST CHILDREN'S ACADEMY
4030 86th SE, Mercer Island
98040 (206)232-2545

SHIRLEY SAWDON
1303 E 4th, Olympia 98506
(206)943-6021

SYLVAN LEARNING CENTER
10317 122nd E, Puyallup
98374 (206)848-0771

EASTSIDE ASSN-CHLDN DSBL
17530 NE Union Hill Rd #101
Redmond 98052 (206)882-0792

ACADEMY-ACAD ACHIEVEMENT
133 Evergreen Bldg
Renton 98055 (206)271-6980

BLISS ALDEN
17016 105th SE, Renton
98066 (206)271-8126

ACADEMIC TUTORING
12500 Riviera Pl NE
Seattle 98125 (206)361-0534

ACHIEVE EDUCATIONAL SVCS
16551 Aurora Ave N
Seattle 98133 (206)542-7147

BASIC EDUCATION TUTORS
2623 E Madison, Seattle
98112 (206)322-2113

EDUCATIONAL OPPORTUNITIES
3050 NW 68th, Seattle 98115
(206)782-1850

HIGHLINE TUTORING LOFT
627½ SW 163rd, Seattle 98166
(206)242-0245

MARK WAHL LEARNING SVCS
2000 Fairview E, Seattle
98102 (206)324-9451

PRINCETON REVIEW
229 Broadway E #17, Seattle
98102 (206)325-1341

READING SKILL CENTER
6329 Ravenna NE, Seattle
98115 (206)522-8311

SOUTHWEST YOUTH SVC BUR
9001 35th SW, Seattle 98126
(206)935-9693

STANLEY H. KAPLAN CENTER
1107 NE 45th #440, Seattle
98105 (206)632-0634

SYLVAN LEARNING CENTER
2 Nickerson #101, Seattle
98109 (206)282-6284

SYLVAN LEARNING CENTER
8001 Lake City Way NE
Seattle 98115 (206)525-8080

MOTIVATIONAL/SELF IMPROVEMENT TRAINING

ADVANTAGE LEARNING SYSTEMS
122 112th NE, Bellevue
98004 (206)455-1109

UNLIMITED POTENTIAL
400 Warren, Bremerton 98310
(206)479-8580

W.E. PORTER & ASSOCIATES
109 N Tower, Centralia 98531
(206)738-0225

SUCCESS MANAGEMENT
ASSOCIATES
10126 NE 132nd, Kirkland
98034 (206)820-2505

PERSONAL BEST/SPOKANE
E 22610 Heroy, Otis Orchards
99027 (509)926-1881

ADVENTURES IN ENLIGHTENMENT
433 Garrard Creek Rd,
Rochester 98579
(206)273-8801

DIANETIC COUNSELING GROUP
2124 3rd, Seattle 98121
(206)443-8888

DIANETICS FOUNDATION HUBBARD
2004 Westlake, Seattle 98121
(206)822-6353

MIND TECHNOLOGIES, INC.
9620 Stone N #201, Seattle
98133 (206)525-1555

SCIENTOLOGY MISSION
4522 University Way NE
Seattle 98105 (206)547-8929

SUMMIT INSTITUTE
8833 Earl NW, Seattle 98117
(206)784-7148

BETTER HEALTH OF SPOKANE
E 235 9th, Spokane 99202
(509)458-8136

BOOKS IN MOTION
E 9212 Montgomery Ave
Spokane 99206 (509)922-1646

APPRENTICESHIP TRAINING PROGRAMS

IBEW Electrical Training
8240 Gage Blvd.
Kennewick 99336
(509)783-0589

Plumbers & Steamfitters 598
1328 Road 28 N.
Pasco 99301 (509)547-6480

Ironworks Apprentice
E 5309 3rd, Spokane 99212
(509)534-5107

Carpenters Employer Training
2201 S 78th, Tacoma 98409
(206)472-2931

Worship

In Seattle, the largest city in Washington, there are over 40 Roman Catholic churches, 16 Jewish, and over 550 Protestant and other churches. There are far too many churches in Washington to be listed here. For a complete listing of churches in your area, consult the Yellow Pages of your local telephone directory.

The following is a partial listing of some of the larger church denominations in the state:

Washington Association of Churches
4759 15th Ave. NE
Seattle 98105 (206)525-1988

**Northwest Regional Christian Church
(Disciples of Christ)**
6558 35th Ave. SW
Seattle 98126 (206)938-1008

**Washington North Idaho Conference
United Church of Christ**
720 14th Ave. E
Seattle 98112 (206)323-8383

**American Baptist Churches of the
Northwest**
321 First Avenue W.
Seattle 98119 (206)285-1034

**Roman Catholic Archdiocese of
Seatle**
910 Marion Street
Seattle 98104 (206)382-4888

**The Synod of Alaska-Northwest
Presbyterian Church (USA)**
233 Sixth Ave N., Suite 100
Seattle 98109 (206)448-6403

**NW Washington Synod
Evangelical Lutheran Church in
America**
5519 Phinney Ave. S
Seattle 98103 (206)783-9292

**Pacific NW Conference United
Methodist Church**
2112 Third Ave., Suite 301
Seattle 98121 (206)728-7674

The Episcopal Diocese of Olympia
P.O. Box 12126, Seattle 98102
(206)325-4200

**Oregon-Washington District
Church of the Brethren**
P.O. Box 16366
Portland, OR 97216-0366
(503)253-6099

**Eastern Washington/Idaho Synod
Evangelical Lutheran Church in
America**
South 314-A Spruce
Spokane 99204 (509)838-9871

Roman Catholic Diocese of Spokane
P.O. Box 1453, Spokane 99210
(509)456-7100

Episcopal Diocese of Spokane
East 245 13th, Spokane 99202
(509)624-3191

Roman Catholic Diocese of Yakima
5301 Tieton Dr. #A
Yakima 98908-3493 (509)965-7117

**South West Washington Synod
Evangelical Lutheran Church in
America**
420 South 121st Court
Tacoma 98444 (206)535-8300

The Media

TELEVISION STATIONS

BELLINGHAM

KVOS-TV   CHANNEL 12
1151 Ellis St, Box 1157
Bellingham, WA 98225
(206)671-1212
Network: CBS

KENNEWICK

KVEW-TV   CHANNEL 42
601 N. Edison. Kennewick,
99336, (509)735-8369
Network: ABC

PASCO

KEPR-TV   CHANNEL 19
2807 W. Lewis, Pasco, WA
99301, (509)547-0547
Network: CBS

PULLMAN

KWSU-TV   CHANNEL 10
Edward R. Murrow Center
WSU, Pullman, WA 99164
(509)335-6588
Network: PBS

SEATTLE

KCTS-TV   CHANNEL 9
401 Mercer, Seattle, WA
98109, (206)728-6463
Network: PBS

KING-TV   CHANNEL 19
333 Dexter Ave, North
Seattle, WA 98109
(206)448-5555
Network: NBC

KIRO-TV   CHANNEL 7
2807 Third Ave, Box C 21326
Seattle, WA 98111,
(206)728-777
Network: CBS

KOMO-TV   CHANNEL 4
100 Fourth Ave N, Seattle,
WA 98109, (206)443-4000
Network: ABC

KTZZ-TV   CHANNEL 22
945 Dexter Ave N, Seattle,
WA 98109, (206)282-2202

SPOKANE

KAYU-TV   CHANNEL 28
Box 8115, Spokane, WA 99203,
(509)448-2828

KHQ-TV   CHANNEL 6
4202 S. Regal St, Spokane,
WA 99203, (509)448-6000
Network: NBC

KREM-TV   CHANNEL 2
4103 S. Regal, Box 8037,
Spokane, WA 99203,
(509)448-2000
Network: CBS

KSPS-TV   CHANNEL 7
3911 S. Regal St, Spokane,
WA 99223, (509)353-5777
Network: PBS

KXLY-TV   CHANNEL 4
W 500 Boone, Spokane,
99201, (509)328-9084
Network: ABC

TACOMA

KCPQ-TV   CHANNEL 13
4400 Steilacoom Blvd. SW
Tacoma, WA 98499,
(206)582-8613
Network: Fox, CBS, NBC

KSTW-TV   CHANNEL 20
1909 S. 341st Pl.
Federal Way, WA 98003,
(206)927-7720

KTPS-TV   CHANNEL 20
Tacoam School District 10
1101 S. Yakima Ave, Tacoma,
WA 98405, (206)272-1528
Network: PBS

TRI-CITIES

KNDU-TV   CHANNEL 25
3312 W. Kennewick Ave.
Kennewick, WA 99302
(509)783-6151
Network: NBC

VANCOUVER

KPDX-TV   CHANNEL 49
910 NE Union
Portland, OR 97232
(206)239-4949

WENATCHEE

KCWT-TV   CHANNEL 27
328 N. Mission St,
Wenatchee, WA 98801
(509)662-5298

YAKIMA

KAPP-TV   CHANNEL 35
1610 S. 24th Ave, Yakima,
98902, (509)453-0351
Network: ABC

KIMA-TV   CHANNEL 29
Box 702, Yakima, WA 98907
(509)575-0029
Network: CBS

KNDO-TV   CHANNEL 23
Box 10028, Yakima, WA 98909
(509)248-2300
Network: NBC

KYVE-TV   CHANNEL 47
1105 S. 15th Ave, Yakima, WA
98902, (509)452-4700
Network: PBS

RADIO STATIONS

ABERDEEN

KAYO-AM 1450 khz
KAYO-FM 99.3 mhz
701 E. Heron, Box 188
Aberdeen, WA 98520
(206)532-1450

KDUX-FM 140.7 mhz
Box 47, 1308 Coolidge Rd.
Aberdeen, WA 98520
(206)533-1320

KXRO-AM 1340 khz
Box 47, 1308 Coolidge Rd.
Aberdeen, WA 98520
(206)533-1320

ANACORTES

KLKI-AM 1340 khz
Box 96, Anacortes, WA 98221
(206)293-3141

AUBURN

KASY-AM 1220 khz
Box 459 Auburn, WA 98071
(206)883-5220

KGRG-FM 89.9 mhz
Green River Community

College, 12401 SE 320th St,
Auburn, WA 98002,
(206)833-5005

BELLEVUE

KASB-FM 89.3 mhz
Bellevue School Dist #405
601-108th Ave SE, Bellevue,
WA 98004, (206)455-6154

KBCS-FM 91.3 mhz
Bellevue Community College
3000 Landerholm Cir, SE.
Bellevue, WA 98007,
(206)641-2424

KLSY-AM 1540 khz
KLSY-FM 92.5 mhz
12011 NE First, Bellevue, WA
98005, (206)454-1540

BELLINGHAM

KBFW-AM 930 khz
Box D, Bellingham, WA 98227
(206)734-8555

KGMI-AM 790 khz
KISM-FM 92.9 mhz
2219 Yew St. Rd.
Bellingham, WA 98226
(206)734-9790

KNWR-FM 104.3 mhz
Box 1170, Bellingham, WA
98227, (206)734-1170

KPUG-AM 1170 khz
Box 1170, Bellingham, WA
98227, (206)734-1170

KUGS-FM 89.3 mhz
Western Washington
University, 410 Viking Union
Bldg, Bellingham, WA 98225
(206)676-2995

BLAINE

KARI-AM 550 khz
4840 Lincoln Rd, Blaine, WA
98230, (206)371-5500

BREMERTON

KBRO-AM 1490 khz
Box 1490, Bremerton, WA
98310, (206)479-1490

CENTRALIA-CHEHALIS

KCED-FM 91.3 mhz
Centraila Community College
600 W. Locust St, Centralia,
WA 98531, (206)736-9391

KELA-AM 1470 khz
1635 S. Gold St, Centralia,
WA 98531, (206)736-3321

KITI-AM 1420 khz
1133 Kresky, Centralia, WA
98531, (206)736-1355

KMNT-FM 102.9 mhz
1635 S. Gold St, Centralia,
WA 98531, (206)736-3321

CHELAN

KOZI-AM 1230 khz
KOZI-FM 93.5 mhz
Box 819, Chelan, WA 98816
(509)682-4033

CHENEY

KEWU-FM 89.5 mhz
Eastern Washington
University, Cheney, WA 99004
(509)359-6390

CLARKSTON

KCLK-AM 1430 khz
KCLK-FM 94.1 mhz
Box 669, Clarkston, WA 99403
(509)758-3361

COLFAX

KCLX-AM 1450 khz
Box 710, Colfax, WA 99111
(509)397-3441

COLLEGE PLACE

KGTS-FM 91.3
Walla Walla College
College Place, WA 99324
(509)527-2991

COLVILLE

KCRK-FM 92.1 mhz
Box 111, Colville, WA 99114
(509)684-5032

KCVL–AM 1240 khz
Box 111, Colville, WA 99114
(509)684-5032

DEER PARK

KAZZ–FM 107.1 mhz
Box 1369, Deer Park, WA
99006, (509)276-8816

EAST WENATCHEE

KYSN–FM 97.7 mhz
960 Valley Mall Parkway
East Wenatchee, WA 98801
(509)884-1555

EDMONDS

KCIS–AM 630 khz
19303 Fremont Ave. N.
Seattle, WA 98133
(206)546-7350

KCMS–FM 105.3 mhz
19303 Fremont Ave. N.
Seattle, WA 98133
(206)546-7350

ELLENSBURG

KQBE–FM 103.1 mhz
Box 1032, Ellensburg,
98926, (509)962-2823

KXLE–AM 1240 khz
KXLE–FM 95.3 mhz
1311 Vantage Highway
Ellensburg, WA 98926
(509)925-1488

ENUMCLAW

KENU–AM 1330 khz
1540 Cole St, Enumclaw,
98022, (206)825-6547

EPHRATA

KGDN–FM 95.9 mhz
55 Alder St. NW, Ephrata,
98823, (509)754-4686

KTBI–AM 810 khz
55 Alder St. NW, Ephrata,
98823, (509)754-4686

KULE–AM 730 khz
910 Basin SW, Ephrata,
98823, (509)754-4661

EVERETT

KRKO–AM 1380 khz
2828 Colby, Everett,
98201, (206)252-1380

KWYZ–AM 1230 khz
Box 1230, Everett, WA 98206
(206)252-5123

FERNDALE

KNTR–AM 1550 khz
Box 308, Ferndale, WA 98248
(206)384-5117

FORKS

KVAC–AM 1490 khz
Box 450, Forks, WA 98331
(206)374-6233

GOLDENDALE

KLCK–AM 1400 khz
Box 305, Goldendale, WA
98620, (206)773-3300

GRAND COULEE

KEYG–AM 1490 khz
KEYG–FM 98.5 mhz
Drawer K, Grand Coulee, WA
99133, (509)633-2020

GRANGER

KDNA–FM 91.9 mhz
Box 800, Granger, WA 98932
(509)854-2222

HOQUIAM

KGHO–AM 1490 khz
KGHO–FM 95.3 mhz
3120 Bay Ave, Hoquiam, WA
98550, (206)532-1200

KELSO

KLOG–AM 1490 khz
Box 90, Kelso, WA 98626
(206)636-0110

KIRKLAND

KARR–AM 1460 khz
Box 682, Kirkland, WA 98033
(206)827-1460

LONGVIEW

KBAM-AM 1270 khz
Box 96, Longview, WA 98632
(206)423-1210

KEDO-AM 1400 khz
1130 14th, Longview, WA
98632, (206)425-1500

KLYX-FM 105.5 mhz
1130 14th, Longview, WA
98632, (206)423-6482

LYNDEN

KLYN-FM 106.5 mhz
1843 Front St, Lynden, WA
98264, (206)354-5596

MERCER ISLAND

KMIH-FM 90.1 mhz
Mercer Island School Dist
#400, 9100 SE 42nd, Mercer
Island, WA 98040,
(206)232-1660

MOSES LAKE

KBSN-AM 1470 khz
KDRM-FM 99.3 mhz
2241 W. Main, Moses Lake,
98837, (509)765-3441

KWIQ-AM 1020 khz
KWIQ-FM 100.3 mhz
Box 999, Moses Lake, WA
98837, (509)765-1761

MOUNTLAKE TERRACE

KKZU-AM 1510 khz
120 Second Ave. S.
Edmonds, WA 98020
(206)771-2343

MOUNT VERNON

KAPS-AM 1470 khz
Box 70, Mount Vernon,
98273, (206)424-7676

KBRC-AM 1430 khz
Box 250, Mount Vernon,
98273, (206)424-4278

KSVR-FM 90.1 mhz
2405 College Way

Mt. Vernon, WA 98273
(206)428-1198

NEWPORT

KUBS-FM 91.5 mhz
Newport High School
Box 68, Newport, WA 99156
(509)447-4931

KMJY-AM 700 khz
Box 1740, Oldtown, ID 83822
(208)743-2502

OAK HARBOR

KJTT-AM 1110 khz
Box 70, Oak Harbor, WA 98277
(206)679-1110

OLYMPIA

KAOS-FM 89.3 mhz
The Evergreen State College
Olympia, WA 98505,
(206)866-6822

KGY-AM 1240 khz
Box 1249 Olympia, WA 98507
(206)943-1240

KQEU-AM 920 khz
2914 Yelm Hwy SE
Olympia, WA 98501
(206)491-9200

KTOL-AM 1280 khz
4414 Pacific SE
Olympia, WA 98503
(206)438-1280

OMAK

KOMW-AM 680 khz
KOMW-FM 92.7
Box 151, Omak, WA 98841
(509)826-0100

OTHELLO

KRSC-AM 1400 khz
Box 566, Othello, WA 99344
(509)488-2791

PORT ANGELES

KAPY-AM 1290 khz
Box 1290, Port Angeles, WA
98362, (206)452-9228

KONP-AM 1450 khz
Box 1450, Port Angeles, WA
98362, (206)457-1450

PROSSER

KACA-FM 101.7 khz
1227 Hillcrest Dr.
Prosser, WA 99350
(509)786-1017

KARY-AM 1310 khz
Rt 1 Box 1310, Prosser, WA
99350, (509)786-1310

PULLMAN

KHTR-FM 104.3 mhz
Box 1, Pullman, WA 99163
(509)332-6551

KQQQ-AM 650 khz
Box 1, Pullman, WA 99163
(509)332-6551

KWSU-AM 1250 khz
Washington State University
Pullmam, WA 99164
(509)335-6500

KZUU-FM 90.7 mhz
Washington State University
Pullman, WA 99164
(509)335-2208

KIRO-AM 710 khz
2807 Third Ave, Seattle,
98111, (206)728-7777

KISW-FM 99.9 mhz
712 Aurora Ave, Seattle,
98109, (206)285-7625

KIXI-AM 880 khz
1100 Olive Way, Seattle,
98101, (206)662-3251

KJET-AM 1590 khz
200 W. Mercer St, Suite 304
Seattle, WA 98119
(206)281-5600

KJR-AM 950 khz
190 Queen Anne N, Seattle,
WA 98109, (206)285-2295

KKFX-AM 1250 khz
2815 Second Ave #550
Seattle, WA 98121
(206)728-1250

KMGI-FM 107.7 mhz
1100 Olive Way, Seattle,
98101, (206)662-3251

KMPS-AM 1300 khz
KMPS-FM 94.1 mhz
1507 Western Ave, Seattle,
WA 98124, (206)662-2312

KNHC-FM 89.5 mhz
Seattle Pacific Schools
10750 30th Ave NE
Seattle, WA 98125
(206)281-6215

KOMO-AM 1000 khz
100 Fourth Ave North
Seattle, WA 98109,
(206)443-4010

KPLZ-FM 101.5 mhz
Tower Building, Seattle,
98101, (206)223-5700

KRPM-AM 770 khz
22220 Marine View Dr.
Seattle, WA 98198
(206)343-9145

KQIN-AM 800 khz
2815 Second, Suite 550
Seattle, WA 98166
(206)443-8200

KRAB-FM 107.7 mhz
2212 South Jackson
Seattle, WA 98144
(206)325-5110

KSEA-FM 100.7 mhz
2807 Third Ave, Seattle,
98111, (206)728-5732

KUBE-FM 93.3 mhz
110 Lakeside, Seattle,
98122, (206)322-1622

KUOW-FM 94.9 mhz
University of Washington
Seattle, WA 98195
(206)543-2710

KVI-AM 570 khz
Tower Building, Seattle,
98101, (206)223-5700

KXRX-FM 96.5 mhz
3131 Elliott Ave. E.
Seattle, WA 98112
(206)283-5979

KZOK-FM 102 mhz
200 W. Mercer St, Suite 304
Seattle, WA 98119
(206)281-5600

SELAH

KYXE-AM 1020 khz
103 W. Naches Ave.
Selah, WA 98942
(509)697-5993

SEQUIM

KJSM-AM 1520 khz
Box 520, Oak Harbor, WA
98277, (206)679-1520

SHELTON

KMAS-AM 1030 khz
Box 760, Shelton, WA 98584
(206)426-1030

SILVERDALE

KITZ-AM 1400 khz
Box 1400, Silverdale, WA
98383, (206)698-1400

SPOKANE

KAGU-FM 88.7 mhz
Gonzaga University
E 502 Boone Ave
Spokane, WA 99258
(509)328-4220

KAQQ-AM 590 khz
E 300 Third, Spokane,
99203, (509)459-9800

KDRK-FM 93.7 mhz
6228 S. Regal, Spokane,
99203, (509)448-8300

KEYF-AM 1050 khz
KEYF-FM 101 mhz
Box 8148, Spokane, WA 99203
(509)448-1111

KEZE-FM 105.7 mhz
Box 8007, Spokane, WA 99203
(509)448-8888

KGA-AM 1510 khz
6228 S. Regal, Spokane, WA
99203, (509)448-2311

KISC-FM 98.1 mhz
#. 300 Third, Spokane, WA
99202, (509)459-9800

KJRB-AM 790 khz
Box 8007, Spokane, WA 99203
(509)448-1000

KKZX-FM 98.9 mhz
S. 5106 Palouse Hwy
Spokane, WA 99223
(509)448-9936

KMBI-AM 1330 khz
KMBI-FM 107.9 mhz
S. 5408 Frya, Spokane,
98223, (509)448-2555

KPBX-FM 91.1 mhz
2319 Monroe St.
Spokane, WA 99205
(509)328-5729

KRSS-AM 1230 khz
1401 N. Ash Spokane,
99201
(509)326-1699

KSFC-FM 91.9 mhz
Spokane Falls Comm. College
W. 3410 Ft George Wright Dr.
Spokane, WA 99204,
(509)459-3825

KSVY-AM 1550 khz
W. 933 Third Ave, Spokane,
WA 99204, (509)455-4080

WTRW-AM 970-khz
S. 5505 Regal, WA 99223
(509)448-5555

KUDY-AM 1280 khz
S. 5106 Palouse Hwy
Spokane, WA 99223
(509)448-1280

KWRS-FM 90.3 mhz
Whitworth College
Spokane, WA 99251
(509)466-1289

KXLY-AM 920 khz
KXLY-FM 99.9 mhz
W. 500 Boone, Spokane, WA
99201, (509)328-6292

KZZU-FM 92.9 mhz
S. 5505 Regal, Spokane, WA
99223, (509)448-5555

SUNNYSIDE

KREW-AM 1210 khz
KREW-FM 96.7 mhz
Box 149, Sunnyside, WA 98944
(509)837-2277

TACOMA

KBRD-FM 103.7 mhz
Box 11335. Tacoma, WA 98411
(206)473-0086

KBSG-FM 97.3 mhz
948 S. Grant, Tacoma, WA
98405, (206)283-9700

KKMO-AM 1360 khz
Box 1277, Tacoma, WA 98401
(206)922-3345

KLAY-AM 1180 khz
10025 Lakewood Dr. SW
Tacoma, WA 98499
(206)581-0324

KNBQ-FM 97.3 mhz
948 S. Grant, Tacoma, WA
98405, (206)383-9700

KPLU-FM 88.5 mhz
Pacific Lutheran University
Tacoma, WA 98447
(206)535-7758

KTAC-AM 850 khz
Box 11335, Tacoma, WA 98411
(206)473-0086

KTPS-FM 91.7 mhz
Tacoma School Dist. #10
1101 S. Yakima, Tacoma, WA
98405, (206)597-7234

KUPS-FM 91.1 mhz
University of Puget Sound
1500 N. Warner, Tacoma, WA
98416, (206)756-3277

KVTI-FM 90.9 mhz
Clover Park School Dist.
4500 Steilacoom Blvd. SW
Tacoma, WA 98499
(206)756-5884

TOPPENISH

KENE-AM 1490 khz
KHYT-FM 92.7 mhz
Box 350, Toppenish, WA 98948
(509)865-5363

TRI CITIES AREA

KALE-AM 960 khz
310 West Kennewick
Kennewick, WA 99336
(509)586-2151

KEYW-FM 98.3 mhz
Box 2838, Tri Cities, WA
99302, (509)547-1100

KFAE-FM 89.1 mhz
Murrow Communication Center
WSU, Pullman, WA 99164
(509)335-6511

KHWK-FM 106.5 mhz
Box 6127, Kennewick, WA
99336, (509)586-4165

KIOK-FM 94.9 mhz
310 West Kennewick
Kennewick, WA 99336
(509)586-2151

KOLU-FM 90.1 mhz
4921 W. Wernett
Pasco, WA 99301
(509)547-2021

KONA-AM 610 khz
KONA-FM 103.5 mhz
Box 2623, Tri Cities, WA
99302, (509)547-1618

KORD-AM 870 khz
Box 2485, Tri Cities, WA
99302, (509)547-9791

KTCR-AM 1340 khz
KOTY-FM 106.5 mhz
Box 6127, Kennewick, WA
99336, (509)586-4165

KTCV-FM 88.1 mhz
Kennewick School Dist. #17
5929 W. Metaline
Kennewick, WA 99336
(509)735-8790

KZZK-FM 102.7 mhz
Box 2485, Tri Cities, WA
99302, (509)547-9791

TUMWATER

KVSN-AM 1500 khz
Box 4207, Tumwater, 98501
(206)943-9834

VANCOUVER

KBMS-AM 1480 khz
Box 5857, Vancouver, WA
98668, (206)228-1480

KKEY-AM 1150 khz
550 E. Fourth Plains Blvd.
Vancouver, WA 98663
(206)693-2526

KKSN-AM 910 khz
POB 9791
Portland, OR 97207
(503)226-9791

KVAN-AM 1550 khz
Box 4638, Vancouver, WA
98662, (206)256-9043

WALLA WALLA

KAFR-FM 97.1 mhz
Box 796, Walla Walla, WA
99362, (509)525-3190

KEXI-FM 93.3 mhz
112 NE Fifth
Milton-Freewater, OR 97862
(503)938-6688

KHSS-FM 100-9 mhz
107 N. 22nd Ave.
Walla Walla, WA 99362
(509)522-5412

KNLT-FM 95.7 mhz
Rt 5, Box 513

Walla Walla, WA 99362
(509)529-8000

KSMX-AM 1320 khz
6 East Alder St.
Walla Walla, WA 99362
(509)525-3162

KTEL-AM 1490 khz
Box 948, Walla Walla, WA
99362, (509)525-4103

KUJ-AM 1420 khz
Rt 5, Box 513
Walla Walla, WA 99362
(509)529-8000

KWCW-FM 90.5 mhz
Whitman College
Walla Walla, WA 99362
(509)527-5283

WENATCHEE

KPQ-AM 560 khz
KPQ-FM 102.1 mhz
32 N. Mission
Wenatchee, WA 98801
(509)663-5121

KKRT-AM 900 khz
POB 79, Wenatchee, 98801
(509)663-5186

KWWW-AM 1340 khz
Box 638, Wenatchee, WA 98801
(509)662-7135

KYJR-FM 104.9 mhz
Box 79, Wenatchee, WA 98801
(509)663-5185

YAKIMA

KATS-FM 94.5 mhz
114 S. Fourth St,
Yakima, WA 98901
(509)457-8115

KBBO-AM 1390 khz
Box 9188
Yakima, WA 98907
(509)248-1390

KFFM-FM 107.3 mhz
Box 1460
Yakima, WA 98907
(509)248-1460

KIHS-FM 99.3 mhz
Box 2498
Yakima, WA 98907
(509)248-4722

KIT-AM 1280 khz
114 S. Fourth St
Yakima, WA 98901
(509)457-8115

KMWX-AM 1460 khz
Box 1460
Yakima, WA 248-1460

KRSE-FM 98.3 mhz
Box 9188
Yakima, WA 98907
(509)248-1390

KUTI-AM 980 khz
Box 2309
Yakima, WA 98907
(509)248-2900

KXDD-FM 104.1 mhz
Box 2309
Yakima, WA 98907
(509)248-2900

KYKA-FM 96.9 mhz
2412 W. Lincoln
Yakima, WA 98902
(509)453-6296

KYSC-FM 88.5 mhz
Yakima School Dist #7
1116 S. 15th Ave
Yakima, WA 98902
(509)575-3333

KZTA-Am 930 khz
Box 2489
Yakima, WA 98907
(509)248-4722

DAILY NEWSPAPERS

ABERDEEN

Aberdeen Daily World
POB 269, Aberdeen, WA 98520
(206)532-4000

AUBURN

Globe-News
c/o Valley Newspapers
POB 130, Kent, WA 98032
(206)872-6650

BELLEVUE

Daily Journal American
POB 90130, Bellevue, WA
98009, (206)455-2222

BELLINGHAM

Bellingham Herald
POB 1277, Bellingham, WA
98227, (206)676-2600

BREMERTON

Bremerton Sun
POB 259, Bremerton, WA 98310
(206)377-3711

CENTRALIA

The Daily Chronicle
POB 580, Centralia, WA 98531
(206)736-736-3311

COLFAX

Daily Bulletin
(4 times a week) POB 770

Colfax, WA 99111,
(509)397-4333

ELLENSBURG

Ellensburg Daily Record
POB 248, Ellensburg, WA
98926, (509)925-1414

EVERETT

The Everett Herald
POB 930, Everett, WA 98206
(206)339-3000

KENT

News-Journal
c/o Valley Newspapers
Box 130, Kent, WA 98032
(206)872-6600

LONGVIEW

Longview Daily News
POB 189, Longview, WA 98632
(206)577-2500

MOSES LAKE

Columbia Basin Herald
POB 910, Moses Lake, WA
98837, (509)765-4561

MOUNT VERNON

Skagit Valley Herald
POB 578, Mount Vernon, WA
98273, (206)424-3251

OLYMPIA

The Daily Olympian
POB 407, Olympia, WA 98507
(206)754-5400

PORT ANGELES

Port Angeles Daily News
POB 1330, Pork Angeles, WA
98362, (206)452-2345

PULLMAN

Daily Evergreen (WSU)
POB 2008, Pullman, WA 99165
(509)335-4573

The Daily News
South 107 Grand Ave, Suite
B, Pullman, WA 99163
(509)334-6397

RENTON

Record-Chronicle
c/o Valley Newspapers
POB 130, Kent, WA 98032
(206)872-6660

SEATTLE

The Daily (UW)
132 Communications U.W.DS-20
Seattle, Wa 98195,
(206)543-2680

Daily Journal of Commerce
POB 11050, Seattle, WA 98111
(206)622-8272

Seattle Post-Intelligencer
101 Elliott Ave, W, Seattle,
WA 98119, POB 1909, Seattle,
WA 98121, (206)464-2121

The Seattle Times
Fairview Ave N. & John St.
POB 70, Seattle, WA 98111
(206)464-2111

SPOKANE

Spokane Chronicle
POB 2160, Spokane, WA 99210
(509)455-7010

The Spokane-Review
POB 2160, Spokane, WA 99210,
(509)459-5060

SUNNYSIDE

Sunnyside Sun Daily News
POB 878, Sunnyside 98944
(509)837-4500

TACOMA

Tacoma Daily Index
POB 1303, Tacoma, WA 98401
(206)627-4853

Tacoma News Tribune
POB 11000, Tacoma, WA 98411,
(206)597-8511

TRI-CITIES

Tri-City Herald
POB 2608, Tri-Cities, WA
99302, (509)586-1500

VANCOUVER

The Oregonian
Clark County News Bureau
208 W. 11th St, Vancouver,
WA 98660, (206)694-1450

Vancouver Columbian
POB 180, Vancouver, WA
98668, (206)694-3391

WALLA WALLA

Union-Bulletin
POB 1358
Walla Walla, WA 99362
(509)525-3300

WENATCHEE

Wenatchee Daily World
POB 1511, Wenatchee, WA
988801, (509)663-5161

YAKIMA

Yakima Herald-Republic
114 N. Fourth St, POB 9668
Yakima, WA 98909,
(509)248-1251

NEWS BUREAUS:

Associated Press
POB 2144, Seattle, WA 98111

MOTION PICTURE PRODUCERS AND STUDIOS

EGS INTERNATIONAL
Edmonds 98020 (206)771-4522

NORTHWEST SUPERLDOPERS
25831 SE 30th, Issaquah
98027 (206)392-4093

PHIL LUCAS PRODUCTIONS
1065 12th NW, Issaquah
98027 (206)392-9482

DJ & COMPANY COMMS SVCS
26550 Ritter Ln NE
Kingston 98346 (206)297-3997

AV PRODUCTION & SERVICES
3823 48th SW, Seattle
98116 (206)361-9606

AMERICAN PRODUCTION SERVICES
2247 15th W, Seattle 98119
(206)282-1776

CAMERA ONE PRODUCTIONS
431 N 34th, Seattle 98103
(206)547-5131

CAMERON PRODUCTIONS, INC.
222 Minor N, Seattle 98109
(206)623-4103

CHARLES A. STEWARD
PRODUCTIONS
201 Galer, Seattle 98109
(206)285-5253

COFFIN & COMPANY
1506 17th E, Seattle 98112
(206)328-2330

CONWAY PRODUCTIONS
14802 Bothell Way NE
Seattle 98153 (206)365-4811

EATON ASSOCIATES, INC.
4712 Fremont W, Seattle
98103 (206)632-6841

FACTOTUM PRODUCTIONS, INC.
POB 31973, Seattle 98121
(206)682-1210

FILM & VIDEO SEMINAR
1001 Lenora, Seattle 98121
(206)682-1210

GRIFFIN PRODUCTIONS
10 Harrison, Seattle 98109
(206)285-1661

HUSKINSON PRODUCTIONS
1809 7th, Seattle 98101
(206)823-8949

JRB MOTION GRAPHICS LDT
4117 Stone Way N, Seattle
98103 (206)547-2552

JAMES MEYER PRODUCTIONS
87 Wall, Seattle 98121
(206)443-4238

JENSEN/HALL, INC.
1201 1st #200, Seattle
98134 (206)682-7005

KALLES CASTING
606 2nd, Seattle 98104
(206)447-8318

KAYE-SMITH PRODUCTIONS
2211 5th, Seattle 98121
(206)728-8651

MAZZOLA & ASSOCIATES, INC.
443 8th N, Seattle 98109
(206)622-8540

MERWIN PRODUCTIONS
206 3rd S, Seattle 98104
(206)621-7552

MIRAMAR PRODUCTIONS, INC.
200 2nd W, Seattle 98119
(206)284-4700

NOREN PRODUCTIONS, INC.
120 Lakeside #240, Seattle
98122 (206)325-5306

NORTH PACIFIC FILM/TAPE
108 Jackson, Seattle 98104
(206)623-3151

NORTHSTAR PRODUCTIONS
700 S Homer, Seattle 98108
(206)762-1605

NORTHWEST VIDEO CENTER
1050 W Nickerson, Seattle
98119 (206)282-9670

OFFSHORE PRODUCTIONS
617 E Thomas, Seattle
98102 (206)323-3040

PAL PRODUCTIONS, INC.
511 2nd W, Seattle 98119
(206)282-2025

ROB ROY PRODUCTIONS, INC.
1513 14th, Seattle 98122
(206)322-2597

TAYLOR J. GRALEY
500 Wall, Seattle 98121
(206)441-6110

THE LEMSMAN COMPANY, INC.
1932 1st, Seattle 98101
(206)441-8077

TOMLEN PRODUCTION
200 W Mercer, Seattle 98119
(206)283-5446

VIDEO PRESENTATIONS, INC.
2326 6th, Seattle 98121
(206)728-9241

VIK-WINKLE PRODUCTIONS
1331 3rd, Seattle 98101
(206)343-9440

VULCAN PACIFIC
6920 Roosevelt Way NE
Seattle 98115 (206)622-1399

WASHINGTON FILM & VIDEO
600 1st, Seattle 98104
(206)682-5495

TRIAD PICTURES CORP.
134 Simdars Rd, Sequim
98382 (206)683-8459

BROADWAY WEST PRODUCTION
W 1229 Broadway, Spokane
99201 (509)327-1833

LON GIBBY PRODUCTIONS
E 113 Magmesium Rd, Spokane
99208 (509)467-1113

MILL MOUNTAIN PRODUCTION
S 126 Division, Spokane
99202 (509)624-3146

MILL MOUNTAIN PRODUCTION
W 915 12th, Spokane 99204
(509)838-1617

PINNACLE PRODUCTIONS, INC.
E 204 Nora, Spokane 99207
(509)326-7030

RLP PRODUCTIONS
N 601 Cedar, Spokane 99201
(509)328-6160

ABATTOIR PRODUCTIONS
1103 South A St, Tacoma
98402 (206)572-4897

SHOOTIST
400 E Evergreen Blvd
Vancouver 98660
(206)639-5444

Legal

(see legal listing under individual county section)

WASHINGTON SMALL CLAIMS COURT

Small claims court is where minor lawsuits are brought. They enable you to by-pass lawyers and much of the time consuming red tape of other more formal courts.

The small claims court judge has only the power to award or deny a judgement for money. He cannot order a person to return an item of property to its original owner. Nor can real estate ownership be ascertained. Nor can he direct a person to do something affirmative, like removing an illegal barrier, or stopped from doing something like cutting down a neighbor's hedge brush. Small claims judges cannot settle domestic disputes between husbands and wives. They do not have the power to sentence your foe to jail for not paying. If your case against the other person or organization involves anything other than the reward of a sum of money, you will not be able to use the small claims court.

The monetary limit for which you can sue for in Washington is $2,000. If your claim is larger than this amount, you will have to either lower it, or take your case to a higher court.

Who can use the Small Claims Court?

Any competent person 18 years or older can use the small claims court. If under the age of 18, individual must be represented by a guardian. Besides age and mental competency, the last requirement is that the party who is being sued and the party who brings the suit must be personally involved in the case.

Lawyers

Lawyers are not permitted to argue your case in small claims court. You and your opponent will have to argue your own cases without being represented by anyone else. You can however have witnesses.

Court Locations

Once you have decided to use the small claims court, your next step is to determine the courthouse where your case must be brought. Each county has one Justice Court with a small claims division. Some of the larger counties are divided into districts with courts and judges assigned to each. **(see court listings under individual counties).** By all means contact the clerk of the district court in the district where your case will be heard.

How to get your opponent to court

The "Notice of Claim," is the process which must be served to get your opponent to court. You must fill out the form at the clerk's office. A copy of your claim and of the claim notice will be returned to you by the clerk.

Delivery of papers

You are not permitted to personally deliver the claim
notice. You should mail the paperwork by certified or
registered mail with a "return receipt requested." If you
believe that hand-delivered service would be better than
certified or registered mail, you can have the county
sheriff or a private messenger service hand-deliver it for
you.

For additional information on the small claims court
contact: Administrator for the Courts, 1206 South Quince
St., EZ-11, Olympia, WA 98504, (206)753-3365

Small Claims Court Guide For Washington: How To Win Your
Case! Self-Counsel Press, Inc., 1704 N. State St.,
Bellingham, WA 98225

PARALEGALS

(Also see Legal listing under each
county for additional assistance)

AUBURN PARALEGAL SERVICES
424 37th St SE, Auburn 98002
(206)393-2664

CIVIL CLAIMS SERVICES
606 110th NE, Bellevue
98004 (206)455-5169

LEGAL SERVICES
4091 State Hwy 3, Bremerton
98312 (206)479-4409

OLYMPIC ACCOUNTING &
PARALEGAL
2614 6th, Bremerton 98312
(206)373-5306

LEGAL ASSOCIATES
3321 Wetmore Ave, Everett
98201 (206)258-4484

SELF COUNSEL PLUS TYPING
607 SE Everett Mall Way
Everett 98208 (206)348-5607

M.L. WEBB & ASSOCIATES
725 Perry Ave, Hoquiam
98550 (206)532-7722

DIVORCE & BANKRUPTCY SVCS-WA
614 196th St SW, Lynnwood
98036 (206)775-1233

DIVORCE & BANKRUPTCY SVCS.
1017 E 4th, Olympia 98506
(206)754-0488

BAYVIEW PARALEGAL SERVICE
581 Bay, Port Orchard
98366 (206)876-1857

FAMILY LEGAL SERVICES
2505 SE State Hwy 160 #C4
Port Orchard 98366
(206)876-8240

LELA'S PARALEGAL SERVICE
2505 SE State Hwy 160
Port Orchard 98366
(206)876-0568

PARALEGAL CLINIC
116 Bay, Port Orchard
98366 (206)895-0939

PARALEGAL ASSOCIATES
212 Wells S, Renton 98055
(206)625-0460

THE PARALEGAL COMPANY, INC.
3233 NE 12th #207, Renton
98058 (206)226-8090

ROTHBAUM & SONS LEGAL COPY
1407 NW 70th, Seattle 98117
(206)789-2188

ABC PARALEGAL SERVICES
8717 S Hosmer, Tacoma 98444
(206)537-7377

WASHINGTON PARA-LEGAL
9618 Gravelly Lake Dr SW
Tacoma 98499 (206)584-1955

MARRIAGE IN WASHINGTON STATE

The legal requirements for marriage in Washington are
outlined in RCW (Revised Code of Wash.) 26.04, as amended in
1973. This law requires that both parties be at least 18
years of age unless they have a court order permitting them
to marry at a younger age.

It is against the law to marry anyone closer than a second
cousin, including an aunt, uncle, grandchild, nephew, or
niece.

Before marriage, a couple must apply for and secure a
license from a county auditor.

Unmarried couples and the law

The State of Washington does not recognize "common-law
marriage" as some states do; which decree that after a set
number of years of living together a couple are considered
married.

Normally in Washington, property acquired by unmarried
couples living together has been for the most part
considered to belong to one or the other of them.

Separation

It is possible, and often common for a couple to separate
without any legal action being taken. However, Washington
law provides a procedure for setting down the terms of a
separation agreement, making them binding on both parties.
Separation agreements are legally very powerful, and should
not be entered into lightly. A separation agreement can be
drawn-up while the parties are still living together.
Neither party can be forced into signing an agreement.

In Washington, separation agreements are not completely
binding regarding custody, visitation, and support of
children, since the courts reserves the right to review
these provisions to make sure that the best interest of the
children is taken into account.

Dissolution of marriage

Washington has an uncomplicated and reasonable set of laws
pertaining to divorce. A non-contested divorce can be
accomplished in 90 days total time. The 1973 amendments to
Washington's divorce laws abolished the previous "grounds"
for divorce and established the present "no fault" system.

"No fault" means that the court will not permit or require
evidence of specific acts of misconduct or fault in granting
a dissolution of a marriage contract.

Initiating a divorce action

An action for divorce, or "dissolution of marriage" as it is referred to in Washington, is initiated by filing a petition for dissolution and a summons and by serving these documents on your marriage partner. It generally makes no difference which spouse files the petition. The summons and petition are filed in the Superior Court of the county where one or both spouses reside. A filling fee is required to be paid at the time of filing.

The petition for dissolution does not have to be complicated. The law only requires that it contain a minimum set of facts. Other facts are permissible, but not mandatory. The minimum information is as follows:

1. A statement that the marriage is irretrievably broken.

2. The last known address of each party.

3. The date and place of marriage.

4. The date on which the parties separated.

5. The names, ages, and addresses of any and all children dependent upon either or both of the spouses.

6. A statement about whether the wife is pregnant.

7. A statement about whether there is property to be disposed of and obligations to be assigned.

8. A statement of the relief sought.

Crime

ARREST BY TYPE OF OFFENSE STATEWIDE 1989
(Source Washington Association of Sheriffs & Police Chiefs)

OFFENSE	SEX	JUVENILE TOTAL	ADULT TOTAL	TOTAL ARRESTS
MURDER	M	11	118	129
	F	2	13	15
MANSLAUGHTER	M	1	33	34
	F	3	2	5
RAPE	M	132	704	836
	F	4	5	9
ROBBERY	M	201	843	1,044
	F	28	81	109
AGGRAVATED ASSAULT	M	497	2,678	3,175
	F	64	398	462
BURGLARY	M	2,592	3,722	6,314
	F	235	267	502
LARCENY	M	8,252	15,174	23,426
	F	3,667	7,303	10,970
MOTOR VEHICLE THEFT	M	969	950	1,919
	F	186	121	307
TOTAL CRIME INDEX	**M**	**12,655**	**24,222**	**49,256**
ARRESTS	**F**	**4,189**	**8,190**	
OTHER ASSAULTS	M	2,411	19,823	22,234
	F	843	4,161	5,004
ARSON	M	159	110	269
	F	11	15	26
FORGERY & COUNTER-FEITING	M	143	895	1,038
	F	56	494	550
FRAUD	M	26	869	895
	F	6	571	577
EMBEZZLEMENT	M	1	15	16
	F	0	15	15
STOLEN PROPERTY	M	784	1,857	2,641
	F	129	398	527
VANDALISM	M	1,602	2,952	4,554
	F	171	402	573

WEAPON-CARRYING POSSESSION	M	303	1,565	1,868
	F	16	138	154
PROSTITUTION	M	12	822	834
	F	56	825	881
SEX OFFENSES	M	300	1,689	1,989
	F	15	81	96
DRUG ABUSE	M	852	9,876	10,728
	F	195	2,298	2,493
GAMBLING	M	0	8	8
	F	0	2	2
OFFENSES AGAINST FAMILY	M	10	424	434
	F	8	96	104
DRIVING UNDER THE INFLUENCE	M	313	28,121	28,434
	F	76	5,288	5,364
LIQUOR LAW	M	3,116	11,110	14,226
	F	1,369	2,180	3,549
DRUNKENESS	M	12	97	109
	F	6	26	32
DISORDERLY CONDUCT	M	237	2,678	2,915
	F	93	507	600
VAGRANCY	M	20	100	120
	F	3	4	7
ALL OTHER OFFENSES	M	3,048	38,385	41,433
	F	773	7,534	8,307
SUSPICION	M	39	185	224
	F	6	22	28
CURFEW-LOITERING	M	76	0	76
	F	42	0	42
RUNAWAY	M	1,030	0	1,030
	F	1,484	0	1,484
CLASS II OFFENSES TOTAL	**M**	**14,494**	**121,581**	**166,490**
GRAND TOTAL	**M**	**27,149**	**145,803**	**215,746**
	F	**9,547**	**33,247**	

DEPARTMENT OF CORRECTIONS

Capitol Center Bldg, FN-61
Olympia 98504-3461
POB 9699, Olympia 98504
(206)753-1573

This department runs the comprehensive system of corrections for convicted law violators within the state. Following is a list of the state's penal institutions.

INSTITUTIONS

Cedar Creek Corrections Ctr
POB 37, Littlerock 98556
(206)753-7278

Cllallam Bay Corrections Ctr
HH 63, POB 5000, Clallam
98326-9775 (206)963-2000

Clearwater/Olympic Corr. Ctr
HC-80, Box 2500, Forks 98331
(206)374-6181

Indian Ridge Corrections Ctr
19601 Nicks Rd, Arlington
98223-9515 (206)339-1860

Larch Corrections Center
15314 NE Dole Valley Rd
Yacolt 98675-9531
(206)696-6341

McNeil Island Corrections Ctr, POB 900, Steilcoom
98388-0900 (206)588-5281

Pine Lodge Corrections Ctr
POB C, Medical Lake 99022
(509)299-5135

Special Offender Center
POB 514, Monroe 98272-0514
(206)794-2200

Twin Rivers Corrections Ctr
POB 888, MS:NM-85
Monroe 98272-0888
(206)794-2400

Washington Corrections Ctr
POB 900, Shelton 98584
(206)858-9101

**Washington Corrections Ctr
For Women,** POB 17, MS:WP-04,
Gig Harbor 98335
(206)858-9101

**Washington State
Penitentiary**
POB 520, Walla Walla 99362
(509)525-3610

Washington State Reformatory
POB 777, MS:NM-83, Monroe
98272-0777 (206)794-2600

Consuming

UNIQUE SHOPPING

SWAP MEETS & SHOPS

BROWSE & SWAP
1101 S Gold, Centralia 98531
(206)736-7772

PUGET SOUND DRIVE-IN
13020 Meridian S, Everett
98204 (206)337-1436

MIDWAY SWAP & SHOP
24050 Pacific Hwy S
Kent 98032 (206)878-1990

DRIVE-IN SWAP SHOP
17325 Hwy 99, Lynnwood 98037
(206)743-2294

OLD HOBBY SHOP
17707 Hwy 99, Lynnwood 98037
(206)743-1033

MONROE FAIRGROUNDS SWAP MEET
Monroe 98272 (206)794-4000

RAINBOWS END CONSIGNMENT
138 S 1st, Montesano 98563
(206)249-6340

THE PUBLIC MARKET
7009 Martin Way E
Olympia 98508 (206)438-2604

STAR-LITE SWAP & SHOP
8301 S Tacoma Way
Tacoma 98499 (206)588-8000

SWAP & SHOP ASSOCIATION
S 84th & S Tacoma Way
Tacoma 98409 (206)588-8621

PERSONAL SHOPPING SERVICES

SHOPPING JUST FOR YOU
Colbert 99005 (509)238-4450

BORN TO SHOP
Ellensburg 98926
(509)925-6328

TIME FOR SALE, INC.
14134 110th Ave NE
Kirkland 98034 (206)488-7696

ROADRUNNERS
Longview 98632 (206)425-8070

FRIENDLY SHOPPER
26605 Ansell Rd NW
Poulsbo 98370 (206)779-9054

SHOPPING ETC
Poulsbo 98370 (206)779-3427

ELITE SERVICES
Richland 99352 (509)627-5115

MOBILE GROCER
15550 27th NE, Seattle 98155
(206)363-7447

COST PLUS DELIVERY
POB 9063, Spokane 99209
(509)325-5030

KEN & RITS'S SHOPPING &
ERRAND, W 4011 27th Ave
Spokane 99204 (509)838-1232

DONNA JEAN'S ENTERPRISES,
INC, POB 97052, Tacoma 98497
(206)581-4033

LIMITED TIME
5820 Montana Ln
Vancouver 98861
(206)694-6613

BARTER AND TRADE

Cascade Trade Association
34 37th NE, Auburn 98002
(206)735-0340

Exchange Enterprises
13620 NE 20th, Bellevue
98005 (206)641-0070

Inter Trade Exchange
320 E Fairhaven Ave #104
Burlington 98233
(206)755-0107

Northwest Internet
4729 W View Dr, Everett
98203 (206)253-4488

Exchange Enterprise
7525 W Deschuter
Kennewick 99336
(509)735-6146

Trade-Mark Bus Barter
7002 Ocean Beach Hwy S.
Longview 98632 (206)423-3823

Cascade Trade Assoc., Inc.
15735 Pacific Hwy S.
Seattle 98188 (206)441-4417

Itex Spokane
N 6619 Cedar, Spokane 99208
(509)328-5200

Advanced Barter
7939 NE St Johns Rd
Vancouver 98665
(206)573-5874

SURVIVAL PRODUCTS

INFLATABLE BOATWORKS
2425 NW Market, Seattle
98107 (206)789-7470

NEPTUNE SAFETY CENTER
3425 16th W, Seattle 98119
(206)282-3111

THE FOOD CUPBOARD
9414 Roosevelt Way NE
Seattle 98115 (206)524-8300

EXPLORATION PRODUCTS, LTD
E 12411 Empire Ln, Spokane
99206 (509)927-8101

ULTIMATE SURVIVAL GAME
6616 150th SW, Tacoma 98439
(206)581-4014

SPRING UNLIMITED
POB 10886, Winslow 98110
(206)842-1506

BANKS

Following is a list of the chartered banks in Washington with total assets of 2 million dollars (1988 totals) or more along with their number of branches.

Washington Mutual Savings Bank
POB 834, 1201 Third Avenue
Seattle, WA 98101
(206)461-2000
Total assets: $5,796,614,000
Branches: 49

Puget Sound Savings Bank
1325 Fourth Avenue
Seattle, Wa 98101
(206)447-5700
Total Assets: $1,548,507,000
Branches: 83

Key Bank of Puget Sound
1000 Second Avenue (98104)
POB 90, Seattle, WA 98111
(206)684-6000
Total Assets: $991,196,000
Branches: 29

Great Western Bank, A Savings Bank
11201 SE 8th Street
Bellevue, WA 98004
(206)451-2000
Total assets: $844,106,000
Branches: 16

University Savings Bank
6400 Roosevelt Way NE
Seattle, WA 98115
(206)526-1000
Total assets: $763,188,000
Branches: 22

**The Mitsui Taiyo Kobe Bank, Ltd.
Seattle Branch**
900 Fourth Avenue, Suite 3900
Seattle, WA 98154
(206)622-0330
Total assets: $643,770,000
Branches: none

**Security Pacific Savings
Bank,** POB 1637, 1102 Commerce
Tacoma, WA 98401
(206)572-5220
Total assets: $625,835,000
Branches: 17

Washington Trust Bank
POB 2127
Spokane, WA 99210
(509)455-4122
Total assets: $538,304,000
Branches: 13

**The Bank of Tokyo, Ltd.
Seattle Branch**
POB 2466
Seattle, WA 98111
(206)382-6000
Total assets: $389,307,000
Branches: none

First Independent Bank
POB C-004
Vancouver, WA 98668
(206)699-4242
Total assets: $360,015,000

The Hokkaido Takushoku Bank
1001 Fourth Avenue
Seattle, WA 98154
(206)624-0920
Total assets: $352,376,000
Branches: none

Korea Exchange Bank
One Union Square Building
600 University St, Suite 2111
Seattle, WA 98101
(206)622-7821
Total assets: $342,324,000
Branches: none

Horizon Bank, A Savings Bank
POB 580
Bellingham, WA 98227
(206)733-3050
Total assets: $266,152,000
Branches: 7

Everett Mutual Savings Bank
1502 Wall Street
POB 569 (98206-0569)
Everett, WA 98201
(206)258-3641
Total assets: $210,157,000
Branches: 7

SINGING TELEGRAMS

AUBURN FLORAL-BRIDAL/TUX
1403 Auburn Way, S, Auburn
98002 (206)735-3115

NORTHERN NOTES TELEGRAM
3025 Meridian, Bellingham
98225 (206)678-0333

ROYAL ENTERTAINMENT
3125 Northwest, POB 1381
Bellingham 98225
(206)647-2789

BILLIES GRAM-O-RAMA
Blaine 98230 (206)332-5376

BAG LADY
1030 S Tower, Centralia
98531 (206)736-1266

M & M BALLOONS
23931 Hwy 99, Edmonds 98020
(206)778-7366

GORILLA GRAMS
3012 N Rd 68, Pasco 99301
(509)547-7648

HAPPY FACE CLOWNS
Port Angeles 98362
(206)452-5961

SPECIAL TIMES SINGAGRAM
1722 W 15th, Port Angeles
98362 (206)457-98362

REPUTATIONS TELEGRAM ETC.
Pullman 99163 (509)332-7032

A-DANCE A-GRAM
7424 140th Pl NE, Redmond
98052 (206)869-1524

APPLEMANIA PRODUCTIONS
106 Union, Seattle 98101
(206)340-1709

CHAMPAGNE AND ROSES LTD.
POB 51172, Seattle 98115
(206)525-525-2339

HELIUM ROSES BALLOON CO.
4531 California Ave SW
Seattle 98116 (206)938-3469

LIVE WIRES
7515 12th NE, Seattle 98115
(206)526-526-6483

WESTERN UNION SIGNING
W 612 Garland, Spokane 99205
(509)325-8863

THE FLOWER MILL
1314 Yakima Valley Hwy
Sunnyside 98944
(509)837-3500

LOIS E. SMITH VAN SOPRANO
601 E 22nd, Vancouver 98663
(206)694-0954

WASHINGTON STATE PUBLIC AUTCIONS

Washington holds public auctions of used state vehicles through the use of "silent bid" (auctions where the bids are written rather than spoken), and sells surplus materials by sealed bid (bids are sent in via mail) by catalogs. The vehicles are auctioned off about every three months. Auctions include all types of used state conveyances, from patrol cars, to trucks, and passenger cars, most having over 100,000 miles on them. There are a few new luxury or confiscated type vehicles.

The "silent bids" are held once a month, and include large quantities of office furniture sold by the pallet, with the exception of typewriters, which are sold individually. You may visit the warehouse to inspect the items beforehand. Payment may be made by cashier check, money order, or cash, but no personal checks are accepted.

For the sealed bids, you may request a catalog of merchandise, which includes everything from vehicles to scrap material, office furniture and equipment, computers, clothing, cleaning fluids, tools, pumps, etc. To receive monthly catalogs and listing of these sales write to:

Office of Commodity Redistribution
2805 C Street, SW, Bldg 5, Door 49
Auburn, WA 98001 (206)931-3931

(example of auction and sealed bid listing)

SURPLUS SALE CATALOG

ITEM		
1:	MISC. CHAIRS Approx 97	BID PER LOT
2:	MISC. TABLES consist- ing of: End Tables, Display Tables, 3x8 Folding Table, Typing Stands, etc. 2 pallets	BID PER LOT
3:	General Electric DEEP FRYER	BID PER EACH
4:	MISC. COMPUTER COMP- ONENTS consisting of: Computer, Xerox Printers Xerox Disk Drives, Xerox Monitors, etc. 5 pallets	BID PER LOT
5:	Harris TERMINALS Approx 37 2 pallets	BID PER LOT

ITEM		
15:	MISC. VIDEO EQUIP. consisting of: Rewinder, Repair Kit, Movie Scope, Kodak Camera, Slide Viewer, Polaroid Camera, Minolta Video Camera, Canon Video Camera, RCA Projector, etc.	BID PER LOT
16:	MISC. ELECTRIC POWER PANEL BOXES consisting of: Junction Boxes and Electric Welding Machines	BID PER LOT
17:	MISC. TABLES AND SHELVING UNITS con- sisting of: Table w/2 drawers, Wood Table, Shelving Units, Mail Slots etc.	BID PER LOT

WASHINGTON'S UNCLAIMED PROPERTY

Does your memory sometimes play tricks on you? Have you ever
forgotten where you put that gift certificate you got for
your birthday or where you put the insurance check that came
in the mail last month? Did you forget to pick up your
utility deposit or close out a bank account when you moved:
if so, you're not along. Since 1955 the Washington
Department of Revenue has received over $70 million in
unclaimed property and the amount turned over to the state
each year continues to grow.

In Fiscal Year 1989 the Unclaimed Property Section received
property worth over $9 million. All funds received through
the program are deposited into a trust account. The
department operates this program as a consumer protection
operation and it's primary purpose is to guard and return
the unclaimed property to the rightful owners or their
heirs.

Filing a Claim

If you think that state is holding unclaimed property
belonging to you, you can obtain a claim form from: The
Department of Revenue, Unclaimed Property Section, ATTN:
Claims Office, POB 448, Olympia, WA 98504. Or you can phone
the claims office at (206)586-2736. There is no time limit
on claiming funds. Property reported in 1955 and thereafter
can still be claimed by the rightful owners or their heirs.

Acting as agents for unclaimed property owners

The Department of Revenue permits individuals and businesses
to act as agents in locating the owners of unclaimed
property. Available upon request is an information
packet describing all the requirements and conditions. If
this interests you, write them at the above address, there
could be lots of money to be made.

Wine

WINERIES

FIDALGO ISLAND WINERY
5303 Doons Way, Anacortes
98221 (206)293-4342

BAINBRIDGE ISLE WINERY
682 State Hwy 305 NE,
Brainbridge Isle 98110
(206)842-9463

HEUBLEIN WINES
1200 112th NE, Bellevue
98004 (206)462-8826

PAUL THOMAS WINES
1717 136th Pl NE, Bellevue
98005 (206)747-1008

SEAGRAMS CLASSICS WINES
1756 114th SE, Bellevue
98004 (206)482-8824

BLACKWOOD CANYON VINEYARDS
Sunset Rd, Benton City 99320
·(509)588-8249

KIONA VINEYARDS WINERY
Sunset Dr, Benton City 99320
(509)588-6716

OAKWOOD CELLARS
Demoss Rd, Benton City 99320
(509)588-5332

MONT ELISE VINEYARDS
315 W Steuben, Bingen 98805
(509)493-3001

WASHINGTON WINE/BEVERAGE
17616 15th Ave SE, Bothell
98012 (206)485-2437

MT BAKER VINEYARDS
4298 Mt Baker Hwy, Deming
98244 (206)592-2300

BISCUIT RIDGE WINERY
Dixie 99329
(509)529-4988

WENATCHEE VALLEY VINEYARD
1111 S Van Sickle
E Wenatchee 98802
(509)884-8235

CASCADE MOUNTAIN CELLARS
606 W 3rd, Ellensburg
98926 (509)925-2998

CHAMPS DE BRIONNE WINERY
98 RD W NW, George 98824
(509)785-6685

CHATEAU STE MICHELLE
Olson Rd, Grandview 98930
(509)882-4438

COVENTRY VALE VINEYARDS
Wilgus & Evans Rds,
Grandview 98930
(509)882-4100

EATON HILL WINERY
530 Gurley Rd, Granger
98932 (509)854-2220

STEWARD VINEYARDS WINERY
Cherry Hill Rd, Granger
98932 (509)854-1882

HOODSPORT WINERY
N 23522 Hwy 101, Hoodsport
98548 (206)877-9894

CHARLES HOOPER FAMILY
Spring Creek Rd, Husum
98623 (509)493-2324

COVEY RUN WINES
107' Central Way, Kirkland
98033 (206)828-3848

SALISHAN VINEYARDS
RR 2 Box 8, La Center 98629
(206)263-2713

L'ECOLE NO 41, 41 Lowden
School Rd, Lowden 99360
(509)525-0940

WOODWARD CANYON WINERY
Lowden 99360
(509)525-4129

FRAN WILHELM LANGGUTH WINERY
2340 Winery Rd, Mattawa
99344 (509)932-4943

VANTAGE VINTNERS
Beverly-Smirne Rd, Mattawa
99344 (509)932-4808

HUNTER HILL VINEYARDS
2752 W McMannamon Rd,
Othello 99344 (509)348-2607

BOOKWATER WINERY
2708 Commerical, Pasco 99301
(509)545-9483

CHATEAU GALLANT WINERY
1355 S Gallant Rd
Pasco 99310 (509)545-9570

MERCER RANCH VINEYARDS
522 Alderdale Rd, Prosser
99350 (509)894-4741

PONTIN DEL ROZA WINERY
Hinzerling Rd, Prosser
99350 (509)786-4449

WASHINGTON ASSN. OF WINE
Prosser 99350
(509)788-2582

YAKIMA RIVER WINERY, INC.
North River Rd, Prosser
99350 (509)786-2805

GORDON BROTHERS
531 Levey Rd, Pasco 99301
(509)547-8224

PRESTON FAMILY, INC.
1124 W Ainsworth, Pasco
99301 (509)547-9411

PRESTON WINE CELLARS
502 E Vineyard Dr, Pasco
99301 (509)545-1990

QUARRY LAKE VINTNERS
2530 Commercial, Pasco 99301
(509)547-7307

COLUMBIA CREST WINERY
River Ridge Winery,
Patterson 99345
(509)875-2061

CHINOOK WINES
Wine County Rd, Prosser
99350 (509)786-2725

HINZERLING VINEYARDS
1520 Sheridan Ave
Prosser 99350 (509)786-2163

HOGUE CELLARS
Lee & Meade Ave, Prosser
99350 (509)786-4557

FACELLI WINERY
12335 134th Ct NE, Redmond
98052 (206)823-9486

CASCADE ESTATES WINERY
1210 Valley, Seattle 98109
(206)624-5310

EB FOOTE WINERY
9354 4th S, Seattle 98108
(206)763-9928

OREGON METHODE CHAMPENOISE,
INC, 5318 22nd NW, Seattle
98107 (206)789-6543

STATON HILLS WINERY
1910 Post Alley, Seattle
98101 (206)443-8084

LOST MOUNTAIN WINERY
730 Lost Mountain Rd
Sequim 98382 (206)683-5229

NEUHARTH WINERY, INC.
148 Still Rd, Sequim 98382
(206)683-9652

QUILCEDA CREEK VINTNERS
6226 Machias Hwy
Snohomish 98290
(206)568-2389

SNOQUALMIE WINERY
1000 Winery Rd, Snoqualmie
98065 (206)888-4000

TAGARIS WINERY
39202 Meadowbrook Way,
Snoqualmie 98065
(206)888-9400

ARBOR CREST WINE CELLARS
N 4705 Fruit Hill Rd,
Spokane 99207 (509)927-9894

LATAH CREEK WINE CELLARS
E 13030 Indiana, Spokane
99216 (509)926-0164

STE MICHELLE WINES
S 5118 Madelia, Spokane
99223 (509)448-5428

WORDEN'S WASHINGTON WINERY
W 7217 45th, Spokane 99204
(509)455-7835

MANFRED VIERTHALER, INC.
17136 State Hwy 410
Sumner 98390 (206)863-1633

CASCADE CREST ESTATES
111 E Lincoln, Sunnyside
98944 (509)839-9463

CHATEAU STE MICHELLE
Bethany Rd, Sunnyside 98944
(509)837-7339

JOHNSON CREEK WINERY
19248 Johnson Cr Rd SE
Tenino 98589 (206)264-2100

VINEYARD GALLERY
101 S Toppenish Ave
Toppenish 98948
(509)865-5002

LEONETTE CELLAR
1321 School, Walla Walla
99362 (509)525-1428

WATERBROOK WINERY
POB 46 Mac Donald Rd
Walla Walla 99362
(509)522-1918

STATON HILLS WINERY
2290 Gangl Rd, Wapato 98951
(509)877-2112

CRYSTAL PHEASANT VINEYARDS
Acme Rd W, White Solmon
98672 (509)493-1629

CHATEAU STE MICHELLE
14111 NE 145th, Woodinville
98072 (206)488-1133

COLUMBIA WINERY
14030 NE 145th, Woodinville
98072 (509)488-2776

FRENCH CREEK CELLARS
17721 132nd Ave NE
Woodinville 98072
(509)486-1900

TUCKER CELLARS
15 W Yakima Ave, Yakima
98902 (509)454-9463

BONAIR WINERY
500 S Bonair Rd, Zillah
98953 (509)829-6027

COVEY RUN WINES
1500 Vintage Rd, Zillah
98953 (509)829-6235

HORIZON'S EDGE WINERY
4530 E Zillah Dr, Zillah
98953 (509)829-6401

HYATT VINEYARDS
2020 Gilbert Rd, Zillah
98953 (509)829-6333

ROSA HILLS VINEYARDS
Zillah 98953
(509)829-6152

ZILLAH OAKS WINERY
Exit 52 off Interstate 82
Zillah 98953 (509)829-6990

Travel

TOURS AND SIGHTSEEING

CROSSROADS TRAVEL, INC.
Crossroads Mall, Bellevue
98007 (206)746-2202

GALAXY TRAVEL INC.
25 102nd NE, Bellevue
98004 (206)454-2020

GRAD WEEK HAWAII
1300-B Bellevue Way NE
Bellevue 98004 (206)643-7175

MAGELLAN TOURS
925 116th NE, Bellevue 98004
(206)453-0722

SKYLINE TOURS USA
10 148th Ave NE, Bellevue
98007 (206)643-8982

BELLINGHAM SEATAC AIRPORTER
4121 Mitchell Way, Bellingam
98226 (206)733-3800

CHRISTY'S SEA-TO SKI CLUB
4855 Guide Meridian
Bellingham 98226
(206)734-9381

PUGET SOUND TOURS
1268 Mt Baker Hwy
Bellingham 98226
(206)734-3570

TLC TOURS, INC.
POB 337, Bellingham 98227
(206)671-7677

ALASKA MOTORCYCLE TOURS
9523 NE 198th, Bothell 98011
(206)487-3219

CAMAS TRAVEL SHOPPE
400 NE 4th, Camas 98607
(206)834-3155

CARNATION RESEARCH FARM
28901 NE Carnation Farm Rd
Carnation 98014
(206)788-1511

LAKE CHELAN BUS CHARTERS
POB 757, Chelan 98815
(206)682-4248

GOLF TOURS NW
11880 Des Moines Memorial Dr
Des Moines 98188
(206)244-6276

BLACK FISH PADDLERS
POB 1084, Eastsound 98245
(206)376-4041

CRUISE CENTER
1703 S 324th, Federal Way
98003 (206)927-7447

FRIDAY HARBOR INN
410 Spring W, Friday Harbor
98250 (206)378-4351

CHAMPS DE BRIONNE WINERY
98 Rd W NW, George 98824
(509)785-6685

FIRST CHOICE TRAVEL
7116 Stinson Ave, Gig Harbor
98335 (206)851-5110

GALAXY TRAVEL, INC.
4135 Providence Point Dr SE
Issaquah 98027 (206)392-2763

CLEARWATER TRAVEL, INC.
4607 W Clearwter Ave
Kennewick 99336
(509)735-9575

CHARTERS NORTHWEST
11504 NE 128th, Kirkland
98034 (206)821-9003

RETCO
907 Front, Leavenworth
98826 (509)548-8923

SUNSHINE VENTURES
2824 Queens Way, Milton
98354 (206)572-9330

ACTION TRAVEL
104-B Broadway, Moses Lake
98837 (509)785-2100

TRAVEL DESK
2114 Riverside Dr, Mt Vernon
98273 (206)424-7063

COMPASS TOURS
6425 Glenwood Dr SW, Olympia
98502 (206)943-7128

CREATIVE DESTINATIONS
POB 10274, Olympia 98502
(206)866-9533

NEWMAN TRAVEL PROGRAMS
1702 E 4th, Olympia 98506
(206)754-8067

PACIFIC TRAVELS NW TOUR
3730 Pacific Ave SE
Olympia 98501 (206)491-2883

OLYMPIC VAN TOURS, INC.
POB 2201, Port Angeles 98362
(206)452-3858

TOURING EXCHANGE
215 Taylor, Port Townsend
98368 (206)385-0667

WHEATLAND TRAVEL
1650 S Grand Ave, Pullman
99163 (509)334-2000

BASSETT TRANSIT
Richland 99352
(509)943-6847

CREATIVE TRAVEL, INC.
1515 Geo Washington Way
Richland 99353 (509)946-0637

ADVENTURE ASSOCIATES
POB 16304, Seattle 98116
(206)932-0620

ALASKA SIGHTSEEING TOURS
Fourth & Battery Bldg
Seattle 98121 (206)441-8887

AM PAC TOURS
8810 Aurora N, Seattle 98103
(206)527-7897

BARBARA J. BORESON & ASSOC.
500 Wall, Seattle 98121
(206)443-0708

BETTY'S TRAVEL & TOURS
444 NE Ravenna Blvd
Seattle 98115 (206)527-3320

BRENNAN TOURS
Fourth & Battery Bldg
Seattle 98121 (206)441-8689

CASUAL CABS
Pioneer Square
Seattle 98104 (206)623-2991

CHINATOWN DISCOVERY
POB 3406, Seattle 98114
(206)236-0654

DON & DIANE FUNTOURS
POB 21007, Seattle 98111
(206)282-3508

EASTERN EUROPE TOURS
600 Steward, Seattle 98101
(206)448-8400

GLACIER BAY TOURS
515 Pine, Seattle 98101
(206)623-7110

GRAY LINE OF ALASKA
300 Elliott W, Seattle 98119
(206)281-3535

GRAY LINE OF SEATTLE
720 S Forest, Seattle 98134
(206)624-5813

HOLDEN PACIFIC WINE TOUR
814 35th Ave, Seattle 98122
(206)325-4324

HOLIDAY WORLD TOURS
701 5th #3488, Seattle
98104 (206)625-8687

IMAGINE TRAVEL ALTERNATIVES
POB 27023, Seattle 98125
(206)624-7112

LEISURE TOURS
300 Elliott W, Seattle 98119
(206)281-3670

LITTLE HOLIDAY
603 Stewart #607, Seattle
98101 (206)622-4575

MAYAN ADVENTURE TOURS
5508 35th NE, Seattle
98105 (206)523-5309

NORTHWEST GREETING & TOUR
SERVICE
419 Queen Anne N, Seattle
98109 (206)285-2730

NORTHWEST TOURS
POB 9388, Seattle 98109
(206)728-1840

POWER TOURS
85 Marion #305, Seattle
98104 (206)682-8864

PROGRESSIVE TRAVELS LTD.
1932 1st, Seattle 98101
(206)443-4225

SCAN TRAVEL LTD.
500 Union #1012, Seattle
98101 (206)622-6412

SENIOR SAFARI, INC.
5033 Pullman NE, Seattle
98105 (206)623-4416

SOCIETY EXPEDITIONS
3131 Elliott, Seattle 98121
(206)285-9400

TROPICAL ADVENTURES
111 2nd N, Seattle 98109
(206)441-3483

TYEE TOURS & TRAVEL
707 E Washington
Sequim 98382 (206)682-3342

EMPIRE TOURS OF SPOKANE
W 910 Sprague, Spokane
99204 (509)455-5055

FOUR SEASONS TRAVEL
N 2104 Hamilton, Spokane
99207 (509)484-1142

JET-SET TRAVEL SERVICE
S 18 Monroe, Spokane 99204
(509)455-5944

NORTHGATE TRAVEL
N 9423 Division, Spokane
99218 (509)467-8539

QUALITY TOURS & TRAVEL
E 12510 Sprague Unit 2
Spokane 99218 (509)926-8532

RODEEN'S GROUP TOURS
W 1212 Washington, Spokane
99201 (509)326-2212

SILVER EAGLE BUS CHARTERS
E 5409 Broadway, Spokane
99212 (509)535-9627

SUNSEEKERS HOLIDAYS
W 4302 Kathleen, Spokane
99208 (509)326-0610

CTT INTERNATIONAL, INC.
3624 Steilacoom Blvd SW
Tacoma 98499 (206)582-5251

TACOMA HARBOR TOURS
535 Dock, Tacoma 98402
(206)572-9858

VALLARTA SUNSCAPES
312 112th S, Tacoma 98444
(206)537-7204

GARRETT-LIPP/ASSOC INC.
1500 Lake Park Dr
Tumwater 98502 (206)754-0978

PRIME TIME FISHING TOURS
Vantage 98950
(509)858-2273

AMERICANA TOURS
15 Boyer Ave, Walla Walla
99362 (509)522-2592

TOURS NORTHWEST
402 E Yakima Ave
Yakima 98901 (509)452-0525

wholesale tours

MANAGEMENT CONTRACTS LTD
925 116th NE #233
Bellevue 98004 (206)455-3261

ADVENTOURS
POB 55791, Seattle 98155
(206)367-3792

GROUP TRAVEL SERVICE WASH.
11556 30th Pl SW
Seattle 98148 (206)244-4091

KOALA TOURS. INC.
632 SW 153th, Seattle 98168
(206)241-7470

MIR CORPORATION
85 S Washington #210
Seattle 98104 (206)624-7289

REGENCY PACIFIC TOURS, INC.
620 SW 150th, Seattle 98166
(206)248-3800

SIMPLEX TOURS
19415 Pacific Hwy S
Seattle 98188 (206)824-5910

HUME WORLD TOURS, INC.
POB 771, Kent 98032
(206)859-1115

BUFFY BUS
611 Market, Kirkland 98033
(206)827-6328

Bed & Breakfast

ANDERSON ISLAND

The Inn at Burg's Landing
8808 Villa Beach Rd, Anderson
Island, WA 98303 (206)884-9185
/488-8682, Ken and Annie Burg,
Two rooms, Private baths, Hydro
tub for two, New log home with
water views, Full gourmet
breakfast.

ANACORTES

Admiral's Hideaway Bed and
Breakfast Inn, 1318 30th St,
Anacortes, WA 98221
(206)293-0106 Leslie Ann Carty,
Modern, Nautical theme, Heated
indoor pool, Hot tub, Mt. Baker
and Fidalgo Bay view.

Channel House
2902 Oaks Ave., Anacortes, WA
98221 (206)293-9382, Dennis and
Patricia McIntyre, A classic
1902 Island home, Six rooms,
4 with private baths and w with
fireplaces.

Oak Brook Inn
530 Old Brook Lane, Ancortes,
98221 (206)293-4768, Dick Ash,
Children welcome, Private baths,
Queen beds, Plenty of walking
trails plus a trout pond set on
9 acres.

ASHFORD

Growly Bear
POB 103, Ashford, WA 98304,
(206)569-2339, Susan Jenny,
Rustic 1890 homestead house one
mile from entrance to Mt. Rainier
National Park.

BAINBRIDGE ISLAND

Bombay House Bed & Breakfast
8490 Beck Road, Bainbridge
Island, WA 98110, (206)842-3926
Bunny Cameron and Roger Kanchuk
A spectacular 30 minute ferry
ride from downtown Seattle.
Recommended by "Fodor".

BELLEVUE

Bellevue Bed & Breakfast
830-100th Ave.,SE., Bellevue,
WA 98004, (206)453-1048, Cy and
Carol Garnett, Hilltop, Mountain
& city views, Private suites or
single rooms, Private baths.

Petersen Bed & Breakfast
10228 SE 8th, Bellevue, WA
98004, (206)454-9334, Eunice
and Carl Petersen, Five minutes
from Bellevue Square, Hotels,
Restaurants, Hot tub on deck.

BELLINGHAM

Bellingham's DeCamm House Bed &
Breakfast
2610 Eldridge Ave., Bellingham,
WA 98225, (206)734-9172, Van and
Barbara Hudson, Victorian rooms,
Private Baths.

North Garden Inn
1014 north Garden St. Bellingham
WA 98225, (206)671-7828, Barbara
and Frank DeFreytas, Historic
Queen Anne Victorian with
sweeping view of Bay and Islands
10 elegant guest rooms.

Schnauzer Crossing Bed &
Breakfast
4421 Lakeway Dr., Bellingham,
98226, (206)733-0055, Sonna and
Monty McAllister, King suite &
queen bedrooms, Jacuzzi and
fireplace, Tennis, Boating,
Bicycling.

CATHLAMET

The Gallery Bed & Breakfast at
Little Cape Horn
4 Little Cape Horn, Cathlamet,
WA 98612, (206)425-7395, Carolyn
and Eric Feasey, Contemporary
home overlooking hiking,
windsurfing beach and ship
channel of Columbia River.

CHELAN

Lake Chelan River House
Rt. 1 Box 614, 307 2nd Ave.,
Chelan, WA 98816, (509)682-5122
Randy and Sue Scofield, Historic
home on riverfront.

CLE ELUM

Moore House Bed & Breakfast County Inn
POB 2861, So. Cle Elum, WA 98943
(509)674-5939, Monty and Connie
Moore, Historic railway hotel
next to Ironhorse State Park,
Stay in real caboose, Golf,
mountain biking, X-country
skiing.

Ramblin' Rose
102 W. Railroad, Cle Elum, WA
98922, (509)674-5224, Cathy and
Steven Kelly, Turn of the
century hotel, 8 unique quest
rooms, private baths, children
welcome.

CLINTON

Home By The Sea
2388 East Sunlight Beach Rd.
Whidbey Island, Clinton, WA
98236 (206)221-2964, Sharon
Fritts and Helen Fritts,
Beachside B & B, Private Baths,
Hot tub, Fireplace, Lakeside
setting.

Kittleson Cove
POB 396, Clinton, WA 98236
(206)221-2734, Al and Penny
Kittleson, New Whidbey Island
home on 300' of secluded salt
waterfront property, Private
suites with kitchen, Living area
Queen bed, bath & covered deck.

The Beach House
7338 S. Maxwelton Rd., Clinton,
WA 98236, (206)321-4335, Judy
Thorsen, West Whidbey Island,
Large waterfront suite on sandy
beach, Immense water and
mountain view, Painted sunsets.

CONCRETE-BIRDSVIEW

Cascade Mountain Inn
3840 Pioneer Lane

Concrete-Birdsview, WA 98237,
(206)826-4333, Ingrid and
Gerhard Meyer, All rooms with
private bath, Hiking, Fishing,
Hunting.

COUPVILLE

The Colonel Crockett Farm Bed & Breakfast
1012 S. Fort Casey Rd
Coupville, WA 98239, (206)678-
3711 Robert and Beulah Whitlow,
130 years of Victorian Edwardian
serenity in a farm-quite island
setting.

DAYTON

Syndicate Hill Bed & Breakfast
403 S. 6th St, Dayton, WA 99328,
(509)382-2688, Len and Sandy
Conlee, Elegant and comfortable
1907 home, Scenic historic area,
All season recreation, Queen bed
Shared bath, Cozy woodstove, Spa

EAST SOUND

Turleback Farm Inn
Route 1, Box 650, East Sound, WA
98245, (206)376-4914, William
Susan Fletcher, Restored farmhouse, Pastoral setting, private
baths, Award winning breakfasts.

ELLENSBURG

Murphy's Country Bed & Breakfast
Route 1, Box 400, Ellensburg, WA
98926, (509)925-7986, Doris
Murphy, Two large guest rooms.

FERNDALE

Anderson House Bed & Breakfast
2140 Main St, POB 1547, Ferndale
WA 98248, (206)384-3450, Dave
Kelly Anderson, Canada only 15
miles away, Enjoy a 2 nation
vacation.

Hill Top Bed & Breakfast
5832 Church Rd., Ferndale, WA
98248, (206)384-3619, Paul and
Doris Matz, Panoramic mountain
view, 8 miles south of Canada,
Private bath, Children welcome.

FORKS

Miller Tree Inn
POB 953, Folks, WA 98331,
(206)374-6806, Ted and Prue
Miller, 1917 country homestead
near Hoh Rain Forest and Rialto
Beach on West Olympia Peninsula
6 guest rooms.

River Inn
Route 3, Box 3858D, Folks, WA
98331, (206)374-6526, Les and
Joanne Klontz, A waterside
Scenic river view, 2.5 miles to
town, Sun deck.

FREELAND

Cliff House & Seacliff Cottage
5440 Windmill Rd, Whidbey
Island, Freeland, WA 98249,
(206)321-1566, Peggy Moore and
Walter O'Toole, Surfside setting

FRIDAY HARBOR

Blair House Bed and Breakfast
345 Blair Ave., Friday Harbor,
WA 98250, (206)378-5907, Jane
Benson and Jeff Zander, Set on
3 1/3 acres in Friday Harbor,
Private or shared baths, Heated
swimming pool.

Duffy House
760 Pear Point Rd., Friday
Harbor, WA 98250, (206)378-5604
Garreth Jeffers, 1926 Tudor
style home, 5 rooms, Shared
baths, View of Olympic Mountains
Gardens, Orchards, Beach cabin.

The Meadows
1980 Cattle Point Rd., Friday
Harbor, WA 98250, (206)378-4004
Dodie and Burr Henion,
Cascade-Griffin Bay view, Two
spacious rooms share bath and
guest house.

Moon and Sixpence
3021 Beaverton Valley Rd, Friday
Harbor, WA 98250, (206)378-4138
Charles and Evelyn Tuller,
Weaving studio, Birding, Biking,
Walking, Nearby lakes, Historic
sites, Whale watching.

Olympic Lights
4531A Cattle Point Rd., Friday
Harbor, WA 98250, (206)378-3186,
Christian and Lea Andrade,
Magnificent view of the sea and
Olympic Mountains, 1895
Victorian farmhouse, 5 rooms.

San Juan Inn Bed and Breakfast
50 Spring St., POB 776, Friday
Harbor, WA 98250, (206)278-2070
Joan and Norm Schwinge, Antiques
Harbor view parlor, Close to
ferries, Shops, Restaurants,
Entertainment.

Tucker House Bed and Breakfast
260 B St., Friday Harbor, WA
98250 (206)378-2783, Joan and
Evelyn Lackey, Mitzi Stack
Victorian, Hot tub/decks, Some
private baths, Fireplace,
Kitchen, Children welcome.

Westwinds Bed and Breakfast
4909 H. Hannah Highlands Rd.,
Friday Harbor, Wa 98250,
(206)378-5283, Christine Durbin
and Gayle Rollins, View of
Strats and Olympic Mountains.

GLENWOOD

Flying L. Ranch
25 Flying L. Lane, Glenwood,
98619, (509)364-3488, Darvel
Lloyd, 160 acres with view of
Mt. Adams, Pond, Hot tubs,
11 rooms, 1 cabin, Cycling,
Cross country skiing.

GOOSE PRAIRIE

The Hopkinson House
862 Bumping River Rd., Goose
Prairie, WA 98937, Ray and
Martha Jean Hopkinson, Mountain
and river view, Ski or hike,
3200 ft. elevation.

GREENBANK

Guest House Cottages
835 E. Christenson Rd.,
Whidlbey Island, Greenbank, WA
98253, (206)678-3115, Don and
Mary Jane Creger, Total privacy
Pool, Spa, Exercise room,
In-room Jacuzzi, Featherbeds,
VCR's, Fireplaces, Wildlife
pond, Near winery.

HAMILTON

Smith House Bed and Breakfast
POB 535, Hamilton, WA 98255,
(206)826-4214, Rick and Loretta
Roetcisoender, Old home built in
1908, Quite scenic setting, Four
bedrooms, Recreation room.

ISSAQUAH

Wildflower Bed & Breakfast Inn
25237 SE Issaquah-Fall City Rd,
Issaquah, WA 98027, (206)392-1196
Laureita Caldwell, Quite country
2-story log home, Spacious rooms,
Private baths.

KIRKLAND

Shumway Mansion
11410 99th Pl. NE, Kirkland,
98033, (206)823-2303, Richard
and Salli Harris, Award winning
1909, 4-story mansion, Seven
bedrooms with private baths,
3 blocks to beach, Tennis,
Jogging trails, Large ballroom
for seminars or social functions.

LACONNER

Downey House
1880 Chilberg Rd, LaConner,
98257, (206)466-3207, Jim and
Kay Frey, 1904 Victorian
farmhouse, Scenic valley view,
5 antique-filled guest rooms,
Hot tub, Near tulip fields.

The White Swan Guest House
1388 Moore Rd, Mt. Vernor,
98273, (206)445-6805, Peter
Goldfarb, Storybook farmhouse,
Bicycle, Birdwatching.

LANGLEY

Blue House Inn & Bed & Breakfast
513 Anthes, Langley, WA 98260,
(206)221-8392, Rod and Mary
Erickson, Traditional Bed &
Breakfast.

Country Cottage of Langley
215 6th St., POB 459, Langley,
WA 98260, (206)221-8709, Trudy
and Whitey Martin, Restored
twenties farmhouse, Mountains
and sea, Private suites and
baths.

Eagles Nest Inn
3236 E. Saratpga Rd., Langley,
WA 98260, (206)321-5331, Nancy
and Dale Bowman, Large rooms,
Private baths, King beds,
Spacious decks, Spa, Library
/lounge.

Log Castle
3273 E. Saratoga Rd, Langley,
98260, (209)321-5483, Senator
Jack and Norma Metcalf, On a
secluded beach on Whidbey Isl
Log lodge, Turret bedrooms,
Private baths.

The Saratoga Inn
4850 S. Coles Rd, Langley, WA
98260, (206)221-7526, Debbie
Jones A Cape Cod Inn overlooks
Saratoga Passage, Spacious rms
with private baths and
fireplaces, English cottage
garden, 5 minutes to tennis,
beach and shopping, 1 hour to
Seattle.

The Whidbey Inn
POB 156, 106 1st St., Langley
98260, (206)221-7115, Shannon
and Richard Francisco, Waterfnt
Inn, Breakfast baskets at your
door.

LEAVENWORTH

Run of the River Bed and Breakfast
9308 E. Leavenworth Rd, POB 448
Leavenworth, WA 98826,
(509)548-7171, Karen and Monty
Turner, Log lodging, Icicle
River setting, Cascade views,
Spa, Private baths, Wood stove
and non smoking rooms, Ski,
Golf, Rafting.

The Old Brick Silo Bed & Breakfast
9028 E. Leavenworth Rd,
Leavenworth, WA 98826,
(509)548-4772, Don and Marge
Marshall, Mountain view, Log
home, Covered porches,
Queen/King beds, Recreation
room, Near Bavarian village.

LOPEZ ISLAND

Inn at Swifts Bay
Port Stanley Rd, Lopez Island,
WA 98261, (206)468-3636, Robert
Herrmann and Christopher
Brandmeir, 4 garden view rooms,
Hot tub, Private beach nearby,
Eagles, Whales, Fireplaces,
Close to ferry.

LUMMI ISLAND

The Willows Inn
2579 West Shore Dr, Lummi
Island, WA 98262, (206)758-2620,
Gary and Victoria Flynn, Small
country Inn, Spectacular sunsets
over Gulf Islands.

West Shore Bed and Breakfast
2781 West Shore Dr Lummi Island,
WA 98262, (206)758-2600, Polly
and Carl Hanson, Rural seaside
farm, Canadian Mountains, Eagles,
Seals, Owner built octagonal
home.

LYNDEN

LeCocq House
719 West Edson, Lynden, WA 98264
(206)354-3032, Bob and Bonnie
Sunday, Short walk to museum,
Dutch Village shops and
restaurants, Spacious Colonial
home.

MAPLE VALLEY

Maple Valley Bed and Breakfast
20020 SE 228th, Maple Valley,
WA 98038, (206)432-1409, Clark
and Jayne Hurlbut, Spacious
grounds, Wildlife pond, Cedar
rooms, Hootnanny pancakes and
hot babies.

MONTESANO

"Sylvan Haus" - Murphy's Bed and
Breakfast
POB 416, Montesano, WA 98563,
(206)249-3453, Michael L. and
JoAnne Murphy, Valley view,
Secluded hilltop, Ocean beaches
30 minutes.

MORTON

St. Helens Manorhouse
7476 US Highway 12, Morton, WA
98356, (206)498-5243, Jack and
Darlene Brown, Antique motif,
Spacious bedrooms.

MOXEE CITY

The Desert Rose
POB 166, Moxee City, WA 98936,
(509)452-2237, Pete and Grace
Optekar, English manor, Two
large guest rooms.

OCEAN SHORES

Ocean Front Lodge
N. Ocean Shores Blvd, POB 1265,
Ocean Shores, WA 98936,
(206)289-3036, Joan Johnson,

ORCAS

Orcas Hotel
POB 155, Orcas, WA 98280,
(206)376-4300, Barbara Johnson
Restored Victorian Inn, 12
guestrooms.

PATEROS

French House Bed and Breakfast
206 W. Warren, Pateros, WA
98846, (509)923-2626 Bob and
Charlene Knoop, Country
setting, 4 distinct seasons.

PORT ANGELES

Glen Mar by the Sea
318 N. Eunice, Port Angeles,
WA 98362, (206)457-6110 or
457-4686 Glenndia and Marvin
Witherow, Waterfront view.

Kennedy's Bed and Breakfast
332 E. 5th, Port Angeles, WA
98362, (206)457-3628 Bob and
Natalie Kennedy, 1896 historic
home, Rides to ferry or
airport, Walking distance to
downtown.

Tudor Inn
1108 S. Oak, Port Angeles, WA
98362, (206)452-3138 Jane and
Jerry Glass 1910 half timbered
English tudor with English

decor, Antiques, Gardens and
mountain views.

PORT TOWNSEND

Heritage House Inn
305 Pierce St., Port Townsend,
WA 98368, (206)385-6822 Jim
and Pat Broughton, Bob and
Carolyn Ellis, Six bedroom
Victorian Inn.

Holly Hill House
611 Polk, Port Townsend, WA
98368, (206)385-5619 Bill and
Laurie Medlicott, The R.C.
House built in 1872, 4 large
bedrooms with queen beds,
Gardens.

Lizzie's
731 Pierce, Port Townsend, WA
98368, (206)385-4168 Bill and
Patti Wickline, 1888 Italanate
Victorian mansion in historic
seaport, 7 large guest rooms,
2 parlors with fireplaces.

Old Consulate Inn (F.W.
Hastings House)
313 Walker at Washington, Port
Townsend, WA 98368,
(206)385-6753 Bob and Joanna
Jackson, National historic
landmark - Victorian-on-the
-Bluff, Fireplaces, 8 guestrooms, Private baths.

Staret House Inn
744 Clay St., Port Townsend,
WA 98368, (206)385-3205 Bob
and Edel Sokol, A national
treasure.

REDMOND

Cedarym-A Colonial Bed and
Breakfast
1011-240th Ave NE, Redmond,
98053, (206)868-4159 Mary
Ellen and Walt Brown, A
Colonial reproduction, Gazebo
covered spa, Wooded path,
Breakfast by candle light.

SEATTLE

Chelsa Station Bed and
Breakfast Inn
4915 Linden Ave N., Seattle,
WA 98103, (206)547-6077 Dick
and Marylou Jones, 1920
Colonial, Hot tub, King beds,
Private baths.

Galer Place Bed and Breakfast
318 W. Galer, Seattle, WA
98119, (206)282-5339 Chris and
Terry Giles, Victorian charm,
All private baths.

Hainsworth House
2657-37th SW, Seattle, WA
98126, (206)938-1020 Carl and
Charlotte Muia, West Seattle's
historic mansion, City views.

Marit's Bed and Breakfast
6208 Palatine Ave N, Seattle,
WA 98103, (206)782-7900 Marit
Nelson, Scandinavian
hospitality, Sound and
mountain view, Walk to park,
zoo and lake.

Mildred's Bed and Breakfast
1202 15th Ave E, Seattle, WA
98112, (206)325-6072 Mildred
J. Sarver, In the heart of
Seattle, 1890 Victorian house,
Park and museum across the
street, Bus at front door.

Queen Anne Hill Bed and
Breakfast
1835 7th West, Seattle, WA
98119, (206)284-9779 Chuck and
Mary McGrew, Turn of the
century home near downtown and
Seattle Center, Mountain and
water views, Minutes from Pike
Place Market.

Salisburg House
750 16th Ave E, Seattle, WA
98112, (206)328-8682 Mary and
Cathryn Wiese, Turn of the
century home, Minutes away
from Seattle.

The Shafer Mansion
907 14th Ave E, Seattle, WA
98112, (206)329-4628 H. Lee
Vennes, Located in Seattle's

Capitol Hill area, once
referred to as "Millionaires
row".

Villa Heidelberg
4845 45th Ave SW, Seattle, WA
98116, (206)938-3658 Barb and
John Thompson, 1909 country
home in West Seattle,
Wrap-around porch, Formal
gardens.

Williams House Bed and Breakfast
1505 4th Ave N, Seattle, WA
98109, (206)285-0810 Susan,
Doug & Danielle Williams,
Turn-of-the-Century style in
city location, Views of city,
lake, and mountain, 5 large
rooms.

SEQUIM

Margie's Bed and Breakfast
120 Forrest Rd, Sequim, WA
98382, (206)683-7011 Margie L.
Vorhies, Large contemporary
ranch style home, 180' of
water frontage, Country
setting.

SNOHOMISH

Countryman Bed and Breakfast
119 Cedar, Snohomish, WA
98290, (206)568-9622 Larry and
Sandy Countryman, Queen Anne
Victorian, Private baths,
Fireplaces, One block from
over 200 antique dealers, Free
limo tour of town.

Noris House
312 Ave. D, Snohomish, WA
98290, (206)568-3825 Thom Ris
and Lee Nokleby, Edwardian
style home, Furnished in
antiques, Convenient to
skiing, lakes, and ferrys.

SNOQUALMIE

The Old Honey Farm Bed and Breakfast and Country Inn
8910 284th Ave SE, Snoqualmie,
WA 98065, (206)888-1637 or
888-9399 Conrad, Mary Jean,
and Marilyn Potter, Pastoral

setting with full view of Mt.
Si and the Cascades, Golf,
Winery, Train, Horse
facilities available.

SPOKANE

Durocher House Bed and Breakfast
W. 4000 Randolph Rd, Spokane,
WA 99204, (509)325-4739 Mary
Dunton Victorian Duocher
House at Historic Fort Wright,
Ten minuets to airport or
downtown.

Town and Country Bed and Breakfast
N. 7620 Fox Point Dr, Spokane,
WA 99208, (509)466-7559 Narda
Johnson, Full "cottage"
breakfast. Near Whitworth
College.

Waverly Place Bed and Breakfast
W. 709 Waverly Place, Spokane,
WA 99205, (509)328-1856 Marge
and Tammy Ardt, Victorian home
built in 1902, Located on
Corbin Park.

Whispering Pines
7504 E. 44th, Spokane, WA
99223, (509)448-1433 Dean and
Almeda Campbell, Super kin &
queen beds, Private and shared
baths, Separate entrance.

TROUT LAKE

Mio Amore Pensione
POB 208, Trout Lake, WA 98650,
(509)395-2264 Tom and Jill
Westbrook, Four distinctive
rooms, Northern Italian
dining, Fishing, Hiking,
Biking, White water rafting
and X-country skiing.

WHITE SALMON

Liama Ranch Bed and Breakfast
1980 Hwy 141, White Salmon, WA
98672, (509)395-2786 Jerry and
Rebeka Stone, Free llama
walks, Children welcome, Queen
beds, Kitchen.

Museums

A LIST OF SELECTED MUSEUMS

ANACORTES

Anacortes Museum of History and Art 1305 Eight, Anacortes, WA 98221 (206)939-2783, Indian artifacts, antique musical instruments, early photographs of area.

AUBURN

White River Valley Historical Society Museum 918 H St SE, Auburn, WA 98002, Early pioneer artifacts, early documents of the White River Valley

BELLEVUE

Bellevue Art Museum 301 Bellevue Sq, Bellevue, WA 98004, (206)454-6021, Twentieth century American art.

BELLINGHAM

Whatcom Museum of History and Art, 121 Prospect St, Bellingham, WA 98225, (206)676-6981, Art and history, anthropology, regional geology.

BOTHELL

Bothell Historical Museum 9919 NE 180th, Bothell, WA 98011, (206)486-1889, Regional historical items.

BREMERTON

Naval Shipyard Museum Wash. State Ferry Terminal Bldg, Bremerton, WA 98310, (206)479-7447, Showcases maritime history of Puget Sound and Naval Shipyard.

COUPEVILLE

Island County Historical Society Museum, Alexander St, POB 305, Couperville, WA 98239, (206)678-4470, Indian artifacts, regional historical items, World War 1 mementos.

CASHMERE

Chelan County Museum 5698 Museum Dr, Cashmere WA 98815, (509)782-3230, Restored historical buildings, Indian artifacts.

CATHLAMET

Wahkikum County History Society, POB 541, Cathlamet, WA 98612, (206)795-3945, Indian artifacts, Regional items, logging tools and photographs.

CHEHALIS

Lewis County Historical Museum, 599 NW Front St, Chehalis, WA 98532, (206)748-0831Regional historical items, Chehalis Indian artifacts.

CHENEY

Eastern Washington University Gallery of Art Eastern Wash. Univ., Cheney, WA 99004, (509)359-2493, Contemporary art exhibits.

CLARKSTON

Valley Art Center 842 Sixth St, Clarkston, WA 99403, (509)758-8331, Historical and Indian Art.

CLE ELUM

Cle Elum Historical Museum 221 East First St, Cle Elum, WA 98922, (206)674-5702, Pioneer items, telephone exhibit, mining displays.

COLFAX

Whitman County Historical Society Museum, 623 North Perkins, Colfax, WA 99111, (509)397-2555, Regional historical items.

DAVENPORT

Lincoln County Historical Museum, POB 585, Davenport, WA 99122, (509)725-6711, Historical artifacts, early agriculture tools.

DUPONT

Du Pont Historical Museum 207 Barksdale, Du Pond 98327, (206)964-2399, Regional historical items.

EASTSOUND

Orcas Island Historical Museum, POB 134, Eastsound 98245, (206)376-4849, Indian artifacts and antiques.

EDMONDS

Edmonds Museum 118 Fifth Ave N., Edmonds, WA 98020, (206)774-0900, Regional historical items.

ELLENSBURG

Kittitas County Museum POB 265, 114 E Third, Ellensburg, WA 98926, (509)925-3778, Kittitas County historical artifacts, regional rocks, housed in the 1889 Cadwell Building.

Museum of Man Central Washington Univ., Dept of Anthropology, Ellensburg, WA 98926, (509)939-3201, Worldwide ethnographic material.

EPHRATA

Grant County Museum 742 Basin St, NW, Box 1141, Ephrata, WA 98823, (509)754-3334, Regional pioneer artifacts.

FORT LEWIS

Fort Lewis Military Museum
Building T4320, Fort Lewis,
WA 98433, (206)967-7206,
History of US Military in
the Northwest, US Military
weapons collections.

FRIDAY HARBOR

San Juan Historical Society
POB 174, Friday Harbor WA
98250, (206)378-4587,
Artifacts related to the
San Juan Islands.

Whale Museum
POB 945, Friday Harbor, WA
98250, (206)378-4710,
Exhibits of marine mammal
materials.

GOLDENDALE

**Klickitat County Historical
Society,** 127 W. Broadway,
Goldendale, WA 98620,
(509)773-4303, Agricultural
and regional artifacts.

Maryhill Museum of Fine Arts
Goldendale 98620,
(509)773-4792, Housed in the
Samuel Hill mansion,
European and American
paintings, glass memorabilia
of European royalty,
sculpture, ceramics, Indian
artifacts.

ISSAQUAH

Issaquah Historical Society
165 SE Andrews, Issaquah, WA
98027, (206)392-3500,
Regional historical items.

KELSO

**Cowlitz County Historical
Society Museum,** 405 Allen,
Kelso 98626, (206)577-3119,
Large selection of regional
birds, restored 1884 cabin,
Indian artifacts.

KENNEWICK

**East Benton Co. Historical
Society Museum,** POB 6710,
Keewaydin Dr, Kennewick, WA
99336, (509)582-7704, East
Benton County pioneer and
Indian artifacts.

LA CONNER

**Valley Museum of Northwest
Art,** 602 N. Second, La
Conner, WA 98257,
(206)466-3365, Indian and
pioneer memorabilia,
implements of early county
industries.

LIND

**Adams County Historical
Society Museum,** Phillips
Bldg, Box 188, Lind, WA
99341, (509)677-3219,
Paintings by local artists,
pioneer artifacts.

NEAH BAY

**Makah Cultural & Research
Center,** POB 95, Neah Bay, WA
98357, (206)645-2711,
Archaeological collection
relating to the Makah and
other Olympic Peninsula
Indians.

NORTH BEND

**Snoquaimie Valley Historical
Museum,** POB 179, North Bend,
WA 98045, (206)888-3200,
Indian artifacts and pioneer
family items.

OLYMPIA

State Capital Museum
211 West 21st Ave, Olympia,
WA 98504, (206)753-2580,
History museum relating to
the Washington State
Capitol; Indian art and
culture, territorial pioneer
and government displays.

PASCO

Franklin County Historical Society Museum, 305 North Fourth, Pasco, WA 99301, (509)547-3714, Regional historical artifacts.

PORT ANGELES

Clallam County Historical Society, 223 East Fourth St, Port Angeles, WA 98362, Historical artifacts and natural history exhibits.

PORT GAMBLE

Port Gamble Historical Museum, Port Gamble, WA 98364, (206)297-2311, Historical memorabilia, series of restored buildings.

PORT TOWNSEND

Jefferson County Historical Society, City Hall, Port Townsend, WA 98368, (206)385-1003, Pioneer exhibits, Indian artifacts, one room devoted to Fort Worden.

Port Townsend Marine Science Center, Fort Worden, WA 98368, (206)385-5582, Programs and exhibits on marine sciences in the Puget Sound region.

PROSSER

Benton County Historical Society Museum, Box 591, Prosser 99350, (509)786-3842, Diorama featuring the House Heaven Hills in earlier times.

PULLMAN

Charles R. Conner Museum Washington State University, 99164, (509)335-1977, Natural history collection of birds and mammals

Museum of Anthropology Washington State University, 99164, (509)335-8556, Archaeological collections from Washington, Alaska, and western US.

Museum of Art Washington State University, 99164, (509)335-1910, American and Pacific Northwest art.

Washington State University Herbarium, Pullman 99164, (509)335-3250, Over 200,000 plant specimens.

PUYALLUP

Ezra Meeker House Puyallup 98371, (206)848-1770, The books of Ezra Meeker, house and furnishings.

Paul H. Karshner Memorial Museum, 309 Fourth NE, Puyallup 98371, (206)841-8748, Rocks, minerals, fossils and Indian items.

REDMOND

Marymoor Museum 6046 Lake Sammamish Parkway NE, POB 162, Redmond, WA 98052, (206)885-3684, Indian artifacts, Pioneer implements, housed in former Cise mansion built in 1907.

RICHLAND

Hanford Science Center POB 800, Richland, WA 99352, (509)376-6374, History of the nuclear industry and activities of the Hanford complex.

SEATTLE

Center for Wooden Boats 1010 Valley, Seattle, WA 98109, (206)382-2628, Classical and historical wooden boats.

Center on Contemporary Art
316 Occidental S. Seattle,
WA 98104, (206)682-4568,
Exhibits, demonstrations,
and classes on contemporary
art.

**Charles & Emma Frye Art
Museum,** 704 Terry Ave,
Seattle, WA 98104,
(206)622-9250, 1850-1900,
Munich school paintings,
American school 19th and
20th centuries.

Children's Museum
112 Occidental South,
Seattle, WA 98104,
(206)441-1767, Hands on
exhibits.

Coast Guard Museum
1519 Alaska Way South,
Seattle, WA 98134,
(206)286-9608, Exhibits and
materials on the role of the
Coast Guard on the Pacific
Coast.

Henry Art Gallery
University of Washington,
Seattle, WA 98195,
(206)543-2280, 19th Century
American & European
paintings, pottery, Japanese
folk pottery.

Museum of Flight
9404 E. Marginal Way,
Seattle, WA 98108,
(206)764-5720, Extensive
selection of restored
historical airplanes;
research library, education
and outreach program.

**Museum of History and
Industry,** 2700 24th Ave
East, Seattle, WA 98112,
Pacific Northwest and Alaska
history and maritime
exhibits.

Nordic Heritage Museum
3014 NW 67th St, Seattle, WA
98117, (206)789-5707, Nordic
heritage in the Pacific
Northwest.

Pacific Science Center
200 Second Ave N, Seattle,
WA 98109, (206)433-2001,
Space, astronomy, and
physical science.

Renton Historical Museum
235 Mill S. Renton, WA
98055, (206)255-2330,
Regional and historical
items.

Seattle Art Museum
Volunteer Park, Seattle
98112, (206)625-8901,
Northwest paintings,
sculpture and art from
around the world.

**Seattle Environmental Art
Museum,** 801 First Ave,
Seattle, WA 98104,
(206)625-0715, Dedicated to
exploring the "designed
environment," focus on
architecture, landscaping

Shoreline Historical Museum
POB 7177, Seattle, WA 98133,
(206)542-7111, Artifacts
depicting the US Navy,
logging, transportation, and
education on the shoreline
of Seattle.

**Thomas Burk Memorial
Washington State Museum**
University of Washington,
Seattle, WA 98195,
(206)543-5590, Northwest
Coast Indian material,
ethnology of the Pacific
Rim, geology and
paleontology of the Pacific
Rim.

Wing Luke Museum
407 Seventh Ave South,
Seattle, WA 98104,
(206)623-5124, Chinese
history and culture.

SEQUIM

Sequim-Dungeness Museum
175 West Cedar, Sequim, WA
98382, (206)683-8110,
Regional historical items.

SILVERDALE

Kitsap County Museum
NW Byron, Silverdale, WA
98383, (206)692-1949,
Regional historical items.

SNOQUALMIE

**Puget Sound Railroad &
Historical Museum,** POB 459,
Snoqualmie, WA 98065,
(206)746-4025, Steam
railroad equipment and train
tours.

SOUTH BEND

**Pacific County Museum and
Historical Society**
1008 W. Robert Bush Dr,
South Bend, WA 98586,
(206)875-5224, Indian
artifacts and pioneer
memorabilia.

SPOKANE

**Cheney Cowels Memorial
Museum,** Eastern Washington
Historical Society, 2316
First Ave, Spokane, WA
99204, (509)456-3931, Indian
art and culture featuring
plateau Indians, history of
Spokane and Inland Empire.

**Museum of Native American
Culture,** E. 200 Cataldo, POB
3044TA, Spokane, WA 99220,
(509)326-4550, Native
American materials
representing the Plains and
Washington State Indians,
Pre Columbian artifacts.

STEILACOOM

Steilacoom Historical Museum
Box 16, Steilacoom, WA
98388, (206)584-8623,
Pioneer items and artifacts
from Fort Steilacoom.

STEVENSON

**Skamania County Historical
Society,** POB 396, Stevenson,
WA 98648, (509)427-5141,
Indian and pioneer
artifacts.

SUMNER

Ryan House Museum
1228 Main, Sumner, WA 98390,
(206)863-8936

SUQUAMISH

Suquamish Museum
Sandy Hook Rd, POB 498,
Suquamish, WA 98329,
Historical photographs,
Puget Sound Salish Indian
culture.

TACOMA

**Puget Sound Museum of
Natural History**
University of Puget Sound,
Tacoma, WA 98416, Collection
of Northwest flora and
fauna.

Tacoma Art Museum
12th & Pacific Ave, Tacoma,
WA 98402, (206)272-4258
American and European contemporary art. Early American
furniture and artifacts.

**Washington State Historical
Society,** 315 N. Stadium
Way, Tacoma, Wa 98403,
(206)593-2830 Pacific Northwest history, Indian artifacts, books, manuscripts,
and photos.

**Western Forest Industries
Museum,** Point Defiance
Park, Tacoma, WA 98407,
(206)752-0047, Restored
logging camp, artifacts of
lumbering in the Pacific NW.

TOPPENISH

**Yakima Nation Cultural
Center,** POB 151, Toppenish,
WA 98948, (509)865-2800,
Exhibits of the Yakima
Nation, dioramas;
Strongheart Collection of
Indian artifacts from
throughout the country.

VANCOUVER

Clark County Historical Museum, 1511 Main St, Vancouver, WA 98660, (206)695-4681, Country store, historical dioramas, Indian artifacts, doctors office.

U.S. Grant Museum
1106 Evergreen Blvd, Vancouver, WA 98660, (206)694-4002, Quarters once occupied by Ulysses S. Grant when stationed at Vancouver Barracks.

WALLA WALLA

Fort Walla Walla Museum Complex, Myra Rd, POB 1616, Walla Walla, WA 99362, (509)525-7703, Thirteen restored buildings including 1859 Ransom Clark cabin, 1867 school house and 1880 Babcock Railway Depot, located on the site of old Fort Walla Walla.

WATERVILLE

Douglas County Historical Society Museum, POB 83, Waterville, WA 98858, (509)745-2581, Pioneer and Indian artifacts.

WENATCHEE

North Central Washington Museum, 127 South Mission, Wenatchee, WA 98902, (509)662-4728, Indian and pioneer artifacts, South Pacific items

YAKIMA

Yakima Valley Museum and Historical Association
2105 Tieton Dr, Yakima, WA 98902, (509)248-0702, Western and Indian artifacts, wagon and horse drawn agricultural implements.

Parks

NATIONAL PARKS AND MONUMENTS

National Park Service, Pacific Northwest Region
83 King St., Suite 212, Seattle, WA 98104, (206)442-5565

National Park Service, Information Office
1018 First Ave, Seattle, WA 98104, (206)442-0170

COULEE DAM NATIONAL RECREATION AREA
POB 37, Coulee Dam 99116, (509)446-9441
Established in 1946 Coulee Dam National Recreational Area covers over100,390 acres, and features 130 mile long Franklin Lake.

EBEY'S LANDING NATIONAL HISTORIC RESERVE
23 Front St., POB 774, Coupeville, WA 98239, (206)678-6084
Established in 1978 by the people of Central Whidbey it covers the community of Coupeville, covers over 17,000 acres.

FORT VANCOUVER NATIONAL HISTORICAL SITE
1501 East Evergreen Blvd, Vancouver, WA 98661, (206)422-7655
Established in 1948, covers over 209 acres, commemorates the western headquarters of the Hudson's Bay Company from 1825 to 1849.

KLONDIKE GOLD RUSH NATIONAL HISTORICAL PARK
117 South Main St, Seattle, WA 98104, (206)442-7220
Established in 1976, depicts the role Seattle played as as staging area for the 1890s gold rush.

MOUNT ST. HELENS NATIONAL VOLCANIC MONUMENT
Monument Visitor Center 3029 Sprit Lake Highway, Castle Rock, WA 98611, (206)274-6644
Established in 1982, covers 110,000 acres. A living laboratory dedicated to the study and viewing of the only active volcano within the continental United States and the natural regenerative processes on lands destroyed by the eruptions in May of 1980.

MOUNT RAINIER NATIONAL PARK
Tahoma Woods, Star Route, Ashford, WA 98304, (206)569-2211
Established in 1899, covers 235,404 acres. Encompasses Mount Rainier (elevation 14,410 feet).

NORTH CASCADES NATIONAL PARK
1205 Highway 20, Sedro Woolley, WA 98284, (206)856-5700
Established in 1968, covers 684,244 acres, beautiful alpine scenery, glaciated canyons. Included within the park are: Lake Chelan Nat. Rec. Area, and Rose Lake Nat. Rec. Area. Over 300 glaciers, mountain streams and lakes.

OLYMPIA NATIONAL PARK
600 East Park Ave, Port Angeles, WA 98362, (206)452-4501
Established in 1938, covers over 914,576 acres. Contained Pacific Northwest rain forest, active glaciers, fifty miles of beautiful ocean shoreline.

SAN JUAN ISLAND NATIONAL HISTORICAL PARK
POB 429, Friday Harbor, WA 98250, (206)378-2240
Established in 1966, covers 1,751 acres, dates the

events on the island from
1853 to 1871 pertaining to
the final settlement of the
nation's northern boundary.
Includes the "Big War" of
1859.

**WHITMAN MISSION NATIONAL
HISTORIC SITE**
Route 2, Box 247 Walla
Walla, WA 99362,
(509)434-6360
Established in 1936, covers
98 acres, commemorates the
pioneer mission landmark on
the Oregon Trail, and Marcus
and Narcissa Whitman who
were killed in the Indian
uprising of 1847.

STATE PARKS

There are hundreds of fine
state parks in Washington
State. Reservations are
required at the following
from Memorial Day through
Labor Day: Belfair, Birch
Bay, Fort Canby, Fort
Flagler, Lake Chelan, Moran,
Pearrygin Lake, Steamboat
Rock, and Twin
Harbors/Grayland Beach. For
additional information on
state parks call:

Campsite Information Center:
8 AM to 5 PM (Summers only)
Toll free from within
Washington: 1-800-562-0990
Out-of-state call:
(206)753-5755

**Washington State Parks and
Recreation Commission**
Public Affairs Office
7150 Clearwater Ln, KY-11
Olympia, WA 98504,
(206)753-2027

Washington Indians

For information on Washington Indian tribes and government contact:

BUREAU OF INDIAN AFFAIRS PACIFIC NORTHWEST AREA
1425 NE Irving, Portland, OR 97208 (503)231-6702

SMALL TRIBES ORGANIZATION OF WESTERN WASHINGTON
520 Pacific, POB 578, Sumner, WA 98390 (206)593-2894

GOVERNOR'S OFFICE OF INDIAN AFFAIRS, 605 11th Ave S, Suite 112, Olympia 98504 (206)753-2411
This office examines and set issues relating to the rights and needs of Washington's Indians. It advises the governor and state agencies on programs, policies, and plans pertaining to their special needs.

BUREAU OF INDIAN AFFAIRS AGENCIES

COLVILLE AGENCY
POB 111, Nespelem 99155 (509)634-4901

OLYMPIC PENINSULA AGENCY
POB 120, Hoquiam 98550 (206)533-9100

PUGET SOUND AGENCY
3006 Colby Ave, Federal Building, Everett 98201 (206)258-2651

SPOKANE AGENCY
POB 389, Wellpinit 99040 (509)258-4561

YAKIMA AGENCY
POB 632, Toppenish 98948 (509)865-2255

INDIAN TRIBES

CHEHALIS BUSINESS COUNCIL
POB 536, Oakville 98568
(206)273-5911

CHINOOK TRIBE
POB 228, Chinook 98614
(206)777-8303

COLVILLE BUSINESS COUNCIL
POB 150, Nespelem 99155
(509)634-4711

COWLITZ TRIBE
5210 12th St E, Suite 103
Tacoma 98424 (206)922-5950

DUWAMISH TRIBE
15507 First Ave S, #3
Seattle 98148 (206)244-0606

HOH TRIBAL BUSINESS COUNCIL
HC 80, Box 917, Folks 98331
(206)374-6582

JAMESTOWN KLALLAM TRIBAL COUNCIL, 305 Old Blyn Hwy,
Sequim 98382 (206)683-1109

KALISPEL BUSINESS COMMITTEE
POB 38, Usk 99180
(509)445-1147

LOWER ELWHA TRIBAL COMMUNITY COUNCIL, 1666 Lower Elwha Rd
Port Angeles 98362
(206)452-8471

LUMMI INDIAN BUSINESS COUNCIL, 2616 Kwina Rd
Bellingham 98226
(206)734-8180

MAKAH INDIAN TRIBAL COUNCIL
POB 115, Neah Bay 98357
(206)645-2201

MARIETTA-NOOKSACK TRIBE
1827 Marine Dr, Bellingham
98226 (206)733-6039

MUCKLESHOOT INDIAN TRIBAL COUNCIL, 39015 172nd SE
Auburn 98002 (206)939-3311

NISQUALLY INDIAN COMMUNITY COUNCIL, 4820 She-Nah-Num Dr
SE, Olympia 98503
(206)456-5221

NOOKSACK INDIAN TRIBAL COUNCIL, POB 157, Deming
98244 (206)592-5176

PORT GAMBLE COMMUNITY COUNCIL, POB 280, Kingston
98346 (206)297-2646

PUYALLUP TRIBAL COUNCIL
2002 E 28th St, Tacoma 98404
(206)597-6200

QUILEUTE TRIBAL COUNCIL
POB 279, La Push 98350
(206)374-6163

QUINAULT INDIAN NATION-BUSINESS COMMUNITY
POB 189, Taholah 98587
(206)276-8211

SAMISH TRIBE
POB 217, Anacortes 98221
(206)293-6404

SAUK-SUIATTLE TRIBAL COUNCIL
5318 Chief Brown Ln
Darrington 98241
(206)435-8366

SHOALWATER BAY TRIBAL COUNCIL, POB 130, Tokeland
98590 (206)267-6766

SKAKOMISH TRIBAL COUNCIL
N 80 Tribal Center Rd
Shelton 98584 (206)426-4232

SNOHOMISH TRIBE
1422 Rosario Rd, Anacortes
98221 (206)293-7716

SNOQUALMIE TRIBE
18525 Novelty Hill Rd
Redmond 98052 (206)885-7464

SPOKANE BUSINESS COUNCIL
POB 100, Wellpinit 99040
(509)258-4581

SQUAXIN ISLAND TRIBAL COUNCIL, SE 70, Squaxin Ln
Shelton 98584 (206)426-9781

STELIACOOM TRIBE
19614 Mountain Highway
Spanaway 98387 (206)847-6448

STILLAGUAMISH BOARD OF DIRECTORS, 3439
Stoulckquamish Ln, Arlington
98223 (206)652-7362

SUQUAMISH TRIBAL COUNCIL
POB 498, Suquamish 98392
(206)598-3311

SWINOMISH INDIAN TRIBAL COMMUNITY, POB 817, LaConner
98257 (206)466-3163

TULALIP BOARD OF DIRECTORS
6700 Totem Beach Rd
Marysville 98270
(206)653-4585

UPPER SKAGIT TRIBAL COUNCIL
2284 Community Plaza
Sedro Woolley 98284
(206)856-5501

YAKIMA TRIBAL COUNCIL
POB 151, Toppenish 98948
(509)865-5121

INDIAN RESERVATIONS

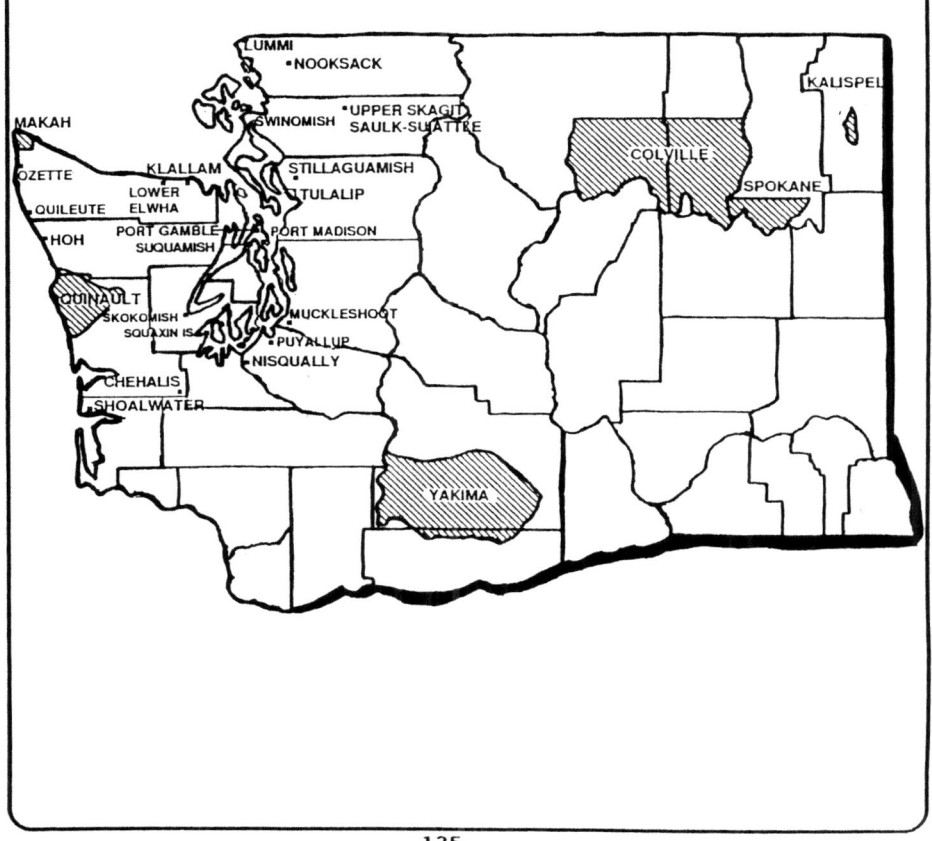

Military

WASHINGTON MILITARY DEPARTMENT

Camp Murray, Tacoma, WA
98430-5000, (206)581-1950

This department is responsible for the overall management, supervision, administration and stationing of National Guard units and personnel within the state. Their primary function is the protection of life and property and the preservation of peace, order and public safety by order of the governor as commander-in-chief.

THE ACTIVE MILITARY

THE ARMY

·FORT LEWIS

Where: 12 miles south of Tacoma off I-5; Zip code 98433, Phone (206)967-1110

Population: 23,857 Active duty soldiers; 35,000 family members.

THE NAVY

BANGOR NSB

Where: 11 miles north of Bremerton off Hwy. 3; Zip code 98315, Phone (206)396-6008

Population: 5,550 active duty sailors; 3,720 family members.

BREMERTON NAVAL HOSPITAL

Where: 4 miles north of Bremerton on Route 3 at the north end of Jackson Park Navy housing; Zip code 98312 Phone (206)479-6600

Population: 506 active duty sailors; 732 family members.

PUGET SOUND NAVAL SHIPYARD

Where: On Route 3 and 16 in Bremerton, 60 miles west of Seattle; Zip code 98314 Phone (206)476-3711

Population: 4,542 active duty sailors; 6,260 family members.

PUGET SOUND NS

Where: Sand Point site is 7 mile northeast of downtown Settle off I-5; Zip code 98115; Phone (206)526-3367

Population: 1,000 active duty sailors; 1,750 family members.

WHIDBEY ISLAND NAS

Where: At Oak Harbor, 60 miles north of Seattle on Route 20; Zip code 98277 Phone (206)257-2211

Population: 7,900 active duty sailors; 13,000 family members.

THE MARINES

SEATTLE CG SUPPORT CENTER

Where: Located within Seattle city limits off Hwy. 99; Zip code 98134; Phone (206)286-9650

Population: 1,000 active duty marines; 500 family members.

THE AIR FORCE

FAIRCHILD AFB

Where: 12 miles west of Spokane off Route 2; Zip code 99011; Phone (509)247-1212

Population: 4,400 active duty airmen; 4,600 family members.

McCHORD AFB

Where: 6 miles south of downtown Tacoma off I-5; Zip code 98438; Phone (206)967-1910.

ARMY RESERVES

124th U.S. Army Reserve Command
Fort Lawton, WA 98199
(206)281-3031

This unit is responsible for the overall management, supervision, administration, and stationing of Army Reserve units and personnel within the state.

Social Service

EMPLOYMENT SECURITY DEPARTMENT

This department operates as part of a national employment
and training system that helps people find jobs. The
department also helps employers find workers and in some
cases provides workers with temporary income while they look
for work.

Employment Services
This department attempts to place people in jobs. These
job placement services are provided through a network of 29
Job Service Centers (JSC) and 34 satellite, outstation and
itinerant offices throughout the state. Job seekers are
screened, offered employment counseling, job search
assistance, testing and referral to training, jobs and other
services.

Corrections Clearinghouse
This department specializes in offender services. It
functions as a vital link between the employment and
training system and the criminal justice system. Projects
operated by the Clearinghouse have focused on
pre-release/work orientation activities in the correctional
institutions, career awareness planning and job placement
activities in the community and statewide coordination of
offender programs and resources.

Unemployment Insurance
This benefit, partially compensates eligible unemployed
workers for loss of wage/salary. In order to qualify,
participants must be unemployed through no fault of their
own, be physically able to work and have worker at least 680
hours in a base year (first four of the last five completed
quarters) for employers covered by the applicable law.
Applicants must be immediately available to accept any
suitable work. In addition, applicants must actively seek
work by making personal contacts with prospective employers.

Federal Bonding Program
This program provides individual fidelity bonds for
applicants denied coverage by commercial carries because of
a record of arrest, conviction or imprisonment; history of

alcohol or drug abuse; poor credit history; lack of
employment history (e.g. youth or displaced homemaker);
Dishonorable Discharge from military; and or special
situations requiring a fidelity bond. To qualify, job offer
must be full-time steady work providing adequate working
conditions and wages.

Targeted Job Tax Credit Program
This program allows employers to receive a tax break for
hiring employees from certain disadvantaged groups.
Employers can claim a credit of 40 percent of the first year
wages up to $6,000.00 (maximum credit of $2,400.00) per
employee. Targeted groups available for the credit are
disadvantaged youth (18-22); Vietnam-era veterans;
ex-felons; summer youth (16-17 and hired between May 1 and
Sep 15); youth 16-19 in a cooperative education program;
Vocational Rehabilitation referrals; Social Security
recipients; General Assistance recipients; recipients of Aid
to Families with Dependant Children; and participants in the
Family Independence or Opportunities Programs.

Veterans' Programs
These programs are offered in four categories. The Disabled
Veteran Outreach Program - provides employment assistance to
disabled and Vietnam-era veterans. The Veterans Job
Training Act - provides monetary incentives to employers who
hire Korean or Vietnan-era veterans. Participants have to
be unemployed at the time of application and unemployed for
10 of the 15 preceding weeks. The Apprenticeship/On-The-Job
Training Program - supplements the veteran's salary for a
period of time with the rate of the employer's contribution
increasing to 100 percent upon completion of training. The
Federal Contractor Job Listing Program - requires that the
party contracting with the United States will take
affirmative action to employ and advance qualified Special
Disabled Veterans and Veterans of the Vietnam-era.

Washinton State Service Corps
This program provides unemployed residents between 18-25
with the opportunity to learn new skills and receive work
and training experience to better complete in today's job
market. The Service Corps also offers its participants the
opportunity to continue their education, both during and
after their tenure with the program. The program pays
participants $525. a month and provides health insurance.
If eligible, tenure may last between 6-12 months.

Family Independence Program
This program is an alternative to the Aid to Families with
Dependent Children program. The Employment Security
Department offers employment and training services to
participants. Applicants must meet the eligibility
requirements of the Aid to Families with Dependant Children
to participate. Services offered through the program are
referral to jobs, basic and vocational education, labor
market information, on-the-job training, job search skill
development, institutional training and work experience

Washington State Opportunities Program
This program serves recipients of the Aid to Families with Dependent Children program. Services may include employment and family counseling, work search assistance, work experience, on-the-job training, institutional training, childcare, and medical and dental services.

Shared Work Program
This program allows an employer to reduce an eligible employees' hours and wages by a mutually agreed percentage, while that employee receives a corresponding percentage of unemployment insurance benefits.

Job Training Partnership Act
This program provides job training and placement services to economically disadvantaged youth and adults. Services available may include job search assistance, on-the-job training, GED completion, work experience, remedial education and basic skills training, institutional skill training and supportive services.

Job Corps
This program is for disadvantaged youth between the ages of 16-21. It provides institutional training for future entry into the job market. Applicants are paid, housed and provided medical benefits while attending training. Services offered by the Employment Security Dept are: outreach and screening applicants, application completion and processing, maintaining contact and support of Job Corps students while in the center and job placement assistance upon completion of training.

First Source Hiring Program
This program is an incentive for employers to hire unemployed individuals, especially those currently on welfare or drawing unemployment compensation. The employer and the prospective employee agree to a 30-day training period. During this period the employer pays no wages and the potential employee continues to receive their public assistance or unemployment insurance benefits.

Migrant and Seasonal Farmworker Program
This program provides placement services in rural agricultural areas directly or refers workers to other appropriate agencies. Bilingual staff are available to assist Spanish-speaking applicants.

Alien Employment Certification
This program makes it possible for an employer to hire a foreign national if it can be proved there are no qualified, available United States workers for the specific employment in question.

DEPARTMENT OF SOCIAL AND HEALTH SERVICES

The Department of Social and Health Services (DSHS) helps people who are unable to protect themselves or to fully provide for their basic needs. This department also protects the general public from hazards such as contagious diseases, radiation and polluted water. Through public education efforts, DSHS promotes activities that contribute to the public health.

The department's offices and facilities are located throughout the state. Grants, medical assistance, and foodstamps can be obtained at 57 Community Services Offices (CSO's) located state-wide.

Public Health
This division works to prevent and control the causes of disease, injury, disability and premature death. The emphasis is on prevention through education and early detection.

Health and Rehabilitative Services
Alcohol and Substance Abuse is a bureau that helps people recover from alcoholism and drug addiction. The bureau contacts with county governments and private providers for various types of treatment.

Vocational Rehabilitation
This bureau assists people with physical or metal disabilities to become employed. Through a variety of individual services, clients are prepared for and places in employment. Ongoing support is arranged to help them remain employed.

Developmental Disabilities
This bureau assists people with developmental disabilities to live as fully and independently as possible. Services are bases on individual need ranging from full-time care to assistance needed to live and work independently. Clients may live on their own, with family, in community group homes or in one of six residential centers operated by the Department.

Mental Health
This bureau oversees a comprehensive system of mental health services intended to provide treatment to people who are mentally ill. Community mental health agencies provide evaluation, therapy, education and some residential services such as group homes, foster care and semi-independent living arrangements. DSHS operates four mental health institutions where people with more severe mental disorders receive care and treatment.

Aging and Adult Services
This bureau assists clients in identifying their needs and arranging for necessary services. They also investigate reports of abuse, neglect, exploitation or abandonment of older persons and adults who are disables. Appropriate services are provided to protect those who are vulnerable to abuse.

ECONOMIC AND MEDICAL SERVICES

Income Assistance
This bureau provides financial assistance and/or food stamps to needy families and individuals such as parents with young children, unemployed adults and those who are disabled and are not employable. In addition, clients enrolled in the Family Independence Program will receive services to help them become employable as well as assistance in such areas as locating child care and making transportation arrangements.

Medical Assistance
This program assures that necessary medical care is available to all eligible low income clients. The program promotes maintenance of good health, monitors quality of care, pays medical service providers and works to control health care costs.

Refugee Assistance
This program provides refugees the opportunity to become economically self-sufficient as quickly as possible after they settle in Washington. Services provided to refugees include cash and medical assistance, English-language training, counseling, help in finding employment and foster care for minors.

CHILDREN, YOUTH AND FAMILY SERVICES

Field Operations
Works directly with families to investigate reports of child abuse and neglect, and to resolve conflict. When necessary to keep a child safe, they arrange for temporary out-of-home placement or as appropriate adoption services. They also arrange for on-going services to support and strengthen families, such as counseling and home visits.

Child Protection/Welfare Programs
This program supports Children's Services field staff through program and policy development, consultation and technical assistance. This area also works with the public, the Legislature and the press to promote a shared understanding of child protection and child development programs.

Parent and Child Health
This program focuses on improving the health and well-being of infants, children, youth, parents and protective parents. Primary efforts include prenatal care, improving diet and nutrition, detecting and preventing childhood illness and disability, preventing unplanned pregnancies and promoting family health.

Juvenile Rehabilitation

This program provides confinement and rehabilitation for youth offenders convicted by juvenile courts. Three institutions and two forestry camps are operated through the Division. These facilities provide education, vocational training, recreation and specific treatment efforts to rehabilitate young offenders. Community-based programs such as homes, learning centers and counseling services provide less-costly alternatives for juvenile offenders who don't require a 24 hour restrictive setting.

DEPARTMENT OF VETERANS AFFAIRS (DVA)

The Washington Department of Veterans Affairs (DVA) is a full-service state agency created to assist veterans, service members, their dependents and survivors. The Department is an advocate for Washington State veterans. Upon request, this department will try to obtain for such persons any benefit to which they are entitled under the laws of the United States, the state of Washington, or any other state or government agency. The department has two residential facilities designed to provide a high level of medical and supportive care to eligible persons who cannot provide for themselves. Services/benefits include, but are not limited to:

Burial Benefits	Employment Preference
Dependents' Benefits	Domiciliary and Nursing Care
Disability Compensation	Insurance
Education	Home/Business Loans
Home Nursing Treatment	Pension
Homeless Veterans	Delayed Stress
Military Retirement Credits	Special Benefits for Disabled
Upgrading of Discharges	Medical/Dental Care

JOB TRAINING PARTNERSHIP ACT

The Job Training Partnership Act (JTPA) is an employment and training program which provides job training and job placement to economically disadvantaged youth (16-21 years of age) and adults (22 years or older).

Available services generally include, but are not limited to:

Job Search Assistance
Job Counseling
On-The-Job Training
GED Completion
Work Experience
Remedial Education and Basic Skills Training
Institution Skill Training
Pre-Apprenticeship Program
Supportive Services

EMPLOYMENT SECURITY DEPARTMENT
212 Maple Park, KG-11
Olympia 98504-5311
(206)753-5116

DEPARTMENT OF SOCIAL AND HEALTH SERVICES
OB-44R, Olympia 98504-0095
(206)753-7039 or 753-2745

DEPARTMENT OF HEALTH
1112 South Quince, ET-21
Olympia 98504
(206)753-5871

COUNCIL FOR THE PREVENTION OF CHILD ABUSE AND NEGLECT
1507 Western Avenue, Suite 605
Seattle 98101 (206)464-6151

DEPARTMENT OF VETERANS AFFAIRS
505 East Union, Republic Bldg
POB 9778, PM-41, Olympia 98504
(206)753-5586

WASHINGTON BASIC HEALTH PLAN
1220 Eastside SE, HL-11
POB 9014, Olympia 98504
(206)586-5332

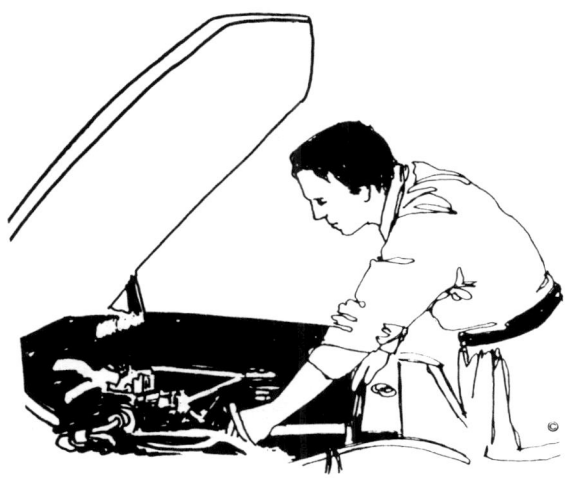

Help Wanted

1·800 Toll·Free Numbers

Adoption 1-800-562-5682
Aeronautics (Seattle) 1-800-552-0666
Aging Services (SHS) 1-800-562-6028
Agriculture (AGR) (Nursery Inspection) 1-800-562-4966
AIDS Hotline 1-800-272-2437
Attorney General (ATG) (Seattle) 1-800-551-4636

Basic Health Plan (low income only) **1-800-826-2444**
Better Business Bureau (SW Wash only) .. 1-800-422-4007
Blind Hotline 1-800-552-7103
Blind Library 1-800-542-0866
Boat Licensing Hotline 1-800-521-9319
Business Assistance Center 1-800-237-1233
Business License 1-800-562-8203
    Pesticides   Cigarettes   Master License
    Trade Names   Liens   Nursery
    Uniform Code   Corporations (license renewal)

Charities (SEC) **1-800-332-4483**
Child Find 1-800-426-5678
Children's Services (SHS) 1-800-562-5624
Commercial Fishing Hotline (July-Nov) 1-800-562-5672
Community Development (DCD) 1-800-562-5677
Consumer Protection (Seattle) 1-800-551-4636
Credit Union (Washington State Emp) 1-800-562-0999

Deferred Compensation (CDC) **1-800-423-1524**
Developmental Disabilities (SHS) 1-800-562-6028
Disability Insurance (SHS) 1-800-562-6074
Domestic Violence Hotline 1-800-562-6025

Emergency Services **1-800-562-6108**
Emission Control 1-800-248-9993
Energy Assistance (DCD) 1-800-562-5677

Fair Housing Discrimination Hotline **1-800-233-3247**
Ferry Information .... 1-800-542-0810 or 1-800-542-7052
Flags (US) 1-800-552-4668
Forest Tax Assistance 1-800-548-8829

Hazardous Substances (ECY) **1-800-633-7585**
Hazardous Waste Hotline 1-800-262-7483
High Risk Health Coverage 1-800-456-0224

Immigration Hotline **1-800-922-4305**
Impaired Physicians Hotline 1-800-552-7236
Industrial Insurance Fraud (L&I) 1-800-547-8367
Information (State) 1-800-321-2808
Insurance Commission (INS) 1-800-562-6900

Labor & Industries:
    Client Relations **1-800-547-8367**
    Contractor Registration 1-800-647-0982
Legislative Hotline (during session only) ... 1-800-562-6000
Litter Control (ECY) 1-800-732-9253
Long Term Care Ombudsman 1-800-562-6028

Lottery (LOT):
Agents only **1-800-732-5101**
Winning numbers (recording) 1-800-545-7510

Natural Resources (RES) **1-800-527-3305**
Nursery Inspection (AGR) 1-800-562-4966
Nursing Home Complaints 1-800-562-6078
Nursing Home Information 1-800-562-6028

Out of State License Fraud (REV) **1-800-854-3119**

Parks (May 1 thru Labor Day) **1-800-562-0990**
Personalized License Plates (DOL) 1-800-228-9847
Plants & Produce (border crossing) 1-800-562-4966
Puget Sound Water Quality Authority
(WQA) 1-800-547-6863

Recycling Hotline (ECY) **1-800-732-9253**
Red Tide Hotline 1-800-562-5632
Refugee Assistance 1-800-732-9029
Revenue (REV) 1-800-647-7706

Secretary of State (SEC) (charities only) ... **1-800-332-4483**
Social Security 1-800-234-5772
State Information 1-800-321-2808
Support Registry (SHS) 1-800-922-4306

Taxpayer Information **1-800-647-7706**
Thurston County Courthouse 1-800-624-1234
Tourism British Columbia 1-800-663-6000
Tourism (in state-ordering
travel book only) 1-800-544-1800
Tourism (out of state) 1-800-541-9274

Uniform Dental Plan **1-800-537-3406**
Uniform Medical & Vision Plan 1-800-762-6004
Uniform Prescription Plan 1-800-628-8881
Union Hotline (during session only) 1-800-562-6102
Utilities & Transportation Commission
(UTC) 1-800-562-6150
Utility Underground Location Center 1-800-424-5555

Veterans Affairs (DVA) **1-800-562-2308**
Vital Statistics:
In State 1-800-331-0680
Out of State 1-800-551-0562

Wash Training Resource Center **1-800-562-0858**
(Train sewage & water treatment plant operators)
Welfare Fraud Hotline 1-800-562-6906
Wildlife (WDW):
Poaching Reports 1-800-562-5626
Whale Sighting 1-800-562-8832
Wood Stove Burning Information (ECY) 1-800-523-4636
Woodcutting Permit (RES) 1-800-562-6010
WSECU (Credit Union) 1-800-562-0999

Washington State Agricultural Facts

WASHINGTON STATE FARMERS PRODUCE $3.8 BILLION WORTH OF AGRICULTURAL PRODUCTS.

- The food processing industry generates $4.5 billion in sales annually.

- 350,000 people are employed in jobs created or induced by agriculture. This includes those who produce, harvest, transport, process and retail agricultural products as well as those who produce and supply farmers with equipment, seed, feed, fertilizer and other inputs.

AGRICULTURE CONTRIBUTES OVER $1.3 BILLION TO STATE EXPORTS.

- Wheat is Washington's most valuable export commodity. Nine out of ten bushels of wheat are exported, primarily to Japan, Korea, and Taiwan.

- Washington exports fresh apples to 30 countries with Taiwan, Hong Kong and Saudi Arabia our most frequent customers.

- Exports exceed $20 million for many individual Washington commodities including hops, potatoes, barley, sweet cherries, vegetable seeds, hay, dairy products, beef, cattle hides, sweet corn and mint oil.

WASHINGTON RANKS 1ST IN:

	Percent of U.S. Production
Apples	50%
Sweet Cherries	43%
Pears	38%
Hops	73%
Dry peas	64%
Lentils	56%
Spearmint Oil	60%
Red Raspberries	54%
Carrots for processing	26%
Concord Grapes	48%

WASHINGTON STATE AGRICULTURE TOP 40 COMMODITIES*
1989 Value of Production

1.	Milk	$559,224,000
2.	Wheat	447,970,000
3.	Apples	436,000,000
4.	Cattle and Calves	402,172,000
5.	Potatoes	321,550,000
6.	Hay	253,260,000
7.	Nursery/Greenhouse Products	140,000,000
8.	All Pears	103,118,000
9.	Eggs	79,131,000
10.	Grapes	69,158,000
11.	Sweet Cherries	67,390,000
12.	Barley	65,366,000
13.	Hops	57,691,000
14.	Asparagus	55,074,000
15.	Chickens and Broilers	51,363,000
16.	Corn, Grain	44,100,000
17.	Sweet Corn, All	38,864,000
18.	Onions	36,001,000
19.	Mint Oil	30,397,000
20.	Green Peas, Processing	25,977,000
21.	Corn, Silage	25,000,000
22.	Dry Edible Beans	23,318,000
23.	Dry Edible Peas	20,129,000
24.	Alfalfa Seed	17,582,000
25.	Red Raspberries	16,269,000
26.	Carrots	14,407,000
27.	Lentils	11,794,000
28.	Kentucky Bluegrass Seed	11,470,000
29.	Peaches	11,212,000
30.	Hogs & Pigs	9,411,000
31.	Wrinkled Seed Peas	9,104,000
32.	Mink	9,080,000
33.	Mushrooms	8,306,000
34.	Lettuce	8,120,000
35.	Cranberries	7,004,000
36.	Strawberries	5,440,000
37.	Sheep, Lambs and Wool	4,624,000
38.	Blueberries	4,326,000
39.	Oats	3,827,000
40.	Cucumbers for Pickles	3,066,000

Total Value of Production: $3,863,033,000

*as compiled by Washington Agricultural Statistics Service

WASHINGTON COUNTIES AND COUNTY SEATS

PART TWO

NOTES

SOUTHEAST

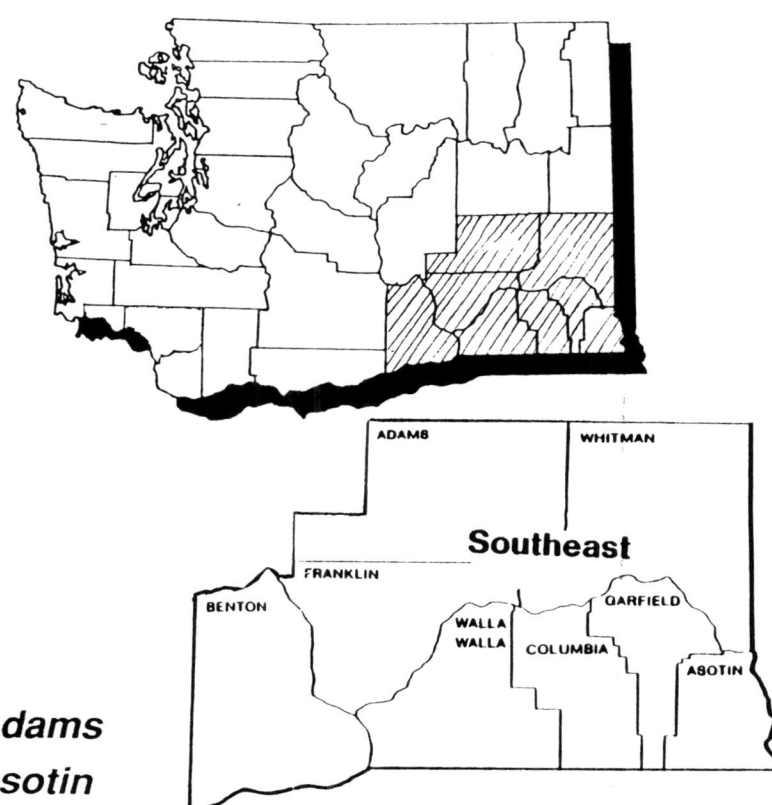

ADAMS

WHITMAN

Southeast

FRANKLIN

BENTON

WALLA
WALLA

GARFIELD

COLUMBIA

ASOTIN

Adams

Asotin

Benton

Columbia

Franklin

Garfield

Whitman

Walla Walla

SOUTHEAST WASHINGTON
TOURISM ASSOCIATION
POB 644, Walla Walla
99362 (509)525-0850

HISTORICAL APPEAL

Asotin County Historical Museum
Asotin

Alpowai Interpretive Center,
Clarkston

Dayton Depot, Dayton

East Benton County Historical
Museum, Kennewick

Franklin County Historical
Museum, Pasco

Sacajawea Interpretive Center
Pasco

Garfield Courthouse, National
Historical Register, Pomeroy

Benton County Historical Museum
Prosser

Washington Archaeological
Research Center, Pullman

Dr. Frank R. Burroughs
Historical Home, Ritzville

Fort Walla Walla Museum
Complex, Walla Walla

Whitman Mission National
Historic Site, Walla Walla

CITIES

ASOTIN
Asotin Chamber of Commerce,
POB 574, Asotin,99402,(509)
243-4222

BENTON CITY
Benton City Chamber of Commerce
POB 401,623 9th St,Benton City
99320,(509)588-3142

CLARKSTON
Clarkston Chamber of Commerce
731 5th St, Clarkston 99403
(509)758-7712

COLFAX
Colfax Chamber of Commerce
N 612 Main St, Colfax 99111
(509)397-3712

CONNELL
Chamber of Commerce, POB 401
600 S Columbia Ave,Connell
99326,(509)234-8731

DAYTON
Dayton Chamber of Commerce
222 E Commercial,Dayton
99326,(509)382-4825

GARFIELD
Garfield Chamber of Commerce
POB 367, 206 California St
Garfield 99130,(509)635-1360

OAKSDALE
Oaksdale Chamber of Commerce
4th & Steptoe 404,Oaksdale
99158,(509)285-6101

OTHELLO
Othello Chamber of Commerce
33 E Larch,Othello 99344,(509)
488-2683

PALOUSE
Palouse Chamber of Commerce
POB 741,E 240 Houghton St
Palouse 99161,(509)878-1269

POMEROY
Pomeroy Chamber of Commerce
POB 947,Pomeroy 99347,(509)
843-1595

PROSSER
Prosser Chamber of Commerce
POB 576,Prosser 99350,(509)
786-3177

PULLMAN
Pullman Chamber of Commerce
N 415 Grand Ave,Pullman 99163

Pullman is the 24th largest
city in Washington, with a
population of 22,300. It is
situated on the South Folk
of the Polouse River, in
Whitman County near the
Washington Idaho border. It
is about 65 miles south of
Spokane and is a trade

center for the surrounding agricultural region. It is the site of Washington State University. It was named in 1884 for George M. Pullman, the railroad car magnate.

RITZVILLE
Ritzville Chamber of Commerce POB 122,107 W Main,Ritzville 99169,(509)659-1035

ROSALIA
Rosalia Chamber of Commerce POB 68,Whitman St,Rosalia 99170,(509)523-3311

TRI-CITIES
Tri-Cities Visitor & Convention Bureau,POB 2241,Tri-Cities 99302,(509)735-8486

BIG BEND...Is Eastern Washington's largest agricultural region. It covers about 7,000 square miles composed of portions of Whitman, Adams, Spokane, Lincoln, Grant, and Douglas Counties. It gets its name from the Big Bend of the Columbia River where it turns southward to westward.

The Kennewick, Pasco and Richland areas comprise what is known as the Tri-Cities areas of Washington. Kennewick, Richland and West Richland are located in Benton County adjacent to the shores of the Columbia River, while Pasco is located in Franklin County opposite the city of Kennewick. The Tri-Cites represent one of the fastest growing areas in the state. Approximately $50 million was invested in major new businesses and existing business expansions in the area during 1988.

*   KENNEWICK
Kennewick, 500 N Moran #1200 Kennewick,99336,(509)736-0510

Kennewick is the 12th largest city in Washington, with a population of 37,000. It is located in Benton County, 185 miles southeast of Seattle. A port on the Columbia River, it is opposite Pasco and southeast of Richland. Together they form what is know as the Tri-Cities Area. The US

Department of Energy Center
in nearby Handford is a
major atomic energy facility
build during World War II.
Large dams, such as McNary
on the Columbia and Ice
Harbor on the Snake River,
provide abundant
hydroelectric power and
irrigation water,
contributing to the city's
booming population. Because
the winters are brief, the
region is one of the best
grape-growing areas in the
state.

* PASCO
Greater Pasco Area Chamber of
Commerce,POB 550,129 N 3rd
Pasco 99301,(509)547-9755

* RICHLAND
Richland Chamber of Commerce
POB 637,700 Geo.Wash.Way
Richland,99352,(509)946-1651

Richland, a city in Benton
County, is the 19th largest
city in Washington, with a
population of 32,970. It is
located on the Columbia
River in the southwestern
part of the state. Richland
is the residential community
for workers at the Handford
Works, and installation,
about 25 miles to the north,
that produces plutonium and
is a center for nuclear
research. Before
establishment of this plant
during World War II,
Richland was a town of a few
hundred persons.

WAITSBURG
Waitsburg Commercial Club
POB 451,721 Main St,Waitsburg
99361,(509)337-6546

WALLA WALLA
Walla Wala Chamber of Commerce
29 E Sumack,Walla Walla
99362,(509)525-0850

**THE HIGHEST TEMPERATURE
EVER RECORDED IN WASH.**
118 degrees. This
occurred twice: 24 July
1928 at Wahluke, and 5
August 1961 at Ice
Harbor Dam, Walla Walla
County.

Walla Walla, the seat of
Walla Walla County, is the 22nd
largest city in Washington,
with a population of 25,700.
It is located on the Walla
Walla River, 120 miles
south-southwest of Spokane.
The major industry is the
processing of vegetables and
grain. Whitman College is in
the city and Walla Walla
College is nearby. Walla
Walla is an Indian term for
"many water." The city grew
around Fort Walla Walla
(1857), near Marcus
Whitman's old mission.

FAIRS AND FESTIVALS

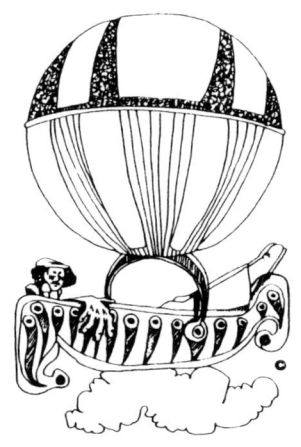

Hot Air Balloon Stampede
Walla Walla
May (509)525-0850

Dayton Days
Dayton
May (509)382-4825

Tri-Cities Int'l Air Show
Pasco, July (509)547-2203

Festival at the Depot
Dayton, July (509)382-4825

Ft. Walla Walla Museum Mountain Man Rendezvous
Walla Walla, July (509)525-7703

Columbia Cup for Unlimited Hydroplanes
Tri-Cities, July (509)547-2203

Wine and Food Fair
Prosser, August (509)786-3177

Benton-Franklin County Fair
Kennewick, August (509)586-9211

Sunfest Downriver Bluegrass Festival
Richland, Richland
(509)946-3131

National Lentil Festival
Pullman, September
(509)334-3565

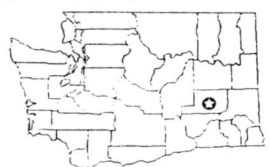

ADAMS COUNTY

Named for John Adams, second president of the U.S.

Created: November 25, 1883

210 West Broadway, Ritzville 99169

AREA: 1,893.5 square miles, State Ranking: 16th

MAJOR ECONOMIC ACTIVITIES
Food Processing and Agriculture

ASSESSED VALUE: $585,861,647

POPULATION: (1989 Estimate): 13,400

Percentage of state: 0.3%
Density: 7.1 persons per square mile

ETHNIC BREAKDOWN:	1988 Estimate
White	11,593
Black	38
Native American	64
Asian and Pacific Islanders	78
Other	2,227

PRIMARY CITIES	Population
Othello	4,550
Ritzville, county seat	1,790

CLIMATE: Ritzville – elevation 1,795 feet

Average	JAN	APR	JUL	OCT
Max Temp (F)	33.8	62.3	88.8	63.6
Min Temp	20.2	35.2	53.2	37.5
Mean Temp	27.0	48.8	71.1	50.6
Precipitation in inches	1.44	.74	.29	1.19

Average Annual Maximum Temperature: 61.4
Average Annual Minimum Temperature: 36.8
Average Annual Mean Temperature: 49.1
Average Annual Precipitation: 11.67 inches

PUBLIC SCHOOL DISTRICTS

Benge School District #122
Benge 99105 (509)887-2370
Enrollment: 9

Lind School District #158
Box 340, Lind 99341 (509)677-3481
Enrollment: 212

Othello School District #147-163-55
615 E. Juniper, Box 588 (509)488-2659
Enrollment: 2,405

Ritzville School District #160-67
Wellsandt Road, Ritzville, 99169
(509)659-659-1660
Enrollment: 497

Washtucna School District #109-43
POB 688, Washtucna 99371 (509)646-3237
Enrollment: 100

HOSPITALS

Othello Community Hospital
350 N. 14th St, Othello
99344 (509)488-2636
Total Beds: 49

Ritzville Memorial Hospital
903 S. Adams, Ritzville
99169 (509)659-1200
Total Beds: 20

THE COURTS

SUPERIOR COURT Area Code (509)
210 W. Broadway, Box 126 Ritzvile 99169
Richard W. Miller, Judge (509)659-0090

JUVENILE COURT
165 N. First St, Othello 99344
Administrator: Wayne Ristau
(509)488-5646

DISTRICT COURTS
Othello - 165 N. First
Charlotte L. DuBois, Judge (509)488-3935

Ritzville - 210 W. Broadway, Box 163, Ritzville
Charlotte L. DuBois, Judge (509)659-0090

CITES OF INTEREST

Mullan Road, Sprague Lake

CRISIS

Community Counseling Service
Othello, 99344, (509) 488-5611
Crisis lines for those in need
of service.

New Success
226 W. 3rd Ave., Moses Lake,
98837 (509)765-1721, Crisis
line, displaced homemakers
programs, 8-5 M-F, those in
need of service, free

MULTIPLE SERVICE CENTERS

Adams County Community Counseling Services
165 N. First, Othello,
99344, (509)488-5162, Certified alcohol/drug, o-p treat, DWI assess., ADATSA, general counseling, 24 hrs, those in need of service, free assessment.

Department of Social & Health Services, 1620 S. Pioneer Way, POB 1399, Moses Lake, 98837 (509) 766-2200 1620 First Northwest, Ephrata, 98823, (509)754-2427 455 East Helmock, Othello, 99344 (509)488-9673

COUNSELING MENTAL/HEALTH

Adams County Health District
103 W. Main, Ritzville, 99169 (509) 659-0090, Health information, limited care and services, HIV testing-all persons free.

Adams County Health District
475 North 14th Ave, Othello, (509) 488-2031, Medical services, Aids testing, children's immunity testing, 24 hrs, those in need of services, free assessment.

Community Counseling, 165 North First, Othello, 99344, (509) 488-5611, Emergency services, substance abuse, o-p treatment all persons, sliding fee.

EMPLOYMENT & TRAINING

Pentad Private Industry Council Inc., 233 N. Chelan Ave., POB 2360, Wenatchee,98801 (509)663-3091

Student Tuition Waivers, Moses Lake,98837, (509)762-5351, Education and tuition waivers, those in need of services

Washington Human Development
410 W. 3rd Ave., Moses Lake 98837 (509) 765-1977

FAMILY PLANNING

Birthright, Moses Lake,98837, (509)765-4425, Family planning, birth control, pregnancy test-hours 11-2, M-F, those in need of service, free.

Birthright, Othello, (509)488-7677 Family planning, those in need of service.

Catholic Family Services
611 W. Columbia St., Pasco, (509)547-0251 Child and youth services, parenting classes, adoption, hours 9-5, M-F, those in need of services, free.

FOOD/CLOTHING/HOUSING

Child Care Food Program
604 W. 3rd Ave., Moses Lake 98837, (509)765-9206, Food nutrition, homeless shelter on weekends, 24hrs, those in need of service, free.

Community Food & Nutrition
604 W. 3rd Ave., Moses Lake 98837, (509)765-9206, Food nutrition, those in need of services.

Quincy Child Development Center, 310 W. St.,Quincy, (509)787-2511, Food and nutrition, those in need of services.

Surplus Commodities, Moses Lake,98837, (509)765-9206 Surplus food distribution center, those in need of services, sliding fee.

WIC Women, Infants and Children, Grant County Courthouse, Ephrata, (509)754-2100, Food and nutrition, those in need of services.

MEDICAL/DENTAL

Columbia Basin Health Association, POB 546, 140 E. Main St., Royal City, (509)

488-5256, Dental care, low income, food, family planning, medical, those in need of services, hours 11-8, M-F, sliding fee.

MISCELLANEOUS

Commission on Hispanic Affairs Olympia, (206)753-3159, Civil rights, those in need of services, free.

Community Corrections, 229 1st Ave., NW, POB 159, Ephrata, 98823, (509) 754-4626, Information & referrals limited to felony offenders sentenced under the Sentencing Reform Act(SRA) who are not receiving supervision within 1 year after release.

Low Income Home Energy Assistance, 604 W. 3rd Ave. Moses Lake, 98837, (509)765-9243, Energy/ Weatherization; hours 9-5 M-F, those in need of services varies.

VETERANS SERVICES

Department of Veteran Affairs North 222 Mission, Rm 134, Spokane, 99205, (509) 456-2803.

For additional information see Grant County

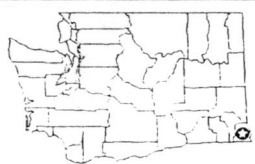

ASOTIN COUNTY

Name derivative of the Indian word "Has-Hu-Tin," meaning "ell."

Created: October 27, 1883
135 Second Street, Asotin 99402

AREA: 633.4 square miles, State Ranking: 34th

MAJOR ECONOMIC ACTIVITIES:
Lumbering, Agriculture,

ASSESSED VALUE: $326,777,263

POPULATION: (1989 Estimate): 17,600

Percentage of state: 0.4%
Density: 27.8 persons per square mile

ETHNIC BREAKDOWN: 1988 Estimate
  White   17,052
  Black   21
  Native American   176
  Asian and Pacific Islanders   70
  Other   81
     Spanish origin (included in above)   180

PRIMARY CITIES   Population
  Asotin, county seat   1,025
  Clarkston   6,700

CLIMATE: Clarkston Heights - elevation 1,186 feet

Average	JAN	APR	JUL	OCT
Max Temp (F)	38.2	64.5	90.5	62.8
Min Temp	23.9	38.2	53.8	38.7
Mean Temp	31.7	51.4	72.2	50.7
Precipitation in inches	1.07	1.16	.51	1.14

Average Annual Maximum Temperature: 63.8
Average Annual Minimum Temperature: 38.9
Average Annual Mean Temperature: 51.4
Average Annual Precipitation: 13.15 inches

PUBLIC SCHOOL DISTRICTS

Asotin-Anatone School District #420
314 First St, Box 489 (509)243-4147
Asotine 99402, Enrollment: 500

Clarkston School District #J 250-185
847 Fifth St, POB 70 (509)758-2432
Clarkston 99403, Enrollment: 2,715

HOSPITAL

**Tri-State Memorial Hospital,
Inc.,** POB 189, 1221 Highland
Ave, Clarkston 99403
(509)758-5511
Total Beds: 62

THE COURTS

SUPERIOR COURT   Area Code (509)
County Courthouse, Box 159,
Asotin 99402
John M Lynde, Judge   243-4182

JUVENILE COURT
1603 Dustan Loop, Clarkston 99403
Administrator: Vonda Campbell
758-1623

DISTRICT COURT
County Courthouse, Box 429, Asotin 99402
William D. Acey, Judge 243-4127

SITES OF INTEREST:

Snake River, Blue Mountain

CRISIS

YMCA Crisis Services
300 Main St, Lewiston,ID 83501
(208)7469655 Sexual assault
programs; those in need of
services

MULTIPLE SERVICE CENTERS

Community Action Agency
124 New 6th St., Lewiston, ID
83501, (208)746-3351, Energy
assistance, referrals, dental,
alcohol & drug referral,
shelter, pre-school assistance, daycare, commodities
distributor; hours 8-5 M-F,
sliding fee.

Department of Social Services
720 6th St., Clarkston, 99403
(509)758-4517

St Vincent de Paul, 834 6th St
Clarkston, 99403, (509)758-7061
Clothing, emergency shelter,
some meals, taxi service;
those in need of services.

COUNSELING MENTAL/HEALTH

**Asotin-Garfield County Mental
Health,** 1603 Dustan Loop,
Clarkston, 99403, (509)
758-3341 Mental health services with treatment, o-p &
group therapy, M-F, all
persons, sliding fee

Rogers Counseling, 900 7th St. Clarkston,99403, (509)758-3341 Counseling, psychotherapy, alcohol & drug counseling; no sexual offender, M-F, all persons, free.

EMPLOYMENT & TRAINING

Eastern Job Training Partnership-Field Operations Division, Mail Stop KG-11, Olympia,98504,(206)586-0898

Employment & Training Center 1603 Dustan Loop,Clarkston 99403, (509) 758-5461, Vocational counseling, job training, work experience, class training, job placement; persons unemployed.

NEWA Rural Resources Development Association, 320 N. Main St., Colville,99114, (509) 684-8421, Vocational counseling & assessment; job training, work experience class training, job placement; low income & disadvantaged.

FOOD/CLOTHING/HOUSING

People Place, 1139 13th St. Clarkston,99403, (509)758-0812 Food bank.

Sulton Company Food Bank 1546 Maple, Clarkston,99403, (509)758-7085, Food bank.

VETERANS SERVICES

Veterans of Foreign Wars 720 W. Court St., Sheridan Bldg, Pasco,99301, (509) 545-8122

VICTIMS

A Women's Place, 640 Jadwin, Suite C, Richard,99352, (509) 582-9841 Domestic violence advocates with counsel, self support groups, shelter, safe house; 265 days a year, answering service, those in need of services, sliding fee, No substance abusers.

MISCELLANEOUS

Center for New Directions Lewis & Clark College, Lewiston, ID 83501, (208)799-2331, Displaced homemakers program; M-F, all persons, free.

Commission on Hispanic Affairs Olympia, (206) 753-3159, Civil Rights; those in need of services, free.

Community Corrections, 730 6th St.,POB 127, Clarkston,99403, (509)758-5870, Information and referrals limited to felony offenders sentenced under the Sentencing Reform Act(SRA) who are not receiving supervision within 1 year after release.

For additional information see Walla Walla / Columbia / Garfield Counties

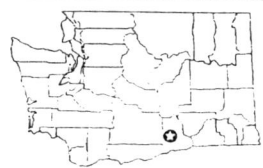

BENTON COUNTY

Named for Thomas Hart Benton, Missouri senator, who favored westward expansion into Oregon county.

Created: March 8, 1905

Courthouse, Dudley Avenue, Prosser 99350

AREA: 1,722.1 square miles, State Ranking: 22nd

MAJOR ECONOMIC ACTIVITIES:
Food Processing, Chemicals, Metal Products, Nuclear Products

ASSESSED VALUE: $2,872,794,287

POPULATION: (1989 Estimate): 104,100

Percentage of state: 2.2%
Density: 60.4 persons per square mile

ETHNIC BREAKDOWN:

	1988 Estimate
White	95,452
Black	781
Native American	722
Asian and Pacific Islanders	1,393
Other	1,752
Spanish origin (included in above)	3,629

PRIMARY CITIES

	Population
Benton City	1,815
Kennewick	36,880
Prosser, county seat	4,010
Richland	29,970
West Richland	3,650

CLIMATE: Prosser – elevation 680 feet

Average	JAN	APR	JUL	OCT
Max Temp (F)	38.7	68.0	90.3	66.6
Min Temp	23.7	38.2	55.6	38.9
Mean Temp	31.2	53.2	72.9	52.8
Precipitation in inches	.94	.55	.17	.92

Average Annual Maximum Temperature: 65.6
Average Annual Minimum Temperature: 39.3
Average Annual Mean Temperature: 52.4
Average Annual Precipitation: 7.77 inches

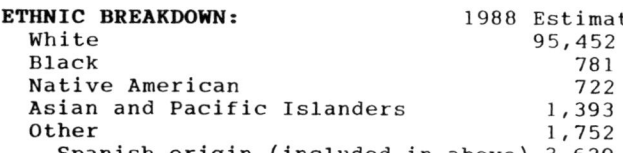

PUBLIC SCHOOL DISTRICTS

Finley School District #53
Route 2, Box 2670, Kennewick 99337
(509)586-3217, Enrollment: 884

Kennewick School District #17
200 S Dayton Street, Kennewick 99336
(509)582-1200, Enrollment: 10,307

Kiona-Benton City School District #52
Box 488, Benton City 99320, (509)588-3717
Enrollment: 1,142

Paterson School District #50
POB 189, Patterson 99345, (509)875-2601
Enrollment: 55

Prosser School District #116
Box 430, Prosser 99350, (509) 786-3323
Enrollment: 2,020

Richland School District #400
615 Snow Avenue, Richland 99352
(509)946-6106, Enrollment: 7,042

HOSPITALS

**Carondelet Psychiatric Care
Center,** 1175 Carondelt Dr
Richland 99352 (509)943-9104
Total Beds: 32

Kadlec Hospital
888 Swift Blvd., Richland
99352 (509)946-4611
Total Beds: 153

Kennewick General Hospital
900 S. Auburn, Kennewick
99336 (509)586-6111
Total Beds: 71

Prosser Memorial Hospital
723 Memorial St, Prosser
99350 (509)786-2222
Total Beds: 74

THE COURTS

SUPERIOR COURT   Area Code (509)
7320 West Quinault St, Kennewick 99336
POB 3051, Tri-Cities, 99302
Carolyn A. Brown, Judge (Kennewick) 783-1471
Fred R. Staples, Judge (Kennewick) 783-1471
Duane E. Taber, Judge (Kennewick) 783-1471
Albert J. Yencopal, Judge (Kennewick) 783-1471
Dennis D. Yule, Judge (Kennewick) 783-2151

JUVENILE COURT
5606 W. Canal Pl.#106, Kennewick 99336
Administrator: Douglas Loree (509)783-2151

DISTRICT COURT
7620 W. Quinault St, Kennewick 99336
Craig Matheson, Pres Judge   738-8476
Eugene F. Pratt, Judge   738-8476

SITES OF INTEREST:

Handford Science Center, McNary Dam

CRISIS

Richard Help Line
(509)843-4357 and
(509)946-4357, 24 hour crisis
line.

MULTIPLE SERVICE CENTERS

**Ben-Frank Community Action
Committee,** 720 W. Court, Pasco
99301, (509)545-4042, Energy
assistance, referrals dental,
alcohol & drug referral,
shelter, pre-school assistance, daycare, commodities
distributor; hours 8-5, M-F,
sliding fee.

COUNSELING MENTAL/HEALTH

**Ben-Frank Community Action
Committee,** 720 W. Court, Pasco
99301, (509)545-4042,
Individual family, relaps &
co-dependent counseling,
intensive out patient
assessment; hours 8-5 M-F,
low income, sliding fee.

**Mid-Columbia Mental Health
Center,** 1175 Gribble Ave,
Richard, 99352, (509)943-9104
Emergency services, substance
abuse, out patient treatment;
all persons, sliding fee.

EMPLOYMENT & TRAINING

**Benton-Franklin-Walla Walla
Private Industry**
6515 W. Clearwater, Suite
238, Kennewick, 99336,
(509)735-8402 (JTPA), job
search assistance, counseling,
OJT, GED, supplemental services; economically dis-
advantaged.

**Columbia Basin Community
College,** 2600 N. 20th Ave,
Pasco, 99301, (509)547-0511
Vocational, academic, GED
testing, career planning, etc;
hours 8-5 M-F, adults 18 +
years, various fees.

Columbia Industries
900 S. Dayton, POB 7396,
Kennewick, 99336,
(509)532-4142, Educational
testing, work training, job
placement; shelter employment;
hours 8-5 M-F, disables
(age 16+years, no fee.

Jackson & Associates,   425 W.
Lewis, Pasco, 99301,
(509)547-2600, Counsel, job
search classes, OJT, TJTC
vouchering; females 16-54 drop
outs.

Washington Human Development
527 W. Court St, Pasco, 99301,
(509)545-4350, Immigration
services, vocational counseling
job development/placement,
ESL/ABE/GED, low income,
migrant seasonal farm workers,
no fee.

FOOD/CLOTHING/HOUSING

Salvation Army
125 W. Bonneville, Pasco 99301
(509)547-2138, Food bank,

clothing; those in need of services.

Tri Cities Food Bank
320 W. 10th, Kennewick, 99336, (509)586-0688.

LEGAL

A Women's Place, 640 Jadwin, Suite C, Richland, 99352, (509)943-2649, Resource services for family law issues, all persons.

MEDICAL/DENTAL

Benton/Franklin Health District
1218 N. 4th, Pasco, 99301, (509)547-9737. 1132 Meade, Prosser, 99350, (509)786-1633 506 McKenzie, Richland, 99352, (509)943-2614, Health info, limited care & services; immunizations, food handler tests, vital statistics, home health care, maternal & child health services, environmental health service, communicable diseases; all persons, variable fees depending on service.

SUBSTANCE ABUSE

Comprehensive Alcohol Program
5219 W. Clearwater Ave, Kennewick, 99336, (509)735-1191, Certified alcohol & drug out patient treatment, information school, DWI client assessment; hours 2-9 M-F, sliding fee, evaluation $50.00.

Psycholgical Consultants
710 George Washington, Richland, 99352, (509)946-9613, Certified out patient drug testing, alcohol career development, psychiatric testing, job training pre-employment screen; all persons, fee varies.

TRANSPORTATION

Ben-Franklin Transit
1000 Columbia Dr, SE, Richland, 99352, (509) 735-4141 $10.50 monthly, 30¢.

Prosser Rural Transit
1225 Pudley, Prosser, 99350, (509)786-1707 35¢ to $1.25.

VETERANS SERVICES

Carondelet Psychiatric Care Center, 1175 Carondelet Dr, Richland, 99352, (509)943-9104 Delayed stress counseling.

Veterans of Foreign Wars
720 W. Court St, Sheridan Bldg, Pasco,99301, (509)545-8122

VICTIMS

Benton/Franklin Rape Relief
640 Jadwin, Richland,99352, (509)946-2377, Resource services for family law issues; sexual assault programs; all persons, hours 8-5 M-F, no fee.

A Women's Place, 640 Jadwin, Suite C, Richland,99352, (509)582-9841, Domestic violence advocates with counsel, self support groups, shelter, safe house; 365 days a year, answering service, those in need of services, sliding fee,

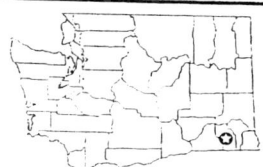

COLUMBIA COUNTY

Named for the Columbia River.

Created: November 11, 1875

341 East Main Street, Dayton 99328

AREA: 859.5 square miles, State Ranking: 31st

MAJOR ECONOMIC ACTIVITIES:
Food Processing, Agriculture, Wood Products

ASSESSED VALUE: $160,531,409

POPULATION: (1989 Estimate): 4,100

Percentage of state: 0.1%
Density: 4.8 persons per square mile

ETHNIC BREAKDOWN: 1988 Estimate
  White   3,971
  Black   0
  Native American   30
  Asian and Pacific Islanders   20
  Other   79
    Spanish origin (included in above)   118

PRIMARY CITIES   Population
  Dayton, county seat   2,640
  Starbuck   190

CLIMATE: Dayton - elevation 1,612 feet

Average	JAN	APR	JUL	OCT
Max Temp (F)	39.2	62.2	87.5	64.6
Min Temp	24.0	38.5	53.8	39.4
Mean Temp	31.6	50.3	70.7	52.0
Precipitation in inches	4.43	1.56	.40	1.89

Average Annual Maximum Temperature: 62.6
Average Annual Minimum Temperature: 39.2
Average Annual Mean Temperature: 50.9
Average Annual Precipitation: 19.53 inches

PUBLIC SCHOOL DISTRICTS

Dayton School District #2
609 S Second St, Dayton 99328 (509)382-2544
Enrollment: 655

Starbuck School District #35
POB 188, Starbuck 99359 (509)399-2381
Enrollment: 50

HOSPITAL

Dayton General Hospital
1012 S. Third St, Dayton
99328 (509)382-2531
Total Beds: 28

THE COURTS

SUPERIOR COURT   Area Code (509)
341 East Main, Dayton 99328
John M. Lyden, Judge (Asotin) 243-2542
    POB 159, Asotin 99402

JUVENILE COURT
310 W. Poplar, POB 1595, Walla Walla
99362, Administrator: (Acting) Michael Bates
527-3275

DISTRICT COURT

41 East Main, Dayton 99328
Charles H. Thronson, Judge   582-4497

SITES OF INTEREST:

Snake River, Blue Mountains

COUNSELING MENTAL/HEALTH

Columbia County Mental Health
129 S.First St,Dayton,99328,
(509)382-2525, Mental health
services, outpatient, medication therapy & crisis intervention; sliding fee.

Columbia County Services
213 W.Clay St,Dayton,99328,
(509)382-2525, Emergency services, substance abuse, outpatient treatment; all persons
sliding fee.

Rogers Counseling, 900 7th St
Clarkston,99403, (509)758-3341,
Counseling, psychotherapy,
alcohol & drug counseling, all
persons, sliding fee.

EMPLOYMENT & TRAINING

**Eastern Job Training
Partnership-Field Operations
Division,** Mail Stop KG-11
Olympia,98504,(206)586-0898

**NEWA Rural Resources
Development Association**
1402 Bridge St,Clarkston,99403
(509)758-5461 Vocational
counseling, assessment, job
training, work experience,
class training, job placement
unemployed persons, low income
and disadvantaged, free.

**Resource Development
Association,** 320 N.Main St
Colville,99114,(509)684-8421,
Vocational counseling, OJT,
job placement, energy assist-

ance, weatherization, legal
aid; low income & disadvantaged, sliding fee.

MEDICAL/DENTAL

**Columbia County Health
District,** 114 N,Second,Dayton
99328,(509)382-2181, Health
information, limited care &
services, immunizations, food
handler testing, WIC, CCS, Aids
testing; all persons, sliding
fee.

**For additional information see Walla Walla
County**

SUBSTANCE ABUSE

Columbia County Services
120 S,1st St,Dayton,99328
(206)382-2524, Certified
alcohol & drug treatment,
information school, DWI client
assessment; those in need of
services.

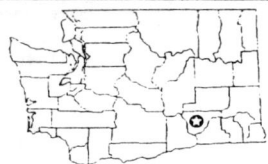

FRANKLIN COUNTY

Named for Benjamin Franklin, author, inventor, and statesman.

Created: November 28, 1883

1016 North Fourth Avenue, Pasco 99301

AREA: 1,259.7 square miles, State Ranking: 27th

MAJOR ECONOMIC ACTIVITIES:
Food Processing, Agriculture, Publishing, Metal Fabrication

ASSESSED VALUE: $1,080,926,822

POPULATION: (1989 Estimate): 34,200

Percentage of state: 0.7%
Density: 27.1 persons per square mile

ETHNIC BREAKDOWN: 1988 Estimate
  White   30,229
  Black   237
  Native American   237
  Asian and Pacific Islanders   454
  Other   3,104
    Spanish origin (included in above) 5,640

PRIMARY CITIES   Population
  Connell   2,015
  Kahlotus   197
  Mesa   275
  Pasco, county seat   17,560

CLIMATE: Eltopia – elevation 920 feet

Average	JAN	APR	JUL	OCT
Max Temp (F)	36.4	68.5	89.7	64.5
Min Temp	22.2	38.1	55.7	37.6
Mean Temp	29.3	52.0	72.8	52.1
Precipitation in inches	.99	.51	.09	.56

Average Annual Maximum Temperature: 63.7
Average Annual Minimum Temperature: 39.1
Average Annual Mean Temperature: 51.5
Average Annual Precipitation: 8.31 inches

PUBLIC SCHOOL DISTRICTS

Kahlotus School District #56
Kahlotus 99335, (509) 282-3338
Enrollment: 100

North Franklin School District #J51-162
POB 829, Connell 99326, (509)234-2031
Enrollment: 1,530

Pasco School District #1
1004 N. 16th Ave
Pasco 99301, (509)547-9531
Enrollment: 6,349

Star School District #54
24180 Pasco-Kahotus Road
Pasco 99301, (509)547-2704
Enrollment: 20

HOSPITAL

Our Lady of Lourdes Hospital
520 N. Fourth Ave, Pasco
99302 (509)547-7704
Total Beds: 125

THE COURTS

SUPERIOR COURT   Area Code (509)
7320 West Quinault St, Kennewick 99336
POB 3051, Tri-Cities 99320
Carolyn A. Brown, Judge   783-1471
Fred R. Staples, Judge   783-1471
Albert J. Yencopal, Judge   783-1471
Dennis D. Yule, Judge   783-1471
Duane E. Taber, Judge   783-1471
JUVENILE COURT
5606 W. Canal Pl.#106, Kennewick 99336
Administrator: Douglas Loree   783-2151

DISTRICT COURT
1015 North Fifth, Pasco 99301
H.W. Felsted, Judge   545-3593

SITES OF INTEREST:

Ice Harbor Dam, Lake Sacajawae

CRISIS

Richland Help Line
(509)943-4357 946-4347,
24 hour crisis line.

545-4042, 545-0855, Detoxification center, treatment, referral services, individual
counseling energy assistance,
block grant; low income &
alcohol abusers, sliding fee.

MULTIPLE SERVICE CENTERS

Ben-Frank Action Community
720 W. Court,Pasco,99301,(509)

COUNSELING MENTAL/HEALTH

Mid-Columbia Mental Health
1175 Gribble Ave,Richland

99352, Adult short term
psychiatric, 24 hour emergency
crisis intervention; drug
& alcohol abusers, sliding fee.

EMPLOYMENT & TRAINING

**Benton-Franklin-Walla Walla
Private Industry**
6515 W. Clearwater,Suite 238
Kennewick,99336,(509)735-8402,
Job search assistance,
counseling, OJT, GED, supplemental services; economically
disadvantaged.

**Colombia Basin Community
College,** 425 W.Lewis,Pasco
99301, (509)547-2600,
Vocational, academic courses,
GED testing; females 16-54
adult drop outs.

Columbia Industries
1350 Grandrich Blvd,Kennewick
99336,(509)735-6347, Education
testing, work training, job
placement, sheltered
employment; alcohol abusers,
sliding fee.

Jackson & Associates
527 W.Court St,Pasco,99301
(509)545-4042, Counseling,
job search classes, OJT, TJTC
vouchering, persons over
55, hispanic/migrant farm
workers, Washington workers;
migrant seasonal farm workers,
no fee.

Washington Human Development
1175 Gribble,Pasco,99302,(509)
943-9104, Immigration services,
vocational counseling, job
development, placement,
ESL/ABE/GED, support services;
all persons, all ages,
sliding fee.

FOOD/CLOTHING/HOUSING

Tri-Cities Food Bank
320 W.10th,Kennewick,99336
(509)586-0688, Food bank;
those in need of services.

LEGAL

A Women's Place, 640 Jadwin
Suite C,Richland,99352,(509)
943-2649, Resource service for
family law issues, all persons.

MEDICAL/DENTAL

**Benton-Franklin Health
District**
409 S.Dayton,Kennewick,99336,
(509)586-0207, Health information, limited care &
services, immunizations, food
handler testing, vital
statistics, home health care,
maternal & child birth health
services, environmental
services & communicable
diseases, shots are $5.00 to
$12.00, other costs are
variable.

SUBSTANCE ABUSE

**Ben-Frank County Alcohol
& Drug Services**
2600 N.20th,Ave,Pasco
(509)547-0511, Individual
family, relaps & co-dependent
counseling, alcohol school,
referrals and outpatient
programs; adults 16+.

Community Alcohol Center
5219 Clearwater Ave,Suite 9
Kennewick,99336,(509)735,1191,
Counseling workshops, alcohol
information, schooling, in
depth alcohol eduction
classes; 9-5 M-F.

**Our Lady of Lourdes Health
Center,** 520 Fourth Ave,Pasco
99320,(509)547-7704, Certified
alcohol & drug outpatient
& inpatient treatment, information school, DWI client
assessment.

TRANSPORTATION

Ben-Franklin Transit
1000 Columbia Dr,SE,Richland
99302,(509)735-4131,
$1050 monthly, 30¢.

Prosser Rural Transit
1225 Pudley,Prosser,99350
(509)786-1707

VICTIMS

A Woman's Place-Columbia
640 Jadwin,Suite C,Richland
99352,(509)582-9841, 943-2649
Domestic violence advocacy,
counseling, support groups,
shelter; 9-5 MF, those in
need of services, sliding
fee but will accommodate
if no money.

For additional information see also Benton County

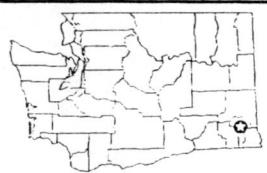

GARFIELD COUNTY

Named for James A. Garfield, president of the U.S., who had just died from an assassination a few weeks before the county was created.

Created: November 29, 1881

County Court House, Pomeroy 99347

AREA: 712.8 square miles, State Ranking: 33rd

MAJOR ECONOMIC ACTIVITIES:
Agriculture

ASSESSED VALUE: $102,337,453

POPULATION: (1989 Estimate): 2,300

Percentage of state: 0.05%
Density: 3.2 persons per square mile

ETHNIC BREAKDOWN:

	1988 Estimate
White	2,385
Black	0
Native American	2
Asian and Pacific Islanders	9
Other	4
Spanish origin (included in above)	5

PRIMARY CITIES   Population
  Pomeroy, county seat   2,385

CLIMATE: Pomeroy - elevation 1,856 feet

Average	JAN	APR	JUL	OCT
Max Temp (F)	39.1	61.4	86.9	65.0
Min Temp	23.8	37.6	52.5	37.8
Mean Temp	31.4	49.5	69.7	51.4
Precipitation in inches	2.02	1.27	.32	1.50

Average Annual Maximum Temperature: 62.4
Average Annual Minimum Temperature: 38.0
Average Annual Mean Temperature: 50.0
Average Annual Precipitation: 16.58 inches

PUBLIC SCHOOL DISTRICTS

Pomeroy School District #110
Box 950, Pomeroy 99347
(509)843-3393
Enrollment: 413

HOSPITAL

**Garfield County Memorial
Hospital,** N. 66 6th St,
Pomeroy 99347 (509)843-1591
Total Beds: 54

THE COURTS

SUPERIOR COURT   Area Code (509)
County Courthouse, POB 915, Pomeroy
99347
John M. Lyden, Judge   Asotin 243-4182
 County Courthouse, POB 159, Asotin 99402
County Clerk, 843-3731

JUVENILE COURT
1603 Dustan Loop, Clarkston 99403
Administrator: Vonda Campbell   758-1623

DISTRICT COURT
County Courthouse, POB 817, Pomeroy
99347
C. Paul Miller, Judge 843-1002
Vannetta I. Jennings, Clerk 843-1002

SITES OF INTEREST:

Snake River Canyon
Blue Mountains

MULTIPLE SERVICE CENTERS

Human Services
856 Main,Pomeroy,99347,(509)
843-3791, Mental counseling,
substance abuse, development
disabilities; those in need of
services, sliding fee.

Information and Assistance
695 Main,Pomeroy,99347,(509)
843-3008, Information and
assistance for those persons
over 60 years of age.

COUNSELING MENTAL/HEALTH

**Garfield County Mental Health
Program,** 856 Main,POB 758
Pomeroy,(509)843-3791
Emergency services, substance
abuse, outpatient treatment;

all persons, sliding fee.

EMPLOYMENT & TRAINING

**Eastern Job Training
Partnership-Field Operations
Division,** Mail Stop KG-11
Olympia,98504,(206)586-0898

Employment & Training Center
1603 Dustan Loop,Clarkston
99403,(509)758-5461,
Vocational counseling &
assessment, job training,
work experience, class
training, job placement,
unemployed, free.

**NEWA Rural Resource Develop-
ment Association,** 320 N.Main
St,Colville,99114,(509)684-8421
Vocational counseling &

assessment, job training, work
experience, class training,
job placement, OJT; low income
& disadvantaged persons.

MEDICAL/DENTAL

**Garfield County Health
Department,** 10th & Columbia
Pomeroy,99347,(509)843-3412,
Health information, limited
care & services, immunizations,
food handler testing; all
persons.

For additional information see also Asotin &

Walla Walla Counties

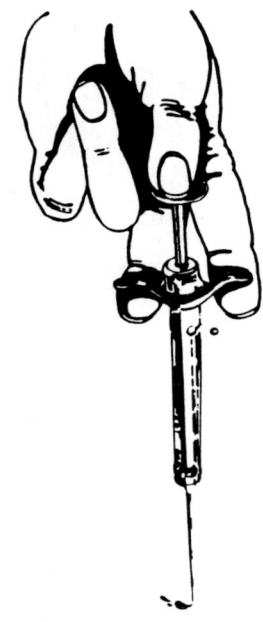

WHITMAN COUNTY

Named for Marcus Whitman, a missionary who
founded Waulatpu Station (Whitman Mission) in
1836.

Created: November 29, 1871

404 North Main Stree, Colfax 99111

AREA: 2,165.5 square miles, State Ranking: 10th

MAJOR ECONOMIC ACTIVITIES:
Wood Products, Agriculture,
Mining, Manufacturing,

ASSESSED VALUE: $973,262,337

POPULATION: (1989 Estimate): 37,600
Percentage of state: 4.0%
Density: 44.0 persons per square mile

ETHNIC BREAKDOWN: 1988 Estimate
  White   36,746
  Black   532
  Native American   243
  Asian and Pacific Islanders   1,137
  Other   342
    Spanish origin (included in above)   561

PRIMARY CITIES   Population
  Albion   675
  Colfax, county seat   2,550
  Palouse   895
  Pullman   22,270
  Tekoa   755

CLIMATE: Pullman – elevation 2,345 feet

Average	JAN	APR	JUL	OCT
Max Temp (F)	33.6	56.5	82.5	60.2
Min Temp	21.1	36.0	49.5	38.3
Mean Temp	27.3	46.3	66.0	49.3
Precipitation in inches	2.67	1.49	.39	1.91

Average Annual Maximum Temperature: 57.4
Average Annual Minimum Temperature: 36.3
Average Annual Mean Temperature: 44.0
Average Annual Precipitation: 20.49 inches

PUBLIC SCHOOL DISTRICTS

Colfax School District #300
N. 1110 Morton St, Colfax 99111
(509)397-3042   Enrollment: 754

Colton School District #306
Colton 99113, (509)229-3385
Enrollment: 187

Endicott School District #308
Endicott 99125,   (509)657-3523
Enrollment: 119

Garfield School District #302
Box 398, Garfield 99130
(509)635-1313   Enrollment: 178

Lacrosse School District #126
Lacrosse 99143   (509)549-3591
Enrollment: 141

Lamont School District #264
RR 2 Box 50, Lamont 99017
(509)257-2463   Enrollment: 30

Oakesdale School District #324
Box 228, Oakesdale 99158
(509)285-5296   Enrollment: 137

Palouse School District #301
Route 1, Box 100, Palouse 99161
(509)878-1521   Enrollment: 206

Pullman School District #267
NW 115 State St., Pullman 99163
(509)332-3581   Enrollment: 2,220

Rosalia School District #322
Box 128, Rosalia 99170
(509)523-3061   Enrollment: 230

St. John School District #322
Box 58, St. John 99171
(509)648-3336   Enrollment: 180

Steptoe School District #304
POB 138, Steptoe 99174
(509)397-3119   Enrollment: 40

Tekoa School District #265
Box 869, Tekoa 99003
(509)284-3401   Enrollment: 190

HOSPITALS

Pullman Memorial Hospital
NE 1125 Washington Ave,
Pullman 99163 (509)332-2541
Total Beds: 42

Whitman Community Hospital
POB 32, Colfax 99111
(509)397-3435
Total Beds: 48

THE COURTS

SUPERIOR COURT Area Code (509)
North 404 Main St, POB 390, Colfax,
WA 99111
Wallis W. Friel, Judge 397-4622
Shirley J. Bafus, County Clerk 397-6240

JUVENILE COURT

N. 400 Main St, POB 230, Colfax, WA
99111
Administrator: Jack W. Lien 397-6246

DISTRICT COURTS
Whitman County
N. 404 Main St, POB 230, Colfax, WA 99111
David J. Frazier, Judge   397-6260
Marlynn Markley, Administrator 397-6260

Pullman Branch Office
City Hall, POB 249, Pullman, WA 99163
David J. Frazier, Judge   332-2065
Marlynn Markley, Administrator 332-2065
                          or   332-2065

SITES OF INTEREST

Steptoe Battlefield
Lower Granite Dam
Palouse Wheat Fields

CRISIS

Pullman Crisis Line
24 hour crisis line
(509)332-1505

MULTIPLE SERVICE CENTERS

**Community Action Center of
Washington,** N 214 Main,Colfax
99111,(509)397-2205, Energy
assistance, referrals, dental,
alcohol & drug referral,
shelter, re-school assistance,
daycare, commodities dis-
tributor; 8-5 M-F, sliding
fee.

COUNSELING MENTAL/HEALTH

**Whitman County Mental Health
Center,** Northeast 340 Maple
#3,Pullman,(509)334-1133,
Emergency services, substance
abuse, outpatient treatment;
sliding fee.

EMPLOYMENT & TRAINING

**Eastern Job Training
Partnership-Field Operations
Division,** Mail Stop KG-11
Olympia,98504,(206)586--0898

Job Service Center, S 405 Grand
POB 549,Pullman,99163,(509)332-
6549

FAMILY PLANNING

Planned Parenthood
W 102 Main,Pullman,99163,(509)
334-1525, Family planning,
pregnancy counseling & prevention.

FOOD/CLOTHING/HOUSING

Emergency Food Bank
POB 107,Colfax,99111,(509)
397-4611, Emergency food bank.

**Whitman County Regional
Planning Council,** Room 8, ONB
Bldg.,Colfax,(509)397-4622,
Emergency shelter.

WALLA WALLA COUNTY

Named for the Walla Walla Indians, whose tribe name means "running water."

Created: April 25, 1854

315 West Main Street, Walla Walla 99362

AREA: 1,267.3 square miles, State Ranking: 26th

MAJOR ECONOMIC ACTIVITIES:
Food Processing, Wood and Paper Products, Agriculture, Manufacturing

ASSESSED VALUE: $1,493,284,007

Population: (1989 Estimate): 48,800
Percentage of state: 1.0%
Density: 38.5 persons per square mile

ETHNIC BREAKDOWN:	1988 Estimate
White	44,586
Black	744
Native American	323
Asian and Pacific Islanders	466
Other	2,181
Spanish origin (included in above)	2,766

PRIMARY CITIES	Population
College Place	5,990
Waitsburg	1,030
Walla Walla, county seat	25,690

CLIMATE: Walla Walla - elevation 949 feet

Average	JAN	APR	JUL	OCT
Max Temp (F)	39.0	63.8	89.2	64.6
Min Temp	27.4	43.7	62.7	45.6
Mean Temp	33.2	53.8	76.0	55.1
Precipitation in inches	1.89	1.40	.21	1.53

Average Annual Maximum Temperature: 63.6
Average Annual Minimum Temperature: 44.7
Average Annual Mean Temperature: 54.2
Average Annual Precipitation: 15.50 inches

PUBLIC SCHOOL DISTRICTS

College Place School District #250

1755 South College Ave., College Place
99324 (509)525-4827 Enrollment: 655

Columbia School District #400
Burbank 99323, (509)545-8571
Enrollment: 774

Dixie School District #101
POB 77, Dixie 99329, (509)525-5339
Enrollment: 30

Prescott School District #402-37
Box 65, Prescott 99348, (509)849-2216
Enrollment: 170

Touchel School District #300
Box 1135, Touchet 99360
(509)394-2352 Enrollment: 180

Waitsburg School District #401-100
Box 217, Waitsburg 99361
(509)337-6301 Enrollment: 250

Walla Walla School District #140
364 South Park, Walla Walla 99362
(509)527-3000 Enrollment: 5,275

HOSPITALS

St. Mary Medical Center
401 W Poplar St, Walla Walla
99362 (509)525-3320
Total Beds: 146

Walla Walla General Hospital
POB 1398, 1025 S Second St,
Walla Walla 99362
(509)525-0488
Total Beds: 72

THE COURTS

SUPERIOR COURT   Area Code (509)
315 West Main, POB 836, Walla Walla,
WA 99362
Yancey Reser, Judge   527-3228
Donald W. Schacht, Judge527-3228
Kathy Martin, County Clerk 527-3221

JUVENILE COURT
310 W. Poplar, POB 1595, Walla Walla
WA 99362, Administrator: 527-3275

DISTRICT COURTS
College Place
317 S. College Ave, Colege Place, WA
99324
R. Gary Ponti, Judge   525-5090
Marian Lindermann, Admin. Clerk 529-1253

Walla Walla
328 W. Poplar, POB 641, Walla Walla, WA 99362
Jerry A. Votendahl, Judge   527-3236
Lonna M. Paul, Administrator 527-3236

SITES OF INTEREST

Whitman Mission
Fort Walla Walla
Lower Monumental Dam

CRISIS

**Crisis Center - Mental Health
Center,** S 216 Palouse,Walla
Walla,99362,(509)5250241,
Information & referrals, out-
patient mental health treat-
ment; sliding fee.

MULTIPLE SERVICE CENTERS

Blue Mountain Action Council
120 E Birch #15, Walla
Walla,99362,(509)529-4980, OJT
classroom training, counseling
job placement assistance,
weatherization assistance,
rent subsidies, food bank;
free.

**Department of Social & Health
Services,** 206 W Poplar,POB 517
Walla Walla,99362,(509)527-4371

Planned Parenthood Center
136 Birch,Walla Walla,99362
(509)529-3570, Health care,
counseling & referrals;
sliding fee.

YWCA, 213 S 1st St,Walla
Walla,99362,(509)525-2570,
After school developmental
daycare program for children
6 to 12, sports, fitness,
educational classes; $3 to $5
per day.

COUNSELING MENTAL/HEALTH

**Catholic Children & Family
Services,** 333 Drunheller
Bldg., Walla Walla,(509)525-
0572, Marriage counseling,
family therapy, individual
counseling; sliding fee.

**Parent Education Resource
Center,** 6 E Whitman,College
Pl,99324,(509)527-2651, Mental
health counseling for children
& families; sliding fee.

Salvation Army Corps
827 W Alder,Walla Walla,99362
(509)529-9470, Provides
personal counseling; free.

**Walla Walla Mental Health
Center,** 216 S Palouse St,Walla
Walla,(509)525-0241, Emergency
services, substance abuse,
outpatient treatment; sliding
fee.

EMPOLYMENT & TRAINING

**Benton-Franklin-Walla Walla
Private Industry**
6515 W Clearwater,Kennewick
99336,(509)735-8402, Job
search assistance, counseling
OJT, GED, supplemental services, economically disadvantaged.

Job Service Center
1530 Stevens,Drawer H,Walla
Walla,99362,(509)527-4390

Job Training Center
120 E Birch,Suite 10,Walla
Walla,99362,(509)529-8050,
Class training, support services, job placement assistance, comprehensive
employment training services;
economically disadvantaged
persons, free.

Walla Walla Community College
500 Tausick Way,Walla Walla

99362,(509)527-4222, Technical, vocational & academic
courses, GED testing, adults
16+ years of age & older,
tuition.

FAMILY PLANNING

Family & Consumer Studies
Walla Walla Community College
Walla Walla,(509)527-4304,
Parenting improvement classes;
sliding fee.

FOOD/CLOTHING/HOUSING

Rescue Mission, 202 W Birch St
Walla Walla,99362,(509)525-7153
Food, clothing, temporary
shelter; free.

St Vincent de Paul Society
308 W Main,Walla Walla,99362
(509)525-3903, Food, clothing,
furniture, medical needs;
free.

V.R.O., Walla Walla
13½ E Main St #203,Walla Walla
99362,(509)527-4504, Helps
disabled state residents obtain
employment; disables, physical &
mental persons; sliding fee.

LEGAL

**Neutral Ground Mediation
Services,** POB 1222,Walla Walla
99362,(509)522-0399,
Mediation, marital, child
custody & legal disputes;
sliding fee.

MEDICAL DENTAL

Health Clinic, 208 N 2nd,POB
515,Walla Walla,99362,(509)
525- 6650, Low income health
& dental care; low income &
migrant workers, sliding
fee.

**Walla Walla County Health
Department,** 310 W Poplar,POB
1753,Walla Walla,99362,(509)
527-3290, Health information,
limited care & services,
immunizations, food handler
testing, basis health services
to all citizens; sliding fee.

SUBSTANCE ABUSE

**Walla Walla Cmty Alcohol &
Drug Abuse Center,** 180 S 5th
Walla Walla,(509)525-7800,
Certified alcohol & drug outpatient treatment, information
school, DWI client assessment,
counseling for alcohol & drug
abusers; sliding fee.

TRANSPORTATION

Valley Transit, 1401 W Rose
Walla Walla,99362,(509)525-
9140, 25¢ and $18.00 monthly.

VICTIMS

**Community Abuse & Assault
Center,** 366 Chase,POB 1773
Walla Walla,99362,(509)529-3377
Resource services for family
law issues, sexual assault
programs, domestic violence &
sexual assault advocacy,
counseling, support groups;
free.

**Neighborhood Community Abuse &
Assault Center & Helpline**
366 Chase St,Walla Walla,99362
(509)529-3300, Victims of
domestic violence & sexual
assault, screening referral
service & emergency aid; free.

For additional information see also
Columbia and Garfield Counties

NORTHEAST

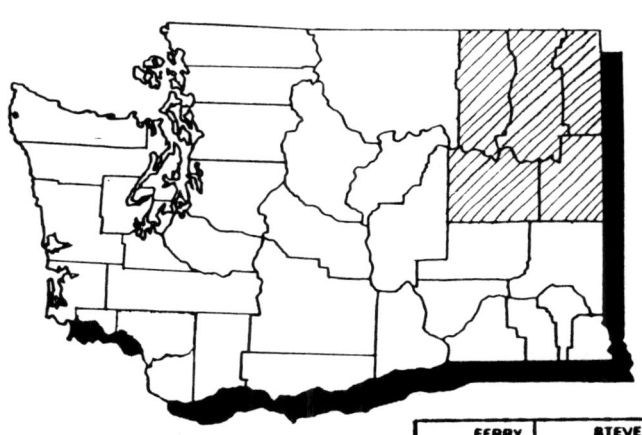

Ferry
Lincoln
Pend Oreille
Spokane
Stevens

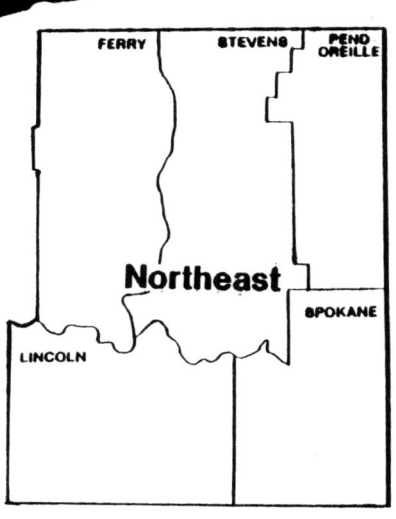

NORTHEAST WASHINGTON
TOURISM ASSOCIATION
POB 312, Spokane 99210
(509)747-2291

HISTORICAL APPEAL

Chewelah Historical Museum
Chewelah

Colville Indian Cultural Center
Colville

Keller Historical Park, Colville

Farm Museum, Davenport

Fairfield Museum, Fairfield

Gifford Inscelium Ferry
Inchelium

St. Paul's Mission, near Kettle
Falls

Pend Oreille County Historical
Museum, Newport

Republic Historical Museum,
Republic

Old Fort Spokane, Roosevelt
Lake at Spokane River

Cheney Cowles Memorial Museum
and Grace Campbell House,
Spokane

Museum of Native American
Cultures, Spokane

| THE HUTTERITIES...Is an Amish like religious denomination. The Hutterite Culture began in the early 1500s in Europe during the Protestant Reformation. A few colonies are located in Eastern Washington and have some of the most productive farms in the state. |

CITIES

CHENEY
Cheney Chamber of Commerce
POB 65,Chaney,99004,(509)235-8480

CHEWELAH
Chewelah Chamber of Commerce
POB 94, 100 N. Park 99109
(509)935-8991

COLVILLE
Colville Chamber of Commerce
POB 267-D,Colville,(509)684-5973

CRESTON
Creston Chamber of Commerce
POB 16,Creston,99117,(509)636-3145

DAVENPORT
Davenport Chamber of Commerce
POB 869,Davenport,99122,(509)
725-1151

DEER PARK
Dear Park Chamber of Commerce
E 316 Crawford,POB 518,Deer
Park,99006,(509)276-5900

FAIRFIELD
Fairfield Chamber of Commerce
POB 345,Fairfield,99012,(509)
263-2301

HARRINGTON
Harrington Chamber of Commerce
POB 126,3rd&Main,Harrington
99134,(509)253-4321

IONE
Ione Chamber of Commerce
POB 518,410 Main St,Ione,99139
(509)442-3424

KETTLE FALLS
Kettle Falls Chamber of
Commerce,205 E 3rd,Kettle
Falls,98141,(509)738-6514

METALINE
Metaline Chamber of Commerce
POB 14,Metaline,991542,(509)
446-4131

NEWPORT
Newport/Old Town Chamber of
Commerce,POB 1795,Newport,99156
(509)447-5812

ODESSA
Oddesa Chamber of Commerce
POB 355,Odessa,99159
(509)982-0049

REPUBLIC
Republic Chamber of Commerce
470 Klondike Rd, Republic
99166, ((509)775-3378

SPOKANE
Spokane Area Chamber of
Commerce,POB 2147,Spokane,99210
(509)624-1341

Spokane Regional Convention &
Visitors Bureau,W 926 Sprague
Spokane,99204,(509)747-3230

THE PANORAMA LAND...
Covers parts of Ferry,
Stevens, and Pend
Oreille Counties, it is
one of the finest
recreational areas in
the United States.

© 1982 VOLK

BIG HORN SHEEP... Can be
seen from December
through February at the
state ran feed station
located at the south
end of Sullivan Lake in
Ione, Pend Oreille
County.

Spokane Valley Chamber of
Commerce,E 10303 Sprague
Spokane,99206,(509)924-4994

Spokane is the second largest
city in Washington and the
county seat of Spokane County.
Spokane is also the largest
city between Seattle and
Minneopolis. It is located in
Northeastern Washington on the
Spokane River, 17 miles from
the Idaho border. It lies in a
scenic area of mountains,
forests, and lakes, and is
noted for its 3,000 acres of
beautiful parks. Spokane Falls,
a series of cascades on the
river in the heart of the city
is a major attraction.

Spokane is the commercial,
industrial, and transportation
hub of the so called **"Inland
Empire"**--The lumbering, mining
and farming region that includes eastern Washington and
parts of Idaho, Montana, and
Oregon. Major industries in or
near Spokane include food
processing, lumber milling,
wood working, aluminum manufacturing, fabricated metal
goods, paper, and electronic
equipment.

Spokane is served by rail,
Interstate Highway 90, and
the Spokane International
Airport.

SPRAGUE
Sprague Chamber of Commerce
Rt 1,Box 40,Sprague,99032
(509)257-2828

WILBER
Wilber Chamber of Commerce
POB 111,Wilbur,99185,(509)
647-2341

**THE
PALOUSE...**Pronounced
Pah-Loose which means
green grassland, is the
best wheatland in the
nation. It's an 85 by
100 mile stretch of
rolling hills which
covers parts of Whitman
and Spokane Counties in
Wash. and Latah County
in Idaho.

FAIRS AND FESTIVALS

Bloomsday Run
Spokane, May (509)838-1579

Lilac Festival
Spokane, May (509)624-1393

Loon's Day Walk
Loon Lake, June
(509)233-2530

Republic Prospectors Days
Republic, June (509)775-3361

Pioneer Days
Davenport, July
(509)725-7021

Chatauqua
Chewelah, July (509)935-8991

Poker Paddle
Usk, July (509)445-1212

Colville Rendezvous Days
Colville, August
(509)684-5973

Interstate Fair
Spokane, September
(509)535-1766

Deutsches Fest
Odessa, September
(509)982-2644

© 1982 VOLK

FERRY COUNTY

Named for Elisha P. Perry, Washington's first governor.

Created: February 18, 1899

County Courthouse, Republic 99166

AREA: 2,202 square miles, State Ranking: 9th

MAJOR ECONOMIC ACTIVITIES:
Mining, Wood Products, Agriculture

ASSESSED VALUE: $255,555,375

POPULATION: (1989 Estimate): 6,100

Percentage of state: 0.1%
Density: 2.8 persons per square mile

ETHNIC BREAKDOWN:

	1988 Estimate
White	4,953
Black	35
Native American	1,061
Asian and Pacific Islanders	7
Other	44
Spanish origin (included in above)	74

PRIMARY CITIES:

	Population
Republic, county seat	1,025

CLIMATE: Republic - elevation 2,503 feet

Average	JAN	APR	JUL	OCT
Max Temp (F)	30.0	58.4	83.5	58.6
Min Temp	14.0	29.5	44.4	30.6
Mean Temp	21.6	44.1	64.1	44.5
Precipitation in inches	1.79	1.13	.78	1.27

Average Annual Maximum Temperature: 56.9
Average Annual Minimum Temperature: 29.4
Average Annual Mean Temperature: 43.2
Average Annual Precipitation: 14.89 inches

PUBLIC SCHOOL DISTRICTS

Curlew School District #50
Curlew 99118, (509)779-4944
Enrollment: 260

Inchelium School District #70
1978 Hornet Ave
Inchelim 99138, (509)722-6181
Enrollment: 250

Keller School District #3
POB 367, Keller 99140
(509)634-4325   Enrollment: 61

Orient School District #65
Orient 99160, (509)684-6873
Enrollment: 107

Republic School District #309
915 Highway 20 E, Republic 99166
(509)775-3173   Enrollment: 527

HOSPITAL

**Ferry County Memorial
Hospital,** POB 365, 470
Klondike Rd, Republic 99166
(509)775-3333
Total Beds: 25

THE COURTS

SUPERIOR COURT   Area Code (509)
215 South Oak, POB 579, Colville 99114
Larry M. Kristianson, Judge (Colville) 684-2181
Fred L. Stewart, Judge (Colville) 684-2181

JUVENILE COURT
350 E. Delaware, Box 751, Republic 99166
Administrator: Ronald C. Delles 684-2549

DISTRICT COURT
320 E. Delaware, Box 214, Republic 99166
Norman G. Sauer, Judge 775-3161, 278 E. Delaware,
Box 348, Republic 99166

SITES OF INTEREST:

Colville Indian Reservation, Roosevelt Kale

CRISIS

**Domestic Violence Shelter
Programs,**
260 N.Oak,Colville,99114,
(509)684-6139, Domestic
violence & abuse shelter.

Family Crisis Network
(509)447-LIVE, 24 hour crisis
line for domestic violence,
rape crisis, may call collect
if necessary.

MULTIPLE SERVICE CENTERS

**Department of Social & Health
Services,** 147 N.Clark,Ave
POB 626, Republic,99166, (509)
735-3155

Ferry County Community Services
Republic,99166,(509)775-3341,
Provides and array of services.

Ferry County Clinic, Courthouse
Republic,99166,(509)775-3161,

Child assissment, immunizations, parenting, carseat loans, maternal and child health care, prenatal program, dental health screening and education, well adult clinic, WIC supplemental food program, services to children with special health care needs, communicable disease control, sexually transmitted disease control, TB testing, health and nutrition education, blood pressure screening, school health services, home assessment visits, AIDSs testing and conseling; 8-4 M-F. Those in need of services, fee.

COUNSELING MENTAL/HEALTH

Community Services, POB 406, Republic,99166,(509)775-3341, Support groups, mental health counseling, drug & alcohol counseling, emergency shelter, domestic violence; 8-4 M-F, all persons.

EMPLOYMENT & TRAINING

Community College Center East 165 Hawthorne,Colville 99114, (509)684-3138, Adult basic education classes, high school completion, community service classes and college credit classes; 7:30-4:40 M-F those in need of services, $57 per credit, $30 per class.

Eastern Job Training Partnership-Field Operations Division, Mail Stop KG-11, Olympia,98504,(206)586-0898

NE Washington Rural Resource Center, 320 N.Main St,Colville 99114,(509)684-8421, Vocational counseling, OJT, job placement; 8-4:30 M-F, low income & disadvantaged persons, free.

FOOD/CLOTHING/HOUSING

Cusick Food Bank, POB 126 Cusick,99119,(509)445-1114,

Food bank; those in need of services.

Inchelium Food Bank, Emergency Medical Services Bldg. Inchelium,99138,(509)772-6831, Food bank; those in need of services.

Keller Food Bank, POB 208 Keller,99140,(509)634-8206, Food bank; those in need of services.

Republic Food Bank, POB 647 Republic,99166,(509)775-3259, Food bank; those in need of services.

MEDICAL/DENTAL

Northeast Tri County Health District, E.347 Astor,Colville 99114,(509)684-5048, Health information, limited care & services, immunizations, food handler testing; all persons.

NE Tri County Health Dist. (Republic Office), POB 584 Republic,99166,(509)775-3161, Health information, limited care & services, immunizations, food handler testing; all persons.

SUBSTANCE ABUSE

County Community Services 4701 N.Klondike Rd,Republic 99166,(509)775-3341, Certified alcohol & drug outpatient & inpatient treatment, information school, DWI client assessment, alcohol referral; 8-4 M-F, those in need of services, sliding fee.

VICTIMS

Ferry County Shelter POB 406,Republic,99166 (509)775-3341, Domestic violence advocacy, counseling and safehome; those in need of services, free.

For additional information see also Stevens & Pend Oreille Counties

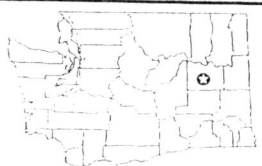

LINCOLN COUNTY

Named for Abraham Lincoln, 16th president of the U.S.

Created: November 24, 1883

450 Logan Street, Davenport 99122

AREA: 2,305.5 square miles, State Ranking: 8th

MAJOR ECONOMIC ACTIVITIES:
Mining, Food Processing, Agriculture

ASSESSED VALUE: $504,625,650

POPULATION: (1989 Estimate): 8,800

Percentage of state: 0.2%
Density: 3.8 persons per square mile

ETHNIC BREAKDOWN:

	1988 Estimate
White	9,508
Black	4
Native American	137
Asian and Pacific Islanders	26
Other	25
Spanish origin (included in above)	78

PRIMARY CITIES

	Population
Davenport, county seat	1,465
Harrington	480
Odessa	940
Reardan	450
Sprague	485
Wilbur	875

CLIMATE: Davenport – elevation 2,450 feet

Average	JAN	APR	JUL	OCT
Max Temp (F)	30.5	59.4	84.4	59.4
Min Temp	18.1	34.0	50.4	35.8
Mean Temp	24.3	46.7	67.4	47.6
Precipitation in inches	2.11	1.07	.53	1.42

Average Annual Maximum Temperature: 57.6
Average Annual Minimum Temperature: 34.8
Average Annual Mean Temperature: 46.2
Average Annual Precipitation: 16.72 inches

PUBLIC SCHOOL DISTRICTS

Almira School District #17
Almira 99103, (509)639-2414
Enrollment: 100

Creston School District #73
POB 17, Creston 99117
(509)636-2721
Enrollment: 100

Davenport School District #207
POB 8, Davenport 99122
(509)725-1481   Enrollment: 370

Harrington School District #204
Box 204, Harrington 99134
(509)253-4331   Enrollment: 134

Odessa School District #105-157-166J
Box 248, Odessa 99159
(509)982-2668   Enrollment: 244

Reardan-Edwall School District #9
POB 255, Readan 99029, (509)796-2721
Enrollment: 570

Sprague School District #8
Box 305, Sprague 99032,
(509) 257-2591   Enrollment: 110

Wilbur School District #200
Box 1090, Wilbur 99185
(509)647-2221   Enrollment: 320

HOSPITALS

Lincoln Hospital
POB 68, 10 Nichols St,
Davenport 99122
(509)725-7101
Total Beds: 93

Odessa Memorial Hospital
502 E Amende, Box 368
Odessa 99159 (509)982-2611
Total Beds: 44

THE COURTS

SUPERIOR COURT   Area Code (509)
450 Logan St, Box 396, Davenport 99122
Phillip W. Borst, Judge   725-3081
Joyce Denison, County Clerk 725-1401

JUVENILE COURT
450 Logan St, POB 5, Davenport 99122
Administrator: William W. Manion 725-7475

DISTRICT COURT
450 Logan St, Box 118, Davenport 99122
Jack R. Buck, Judge   725-2281
Donna Sitko, Chief Clerk   725-2281

SITES OF INTEREST:

Fort Spokane, Grand Coulee Dam,
Roosevelt Lake

COUNSELING MENTAL/HEALTH

**Lincoln County Community
Services**
Professional Bldg, Box 278
Davenport, (509)725-3001
Emergency services, substance
abuse, outpatient, sliding fee.

Lincoln County Counseling Center
100 3rd St, POB 278, Davenport
00122, (509)725-3001, certified
outpatient drug treatment, 24
hour crisis line, sliding fee.

For additional information see also Spokane
County

EMPLOYMENT & TRAINING

**Eastern Job Training
Partnership-Field Operations
Division,** Mail Stop
KG-11, Olympia, 98504
(206)586-0898

**NEWA Rural Employment &
Training Center**
320 N Main, Colville, (509)684-
8421, Vocational counseling &
assessment, job training, work
experience, classroom training,
job placement, OJT; 8-4:30 M-F,
low income & disadvantaged
persons, free.

MEDICAL/DENTAL

Lincoln County Health Department
507 7th St, Davenport, 99122
(509)725-1001, Health information, limited care & services,
immunizations, food handler
testing; all persons.

SUBSTANCE ABUSE

Lincoln County Alcohol Center
407 Morgan St, Davenport, 99122
(509)725-2111, Certified alcohol
& drug outpatient treatment,
information school, DWI client
assessment, ADATSA; 8-5 M-F,
sliding fee.

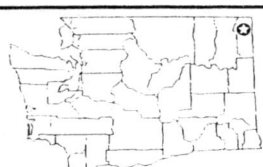

PEND OREILLE COUNTY

Named for the Pend Oreille Indians.

Created: March 1, 1911

625 West Fourth, P.O. Box 409
Newport 99156
Hall of Justice, Garden Avenue, Newport 99156

AREA: 1,402 square miles, State Ranking: 25th

MAJOR ECONOMIC ACTIVITIES:
Wood Products, Agriculture,
Mining

ASSESSED VALUE: $378,090,438

POPULATION: (1989 Estimate): 8,900

Percentage of state: 0.2%
Density: 6.3 persons per square mile

ETHNIC BREAKDOWN:	1988 Estimate
White	8,519
Black	7
Native American	240
Asian and Pacific Islanders	23
Other	47
Spanish origin (included in above)	119

PRIMARY CITIES	Population
Cusick	236
Lone	520
Metaline	182
Metaline Falls	265
Newport, county seat	1,590

CLIMATE: Newport – elevation 2,135 feet

Average	JAN	APR	JUL	OCT
Max Temp (F)	31.4	60.0	86.0	59.0
Min Temp	17.3	30.4	44.7	32.5
Mean Temp	24,0	45.2	65.4	45.8
Precipitation in inches	3.50	1.71	.61	2.76

Average Annual Maximum Temperature: 58.4
Average Annual Minimum Temperature: 31.3
Average Annual Mean Temperature: 44.9
Average Annual Precipitation: 27.16 inches

PUBLIC SCHOOL DISTRICTS

Cusick School District #59
Cusick 99119, (509)445-1125
Enrollment: 329

Newport School District #56-415
POB 70, Newport 99156, (509)447-3167
Enrollment: 1,200

Selkirk School District #70
POB 129, Metaline Falls 99153
(509)446-2951 Enrollment: 420

HOSPITAL

Newport Community Hospital
Box 669, Newport 99156
(509)447-2441
Total Beds: 74

THE COURTS

SUPERIOR COURT   Area Code (509)
Hall of Justice, 229 S. Garden Ave
POB 5000, Newport 99156
Larry M. Kristianson, Judge 447-4317
Fred L. Stewart, Judge 447-4317
Winnie Sounseth, County Clerk 447-2435

JUVENILE COURT
Hall of Justice, 229 S. Garden Ave
POB 5000, Newport 99156
Administrator: Ronald C. Delles 684-2549

DISTRICT COURT
239 S. Garden, POB 5000, Newport 99156
Ralph L. Perkins, Judge 447-4110
Kathleen Williams, Clerk 447-4110

SITES OF INTEREST

Boundary Dam, Gardner Caves
Manresa Grotto
Pacific NW Geophysical Observatory

MULTIPLE SERVICE CENTERS

County Clinic
321 S Garden Ave,Newport,99156
(509)447-3175, Child assessment
immunizations, parenting, carseat loans, maternal & child
health care, prenatal program,
dental health screening & education, well adult clinic, WIC
supplemental food program,
services to children with
special health care needs,
communicable disease control,
sexually transmitted disease
control, TB testing, health
& nutrition education, blood
pressure screening, school
health services, home assessment visits, AIDS testing &

counseling; 9-12 & 1 - 3:30
M-F, free.

Department of Social & Health
Services, 147 N Clark Ave,POB
570,Newport,99156,(509)447-
3192.

COUNSELING MENTAL/HEALTH

**Pend Oreille Community Mental
Health Center,** 230 S Gordon
Ave,POB 5000,Newport,99156
(059)447-3175, Emergency services, substance abuse, outpatient treatment, sliding fee.

EMPLOYMENT & TRAINING

**Eastern Job Training Partner-
ship**
Employment Security Department,
Olympia,(206)586-0898, JTPA,
job search assistance, counseling, OJT, GED, supplement
services; economically disadvantaged.

Job Service Center
418 S Scott Ave,Newport,99156
(509)447-2771

**Resource Development
Association**
320 N Main St,Colville,99114
(206)684-8421, Vocational
counseling, OJT, job placement;
low income & disadvantaged
persons.

FOOD/CLOTHING/HOUSING

Hospitality House
216 S Washington Ave,Newport
99156,(509)447-3812, Food bank.

MEDICAL/DENTAL

Northeast Tri-County Health
District, East 347 Astor
Colville,99114,(206)684-5048,
POB 584,Republic,99166,(206)
775-3161, Health information,
limited care & services,
immunizations, food handler
testing.

SUBSTANCE ABUSE

Mental Health Department
231 S Garden Ave,Newport,99156
(206)447-3175, Drug & alcohol
counseling, crisis services,
individual & family counseling
8-4:30, sliding fee.

**Pend Oreille County Community
Alcoholism Center**
S 230 Garden Ave,Newport,99156
Certified alcohol & drug out-
patient treatment, information
school, DWI client assessment,
ADFATSA.

VICTIMS

Alternative to Violence
260 N Oak,Colville,99114,(206)
684-3796, Resource services for
family law issues, crisis
intervention, domestic violence, sexual abuse & prevention, family support center;
8-5 M-F, free.

Family Crisis Network
POB 959,Newport,99156,(206)
447-5483, Domestic violence &
sexual assault advocacy,
counseling, support resource
services for family law
issues, sexual assault programs; 8-2 M-F, 24 hour
emergency line, free.

**For additional information see also Ferry
and Stevens Counties**

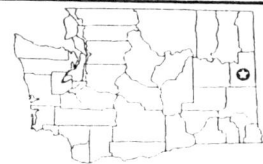

SPOKANE COUNTY

Named for the Spokane Indians, whose tribal name means "child of the sun."

Created: January 29, 1858

West 1116 Broadway, Spokane 99260

AREA: 1,758.3 square miles, State Ranking: 19th

MAJOR ECONOMIC ACTIVITIES:
Wood Products, Agriculture,
Apparel and Textile Manufacturing
Metal Fabrication, Electronics
Machinery Manufacturing, Publishing
Food Processing

ASSESSED VALUE: $9,733,211,671

POPULATION: (1989 Estimate): 358,000

Percentage of state: 7.7%
Density: 203.6 persons per square mile

ETHNIC BREAKDOWN: 1988 Estimate
  White   336,011
  Black   4,657
  Native American   4,481
  Asian and Pacific Islanders   5,262
  Other   3,689
    Spanish origin (included in above) 5,728

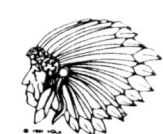

PRIMARY CITIES   Population
  Airway Heights   1,905
  Cheney   7,630
  Deer Park   2,380
  Medical Lake   3,790
  Millwood   1,680
  Spokane, county seat   170,700

CLIMATE: Spokane – elevation 1,982 feet

Average	JAN	APR	JUL	OCT
Max Temp (F)	35.5	61.4	88.4	61.8
Min Temp	24.2	38.4	56.7	39.6
Mean Temp	29.9	49.9	72.6	50.7
Precipitation				
in inches	2.03	1.31	.40	1.17

Average Annual Maximum Temperature: 60.9
Average Annual Minimum Temperature: 39.7

Average Annual Mean Temperature: 50.3
Average Annual Precipitation: 17.41 inches

PUBLIC SCHOOL DISTRICTS

Central Valley School District #356
E 19307 Cataldo, Greenacres 99016
(509)922-6700   Enrollment: 10,100

Cheney School District #360
520 Fourth St, Cheney 99004
(509)359-6433   Enrollment: 3,146

Deer Park School District #414
POB 490, Deer Park 99006
(509)276-5051   Enrollment: 1,475

East Valley School District #361
N 3415 Pines Rd, Spokane 99206
(509)924-1830   Enrollment: 4,065

Freeman School District #358
S. 14626 Jackson Rd, Rockford 99030
(509)291-3695   Enrollment: 665

Great Northern School District #312
N. 3115 Spotted Rd., Spokane 99204
(509)747-7714   Enrollment: 33

Liberty School District #362
S. 29818 N. Pine Creek Rd
Spangle 99031,   (509)245-3223
Enrollment: 550

Mead School District #354
N. 12508 Freya, Mead 99021
(509)466-6800   Enrollment: 6,664

Medical Lake School District #326
Box 128, Medical Lake 99022
(509)299-3156   Enrollment: 1,850

Nine Mile Falls School District #325
W. 10103 Charles Rd., Nine Mile Falls,
99026,   (509)466-5512   Enrollment: 1,155

Orchard Prairie School District #123
N. 7626 Orchard Prairie Rd,
Spokane 99207,   (509)467-9517
Enrollment: 52

Riverside School District #416
Route 1, Box 287, Chattaroy 99003
(509)292-0200,   Enrollment: 1,670

Spokane School District #81
N. 200 Bernard, Spokane 99201
(509)353-5242   Enrollment: 27,757

West Valley School District #363
N. 2805 Argonne Rd.,POB 11739
Spokane 99211, (509)924-2150
Enrollment: 2,851

HOSPITALS

Deaconess Medical Center
800 W Fifth Ave, Spokane
99210 (509)458-5800
Total Beds: 388

**Deer Park Health Center And
Hospital,** Forest and D St,
Deer Park 99006
(509)276-5061
Total Beds: 26

Holy Family Hospital
N 5633 Lidgerwood, Spokane
99207 (509)482-0111
Total Beds: 272

**Mountain View Hospital
(Alcoholism Hospital)**
POB 598, 628 S Cowley
Spokane 99210 (509)624-3226
Total Beds: 34

Scared Heart Medical Center
W 101 Eight Ave, Spokane
99220 (509)455-3131
Total Beds: 607

St. Luke's Memorial Hospital
POB 288, S 711 Cowley
Spokane 99210 (509)838-4771
Total Beds: 146

**Shriners Hospital For
Crippled Children**
N 820 Summit Blvd,
Spokane 99201 (509)327-9521
Total Beds: 30

**Valley Hospital And Medical
Center,** 12606 E Mission Ave,
Spokane 99216 (509)924-6650
Total Beds: 123

THE COURTS

SUPERIOR COURT Area Code (509)
West 1116 Broadway, POB 470, Spokane, WA
99260
Robert D. Austin, Judge   456-4709
Herald D. Clarke, Judge   456-5713
Michael E. Donohue, Judge   456-5784
William J. Grant, Judge   456-5717

Marcus M. Kelley, Judge   456-5792
Richard J. Schroeder, Judge 456-4766
Thomas E, Merryman, Judge   456-4795
James M. Murphy, Judge   456-4712
Kathleen M. O'Connor, Judge 456-4707
John A. Schultheis, Judge   456-4704
Thomas R. Fallquist, County Clerk:
                            456-2211

JUVENILE COURT
West 1208 Mallon, Spokane, WA 99201
Administrator: Thomas J. Davis 456-4742

DISTRICT COURTS
Chaney
611 Second St, Cheney, WA 99004
Daniel T. Maggs, Judge   235-6228
Patricia M. Warnick, Clerk 235-6228
Deer Park
316 Crawford, Deer Park, WA 99006
John J. Madden, Judge   456-2297
Christine McCoy, Clerk   276-8802
Millwood
East 9103 Frederick, Spokane, WA 99206
Donna K. Wilson, Judge   924-9858
Julie Curtis, Court Administrator:
                            456-2287

Spokane
West 1100 Mallon, Public Safety Bldg.,
Spokane   99260

Christine Cary,   Judge   456-4723
Sam F. Cozza, Judge   456-2281
John J. Madden, Judge   456-2297
Daniel T. Maggs, Judge   456-2280
John P. Nollette, Judge   456-4217
Richard B. White , Judge 458-2527
Raymond R. Tanksley, Judge 456-2277
Richard F. Wrenn, Judge   456-2276
Terrence D. Edwards, Court Administrator:
                            456-2287

223 E Fourth St, Port Angeles 98362
Richard A. Headrick, Judge   452-7831

Clallam County Two
Fifth & Division, POB 1937, Folks 98331
Susan J. Owens, Judge   374-6383

SITES OF INTEREST

Long Lake Dam
Mount Spokane
Spokane Plains Battlefield
Spokane House

CRISIS

AIDS Hotline
Airdustrial Park,Bldg 14,LJ
17,Olympia,98504,(800)272-AIDS
Recorded information on AIDS,
specifically HIV aids, referral and out of state health
officials available to answer
questions; free.

Alcohol & Drug Help Line
Spokane,(800)562-1240, Information and referral, alcohol
& drug crisis counseling by
phone; free.

Child Find, Inc., 7 Innis Ave
POB 277,New Paltz,NJ,12556,
(800)426-5678, Locate children, parents, information to
public, missing children,
mediation program for parents
in flight; parents with
custody, $10.00.

Crisis Service, South 107
Division,Spokane,99202,(509)
838-4428, Emotional support &
intervention to individuals
in crisis, information & referral services; free.

Dial Help, 1175 Caronadalet Dr
Richland,99352,(509)946-4357,
Telephone crisis intervention &
referrals, check line also; 24
hours; free.

Drug Crisis Line, West 1101
College,Spokane,99201,(509)
326-9550, Emergency response
with crisis team for drug
abuse, therapist on duty;
24 hour paging; sliding fee.

Family Reconciliation Services
North 1425 Washington,Spokane
99201,(509)456-4451, Crisis
intervention to families with
juveniles in crisis; children
ages 12 to 18 free.

Gay Referral Line, POB 9639
Spokane,99204,(509)489-2266,
Crisis counseling for problems
with sexual identify & referrals; 24 hours; free.

Rape Crisis Network, South 7
Howard,Suite 200,Spokane,99201
(509)624-7273, Rape crisis
line, trained volunteers &
professional counselors; 24
hour phone, victims of sexual
assault; sliding fee.

MULTIPLE SERVICE CENTERS

**American Indian Community
Center**
East 801 2nd Ave,Spokane,(509)
535-0886, ABE, GED, cultural
heritage, food bank; must be
native american for JTPA,
otherwise all persons, free.

**Department of Social & Health
Services,** N 1425 Washington
POB TAF C-37,Spokane,99220
(509)458-4404, 300 S Main,POB
149,Colfax,99111,(509)397-4326
S 121 Authur,POB TAF C-40
Spokane,99220,(509)536-1257, E
232 Lyons,POB TAF C-41,Spokane
99220,(509)483-5600, N 1313
Maple,POB TAF C-42,Spokane
99220,(509)458-2191, POB 640
Davenport,99122,(509)725-5501

Displaced Homemakers Center
W 3305 Ft Geo Wright,Spokane
(509)459-3757, Assistance to
women with divorce, job search
referrals & help line; free.

Family Service Offices
1403 Broadway,Spokane,99201
(509)458-5516, Food, clothing,
furniture, rental aid, counseling; by appointment only,
low income persons, free.

Information & Referral Center
N 507 Howard,Spokane,99201
(509)624-2277, Referrals for
social services in the greater
Spokane area; 24 hour a day 7
days a week; free.

Isabella House, W 2308 3rd Ave
Spokane,99202,(509)624-1244,
Re-entry career development,
drug program, up to 6 month
stay, intensive group therapy;
8-5 M-F.

**SPARC & Womens Service
Programs,** S 812 Walnut,Spokane
99204,(509)624-3251, Basic
services for women after care
from alcohol treatment programs, outpatient counseling,
prenatal limited care; 8-5 M-F
sliding fee.

Spokane DCFS Center
N 1425 Washington,Spokane,99201
(509)456-3986, Child protective
services, foster care, day care
licensing, homefinders; 8-5 M-F
free.

Spokane Neighborhood Centers
2116 E 1st,Spokane,99202,
(509)456-7111, Energy assistance, daycare, commodities
distributor; 8-5 M-F; sliding
fee.

St Joseph's Family Center
1016 N Superior,Spokane,99202
(509)483-6495, Psychological,
educational & spiritual services; sliding fee.

COUNSELING MENTAL/HEALTH

Community Mental Health Center
S 107th Division,Spokane,99202
(509)838-4651, Crisis line
838-4428; emergency services
for drug abusers 60+ years of
age, outpatient extended care
program; 24 hours a day crisis
line; sliding fee.

**Family Counseling Service of
Spokane County,** W 421 Riverside
Spokane,(509)838-4128, Counseling individuals couples,
families, groups; family emergency family shelter for 3
days, food bank & medical
transportation; 9-5 M-F;
sliding fee.

Parkview Associates
S 601 Division,Spokane,99202
(509)747-1102, Program for
sexual offenders & family
members, counseling; 24 hour
phone, sexual abuse victims;
flat rate.

**Regional Center for Child
Abuse and Neglect**
POB 248,Spokane,99210,(509)
623-7501, Child abuse counseling.

Samaritan Center, 33rd & Grand
Spokane,99203,(509)747-8214,
Individual, family and marriage
counseling, divorce recovery
group; 8-4:30; sliding fee.

**Spokane Community Mental
Health Center,** S 107 Division
Spokane,(509)838-4651,
Emergency services, substance
abuse, outpatient treatment;
sliding fee.

**Spokane Community Rape
Emergency Action Program**
S 7 Howard,Symans Bldg,Spokane
99201,(509)6247273, Counseling
liaison between victim & law,
medical personnel; 24 hours,
victims of rape, sliding fee.

EMPLOYMENT & TRAINING

Adult Education Center
W 3305 Ft Geo Write Dr,Spokane
(509)459-3759, N 4001 Cook
Spokane,99207,(509)487-1603, N
2310 Monroe St,Spokane,99205
(509)459-3745, GED & ABE preparation, ESL, business skills
classes, referral service;
free.

Affirmative Action Office
W 808 Spokane Falls Blvd
Spokane,99201,(509)456-4368,
Assistance on minorities &
females in the work place,
women seeking non-traditional
employment, minorities &
females, free.

**Building Trades Training
Program,** N 2110 Fracher,Spokane
99210,(509)534-5986, Con-
struction craft apprenticeship;
low income Spokane residents,
free.

Career Path Services, N 1020
Washington St,Spokane,99201
(509)326-7520, Job placement
assistance, OJT, work

counseling, GED testing, disadvantaged & low income persons, free.

Cutler Counseling, N 1306 Post POB 8282,Spokane,99205,(509) 327-1929, Vocational rehabilitation programs, OASYS computerized job search; sliding fee.

Employment & Training, 1313 N Maple,Spokane,99220,(509)458-3237, Job orientation program resumes, interview tips, job search; DSHS recipients free.

Goodwill Industries, E 130 3rd Ave,Spokane,99202,(509)838-4246, Vocational evaluation, job training, sheltered employment, retail shop & placement services; 8-5 M-F, vocationally handicapped persons, free.

Help Line, W 3305 Ft Geo Wright Dr,Spokane,99204,(509)459-3752, Re-entry into college, financial aid, career testing, job search, resume preparation & job referrals; free.

Inland Northwest Education – Job Information Center
Spokane Public Library, W 906 Main Ave,Spokane,99201,(509) 838-3361 Job information, GED & SAT testing, Civil Service testing & counseling; free.

Job Resource Center, 905 W Riverside,#601,Spokane,99201, (509)747-3071, Job placement & employment orientation training.

Job Service Center
130 S Authur, Spokane,99220 (509)536-1499.

Manpower, S 210 Washington Spokane,99204,(509)838-8531, Temporary jobs; adults 18+ years of age, free.

Martin Luther King Memorial Center, S 845 Sherman,Spokane 99202,(509)455-8722, Career

assessment, counseling, recreation, summer day camp, parenting & developmental skills; free.

Project Read – Spokane Public Library, S 500 Stone,Spokane 99202,(509)838-3365, One-on-one tutoring reading below 5th grade; 10-6 Tue & Sat, reading level below 5th grade, free.

S.L. Start & Associates
E 123 Indiana,Spokane,99207 (509)328-2740, Skill assessment, job placement, job finding & counseling; flat rate.

Spokane Community College
N 1810 Greene St,Spokane 99201,(509)536-7000, Academic & vocational courses, GED testing.

Spokane County Employment & Training Consortium
W 808 Spokane Falls Blvd Spokane,99201,(509)458-2217.

V.R.O., Spokane Community College, 1810 N Green St,MS 2,Spokane,(509)536-7345, Spokane Main,510 Hutton Bldg.,Spokane,99204,(509) 456-3160, Helps disabled states residents obtain employment; disabled, physical & mental persons, free.

Washington Community College District #17, N 1810 Greene St,Spokane,99207,(509)536-7000 Academic & vocational courses, GED testing; sliding fee.

Women's Information Network – Spokane, S 130 Arthur,Spokane (509)536-1364, Job counseling, OJT, job placement; AFDC grants.

Women's Center (SFCC), W 3410 Ft Geo Wright Dr,Spokane,(509) 459-3752, Displaced homemakers multi-service center, workshops, mini courses; free.

FAMILY PLANNING

Catholic Family Services
W 1023 Riverside,Spokane
99201,(509)456-7160,
Counseling groups for effective parenting; no sex
offenders; sliding fee.

Mothers Are Special, Spokane
(509)456-8498, Support group
for mothers, informal
meetings; all mothers free.

Planned Parenthood of Spokane
W 521 Garland,POB 9460,Spokane
(509)326-2142, Counseling &
family planning clinic; hours
variable; sliding fee.

Support Enforcement Office
W 601 Mallon,Spokane,99221
(509)456-4293, Enforcement
of family support obligations;
PA recipients, free.

FOOD/CLOTHING/HOUSING

Alberta Apartments
S 172½ Madison,Spokane,99204
(509)838-1236, Temporary
crisis housing, parole
sponsorship, counseling referral; 18+ years of age,
free.

Bailie Memorial Youth Ranch
131 Memorial Ln,Basin City
99200,(509)269-4211, Ranch
with long term care for abused,
neglected & needed children;
8-5 M-F, girls 6-10, boys 6-14,
sliding fee.

Better Living Center
N Division & Foothills Blvd
Spokane,99207,(509)325-0666,
Food, clothing & bedding bank,
classes in smoking, stress
management; sliding fee.

Community Service Center, E 15
Buckeye,Spokane,99207,(509)325-
1258, Clothing, quilts, mends
clothing, furniture for needy;
free.

**Expanded Food & Nutrition
Education Program**
N 222 Havana,Spokane,99202
(509)456-3651, Young, low
income, homemakers learn
about buying & cooking food,
low income families with
children, free.

Food Bank Lists
W 2011 Maxwell,Spokane,99204
(509)328-2881, Food banks in
area, call for listing, free.

King Gardener Ministries
Spokane,99212,(509)924-9635,
Food bank, counseling.

Manito Presbyterian Church
E 401 30th Ave,Spokane,99203
(509)838-3559, Food bank,
clothing bank, low income
emergencies, free.

Miriam's House of Transition
E 227 Mission,Spokane,99202
(509)328-1632, Place for women
leaving jail to stay and
adjust; drug free environment,
house rules, sliding fee.

**North County Neighborhood
Center,** N 34515 Newport Hwy
Chattercy,99003,(509)466-6120,
Food bank, emergency services,
some home repair, weather-
ization, free.

Ogden Hall, W 2825 Dean
Spokane 99201,(509)327-7737,
Provides emergency short-term
lodging for women and
children, 24 hours, free.

Riverside Neighborhood Center
N 34515 Newport Hwy,Elk,99003
(509)292-2657, Food bank,
emergency services, home
repairs, low income families,
free.

**Salvation Army Family
Emergency Center**
W 1403 Broadway,Spokane, Food
bank, financial aid, family
housing; 5 days a week, all
in need, donations.

Spokane Food Bank
W 2011 Maxwell,Spokane,99201
(509)328-2881, Food bank,
free.

Spokane Housing Authority
W 55 Mission,Rm 104,Spokane
99201,(509)328-2953, Financial
assistance to low income in
rental housing, subsidies rent;
low income elderly, free.

St Vincent de Paul, E 2901
Trent,Spokane,99202,(509)
535-2491, Emergency assistance
with food, clothing, furniture, fuel, free.

**Valley United Church Welfare
League,** Spokane,99212,(509)
926-3021, Emergency food,
clothing, bedding, financial
assistance; 24 hour service,
low income in the valley,
free.

Volunteers of America
YMCA,Spokane,99201,(509)624-
2378, Assistance with clothing,
furniture, bedding & financial
aid, free.

**Westminister Congregational
Church,** S 411 Washington
Spokane,(509)624-1366, Food
bank, clothing, layettes,
housing for relatives of
hospitalized; sliding fee.

**Westminister Presbyterian
Church Outreach,** W 2705 Boone
Spokane,(509)328-5002, Food
and clothing banks, free.

Windsor Baptist Church, W 4404
Hallett Rd,Spokane,99204
(509)455-7816, One time
emergency financial
assistance, food & clothing,
free.

LEGAL

Law Library, W 421 Riverside
Suite 1020,Spokane,99201
(509)456-3680, Law library
for public use, photo copying
available; 8-5 M-F, free.

Lawyer Referral Services
County Courthouse, POB 470
Spokane,(509)456-6032, Referral to lawyer specializing
in type of problem, $15.00.

Legal Services Center
N 14 Howard,Suite 310,Spokane
99201,(509)838-3671, Free
legal services for low income
civil matters only; 8:30-12
M-F for new clients.

MEDICAL/DENTAL

Emergency Dental Clinic
S 500 Stone,Spokane,99202
(509)456-7110, Low income
emergency dental care; low
income persons, sliding fee.

**EWU-Department of Dental
Hygiene,** W 407 Riverside
Spokane,99204,(509)458-6262,
252 Paulsen,Spokane,99204,
Cleaning, fluoride, x-rays,
minor fillings, dental care;
5 days a week; flat fee.

**Sexually Transmitted
Diseases,** W 1101 College
Spokane,99201,(509)456-3640,
Information, diagnosis &
treatment of sexually transmitted diseases, HIV testing,
immunizations; 8-4 M-F;
fixed fee.

Spokane Aids Network, W 1801
Broadway,Spokane,99201,(509)
326-2457, Major referral for
AIDS resources, counseling &
support; 24 hour phone, AIDS
victims & families, free.

Spokane County Health District
W 1101 College Ave,Spokane
(509)456-3630, Health information, limited care & services, immunizations, food
handler testing; 8-5 M-F;
sliding fee.

**Spokane Dental Emergency
Clinic,** E 42 Wallasley,Spokane
99207,(509)487-1270,
Emergency dental care; 8-5 M-F;
flat fee.

Venereal Disease Clinic, W 1101
College,Spokane,99201,
Diagnostic & treatment of
venereal disease; free.

MISCELLANEOUS

Adult Probation & Parole
1717 W Broadway,Spokane,99201
(509)456-3260, Supervision of
adult offenders on parole or
probation;free.

Gamblers Anonymous
W 829 Broadway,Spokane,99201
(509)922-9336, Self-help group
for gamblers and family; 24
hours; free.

Language Bank, S 507 Washington
Spokane,99204,(509)624-0151,
Foreign language services,
into and from a foreign land;
9-5 Tue-Sat, those in need of
services, free.

Library Services, N 2901
Argonne,Spokane,99212,(509)
924-4122, Free loan books,
records & tapes; 10-6 M-F,
county residents, free.

Probation & Parole Volunteers
N 1801 Monroe,Spokane,99202
(509)456-3260, one-to-one
friendship with persons on
probation or parole; 8-4 M-F;
free.

SUBSTANCE ABUSE

Al-Anon Family Groups
Spokane,(509)458-7809, Programs
for family members of alcoholic
homes; interested persons,
free.

Alano Club, W 119 7th St
Spokane,99202,(509)624-2400,
Private club for alcoholics,
dry for 90 days, free.

Alcohol Consultation Services
1504 NW Blvd,Spokane,99205
(509)326-2301, Outpatient
counseling, workshops,
diagnostic evaluation of
alcohol; sliding fee.

Alcohol Information Network
W 1101 College Ave,Spokane
99201,(509)458-2528, Certified
alcohol & drug treatment,
DWI client assessment,
ADATSA public assistance;
8-5 M-F; sliding fee.

Alcoholics Anonymous
S 404 Walnut,Spokane,99204
(509)624-1442, Alcohol support
group, literature; free.

Alcoholism Outpatient Service
E 905 3rd Ave,Spokane,99202
(509)534-3132, Certified
alcohol & drug information
school, DWI client assessment;
sliding fee.

Booth Care Centers, W 3400
Garland,Spokane,99201,(509)
458-5516, Alcohol treatment
center for those who have had
prior treatment and want help,
in & out patient care,
18+ years of age, sliding fee.

Center for Drug Treatment
W 1625 4th Ave,Spokane,99204
(509)458-7437, Certified
alcohol & drug outpatient
treatment; sliding fee.

**Community Alcohol United
Services,** E 2211 Sprague
Spokane,99203,(509)534-5070,
Alcohol outpatient information
school, recovery program;
sliding fee.

Daybreak of Spokane, E 918
Mission,POB 8616,Spokane
99203,(509)483-0107, 442 Dyer
Rd,Spokane,99203,(509)
448-1255, Certified alcohol
outpatient treatment, outpatient youth drug treatment,
residential treatment;
9-7 M-F, those in need of
service and juvenile under 18
years of age, financial aid
available & flat rate.

**Deaconess Hospital - Chemical
Dependency Program,** W 800 5th
Ave,Spokane,99210(509)458-7000,
Certified alcohol & drug in-
tensive inpatient treatment &

detoxification, 24 hour service; flat rate.

Genesis Counseling Services, Inc., N 10103 Division,Suite 100,Spokane,99218,(509)466-1092, Certified alcohol & drug outpatient treatment; 24 hour recording; flat rate.

Greater Spokane Substance Abuse Council, E 245 13th,Spokane (509)624-5156, Substance abuse counseling, recording machine; free.

Hope Forever, POB 94,Green Acres,99016,(509)924-1058, Recovered addicts band together for support on a 1 to 1 basis; free.

Isabella House, 2308 W 3rd Spokane,90204,(509)624-1244, Intensive residential drug treatment program; 24 hours; sliding fee.

Mountainview Hospital – Chemical Dependency Program, S 628 Cowley,Spokane,99202 (509)458-7767, Medical detoxification alcohol, counseling & therapy, outpatient for alcohol & drugs, education programs; 24 hour phone; flat rate.

Narcotics Anonymous, POB 807 Spokane,99210,(509)458-7767, Addiction to any drug prescription or street drugs, 12 step recovery; free.

Salvation Army Booth Care Center, W 3400 Garland,Spokane 99205,(509)458-5516, Certified alcohol recovery house & extended care recovery; 5 days a week; donations.

SPARC Outpatient Services S 812 Walnut,Spokane,99204 (509)624-5228, Certified alcohol & drug information school, DWI client assessment, alcohol outpatient treatment; sliding fee.

Spokane Alcohol & Rehabilitation Center W 1513 8th Spokane,(509)624-3251, Inpatient treatment, therapy, counseling, 90 day inpatient program for women; sliding fee.

Spokane Alcoholism Care Services, E 415 Sprague,Spokane 88202,(509)838-2771, Certified alcohol detoxification & drug referrals; 24 hours; sliding fee.

STEPPS Methadone Program W 1101 College,Spokane,99201 (509)326-9550, Outpatient therapy opiate addiction, 10 day program, outpatient counseling for alcohol & drug methadone program; 24 hour phone; sliding fee.

TASC of Spokane County, 1320 N Ash,Spokane,99204,(509)326-7740, Certified alcohol & drug outpatient treatment.

The Colonial Clinic, W 315 9th Ave,Suite 201,Spokane,(509) 838-6004, Certified alcohol & drug outpatient treatment, information school, DWI client assessment.

Women for Sobriety 628 S Cowley,Spokane,(509)624-3226, Support group for women's sobriety; free.

VETERANS SERVICES

House of Charity, W 9 Main Spokane,99201,(509)624-7821, Drop in center, information & referrals, sleeping rooms in winter, noon meal and a doctor veterans, free.

Veterans Administration Hospital, 4315 N Assembly,Spokane,99205 (509)323-4521, Medical services, alcohol outreach program, certified alcohol & drug information school, alcohol outpatient treatment; 8-4:30 M-F, vets with service disability, free.

Veterans Services
1102 W College,Spokane,99201
(509)453-3690, Emergency aid,
educational benefits for
children of deceased veterans;
8-4:30 M-F, vets & dependents,
free.

Veterans for Sobriety
POB 5118,Spokane,99205,(509)
325-1803, Support group for
veterans completed with alcohol
treatment.

Vietnam Veterans Outreach
25 W Mission,Spokane,99207
(509)327-0274, Support group
for Vietnam veterans, also
women support groups;
8:30-4:30 M-F, vets & dependents, free.

VICTIMS

Alternative to Domestic Violence Program
W 829 Broadway,Spokane
(509)327-9534, Support
services to victims of
domestic violence, safe
shelter, anger management;
sliding fee.

Parents Anonymous – Childrens Home Society
S 4315 Scott,Spokane,(509)
456-2655, Abuse or fear of
abuse for children,
babysitting arrangements,
group meeting; 8:30-5 M-F;
free.

Spokane Child Abuse & Neglect Prevention Center
S 500 Stone,Spokane,(509)
458-7445, Services for family
experiencing abused and
neglected children; sliding
fee.

Vanessa Behan Crisis Nursery
E 1004 8th St,Spokane,99202
(509)535-3155, Short-term care
for young children, abuse
prevention; 8:30-5:30 M-F,
children 1 month to 6 years,
free.

YWCA, W 829 Broadway,Spokane
99201,(509)326-1190, Domestic
violence counseling, child
care; sliding fee.

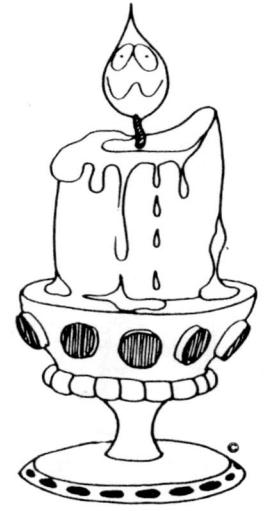

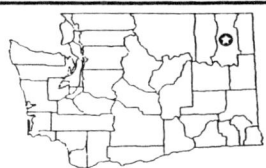

STEVENS COUNTY

Named for Isaac Stevens, first governor of the
Territory of Washington.

Created: January 20, 1863
215 South Oak Street, Colville 99114

AREA: 2,481.2 square miles, State Ranking: 5th

MAJOR ECONOMIC ACTIVITIES:
Wood Products, Mining
Metals Processing

ASSESSED VALUE: $915,662,977

POPULATION: (1989 Estimate): 30,500
Percentage of state: 0.7%
Density: 12.3 persons per square mile

ETHNIC BREAKDOWN:	1988 Estimate
White	28,170
Black	29
Native American	1,622
Asian and Pacific Islanders	123
Other	256
Spanish origin (included in above)	373

PRIMARY CITIES	Population
Chewelah	1,940
Colville, county seat	4,740
Kettle Falls	1,256

CLIMATE: Colville - elevation 1,635 feet

Average	JAN	APR	JUL	OCT
Max Temp (F)	30.3	64.5	86.6	59.6
Min Temp	17.2	33.9	49.1	34.6
Mean Temp	23.5	48.6	68.0	46.8
Precipitation in inches	2.05	1.07	.71	1.69

Average Annual Maximum Temperature: 59.4
Average Annual Minimum Temperature: 34.0
Average Annual Mean Temperature: 46.5
Average Annual Precipitation: 17.36 inches

PUBLIC SCHOOL DISTRICTS

Chewelah School District #36
Box 47, Chewelah 99109 (509)935-8671
Enrollment: 1,084

Columbia School District #206
Hunters 99137, (509)722-3871
Enrollment: 230

Colville School District #115
430 E. Hawthorne
Colville 99114, (509)684-2536
Enrollment: 2,068

Evergreen School District #205
POB 7, Hunters 99137, (509)722-3871
Enrollment: 25

Kettle Falls School District #212
Kettle Falls 99141, (509)738-6625
Enrollment: 840

Loon Lake School District #183
Loon Lake 99148, (509)233-2212
Enrollment: 80

Mary Walker School District #207
POB 159, Springdale 99137
(509)258-4534 Enrollment: 441

Northport School District #211
Northport 99157, (509)732-4251
Enrollment: 290

Onion Creek School District #30
Route 2, Box 301, Colville 99114
(509)732-4240 Enrollment: 44

Summit Valley School District #202
HCR Box 10A, Addy 99101,
(509)935-6362 Enrollment: 45

Valley School District #070
POB 157, Valley 99181
(509)937-2791 Enrollment: 195

Wellpinit School District #49
POB 390, Wellpinit 99040
(509)258-4535 Enrollment: 240

HOSPITALS

Mount Carmel Hospital
928 E Columbia, Colville
99114 (509)684-2561
Total Beds: 55

**St. Joseph's Hospital Of
Chewelah,** E 500 Webster St
Chewelah 99109 (509)935-8211
Total Beds: 65

THE COURTS

SUPERIOR COURT   Area Code (509)
215 S. Oak, POB 579, Colville, WA 99114
Larry M. Kristianson, Judge 684-2181
Fred L. Stewart, Judge   684-2181
Patricia Chester, County Clerk 684-6111

JUVENILE COURT
215 S. Oak, POB 266, Colville, WA 99114
Administrator: Ronald C. Delles 684-2549

DISTRICT COURT
215 S. Oak, POB 163, Colville, WA 99114
David E. McGrane, Judge   684-5249
Delores J. Susemiehl, Chief Clerk 684-5249

SITES OF INTEREST

Fort Colville
Roosevelt Lake
Little Pend Oreille National Wildlife Range

MULTIPLE SERVICE CENTERS

County Clinic
347 E Astor,Colville,99114
(509)684-5048, Child assessment, immunization, parenting,
carseat loans, maternal &
child health care, prenatal
program, dental health screening & eduction, well adult
clinic, WIC supplemental food
program, services to children
with special health care needs,
communicable disease control,
sexually transmitted disease
control, TB testing, health
& nutrition education, blood
pressure screening, school
health services, home assessment visits, AIDS testing &
counseling; 8-4 M-F, those in
need of services, fee.

**Department of Social & Health
Services,** 1100 S Main,Rt 3
Colville,99114,(509)684-5261.

**Stevens County Counseling
Services** 1707 E Birch Ave
Colville,(509)684-4597,
Individual counseling, alcohol
& drug information, mental
health counseling; 8-4:30 M-F;
sliding fee.

COUNSELING MENTAL/HEALTH

Stevens County Services
603 South Infirmary Rd
Colville,(509)684-4597,
Emergency services, subst'ance
abuse, outpatient treatment;
sliding fee.

EMPLOYMENT & TRAINING

**Eastern Job Training
Partnership-Field Operations
Division,** Mail Stop KG-11
Olympia,98504,(206)586-0898

Job Service Center
162 S Wynne St,POB 112
Colville,99114,(509)684-2557

**Resource Development
Association,** 320 N Main St
Colville,99114,(509)648-8421,
Vocational counseling, OJT,
job placement; 8-4 M-F, low
income & disadvantaged
persons.

**Northest Tri-Counties Health
District,** E 347 Astor,Colville
99114,(509)684-5048, POB 584
Republic,99166,(509)775-3161,
Health information, limited
care & services, immunizations,
food handler testing; 8-4:30

M-F, those in need of services, $5.00.

SUBSTANCE ABUSE

Narcotics Anonymous
Spokane & North Idaho
(509)458-7767, Narcotics
abusers; those in need of
services.

**Spokane Tribe of Indians
Alcoholism Program,** POB 212
Wellpinit,99040,(509)258-4513,
Certified alcohol & drug
information school, DWI client
assessment, alcohol outpatient
treatment; $25.00 evaluation.

VETERANS SERVICES

Dr Clark Ashworth, Route 2,Box
379,Colville,99114,(509)684-
8368, Delayed stress counseling.

**Stevens County Counseling
Service,** 603 South Infirmary
Road,Colville,(509)684-4598,
Delayed stress counseling.

Family Support Center, 260 N
Oak,Colville,99114,(509)684-
3796, Domestic violence & sexual assault advocacy, counseling, safehome.

**For additional information see also Ferry and
Pend Oreille Counties**

NORTH CENTRAL

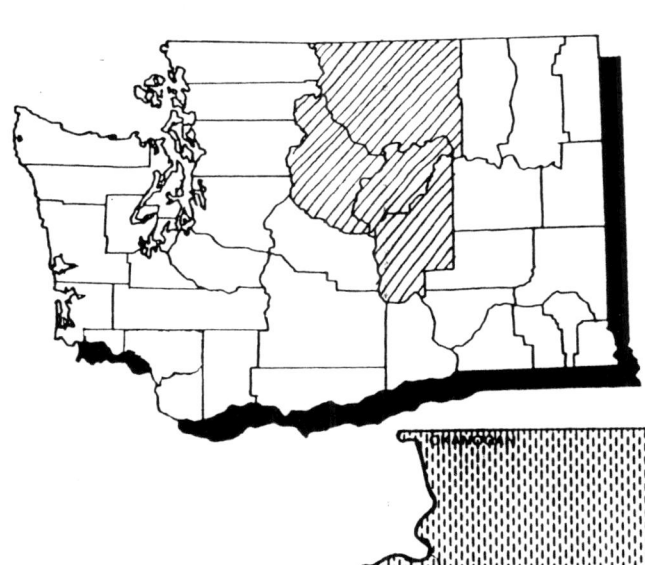

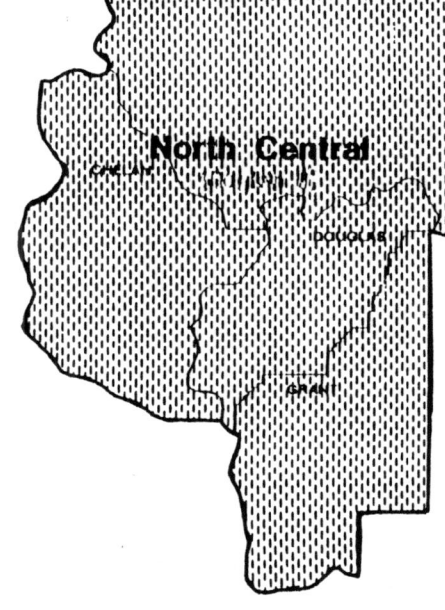

Chelan
Douglas
Grant
Okanogan

North Central

NORTH CENTRAL
WASHINGTON TOURISM
ASSOCIATION
324 S. Pioneer Way
Moses Lake 98837
(509)765-7888 or
1-800-9926234

HISTORICAL APPEAL

Fort Okanogan, Brewster

Chelan County Historical Society Pioneer Village, Cashmere

Chelan Historical Museum Chelan

Grant County Historical Museum Ephrata

Okanogan County Historical Museum, Okanogan

Ghost Town and Molson Museum near Oroville

Othello Community Museum Othello

Old Oroville Depot Museum, Oroville

Historical Museum, Waterville

Apple Industry Museum Wenatchee

North Central Washington Museum Wenatchee

Shafer Museum, Winthrop

CITIES

BREWSTER
Brewster Chamber of Commerce
POB 1087,Brewster,98812

BRIDGEPORT
Bridgeport Chamber of Commerce
2520 Foster Creek Ave
Bridgeport,98813,(509)686-5191

CASHMERE
Cashmere Chamber of Commerce
POB 834,Cashmere,98815,(509)
782-3039

CHELAN
Lake Chelan Chamber of Commerce
POB 216,206 E Johnson Ave,Lake
Chelan 98816,(509)682-2022

HIRAM F. SMITH...AKA "Okanogan Smith," developed the first orchards in Wash. around 1857. He planted about 1200 trees. He is also know as the Johnnie Appleseed of Washington State.

©

THE DEEPEST BODY OF WATER IN WASHINGTON... Is Lake Chelan. It is known to be 1,500 feet deep and 55 miles long. It is said to have some of the purest water anywhere in the world.

CONCONULLY
Conconully Chamber of Commerce
POB 231,Conconully,98819

COULEE CITY
Coulee City Chamber of Commerce
POB 896,Coulee City,99115,(509)
632-5713

EAST WENATCHEE
East Wenatchee Chamber of
Commerce, POB 7195, East
Wenatchee, 98801,(509)884-2514

EPHRATA
Ephrata Chamber of Commerce
112 Basin St SW,Ephrata,98823,
(509)754-4656

GRAND COULEE DAM AREA
Chamber of Commerce
POB 760, Grand Coulee 99133
(509)633-3074

LEAVENWORTH
Levenworth Chamber of Commerce
POB 327,Levenworth,98826,(509)
548-7914

MATTAWA
Chamber of Commerce
POB 1446, 518 Government Rd,
99344, (509)932-4904

MOSES LAKE
Mose Lake Chamber of Commerce
324 S Pioneer Way,Moses Lake
98837,(509)765-7888

OKANOGAN
Chamber of Commerce
233 Second S, POB 1125,
98840, (509)422-0441

OROVILLE
Oroville Chamber of Commerce
POB 536,1728 Main St,Oroville
98844,(509)476-2972

PATEROS
Patero Chamber of Commerce
Pateros 98846,(509)923-2358

QUINCY
Quincy Chamber of Commerce
POB 668,Quincy,98848,(509)
787-2140

**THE COLUMBIA NATIONAL
WILDLIFE REFUGE...**Is
located in Grant County
between Moses Lake and
Potholes State Park. It
covers about 35,000 acres
on the Pacific Flyway
with more than 200
different varieties of
birds.

**GRAND COULEE LASER
LIGHT SHOW...**Held every
night at 9:30 between
mid June and Labor Day
is the largest single
laser light show in the
United States, the
system cost $785,000.

ROYAL CITY
Royal City Chamber of Commerce
POB 152,Royal City,99357,(509)
346-9558

SOAP LAKE
Soap Lake Chamber of Commerce
POB 433,11 Main Ave E,Soap
Lake,98851,(509)246-1821

TONASKET
Tonasket Chamber of Commerce
POB 523,Tonasket,98855,(509)
486-2295

TWISP
Twisp Chamber of Commerce
POB 686,Twisp,98856,(509)
997-2926

WATERVILLE
Waterville Chamber of Commerce
POB 628,Waterville,98858
(509)745-8866

WENATCHEE
East Wenatchee Chamber of
Commerce,POB 7195, E Wenatchee
98801,(509)884-2514

> **THE HIGHEST CITY**
> ...Waterville, Douglas
> County is 2,640 feet
> above sea-level.

Wenatchee is the 27th
largest city in Washington,
with a population of 20,000.
It is in Chelan County,
located on the Columbia
River just below the mouth
of the Wenatchee River
(Wenatchee is Indian for
"river issuing from a
canyon"); at an altitude of
636 feet. Situated at the
geographical center of the
state, it is almost
equildistant from Spokane
and Seattle. It is know as
the "Apple Capitol of the
World" because of the
extensive apple orchards in
the district.

As a gateway to central
Washington's recreational
facilities in the Cascade
Range--swimming, boating,
fishing, camping, and
skiing--Wenatchee receives a
large number of tourists. It
is the site of Wenatchee

> **THE GEOGRAPHIC CENTER
> OF WASHINGTON...**Is
> located about ten miles
> west by southwest of
> Wenatchee in Chelan
> County.

Valley College, Washington
State University Tree Fruit
Experiment Station, The
United States Public Health
Service Toxicology
Laboratory, The North
Central Washington Museum,
and the North Central
Regional Library serving a
five-county area of 15,000
square miles.

WINTHROP
Chamber of Commerce
POB 39, 98862, (509)996-2125

**THE HIGHEST HIGHWAY
MOUNTAIN PASS IN WASH.**
..Is Hart's Pass near
Winthrop, Okanogan
County in Mt Baker/
Snoqualmie National
Forest is 6,197 feet.

FAIRS AND FESTIVALS

Twisp Freeze Yer Buns Run
Twisp, January (509)997-2926

Apple Blossom Festival
Wenatchee, April
(509)662-3616

Maifest
Levenworth, May
(509)548-7914

Moses Lake Spring Festival
Moses Lake, May
(509)765-8248

Memorial Day Festival
Grand Goulee, May
(509)633-3074

Sage N' Sunfest
Ephrata, June
(509)754-4656

**Okanogan County Hot Air
Balloon Rendezvous**
Omak, June (509)826-5107

Omak Stampede & Suicide Race
Omak, August (509)826-1983

**Quincy Farmer Consumer
Awareness Day**
Quincy, September
(509)787-2140

**THE LOWEST TEMPERATURE
EVER RECORDED IN WASH.**
48 below zero at
30 December 1968, Win-
throp, Okanogan County.

CHELAN COUNTY

Name derived from an Indian word meaning "deep water."

Created: March 13, 1899

County Courthouse, Washington and Orondo Streets
Wenatchee 98801

AREA: 2,925.8 square miles, State Ranking: 3rd

MAJOR ECONOMIC ACTIVITIES:
Agriculture, Aluminum Manufacturing, Wood
Products, Food Processing

ASSESSED VALUE: $1,936,883,375

POPULATION: (1989 Estimate): 48,600

Percentage of state: 1.0%
Density: 16.6 persons per square mile

ETHNIC BREAKDOWN: 1988 Estimate
  White   47,484
  Black   57
  Native American   421
  Asian and Pacific Islanders   300
  Other   1,438
    Spanish origin (included in above) 1,972

PRIMARY CITIES   Population
  Cashmere   2,430
  Chelan   2,830
  Entiatr   435
  Leavenworth   1,600
  Wenatchee, county seat   19,950

CLIMATE: Wenatchee – elevation 700 feet

Average	JAN	APR	JUL	OCT
Max Temp (F)	32.9	65.2	87.4	63.1
Min Temp	19.5	39.2	59.4	39.0
Mean Temp	26.2	52.2	73.4	51.1
Precipitation in inches	1.16	.47	.11	.73

Average Annual Maximum Temperature: 61.8
Average Annual Minimum Temperature: 39.5
Average Annual Mean Temperature: 50.6
Average Annual Precipitation: 9.00 inches

PUBLIC SCHOOL DISTRICTS

Cascade School District #228
Central & Evans Sts, Leavenworth 98826
(509)548-5885, Enrollment: 1,193

Cashmere School District #222
210 S Davision, Cashmere 98815 (509)782-3355
Enrollment: 1,121

Entiat School District #127
2650 Entiat Way, Entiat 98822 (509)784-1800
Enrollment: 262

Lake Chelan School District #129
Box 369, Chelan 98816 (509)682-2912
Enrollment: 922

Manson School District #19
Box A, Manson 98831 (509)687-3140
Enrollment: 410

Stehekin School District #69
Stehekin, 98852 Enrollment: 6

Wenatchee School District #246
235 Sunset Ave, POB 1767
Wenatchee 98807 (509)663-8161
Enrollment: 4,630

HOSPITALS

Cascade Medical Center
POB 330, 817 Commerical St.
Leavenworth 98826
(509)548-5815
Total Beds: 33

Central Washington Hospital
1300 Fuller St, Wenatchee
98801 (509)662-1511
Total Beds: 48

**Lake Chelan Community
Hospital**, POB 908
503 E. Highland, Chelan
98816 (509)682-2531
Total Beds: 34

THE COURTS

SUPERIOR COURT   Area Code (509)
401 Washington St, POB 880, Wenatchee
98801, John E. Bridges, Judge   664-5271
Charles W. Cone, Judge   664-5208
Fred L. Van Sickle, Judge   664-5211
    POB 990, Wenatchee 98801

JUVENILE COURT
316 Washington St, Wenatchee 98801
Administrator: Marlene Smith (509)664-5350

DISTRICT COURT

Chelan County Courthouse, Fourth Floor
POB 2182, Wenatchee 98801
Robert E. Graham, Judge   664-5393
Thomas C. Warren, Judge   664-5491

SITES OF INTEREST:

Rock Island, Lake Chelan, Site of Camp Chelan
Old Minning Arrastra

CRISIS

Wenatchee Crisis Line
(509)662-7105, 24 hour crisis
line.

**Che/Dou County Mental Health
Center,** 710 Miller, Wenatchee
98801, (509)662-7145, Out
patient mental health
counseling & crisis line; all
persons, sliding fee.

**Rape Crisis & Domestic Violence
Center,** 327 Penny Rd, POB 2704
Wenatchee,98801, (509)663-7446
Crisis line, advocacy &
counseling to victims of rape
and abuse.

MULTIPLE SERVICE CENTERS

**Chelan-Douglas Community Action
Council,** 620 Lewis St, Wentchee
98801, (509)662-6156, Energy
assistance, referrals, dental,
alcohol & drug referral,
shelter, pre-school assistance,
daycare, commodities
distributor; hours 8-5 M-F,
sliding fee.

**Department of Social Health
Services,** 805 S. Mission,
POB 3088, Wenatchee,98801,
(509)662-0511

Family Planning Association
900 Ferry St, Wenatchee,98801
Provides education, health
care, family planning,
physicals, counseling with
sexual offenders.

COUNSELING MENTAL/HEALTH

**Chelan-Douglas Community Mental
Health Council,** 701 N. Miller
St, Wenatchee,98801, (509)
662-7195 Emergency services,
substance abuse, out patient
treatment; all person, sliding
fee.

EMPLOYMENT & TRAINING

Displaced Homemakers, 233 N.
Chelan, Wenatchee, 98801, (509)
572-4575, Outreach services to
help women re-enter the job
market.

H.O.M.E., 212 First St,
Wenatchee,98801, (509)332-6232
Education help for low income &
welfare recipients.

Job Service Center, 215 Bridge
St, POB 1927, Wenatchee, 98807,
(509)662-0413

**Job Training Center
(Pentad Corp.),** 233 N. Chelan,
Wenatchee, 98801, (509)663-3091
Vocational counseling & testing
job orientation, assessment &
training, supportive services;
unemployed and disadvantaged
persons.

**Pentad Private Industry
Council.,Inc,** 233 N. Chelan Ave
POB 2360, Wenatchee,98801.

**Vocational Rehabilitation
Offices,** South 5 Wenatchee Ave

Wenatchee,98801, (509)662-1439,
Helps disable state residents
obtain employment.

FAMILY PLANNING

Birthright, 5 N. Wenatchee
Wenatchee, 98801, (509)662-0652
Non judgmental counsel &
support services for unplanned
pregnancy; hours 10-2 M-F,
those in need free.

**Catholic Family & Child
Services,** 23 S. Wenatchee Ave
Wenatchee, 98801, (509)662-6761
Counseling foster placement,
aid unwed mothers, those in
need of services.

FOOD/CLOTHING/HOUSING

**Food/Nutrition Distribution
Center of NCW,** 962 S. Columbia
St, Wenatchee, 98801, (509)
662-7830, Provides food,
clothing, furniture & household
goods, hours 10-1 M-F, those
in need no fee.

Goodwill Industries, 615 S.
Wenatchee Ave, Wenatchee, 98801
(509)663-7636, Thrift store of
clothing, furniture & household
goods and community services,
hours 9-6 M-F, all persons,
free.

The Salvation Army, 809 S.
Wenatchee Ave, Wenatchee, 98801
(509)662-5103, Provides lodging
for single women & families,
clothing, furniture; hours
8:30-3, 7 days a week, those
in need of service, sliding
fee.

**Seventh Day Adventist Community
Center,** 606 N. Western Ave,
Wenatchee, 98801, (509)663-4032
Assists low income persons in
need of clothing, furniture,
etc., references; hours 9-12
Tue emergency only.

St. Vincent de Paul Store
518 S. Wenatchee Ave,
Wenatchee,98801, (509)662-6010
Free distribution of clothing,

household items, furniture to
the needy; hours 9:30-5:30 M-F
those in need of services,
community services.

LEGAL

**Community Action Council
Chelan-Douglas,** 620 Lewis St,
Wenatchee, 98801, (509)663-6156
Services & legal aid to low
income & underprivileged, job
placement legal counseling and
information; those in need of
services free.

MEDICAL/DENTAL

Chelan-Douglas EMS Council
Chelan, 98816, (509)682-2531,
Emergency medical services;
those in need of services,
sliding fee.

Chelan-Douglas Health District
316 Washington St, Wenatchee
98801, (509)664-5306, Health
information, limited care &
services, immunizations, food
handler tests; hours 8-5 M-F,
all persons.

Community Health Center
1630 N. Wanatchee, 98801,
(509)662-5163, Medial care for
migrant, low income families,
open to public; hours
8:30-5:30 M-F.

**North Central Washington EMS
Council,** Cashmere, 98815, (509)
782-2772, Emergency medical
services, those in need of
services.

SUBSTANCE ABUSE

Alano Club/AA of Wenatchee
15 Palouse St, Wenatchee, 98801
(509)663-4567 Aid & assist
alcoholics in sobriety and in
all other ways, no fee.

Cascade Community Counseling
1201 S. Mission, Wenatchee,
98801, (509)662-5239, Certified
alcohol & drug out patient
treatment, information school,
DWI client assessment.

**Chelan County District Court
Probation Department**
415 Washington St, Office #210
Wenatchee, 98801, (509)664-5239
Certified alcohol & drug, DWI
client assessment, M-F, sliding
fee.

**Chelan-Douglas County Alcohol
& Drug Abuse Services
Association,** 327 Okanogan Ave,
Wenatchee,98801, (509)662-9673
Certified alcohol & drug out
patient treatment, information
school, DWI client assessment,
prevention, treatment, alcohol
& drug counseling and ed-
ucation; M-F, sliding fee.

Lake Chelan Community Hospital
503 E. Highland Ave, Chelan
98815, (509)682-2531, Certified
intensive inpatient alcohol &
drug treatment; 24 hours a day,
private non-profit organization.

VETERANS SERVICES

American Legion, 406 Doneen
Building, Palouse & Wanatchee
Ave, Wenatchee (206)663-0563

VICTIMS

Adult Protective Services
805 S. Mission, Weantchee,
98801, (509)662-0511, Respond
& investigate complaints of
adults in danger to self or
others, no fee.

**Wenatchee Rape Crisis &
Domestic Violence,** POB 2704,
Wenatchee, 98801, (509)663-7446
Domestic violence & sexual
assault advocacy, counseling
and support services.

For additional information see Douglas County

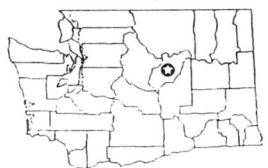

DOUGLAS COUNTY

Named for Steven A. Douglas, Illinois senator from 1847 to 1861.

Created: November 28, 1883

County Courthouse, Waterville 98858

AREA: 1,839.3 square miles, State Ranking: 17th

MAJOR ECONOMIC ACTIVITIES:
Medals Industries, Agriculture

ASSESSED VALUE: $813,133,891

POPULATION: (1989 Estimate): 25,400

Percentage of state: 0.5%
Density: 13.8 persons per square mile

ETHNIC BREAKDOWN:	1988 Estimate
White	23,187
Black	24
Native American	204
Asian and Pacific Islanders	129
Other	556
Spanish origin (included in above)	892

PRIMARY CITIES	Population
Bridgeport	1,405
East Wenatchee	1,785
Rock Island	470
Waterville, county seat	935

CLIMATE: Waterville - elevation 2,605 feet

Average	JAN	APR	JUL	OCT
Max Temp (F)	29.7	57.4	80.8	58.4
Min Temp	14.7	34.6	52.5	36.5
Mean Temp	22.2	46.0	66.6	47.4
Precipitation in inches	1.35	.68	.22	.88

Average Annual Maximum Temperature: 55.7
Average Annual Minimum Temperature: 34.5
Average Annual Mean Temperature: 45.1
Average Annual Precipitation: 11.57 inches

PUBLIC SCHOOL DISTRICTS

Bridgeport School District #75
Box 1060, Bridgeport 98813
(509)686-2201   Enrollment:420

Eastmont School District #206
460 Ninth St NE
East Wematcjee 98802, (509)884-7169
Enrollment: 3,756

Mansfield School District #207
Box 188, Mansfield 98830
(509)683-1012   Enrollment: 99

Orondo School District #13
HC Route, Box 18, Orondo 98843
Enrollment: 165

Pallsades School District #102
HCR #83, Palisades 98845
(509)884-8071   Enrollment: 36

Waterville School District #209
Box 490, Waterville 98858
(509)745-8584   Enrollment: 265

THE COURTS

SUPERIOR COURT   Area Code (509)
203 South Rainer, Waterville 98858
John E. Bridges, Judge (Wenatchee) 664-5472
Charles W. Cone, Judge (Weantchee) 664-5208
Fred L. Van Sickle, Judge (Wenatchee) 664-5211

JUVENILE COURT
110 Third St NE, East Wenatchee 98801
Administrator: William E. McDonald 884-3545

DISTRICT COURTS
Bridgeport Branch
1206 Columbia Ave, POB 730
Bridgeport 98813
John R. Harmon, Judge   686-4041

Douglas County
110 Third St NE, East Wenatchee 98801
H.B Hanna, Judge   884-3536

SITES OF INTEREST:

Rocky Reach Dam, Rocky Island Dam, Wells Dam,
Chief Joseph Dam, Grand Coulee Dam, Banks Lake

CRISIS

Crisis Line, N.701 Miller
Wenatchee,98801,(509)662-7105
Telephone crisis services.

**Rape Crisis & Domestic
Violence Center,** 327 Penny Rd
Wenatchee 98801,(509)663-7446
Crisis line, advocacy & coun-
seling to victims of rape and
9-5 M-F, free.

**Wematcjee Rape & Domestic
Violence Center,** POB 2704
Wenatchee,98801 (509)663-7446,
Domestic violence & sexual
assault advocacy, counseling
and support services, family
resource shelter, food and
clothing; 9-5 M-F, free.

MULTIPLE SERVICE CENTERS

**Che-Dou County Mental Health
Center,** 701 Miller,Wenatchee
98801,(509)662-7105, Out-
patient mental health services
and counseling and crisis line;
all persons.

Family Planning Association
900 Ferry St,Wentchee,98801
(509)662-2013, Provides
education, health care, family
planning, physicals,
counseling with sexual abusers.

Women's Resource Center
20 Adams St,Wenatchee,98801
(509)662-0121, Network of
information & support for
women, education referrals,
counseling, food & shelter;
10-5 M-F, free.

EMPLOYMENT & TRAINING

**Community Action Counsel
Chelan-Douglas,** 620 Lewis St
Wenatchee,(509)663-6156,
Services to low income &
underprivileged to include
legal aid, job placement.

Displaced Homemakers
233 N,Chelan,Wenatchee,98801
(509)572-4575, Outreach

services to help women
re-enter job market.

H.O.M.E. 212 First St
Wenatchee,98801,(509)332-6232
Education help for low income
& welfare recipients.

**Job Training Center (Pentad
Corporation),** 233 N,Chelan
Wenatchee,(509)663-3091,
Vocitional counseling,
testing, job orienation,
assessment, training &
support services; 8-5 M-F,
unemployed & disadvantaged
persons, no fee.

**Pentad Private Industry
Counsel, Inc,** 233 N,Chelan Ave
POB 2360,Wenatchee,98801,(509)
663-3091

Washington Human Development
103 S,Mission,Wenatchee,98801,
(509)662-6211 Immigration
services, cocational
counseling, job development,
placement, ESL/ABE/GED; support
services; 8-5 M-F, migrant
seasonal farm workers, free.

Wenatchee Valley College
1300 Fifth St,Wenatchee,98801
(509)662-1651, Academic and
vocational courses, GED testing; adults 16+.

FAMILY PLANNING

Birthright, 5 N.Wenatchee,98801
(509)663-0563, Non-judgmental
counseling & services for unplanned pregnancy, those in
need of services free.

**Catholic Family & Child
Services,** 23 S.Wenatchee,Ave
Wenatchee,(509)662-6761,
Counseling, foster placement,
assistance to unwed mothers.

FOOD/CLOTHING/HOUSING

Bridgport Food Bank
1300 Foster, POB 909,Bridgeport
98813,(509)686-3371, Food Bank;
those in need of services.

Food/Nutrition Distrubtion Center of NCW, 8th & Kansas E.Wenatchee, (509)884-4339, Provides food, clothing, furniture, information and referrals, free.

Goodwill Industires 625 S.Wenatchee Ave,98801, (509)663-7636, Thrift store of clothing furniture & household goods, all persons.

The Salvation Army 809 S.Wenatchee Ave,Wenatchee 98801,(509)662-5103, Provides lodging for single women & families, clothing, furniture and emergency lodging, family services; 8:30-5 M-F, those in need of services, free.

Seventh Day Adventist Community Center, 606 N.Western Ave Wenatchee,(509)663-4032, Assistance to low income persons in need of clothing, furnishings, etc.,refernces, emergency services on call; 9-12 Tues, free.

St. Vincent de Paul Council 504 S.Chelan,Wenatchee,98801, (509)662-4569, Aid to needy with food, clothing, household items, gas vouchers, referral when needed; those in need of services, free.

W.I.C., 1630 N.Wenatchee,98801 (509)664-3771 Food program for pregnant or nursing mothers, infants & children 3 to 12; 8:30-5:30 M-F, those that qualify, free.

LEGAL

Community Action Center 620 Lewis St,Wenatchee,98801 (509)662-6156, Legal aid to indigent & low income people; legal counseling and information.

MEDICAL/DENTAL

Chelan-Douglas EMS Council 98816,(509)682-2531,(800)223-

0045 Emergency medical services; 24 hours; those in need of services, non-profit organization.

Chelan-Douglas Health District, 316 Washington St Wenatchee,98801,(509)664-5306, Health information, limited care & services, immunizations food handlers testing; all persons.

Community Health Center 1630 N.Wenatchee,98801,(509) 662-5163, Medical care for migrant, low income families; those in need of services, sliding fee.

MISCELLANEOUS

Adult Protective Services 805 S.Mission,Wenatchee,98801 (509)662-0511, Respond & investigate complaints of adults in danger to themselfs and others.

SUBSTANCE ABUSE

Alano Club/AA of Wenatchee 15 Palouse St,Wenatchee,98801 (509)663-4567, Aid and assist alcholics in sobriety and in all other ways.

Chelan-Douglas County Alcohol & Drug Abuse Services Association, 327 Okanogan St Wenatchee,98801,Prevention, treatment and education regarding alcohol & drugs, counseling.

For additional information see Chelan County

GRANT COUNTY

Named for Ulysses S. Grant, Union general and
18th president of the U.S.

Created: February 24, 1909

C Street NW, POB 37, Ephrata 98823

AREA: 2,680.2 square miles, State Ranking: 4th

MAJOR ECONOMIC ACTIVITIES:
Food Processing, Agriculture

ASSESSED VALUE: $1,779,692,077

POPULATION: (1989 Estimate): 51,900

Percentage of state: 1.1%
Density: 19.4 persons per square mile

ETHNIC BREAKDOWN:	1988 Estimate
White	45,775
Black	602
Native American	565
Asian and Pacific Islanders	654
Other	5,104
Spanish origin (included in above)	7,025

PRIMARY CITIES	Population
Electric City	910
Ephrata, county seat	5,440
Grand Coulee	975
Moses Lake	10,810
Quincy	3,519
Soap Lake	1,175
Warden	1,455

CLIMATE: Ephrata – elevation 1,272 feet

Average	JAN	APR	JUL	OCT
Max Temp (F)	33.7	65.3	90.5	65.3
Min Temp	21.1	41.4	62.4	42.9
Mean Temp	27.5	53.2	76.5	42.9
Precipitation in inches	1.05	.56	.20	.77

Average Annual Maximum Temperature: 63.1
Average Annual Minimum Temperature: 41.9
Average Annual Mean Temperature: 52.5
Average Annual Precipitation: 8.42 inches

PUBLIC SCHOOL DISTRICTS

Coulee-Hartline School District #151
POB 428, Coulee City, 99115
(509)632-5231
Enrollment: 229

Ephrata School District #165
POB 788, Ephrata 98823 (509)754-2474
Enrollment: 1,800

Grand Coulee Dam School District #301J
Stevens & Grant
Coulee Dam 99116, (509)633-2143
Enrollment: 968

Moses Lake School District #161
1318 W. Ivy Ave, (509)765-3485
Moses Lake, 98837
Enrollment: 5,000

Quincy School District #144-101
119 J St SW, Quincy 98848
(509)787-4571
Enrollment: 1,460

Royal School District #160
POB 486, Royal City 99357
(509)346-2222
Enrollment: 745

Soap Lake School District #156
POB 158, Soap Lake 98851
(509)246-1822
Enrollment: 325

Wahluke School District #73
POB 907, Mattawa 99344
(509)932-4565
Enrollment: 505

Warden School District #146-161
POB 308, Warden 98857, (509)349-2366
Enrollment: 678

Wilson Creek School District #167-202
Navar St, POB 46, Wilson Creek 98860
(509)345-2541,   Enrollment: 90

HOSPITALS

Columbia Basin Hospital
200 Southeast Blvd, Ephrata
98823 (509)754-4631
Total Beds: 58

Coulee Community Hospital
POB H, 411 Fortuyn Rd

Grand Coulee 99133
(509)633-1753
Total Beds: 48

Quincy Valley Hospital
908 10th Ave SW, Quincy
98848 (509)787-3531
Total Beds: 16

Samaritan Hospital
801 E. Wheeler Rd
Moses Lake 98837
(509)765-5606
Total Beds: 50

THE COURTS

SUPERIOR COURT   Area Code (509)
Division & "C" Sts, NW, POB 37,
Ephrata 98823
Jerry J. Moberg, Judge   754-2011
Evan E. Sperline, Judge   754-2011
Minde Finke, Administrator   754-2011

JUVENILE COURT
4 Cyrus Road, POB 5, Ephrata 98823
Administrator: Robert J. Cornwell
                754-2011

DISTRICT COURT
Division & "C" Sts NW, POB 37,
Ephrata 98823
W. Edward Allan, Judge   754-2011
Janis Witener-Moberg, Judge

SITES OF INTEREST:

Grand Coulee Dam
Dry Falls
Potholes Reservoir

CRISIS

Crisis Line, Moses Lake, 98837
(509)762-1717, Crisis counseling; those in need of
services, free.

MULTIPLE SERVICE CENTERS

**Department of Social & Health
Services,** 1620 S.Pioneer Way
POB 1399,Moses Lake,98837
(509)766-2200 229 First Northwest,Ephrata,99334,
(509)754-2427, 455 E.Helmock,
Othello,99344,(509)488-9673

**Grant County Community Action
Agency,** 604 W.Third,Ave,Moses
Lake,(509)765-9206, Energy
assistance, referrals, dental,
alcohol & drug referral services, outpatient counseling,
daycare, drug counseling,
geriatric services, all
persons.

One Place, 1000 Ivy,St,Moses
Lake,98837,(509)765-1214,
Crisis line, provides advocacy
information & referrals, sexual
assault programs, domestic
violence shelter program;

those in need of services, no
fee for 15 days, otherwise
sliding fee.

COUNSELING MENTAL/HEALTH

**Grant County Mental Health
Center,** 1638 W.Ivy,Moses Lake
98837,(509)765-9239, Counseling, emotional support,
information & referrals, all
persons, fee.

Big Bend Community College
2402 28th St,Moses Lake,98837
(509)762-5581, Academic
& vocational courses, GED
testing, 8-4:30 W-F, adults
16-22 fee.

**Columbia Basin Job Corps
Center,** 2402 24th St,Moses
Lake,98837,(509)662-9681,
Remedial & basic education,
GED, skills training, job
counseling & placement; dis-
advantaged persons 16-22
years of age.

Learning Assistance Center
1616 Pioneer Way,Moses Lake
98837,(509)762-5351, Education
ABE,GED,ESL classes; 8-4:30
M-F, those in need of services
free.

Pentad Private Industry Counsel
226 W.3d Ave,Moses Lake,98837
(509)765-1721, Vocational
counseling and assessment,
employment orientation, OJT
and placement; unemployed &
disadvantaged persons.

Student Tuition Waivers-BBCC
28 Chanote,Moses Lake,98837
(509)762-5351, Education
& tuition waivers; those in
need of services, sliding fee.

Training and Learning Center
Quincy,98848,(509)787-4449,
Education, training and learn-
ing; those in need of services.

**Vocational Rehabilitation
Office,** 1620 S.Pioneer Way
Moses Lake,98837,(509)766-2223
Helps disable state residents

obtain employment; 8-5 M-F,
disabled physical & mental
persons, free.

Washington Human Development
410 W.3rd St,Moses Lake,98837
(509)765-1977, Vocational
counseling; job development,
placement, ESL/ABE/GED support
services; migrant seasonal
farm workers & those in need of
services.

FAMILY PLANNING

Assistance to Pregant Teens
POB 1626, Bldg 9000,Moses Lake
(509)762-9887, Child & youth
services.

Birthright, 402 S.Clover,Moses
Lake,98837,(509)765-4425, Some
free baby clothes & furniture,
crisis pregnancy services,
pregnancy counseling; 9-5 M-F.

Grant County Health District
Courthouse,Ephrata,98823,(509)
754-2011, Prenatal care,
coordinate child services.

Grant County Head Start
POB 389, Bldg 9000,Moses
Lake,98837,(509)762-5506,
Child and Youth services.

FOOD/CLOTHING/HOUSING

Child Care Food Program
604 W.3rd Ave,Moses Lake,98837
(509)765-9206, Food &
nutrition, community nutrition
program, community emergency
services, headstart program.

Community Food & Nutrition
604 W.3rd Ave,Moses Lake,98837
(509)765-9206, Food &
nutrition; those in need of
services.

**Community Services of Moses
Lake,** Moses Lake, (509)765-8101
Clothing; those in need of
services.

Food Bank:
214 N.4th,Coulee
City,99115,(509)632-5696

Basin St,Ephrata,98823,(509) 754-5772 Grand Coulee,99133 (509)633-3279 Lind, 99341 (509)677-3320 606 W.Broadway Moses Lake,98837,(509)765-8101 335 N.3rd,Othello,99344,(509) 488-5256 Quincy,98848,(509) 787-3865 302 Fern St,Royal City,99352,(509)346-2670, Soap Lake,98851,(509)246-0332.

GCCAC, 604 W.3rd Ave,Moses Lake,98837,(509)765-9206, Emergency housing; those in need of serives.

Moses Lake Community Health 1004 W.Broadway,Moses Lake 98837,(509)765-0674, Food & nutrition; those in need of services.

Othello Migrant Headstart 550 N. 7th St,Othello,99344 (509)488-5256, Food & nutrition; those in need of services.

Quincey Child Development Center, 310 H.St,SW,Quincy 98848,(509)787-2511, Food & nutrition, handouts to children in need of services.

Surplus Commodities, 604 W.3rd Ave,Moses Lake,98848,(509) 765-9206, Surpus for distri- bution center, energy weatherization, child services 8-5 M-F.

LEGAL

GCCAC, 604 W.3rd Ave,Moses Lake,98837, (509)765-9206 Legal services, consult and screening.

MEDICAL/DENTAL

Columbia Basis Health Association, 140 E.Main St Othello,99344,(509)488-5256, 1395 Camlela St,Royal City,99357,(509)346-2237 Dental care, family planning, medical services, low income persons & families, free.

Grant County Health District County Courthouse,Ephrata 98823,(509)754-2011, Health information, limited care & services, immunizations, food handler testing, WICK, child care services, developmental disabled services; all persons sliding fee.

Moses Lake Community Health Services, 1005 W.Broadway Moses Lake,(509)765-0674, Dental care for low income persons, acute care Saturday mornings; 8-5 M-F, sliding fee.

SUBSTANCE ABUSE

Grant County Alcohol & Drug Center, 1038 W.Ivy Ave POB 3208, Moses Lake,98837 (509)765-5402, Certified alcohol & drug outpaient treatment, information school, DWI client assessment, ADATSA also an outreach program, 8-5 & 6-10 evenings M-F, those in need of services, fee.

MISCELLANEOUS

Radio KDNA, POB 800,Granger 98932(509)854-2222, Broadcast services for Spanish speaking; public education radio station.

VICTIMS

Our Place, 1000 W.Ivy St,Moses Lake,98837,(509)765-1214 Domestice violence & sexual assault advocacy, counseling, self support groups, resources for family law issues; 24 hour hot line, 8-5 M-Thur, first hour free than sliding scale.

For additional information see also Adams County

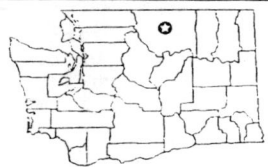

OKANOGAN COUNTY

Named derived from an Indian word meaning
"rendezvous."

Created: November 28, 1883

149 Third North, Okanogan 98840

AREA: 5,300.6 square miles, State Ranking: 1st

MAJOR ECONOMIC ACTIVITIES:
Wood Products, Agriculture

ASSESSED VALUE: $871,285,941

POPULATION: (1989 Estimate): 31,700

Percentage of state: 0.7%
Density: 6.0 persons per square mile

ETHNIC BREAKDOWN:	1988 Estimate
White	27,583
Black	33
Native American	3,414
Asian and Pacific Islanders	88
Other	582
Spanish origin (included in above)	725

PRIMARY CITIES	Population
Brewster	1,588
Okanogan, county seat	2,395
Omak	3,870
Oroville	1,495
Tonasket	1,045

CLIMATE: Okanogan – elevation 835 feet

Average	JAN	APR	JUL	OCT
Max Temp (F)	31.0	67.8	92.1	65.2
Min Temp	17.4	38.4	57.9	38.6
Mean Temp	24.2	53.1	75.0	51.8
Precipitation in inches	1.23	.88	.28	.89

Average Annual Maximum Temperature: 63.2
Average Annual Minimum Temperature: 38.2
Average Annual Mean Temperature: 50.7
Average Annual Precipitation: 11.65 inches

PUBLIC SCHOOL DISTRICTS

Brewster School District #111
Box 97, Brewster 98812
(509)689-2414 Enrollment: 565

Methow Valley School District #350
Twisp 98856, (509)997-3371
Enrollment: 631

Nespelem School District #14
Box 291, Nespelem 99155
(509)634-4551 Enrollment: 220

Okanogan School District #105
Okanogan 98840, (509)422-3629
Enrollment: 890

Omak School District #19
Box 833, Omak 98841, (509)826-0320
Enrollment: 1,909

Oroville School District #410
Tenth & Ironwood, Oroville 98844
(509)476-2281 Enrollment: 785

Pateros School District #122
Pateros 98846, (509)923-2751
Enrollment: 262

Tonasket School District #404
POB 468, Tonasket 98855
(509)486-2126 Enrollment: 1,050

HOSPITALS

Mid-Valley Hospital
810 Valley Way, Omak 98841
(509)826-1760
Total Beds: 44

North Valley Hospital
POB 488, Second and Western
Tonasket 98855 (509)486-2151
Total Beds: 97

**Okanogan-Douglas County
Hospital,** Box 577, 703 NW
Second, Brewster 98812
(509)689-2517
Total Beds: 43

THE COURTS

SUPERIOR COURT Area Code (509)
149 Third N. POB 112, Okanogan 98840
James R. Thomas, Judge   422-3980
Jackie L. Bradley, County Clerk   422-3650

JUVENILE COURT
227 Fourth N, POB 432, Okanogan 98840
Administrator: Bruce Moran   422-3462

DISTRICT COURT
149 Third N, POB 1096, Okanogan 98840
Christopher E. Culp, Judge   422-2944
David S. Edwards, Judeg 422-2944
Carolyn Bonar, Administrator 422-2944

SITES OF INTEREST:

Fort Okanogan, Grand Coulee Dam,
St. Mary's Mission
Colville Indian Reservation

CRISIS

Che-Dou County Mental Health Center
701 N Miller,Weatchee,98801
(509)662-7105, Outpatient
mental health counseling &
crisis line; all persons,
sliding fee.

MULTIPLE SERVICE CENTERS

Department of Social Health Services, Rt 1,Box 1234,S
2nd,Okanogan,98840,(509)422-0082

Farm Worker Clinic, 716 S 1st
Okanogan,98840,(509)422-5700
WIC, Child, food bank, medical,
dental services, bilingual staff.

Northeast Washington Rural Resources, 320 N Main,Colville
99114,(509)684- 8421, Energy
assistance, referrals, dental,
alcohol & drug referral,
shelter, pre-school assistance
daycare, commodities
distributor; 8-5 M-F, sliding
fee.

Okanogan Community Action Council
POB 1067,Okanogan,98840,(509)
422-4041, Energy assistance,
referrals, dental, alcohol &
drug referral, shelter, pre-
school assistance, daycare,
commodities distributor; 8-5
M-F, sliding fee.

Senior Information & Assistance
1300 5th St,Wenatchee,98801

(509)664-2576, Information &
referrals, assistance provided.

COUNSELING MENTAL/HEALTH

Family Counseling & Mental Health Center
107 W Apple,POB 3208,(509)826-
6191,Omak, Emergency services,
substance abuse, outpatient
treatment, all persons, sliding
fee.

EMPLOYMENT & TRAINING

Job Service Center
1234 S 2nd,POB 980,Okanogan
98840,(509)422-1300

Job Training Center (Pentad Corporation)
233 N Chelan,Wenatchee,98801
(509)663-3091, Vocational
counseling & testing, job
orientation, assessment,
training, supportive services;
unemployment & disadvantages
persons.

Washington Human Development
103 S Mission,Wenatchee,98801
(509)662-6211, Immigration
services, vocational counseling
job development & placement,
ESL, ABE, GED, support services
OJT, adult experience; migrant
seasonal farm workers & ex
offenders.

Wenatchee Valley College
1300 5th St,Wenatchee,98801
(509)622-1651, Academic &

vocational courses, GED testing adults 16+ years of age.

FAMILY PLANNING

Family Planning, 123 S 3rd Okanogan,98840,(509)422-1624, Family planning center.

FOOD/CLOTHING/HOUSING

Brewster Food Bank
St Zenes Episcopal Church Basement, POB 1107,Brewster 98812,(509)689-3343,
Food bank.

Okanogan County Community Action Council
POB 1067,Okanogan (509)422-4041, Emergency food bank & shelter.

Omak Food Bank, 2 N Ash POB 137 Omak,98841 (509)826-4689, Food Bank.

Oroville Food Bank
Basement of Adventist Church on So. Main, POB 277,Oroville 98844 (509)476-2878.

SOS Ministries, 953B 2nd St S POB 1425,Okanogan,98840 (509)422-1243, Food Bank.

Tonasket Food Bank, 31663 N Highway 97, Tonasket,98855 (509)486-2632.

MEDICAL/DENTAL

North Central Washington EMS Council,
Cashmere,98815,(509)782-2772, Emergency medical services.

Oranogan County Health Department
237 N 4th St,Okanogan (509)422-3867, Health information, limited care & services, immunizations, food handler testing, aids testing, pregnancy testing, SDS, sliding fee.

SUBSTANCE ABUSE

ORANOGAN COUNTY ALCOHOL PROGRAM
107 W Apple,Omak,98841 (509)826- 5600, Certified alcohol & drug outpatient treatment, information school, DWI client assessment, ADATSA, set fee.

VICTIMS

Support Center, POB 2058,Omak 98841,(509)826-3221, Domestic violence advocacy, counseling, work shops, shelter, resources available with family law issues, sexual assault programs; 8-5 M-F, 24 hour hot line, free.

HANDLE WITH CARE

SOUTH CENTRAL

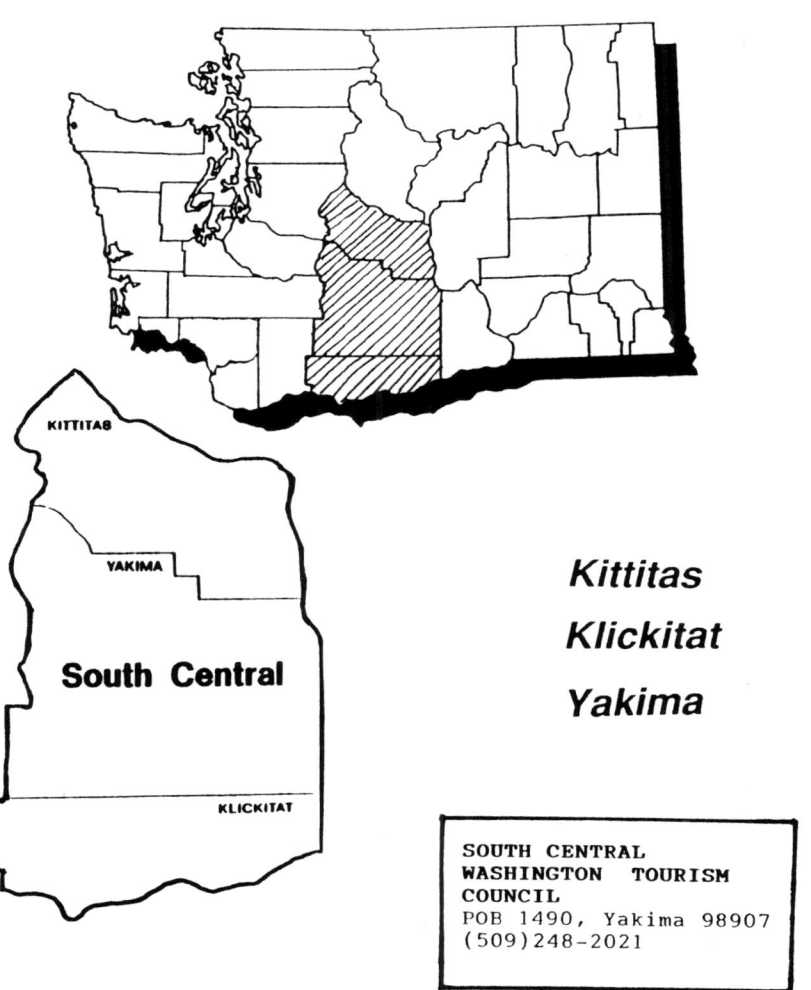

Kittitas

Klickitat

Yakima

SOUTH CENTRAL
WASHINGTON TOURISM
COUNCIL
POB 1490, Yakima 98907
(509)248-2021

HISTORICAL APPEAL

Cle Elum Telephone Museum,
Cle Elum

Kittitas County Museum,
Ellensburg

Olmstead Place Heritage Area
Ellensburg

Klickitat County Historical
Museum, Goldendale

Maryhil Museum and Stonehenge
Maryhill/Goldendale

Roslyn Museum, Roslyn

Sunnyside Museum, Sunnyside

Fort Simcoe State Park, White
Swan

H.M. Gilbert Home Place, Yakima

Yakima Valley Museum, Yakima

CITIES

BINGEN
Mt Adams Chamber of Commerce
POB 449,White Salmon,98672,
(509)493-3630

CLE ELUM
Cle Elum Chamber of Commerce
POB 43,221 E First St,Cle
Elum,98922,(509)674-5958

ELLENSBURG
Ellensburg Chamber of Commerce
436 North Sprague,Ellensburg
98926, (509)925-3137

GLENWOOD
Mt Adams Chamber of Commerce
POB 449,White Solmon,98672,
(509)493-3630

GOLDENDALE/STATUS PASS
Greater Goldendale Area Chamber
of Commerce,POB 524,Goldendale,
98620,(509)773-3400

THE YAKIMA VALLEY MUSEUM...Has the most extensive collection of horse drawn wagons in the Western United States.

THE ELLENSBURG RODEO... Is one of the finest rodeos in the world. It is held during the Kittitas County Fair which begins the Friday before and ends on Labor Day each year. It includes a Western Parade, as well as the world's top rodeo performers.

GRANDVIEW
Grandview Chamber of Commerce
POB 666,Grandview,98930,(509)
882-2201

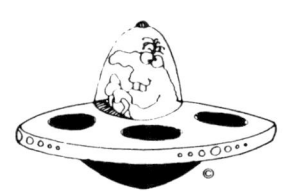

HUSUM
Mt Adams Chamber of Commerce
POB 449,White Salmon,98672,
(509)493-3630

LYLE
Mt Adams Chamber of Commerce
POB 449,White Salmon,98672,
(509)493-3630

SELAH
Selah Chamber of Commerce
216 1st St,Selah,98942
(509)697-6877

SUNNYSIDE
Sunyside Chamber of Commerce
POB 141,812 E Edison,Sunnyside
98944,(509)837-5939

TOPPENISH
Toppenish Chamber of Commerce
POB 28,Toppenish,98948
(509)865-3262

TROUT LAKE
Mt Adams Chamber of Commerce
POB 449,White Salmon,98672,
(509)493-3630

UNION GAP
Visitor Information,102 W
Ahtanum, Union Gap,98903
(509)248-0432

WAPATO
Wapato Chamber of Commerce
POB 157,Watato,98951
(509)877-4404

WHITE SALMON
Mt Adams Chamber of Commerce
POB 449,White Salmon,98672,
(509)493-3630

**THE LARGEST PUBLIC
TELESCOPE...**In the
nation is located at
the Goldendale
Observatory just north
of Goldendale, near
Maryhill, Klickitat
County. The main mirror
is 5 inches thick, weighs
300 pounds, and is $24\frac{1}{2}$
inches in diameter.

© 1982 VOLK

ELK... Can be seen
during the winter
months at the Oak Creek
Winter Feed Station
located about 7 miles
west of Naches, Yakima
County on Hwy 12. About
600 animals can be seen
daily.

APPLES... The city of
Wenatchee is designated
the "Apple Capitol of
the World."

YAKIMA

Greater Yakima Chamber of Commerce, 10 N 9th St, Yakima 98901, (509)248-2021

Yakima is the seventh largest city in Washington with a population of 50,610. It is the Seat of **Yakima County.** It is located on the Yakima River, 110 miles southeast of Seattle. The city is the trading center for the agriculture and fruit-growing Yakima Valley. Yakima has packing plants and canneries and produces clothing and lumber products. The Yakima Indian reservation is nearby. Yakima was settled in 1861. In 1885 the town moved four miles to the northwest to be on the Northern Pacific Railroad.

ZILLAH

Zillah Chamber of Commerce POB 1294, Zillah, 98953, (509) 829-5911

FAIRS AND FESTIVALS

Speelyi-Mi Arts & Crafts Trade Fair
Toppenish, March
(509)865-2800

Yakima Valley Air Fair
Yakima, June (509)248-0246

National Western Art Show & Auction
Ellensburg, May
(509)925-3137

Mayfest
Salmon, May (509)493-2391

Community Days
Goldendale, July
(509)773-3400

Ellensburg Rodeo/Kittitas County Fair
Ellensburg, July
(509)925-3137

THE BLUEBIRD CAPITOL
...Of America is Bickleton, Klickitat County. They arrive in droves in February and then head south in October. The have more bluebirds there than anyplace else in the world.

WHAT IS THE TEAPOT SER-VICE STATION...It is a gas station that's shaped like a giant teapot in Zillah. It was build in 1922 to symbolize the Tea Pot Dome Scandal. It was declared a National Historic Site in 1985.

Antique Show
Yakima, August
(509)248-7160

Run to Roslyn Antique Car Show
Roslyn, August
(509)649-2785

Wine & Food Fest
Yakima, November
(509)248-2021

KITTITAS COUNTY

Name derived from the Indian word meaning "plenty food."

Created: November 24, 1883

Fifth and Main, Ellensburg 98926

AREA: 2,320.0 square miles, State Ranking: 7th

MAJOR ECONOMIC ACTIVITIES:
Food Processing, Wood Products, Agriculture, Metal Fabrication

ASSESSED VALUE: $827,838,295

POPULATION: (1989 Estimate): 25,400

Percentage of state: 0.5%
Density: 10.9 persons per square mile

ETHNIC BREAKDOWN:	1988 Estimate
White	24,189
Black	141
Native American	213
Asian and Pacific Islanders	204
Other	253
Spanish origin (included in above)	327

PRIMARY CITIES	Population
Cle Elum	1,760
Ellensburg, county seat	11,730
Kittitas	750
Roslyn	840
South Cle Elum	480

CLIMATE: Ellensburg – elevation 1,597 feet

Average	JAN	APR	JUL	OCT
Max Temp (F)	35.2	61.8	83.9	63.0
Min Temp	19.3	35.2	52.8	36.1
Mean Temp	24.6	48.1	68.9	48.9
Precipitation in inches	1.26	.49	.13	.66

Average Annual Maximum Temperature: 60.2
Average Annual Minimum Temperature: 35.9
Average Annual Mean Temperature: 47.7
Average Annual Precipitation: 8.86 inches

PUBLIC SCHOOL DISTRICTS

Cle Elum-Roslyn School District #404
HC60, Box 5010, (509)649-2393
Cle Elum 98922,   Enrollment: 800

Damman School District #7
Route 6, Box 1266, (509)925-4567
Ellensburg 98926,   Enrollment: 35

Easton School District #28
Box 8, Easton 98925, (509)656-2317
Enrollment: 59

Ellensburg School District #401
1300 E. Third,   (509)925-0848
Ellensburg 98926,   Enrollment: 2,304

Kittitas School District #403
POB 599, Kittitas 98934
(509)968-3014,   Enrollment: 500

Thorp School District #400
Box 155, Thorp 98946
(509)964-2107,   Enrollment: 156

HOSPITAL

**Kittitas Valley Community
Hospital,** 603 S Chestnut
Ellensburg 98926
(509)962-9841
Total Beds: 50

THE COURTS

SUPERIOR COURT Area Code (209)
205 West Fifth, Ellensburg 98926
Michael E. Cooper, Judge   962-7533
Anna M. Barnaby, Administrator
                        962-7533

JUVENILE COURT
205 West Fifth, Ellensburg 98926
Administrator: Gerald W. Bailey
                        962-7516

DISTRICT COURTS
Lower Kittitas
205 West Fifth, Ellensburg 98926
Thomas Haven, Judge   962-7511

Upper Kittitas
301 West First, #4 Cle Elum 98922
Paul P. Pangrazi, Judge   674-5533

CRISIS

Central Washington Comprehensive Mental Health 321 E Yakima Ave,Yakima,98902 (509)575-4084, (800)572-8122, Mental health counseling, 24 hour crisis line.

Crisis Line, W.507 Nanum Ellensburg,98926,(509)925-4168, Telephone crisis services.

MULTIPLE SERVICE CENTERS

Department of Social & Health Services, 521 Mountain View,POB 366,Ellensburg,98926,(509)925-9834

Kittitas County Action Council 115 W 3rd Ave,Ellensburg,98926 (509)925-1448, Energy assistance, referrals, dental, alcohol & drug referral, shelter, pre-school assistance, daycare, commodities distributor; 8-5 M-F, sliding fee.

COUNSELING MENTAL/HEALTH

Central Washington Comprehensive Mental Health 505 Power St,Cle Elum (509)647-2340, 220 W 4th Ave,Ellensburg,98926,925-9861 Crisis intervention, outpatient therapy, adult day treatment, inpatient care, referral services, 24 hours; sliding fee

EMPLOYMENT & TRAINING

Job Service Center, 521 Mountain View Rd,POB 38,Ellensburg 98926,(509)925-6166.

S. L. Start & Associates 1111 N 1st St,Yakima,98901 (509)452-4571, Skill assessment job placement, finding & counseling; disadvantaged persons, free.

Yakima County Department of Employment & Training Yakima County Courthouse Yakima,98901,(509)575-4252.

FOOD/CLOTHING/HOUSING

Kittitas County Action Council, Inc., 115 W 3rd,Ellensburg 98926 (509)925-1448, Emergency food bank and shelter.

MEDICAL/DENTAL

Kittitas County Health Department 505 Power St,Cle Elum,98922 (509)674-5513, 507 Nanum Ellensburg,98926 (509)962-6811, Health information, limited care & services, immunizations, food handler testing, sliding fee.

VICTIMS

Domestic Violence/Rape Relief 220 W 4th Ave,Ellensburg,98926 (509)925-4168, Resource service for family law issues, assault, sexual programs.

Lower Valley Crisis & Support Services Sunnyside,98944,(509)837-6689, Domestic violence, sexual assault, counseling.

KLICKITAT COUNTY

Named for the Klicktat Indians, whose tribal name means "robber of thief."

Created: December 20, 1859

205 South Columbus, Goldendale 98620

AREA: 1,907.8 square miles, State Ranking: 15th

MAJOR ECONOMIC ACTIVITIES:
Wood Products, Agriculture, Metal Industries

ASSESSED VALUE: $538,437,319

POPULATION: (1989 Estimate): 17,700

Percentage of state: 0.4%
Density: 8.8 persons per square mile

ETHNIC BREAKDOWN:	1988 Estimate
White	15,572
Black	21
Native American	505
Asian and Pacific Islanders	131
Other	371
Spanish origin (included in above)	576

PRIMARY CITIES	Population
Bingen	675
Goldendale, county seat	3,730
White Salmon	2,050

CLIMATE: Goldendale - elevation 1,635 feet

Average	JAN	APR	JUL	OCT
Max Temp (F)	36.5	61.5	84.3	63.4
Min Temp	22.3	34.4	49.5	36.0
Mean Temp	29.4	48.0	66.9	49.7
Precipitation in inches	2.93	.85	.15	1.64

Average Annual Maximum Temperature: 61.0
Average Annual Minimum Temperature: 35.9
Average Annual Mean Temperature: 48.4
Average Annual Precipitation: 17.41 inches

PUBLIC SCHOOL DISTRICTS

Bickleton School District #203
Box 10, Bickleton 99322 (509)896-5473
Enrollment: 63

Centerville School District #215
401 Centervill Hwy,POB 357
(509)773-4893 Enrollment: 68

Glenwood School District #401
Box 12, Glenwood 98619, (509)364-3595
Enrollment: 150

Goldendale School District #404
603 S. Roosevelt, Goldendale 98620
(509)773-5177 Enrollment: 1,300

Klickitas School District #402
Box 37, Klickita 98628
(509)369-4145 Enrollment: 150

Lyle School District #406
Seventh & Keasey Sts
Lyle 98635, (509)365-2191
Enrollment: 400

Roosevelt School District #403
POB 248, Roosevelt 99356
(509)374-5462 Enrollment: 16

Trout Lake School District #R-400
31 Little Mountain Rd. (509)395-2571
Trout Lake 98650 Enrollment: 140

White Salmon Valley School District #405-17
Box 157, White Salmon 98672
(509)493-1500 Enrollment: 1,200

Wishram School District #94
Box 268, Wishram 98673
(509)748-2551 Enrollment: 78

HOSPITALS

Klickitat Valley Hospital
Roosevelt and Allyn Sts
POB 5, Goldendale 98620
(509)773-4022
Total Beds: 31

Skyline Hospital
POB 99, 211 Skyline Dr
White Solom 98672
(509)493-1101
Total Beds: 32

THE COURTS

SUPERIOR COURT   Area Code (509)
205 S Columbus Ave, #206
Goldendale 98620
Ted Kolbaba, Judge   773-5755
Administrator: Christine Jaekel
                        773-5755

JUVENILE COURT
228 W. Main St, Rm 120,
Goldendale 98620
Administrator: Keith J. Anderson
                        773-3355

DISTRICT COURTS
East District Court
205 S. Columbus Ave, #107
Goldendale, 98620
Joe V. Churchill, Judge 773-3311

West District Court
180 NW Lincoln St., POB 435
White Salmon 98672
Robert D. Weisfield, Judge 493-1190

SITES OF INTEREST:

Maryhill Museum, Stonehenge,
Goldendale Observatory

MULTIPLE SERVICE CENTERS

Counseling & Resource Center
112 W Main,Goldendale,98620
(509)773-5801, Mental health,
drug & alcohol abuse counseling,
outpatient information & referral, certified alcohol &
drug outpatient treatment,
information school, DWI client
assessment, ADATSA; 24 hours,
sliding fee.

**Department of Social & Health
Services,** 106 E Main,POB
185,Goldendale,98620,(509)773-
5835, 221 N Main,POB 129,White
Salmon,98672,(509)493-1012.

**Klickitat-Skamania Community
Action Council,** POB 1580,White
Salmon,(509)493-2662, Energy
assistance, referrals, dental,
alcohol & drug referral,
shelter, pre-school assistance,
daycare, commodities dis-
tributor; 8-5 M-F, sliding fee.

COUNSELING MENTAL/HEALTH

**Klickitat Counseling & Resource
Center,** 228 W Main,Goldendale
98620,(509)773- 5801, Emergency
services, substance abuse,
outpatient treatment, sliding
fee.

EMPLOYMENT & TRAINING

Job Service Center
114 W Steuben,POB 387,Bingen
98605,(509)493-1210

**Klickitat & Skamanla Employment
& Training Center**
114 W Steuben, Counseling, self
assessment, employment orientation, OJT, classroom training,
support groups, GED, SS program,
ESL; 8-5 M-F, unemployed, disadvantaged persons, sliding fee.

S. L. Start & Associates, Inc.,
Yakima County Courthouse,98901
(509)452-4571, Job placement,

finding & counseling, disadvantaged persons, free.

**Yakima City Division of
Employment & Training**
Yakima County Courthouse,Yakima
98901,(509)575-4252, JTPA,
job search assistance, counseling, OJT, GED, supplemental
services; economically
disadvantaged persons, free.

FOOD/CLOTHING/HOUSING

**Klickitat-Skamania Community
Development Council**
1003 E Jewett,(509)493-2662,
POB 1580,White Salmon,98672
(509)493-3954, Emergency food
and shelter.

MEDICAL/DENTAL

**Goldendale/Klickitat County
Health Center**
228 W Main,Goldendale
(509)773- 4565, Health information, limited care & services, immunizations, food
handler testing, STD, family
planning; all persons, some
free services otherwise sliding
fee.

**White Salmon/Klickitat County
Health Center**
170 N Lincoln St,White Salmon
98672,(509)493-1558, Health
information, limited care &
services, immunizations, food
handler testing, AIDS testing,
STD, WIC, must call for an
appointment, sliding fee.

SUBSTANCE ABUSE

Counseling & Resource Center
40 Skyline Hospital,White
Salmon,98672,(509)493-3400,
Certified alcohol & drug outpatient treatment, information
school, DWI client assessment.

VICTIMS

**Skamania County Council on
Domestic Violence**
POB 477, Stevenson,(509)427-
5636, Domestic violence &
sexual assault advocacy,
counseling, support, resource
services for family law issues,
sexual assault programs, free.

For additional information see also
Skamania County

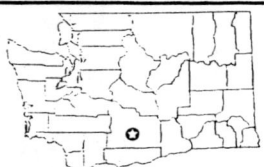

YAKIMA COUNTY

Named for the Yakima Indians.

Created: January 21, 1865

North Second and East B Streets
Yakima 98901

AREA: 4,271.1 square miles, State Ranking: 2nd

MAJOR ECONOMIC ACTIVITIES:
Wood Products, Agriculture,
Food Processing, Manufacturing,

ASSESSED VALUE: $4,445,167,391

POPULATION: (1989 Estimate): 187,800

Percentage of state: 4.0%
Density: 44.0 persons per square mile

ETHNIC BREAKDOWN: 1988 Estimate
  White   148,296
  Black   1,743
  Native American   7,142
  Asian and Pacific Islanders   1,527
  Other   27,592
    Spanish origin (included in above) 31,642

PRIMARY CITIES   Population
  Grandview   6,350
  Granger   1,825
  Mabton   1,245
  Selah   4,980
  Sunnyside   9,730
  Toppenish   6,600
  Union Gap   3,230
  Wapato   3,370
  Yakima, county seat   50,610
  Zillah   1,835

CLIMATE: Yamima – elevation 1,061 feet

Average	JAN	APR	JUL	OCT
Max Temp (F)	36.0	63.9	88.3	64.2
Min Temp	19.3	35.4	53.5	35.6
Mean Temp	28.1	49.7	70.9	50.0
Precipitation in inches	1.22	.62	.16	.47

Average Annual Maximum Temperature: 62.8

Average Annual Minimum Temperature: 36.3
Average Annual Mean Temperature: 49.6
Average Annual Precipitation: 8.03 inches

PUBLIC SCHOOL DISTRICTS

East Valley School District #90
2002 Beaudry Rd, Yakima 98901
(509)248-7757 Enrollment: 1,846

Grandview School District #116-200
913 W. Second St, Grandview 98930
(509)882-2271 Enrollment: 2,312

Granger School District #204
Box 400, Granger 98932
(509)854-1515 Enrollment: 858

Highland School District #203
POB 38, Cowiche 98923
(509)678-4173 Enrollment: 804

Mabton School District #120
Box 37, Mabton 98935, (509)894-4852
Enrollment: 554

Mount Adams School District #209
POB 578, White Swan 98952
(509)874-2611 Enrollment: 844

Moxee School District #90
(see East Valley School Dist. #90)

Naches Valley School District #JT3
POB 99, Naches 98937, (509)653-2220
Enrollment: 1,310

Selah School District #119
POB 610, Selah 98942
(509)697-7243 Enrollment: 3,045

Sunnyside School District #201
1110 S. Sixth Street, Sunnyside
98944 (509)837-5851
Enrollment: 3,610

Toppenish School District #202
106 Franklin Ave., Toppenish 98948
(509)865-4455 Enrollment: 2,577
Enrollment: 2,577

Union Gap School District #2
3200 S. Second St., Union Gap 98903
(509)248-3966 Enrollment: 405

Wapato School District #207
Box 38, Wapato 98951
(509)877-4181 Enrollment: 2,516

West Valley School District #208
8902 Zier Rd., Yakima 98908
(509)965-2000 Enrollment: 3,445

Yakima School District #7
104 N. Fourth Ave., Yakima 98902
(509)575-3208 Enrollment: 11,900

Zillah School District #205
POB 225, Zillah 98953
(509)829-5911 Enrollment: 800

HOSPITALS

Community Hospital
3003 Tieton Dr, Yakima
98902 (509)453-6561
Total Beds: 30

**Providence Center Memorial
Hospital,** POB 672, 504 W 4th
Ave, Toppenish 98948
(509)865-3105
Total Beds: 63

St. Elizabeth Medical Center
110 S 9th Ave, Yakima 98902
(509)575-5000
Total Beds: 214

Sunnyside Community Hospital
10th and Tacoma, Sunnyside
98944 (509)837-2101
Total Beds: 38

**Yakima Valley Memorial
Hospital,** 2811 Tieton Dr,
Yakima 98902 (509)575-8000
Total Beds: 226

THE COURTS

SUPERIOR COURT   Area Code (509)
North Second & "B" Sts, #323
Yakima 98901
Stephen M. Brown, Judge   575-4222
F. James Gavin, Judge   575-4223
Robert N. Hackett, Judge   575-4223
Susan L. Hahn, Judge   575-4222
Michael W. Leavitt, Judge   575-4222
Heather K. Van Nuy, Judge   575-4133

JUVENILE COURT
1728 Jerome Ave., Yakima 98902
Administrator: Paul W. Peterson
                         575-4030

DISTRICT COURTS

SUNNYSIDE
505 South Seventh St., Sunnyside 98944
George Wynn Colby, Judge   837-3713
Gloria Hintze, Admin.   865-5070

YAKIMA COUNTY
North Second & East "B" Sts, #225
Yakima 98901
Rod Fitch, Judge   575-4013
Dirk A. Marler, Judge   575-4036
Randall L. Marquis, Judge 575-4036
N.L. Pat Teague, Admin.   575-4016

SITES OF INTEREST:

Fort Simcoe
Priest Rapids
White Pass Ski Area
Yakima Indian Agency

CRISIS

Crisis Line, Yakima,(509)575-4200, Telephone crisis services; free.

MULTIPLE SERVICE CENTERS

Calvary Rescue Mission
1225 S 6th St,Yakima,98901
(509)248-0120, Counseling,
food box, limited overnight
housing, families, men; free.

**Department of Social & Health
Services,** 1002 N 16th Ave,POB
9428,Yakima,98909, 208 S 8th
St,POB 818,Sunnyside,98944
(509)837-3531, 306 Bolin Dr
POB 470,Toppenish,98948
(509)865-2805

Displaced Homemakers Program
15 N Naches Ave,Yakima,98901
(509)248-7796, Information &
referral, pre-employment
classes, women's shelter,
food, clothing, legal
assistance; 8:30-7 M-F,
females & children, sliding
fee.

Friendship House
A-7S Toppenish,98948
(509)865-4745, Counseling,
referral & support help,

clothing if needed; free.

Salvation Army, 9 S 6th
Ave,Yakima,98907,(509)453-3139
Spiritual & physical needs,
emergency food & shelter; free.

**Treatment Alternative to Street
Crime,** 128 N 2nd St,Rm 6,Yakima
(509)575-4476, Counseling,
alternative to crime; adult
felons, sliding fee.

Yakima-Kittitas Wark Release
2011 S 64th Ave,Yakima,98903
(509)575-4352, Residence,
transportation, counseling,
training, transition time,
adult felons and misdemeanors.

**Yakima Valley Farmworkers
Clinic,** POB 831,Toppenish,98948
(509)865-3054, Energy assis-
ance, referrals, dental,
alcohol & drug referral,
shelter, pre-school assistance
daycare, commodities dis-
tributor; sliding fee.

Yakima Valley OIC
1201 Fruitvale Blvd,Yakima
98902,(509)248-6751,
Energy assistance, referrals,
dental, alcohol & drug referral
shelter.

COUNSELING MENTAL/HEALTH

Catholic Family & Child Services, 303 Division Grandview,98930,(509)882-3050 5301C Tieton Dr,Yakima,98908 (509)965-7100, Counseling for family restoration, child mental health services.

Central Washington Comprehensive Mental Health 321 E Yakima Ave,Yakima,(509) 575-4024, Emergency services, substance abuse, outpatient treatment; sliding fee.

Hope Counseling Service 1015 S 40th Ave,Yakima,98908 (509)966-4744, Counseling for family, individuals & groups.

Lutheran Counsel Services of Yakima, 1604 W Yakima Ave Yakima,(509)575-0161, Individual, marriage & family counseling, therapy; sliding fee.

EMPLOYMENT & TRAINING

CAP, S 130th Arthur,Spokane 99202,(509)536-1518, Works with clients in vocational rehabilitation; 8-5 M-F; free.

City University, 501 N Naches Ave #8,Yakima,98901,(509)453-0303, Adult education, college classes toward BA & MA, working adults; adults in need of services, sliding fee.

Community Education & Counseling Services, 315 S Elm St,Toppenish (509)865-3054, Services for tutoring guidance, counseling, financial aid assistance, housing assistance, academic youth work programs; low income & those in need of services, free.

Fort Simcoe Job Corps Center Rt 1 (Hwy 220),White Swan 98952,(509)874-2244, GED preparation, skills training job counseling & placement;

youths 16 to 21 years of age, free.

Heritage College, Fort Rd at McKinley,Toppenish,98948,(509) 865-2244, Adult education, college classes; adults; sliding fee.

Job Service Center 800 E Custer,POB 747,Sunnyside 98944,(509)837-4904, 306 Division St,Yakima,98902,(509) 575-2700

Opportunities Industrialization Center, 815 Fruitvale Blvd Yakima,98902,(509)248-6936, Various programs for GED, upgrading, skill searches; low income & the unemployed, free.

People for People 302 W Lincoln,Yakima,98902 (509)248-6726, Referral service OJT, occupational internship; disadvantaged & low income persons; non-profit organization.

Perry Technical Institute 2011 Washington Ave,Yakima 98903,(509)453-0374, Training in specialized areas; adults, sliding fee.

S.L. Start & Associates 1116 B East Lincoln Ave,Yakima 98902,(509)452-4571, Skill assessment, job placement & counseling; disadvantaged youths 16 to 21 years of age, free.

Trend College, 112 Pierce Ave Yakima,98902,(509)248-4806, Training in vocational skills, business related fields; adults, siding fee.

V.R.O. 308 Monroe Ave Toppenish 98909,(509)865-5322, 1002 N 16th Ave,Yakima 98909,(509)575-2159, Helps disables state residents obtain employment; disabled physical & mental persons, free.

Washington Employment Opportunity Program,
306 Division,Yakima
(509)575-2702, Training,
education, job placement
& training.

Washington Human Development
16514 Eastway,Sunnyside,98944
(509)837-8363, 516 W 1st Ave
Toppenish,(509)865-3962, 2812
Main St,Union Gap,98903
(509)453-6771, Immigration,
OJT, job placement &
counseling; migrant seasonal
farm workers, free.

Women's Program YYCC, 16th Ave
W Nob Hill Blvd.,Yakima,98907
(509)575-2915, Aid in transition of women to school &
employment; sliding fee.

**Yakima County Employment &
Training,** Yakima County
Courthouse,Yakima,(509)575-
4252, Job search & assistance
counseling, OJT, GED, supplemental services; economically
disadvantaged persons, free.

Yakima Valley Community College
16th & Nob Hill Blvd.,Yakima
98907,(509)575-2350, Academic
& vocational courses, GED
testing, clerical skills &
English; sliding fee.

**Yakima Valley Opportunity
Individual Center,** 1815 Fir
Yakima,98902,(509)248-6751,
Training in sales & home energy,
GED, employment counseling,
disadvantaged & low income
persons, ex-offenders.

FOOD/CLOTHING/HOUSING

Union Gospel Mission
13 S Front St,Yakima,98907
(509)248-4510, Facilities to
house & feed on temporary
basis; free.

**United Indian Association of
Central Washington**
101 Butterfield Rd,Yakima
98901,(509)575-0835, Emergency
food, clothing & job placement

assistance; Urban Indians free.

LEGAL

American Civil Liberties Union
1720 Smith Tower,Seattle,98104
(206)624-2180, Advocacy for
those who believe rights have
been violated; free.

MEDICAL DENTAL

Yakima County Health District
1319 Saul Rd,Sunnyside,98944
(509)837-3411, Health information, limited care &
services, immunizations, food
handler testing; sliding fee.

MISCELLANEOUS

**Lower Valley Energy Services
Center,** 601 W First St
Toppenish,98902,(509)865-4210,
Help low income families
weatherize their homes; 8-5
M-F, low income families
free.

SUBSTANCE ABUSE

**Central Washington
Comprehensive Mental Health**
321 E Yakima Ave,(509)575-4084
220 W 4th Ave,Ellensburg,98926
(509)925-9861, Certified drug
outpatient treatment,
methadone treatment, crisis
intervention, outpatient
treatment; sliding fee.

Chemical People, 909 Coach
Court,Yakima,98908,(509)966-
7527, Provides information on
drug abuse, liaison agencies
involved in prevention; free.

Community Alcohol & Drug Center
102 S Naches,Yakima,98901,(509)
248-1800, Alcohol & drug
evaluation, DWI assessments,
deferred prosecution
evaluations, employee assistance, information & referrals,
intensive outpatient treatment,
support groups.

James Oldham Treatment Center
308 N 4th St,Yakima,98901
(509) 457-1623, 30 day
intensive inpatient treatment,
60 day recovery house, extended
care recovery house, information & referrals.

Omni Clinic, 401 S 5th,Ave
98907,(509)453-2900, Certified
alcohol & drug outpatient
treatment, information school,
DWI client assessment, referrals & counseling; sliding
free.

Substance Abuse Program
604 W Fourth,Toppenish,98948
(509)865-5352, 321 E Yakima
Ave,Yakima,98907,(509)575-4084,
1319 Saul Rd,Sunnyside,98944
(509)837-2089, Outpatient
alcohol & drug treatment
program, crisis intervention,
outpatient theraphy, family
counseling; sliding fee.

Sundown M Ranch, 2280 SR A21
POB 217,Yakima,98942
(509)457-0990, Certified
alcohol & drug inpatient
treatment, DWI client assessment, family counseling.

TASC of Yakima County
128 N 2nd St,Yakima,98901
(509)575-4472, Alcohol & drug
assessment & treatment, court
monitoring, patient referrals;
sliding fee.

The Promise, Highland Dr,Buena
98921,(509)865-2000, Certified
alcohol & drug inpatient
treatment.

Valley Alcohol Council
702 Franklin,POB 291,Sunnyside
98944,(509)837-7700, Certified
alcohol & drug information
school, DWI client assessment,
outpatient treatment.

**Yakima County DWI Assessment
Service,** Yakima County
Courthouse,Yakima,98901,
Certified alcohol & drug out-
patient treatment, DWI client
assessment.

**Yakima Indian Nation
Comprehensive,** POB 523
Toppenish,98948,(509)865-4333
Provides services to families
affected by alcohol,
detoxification, information
school.

TRANSPORTATION

Yakima Transit
2301 Fruitvale Blvd.
Yakima,98902,(509)575-6175,
35¢, $12.00 monthly.

VETERANS SERVICES

Ms Linda Ettl
654 Brathovde Rd,Selah,98942
(509)697-3815, Delayed stress
counseling.

Veterans Affairs Office
16th & Nob Hill Blvd.,Yakima
98907,(509)575-2372,
Assistance to all veterans in
eduction; free.

VICTIMS

**Crisis & Support Services
Lower Valley,** 1319 Saul Rd
Sunnyside,98944,(509)837-6689,
Counseling victims of abuse,
treatment, domestic violence &
sexual assault, anger
management; sliding fee.

Sexual Assault, 321 E Yakima
Ave,Yakima,98907,(509)575-4084,
Assistance with sexual assault
victims and families, public
education, family law resources
sexual assault victims, sliding
fee.

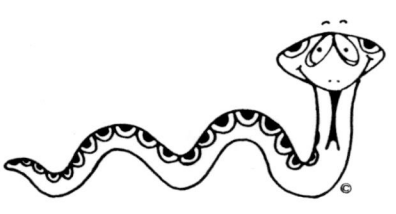

NORTHWEST

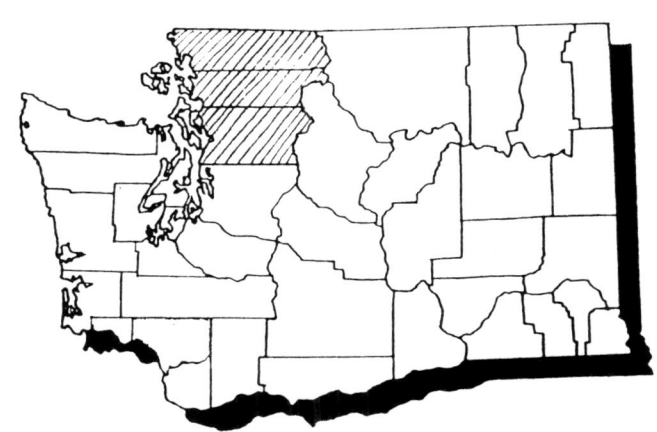

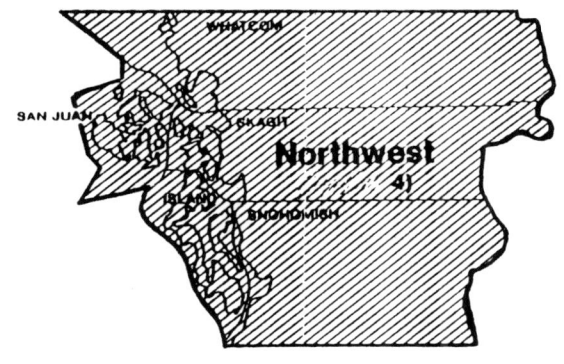

NORTHWEST WASHINGTON
TOURISM ASSOCIATION
POB 922, Langley 98260
(206)221-TOUR

Island

San Juan

Skagit

Snohomish

Whatcom

HISTORICAL APPEAL

Western Washington Museum of
History and Art, Bellingham

Peace Arch Park, Blaine

Orcas Island Historical Museum
Eastsound

Edmonds Museum, Edmonds

Snohomish County Historical
Museum, Everett

Hovander Homestead, Ferndale

Pioneer Park, Ferndale

San Juan Historical Museum
Friday Harbor

© 1981 VOLK

The Whale Museum, Friday Harbor

Skagit County Historical Museum
La Conner

Lopez Historical Museum, Lopez
Village

Lynden Pioneer Museum, Lynden

San Juan Island National
Historic Park, San Juan Island

Blackman Museum, Snohomish

> **THE MOUNTAIN PASSES...**
> The five main mountain
> passes through the
> Cascade Range is:
> Stevens, White, Cayuse,
> Blewitt, and Snoqualmie

CITIES

ANACORTES
Chamber of Commerce
1319 Commercial Ave, 98221
(206)293-3832

ARLINGTON
Arlington Chamber of Commerce
POB 102,Arlington,98223,(206)
435-3708

BELLINGHAM
Bellingham/Whatcom County
Visitors & Convention Bureau
904 Potter St,Suite D
Bellingham,(206)671-3990

Whatcom Chamber of Commerce,POB
958,Bellingham,98226,(206)734-
1330

Bellingham is the eighth
largest city in Washington
with a population of 47,290.
It is the seat of **Whatcom
County** and a port of entry.
It is located on Bellingham
Bay, 80 miles north of
Seattle, near the Canadian
Border. Products include
lumber, paper, and canned
salmon. It is the home of
Western Washington
University.

BIRCH BAY
Birch Bay Chamber of Commerce
4897 Birch Bay-Lynden Rd, Birch
Bay,98230,(206)371-7675

BLAINE
Blaine Chamber of Commerce
POB 1718,Blaine,98230,(206)
332-6484

BURLINGTON
Burlington Chamber of Commerce
POB 522,145 W Rio Vista
Burlington,98233,(206)755-9382

CAMANO ISLAND
Camano Island Chamber of
Commerce,4008 SW Camano Dr
Camano Island,98292,(206)
387-7475

CONCRETE
Concrete Visitor's Center
115 Railroad Ave,Concrete
98237,(206)853-8400

DARRINGTON
Darrington Chamber of Commerce
POB 351,Darrington,98241
(206)436-1260

EDMONDS
Edmonds Chamber of Commerce
POB 146,Edmonds 98020
(206)776-6711

EVERETT
Everett Area Chamber of
Commerce, POB,1086,Everett
98206, (206)252-5181

TALLEST BUILDING...
The Columbia Center
Building in Seattle is
the tallest building
west of Chicago. It is
943 feet high and has
76 Stories.

The largest building in
the world is the Boeing
Assembly Plan in
Everett, Snohomish
County.

**THE LARGEST MARINA IN
WASH...**Is the Port of
Everett, Snohomish
County. One of the
Founding Fathers of
Everett was John D.
Rockefeller.

**WHAT IS THE LARGEST
BUILDING IN WASH?...**
The Boeing 747 and 767
Aircraft Assembly Plant
in Everett, Snohomish
County, is the largest
building in the world.
It's 11 stories covers
62 acres and can house
8 747s and 8 767s at
the same time.

Everett is the fifth largest city in Washington with a population of 64,170. It is the seat of **Snohomish County**. Everett is located on Puget Sound, 30 miles north of Seattle, and has an excellent port. The city has lumber and paper mills, and also produces machinery, fabricated metal products, and foods. A large Boeing Aircraft plant is located here.

FERNDALE
Ferndale Chamber of Commerce
5640 Riverside Dr,Ferndale
98248, (206)384-3042

GLACIER
Mt Baker Foothills Chamber of
Commerce,POB 5,Glacier,98244,
(206)599-2991

LA CONNER
LaConner Chamber of Commerce &
Visitor Information Center
Limedock Bldg 109 1st St,POB
644,LaConner,98257
(206)466-4778

LAKE STEVENS
Greater Lake Stevens Chamber
of Commerce, 809 Vernon Rd
POB 1092, Lake Stevens 98258
(206)334-0433

LYNDEN
Lynden Chamber of Commerce
POB 647,1775 Front St,Lynden
98264

LYNNWOOD
Snohomish Visitor Information
Center, 1331 164th St,SW
Lynnwood 98036,(206)745-4133

MARBLEMOUNT
Marblemount Chamber of Commerce
c/o Marblemount Community Club,
Marblemount 98267,(206)873-4274

MARYSVILLE
Marysville Chamber of Commerce
POB 151,1324 4th St,Marysville
98270, (206)659-7700

SKAGIT EAGLE RESERVE...
Located in Skagit County, this reserve's 1500 acres has one of the largest wintering populations of Bald Eagles in the nation.

THE WONDERLAND TRAIL...
This is a 90 mile hiking trail that circles Mt Rainier.

THE RAINBOW BRIDGE...
It is almost the exact color as the Golden Gate Bridge in SF Calif. It was build in 1958 and crosses the Swinomish Channel in La Conner.   Skagit

MONROE
Sky Valley Chamber of Commerce
211 E Main St,Monroe,98272
(206)794-5488

MOUNT VERNON
Mount Vernon Chamber of
Commerce,325 E College Way,POB
1007,Mt Vernon,98273,(206)428-
8547

POINT ROBERTS
Point Roberts Chamber of
Commerce,79 Tyee Dr,Box 128
Point Roberts,98281
(206)945-2313

SAN JUAN ISLANDS

* LOPEZ ISLAND
Lopez Island Chamber of
Commerce,POB 102,Lopez
Island,98261,(206)468-3800

* ORCAS ISLAND
Orcas Island Chamber of
Commerce,POB 252,Eastsound
Orcas Island,98245

* SAN JUAN ISLAND

** Friday Harbor

** Roche Harbor

SEDRO WOOLLEY
Sedro Woolley Chamber of
Commerce,714 Matcalf St,Sedro
Woolley,98284

SMOKEY POINT
Smokey Point Area,POB
188,Lakewood,98259
(206)652-6637

SNOHOMISH
Snohomish Chamber of Commerce
116 Ave B,Snohomish,98290
(206)568-2526

STANDWOOD
Stanwood Chamber of Commerce
711 90th Ave NE.POB 641
Standwood,98292,(206)629-4525

SULTAN
Sultan Business Associates
Chamber of Commerce,POB
46,Sultan,98294,(206)793-2215

THE WASHINGTON CHEESE COMPANY...Located in Mt Vernon, Skagit County, makes about 65,000 pounds of cheese annually. It has over 12 wonderful varieties.

KILLER WHALES...
Lime Kiln State Park on San Juan Island is the only park in the nation established solely for the purpose of watching whales. At the south tip of the Island is Cattle Point, a nice place to see Minke Whales.

WHIDBEY ISLAND
Central Whidbey Chamber of
Commerce,POB
152,Coupeville,98239
(206)678-5434

* **CLINTON**

* **COUPEVILLE**

* **FREELAND**
Freeland Chamber of
Commerce,POB631,Freeland,98249
(206)221-3171

* **GREENBANK**

* **LANGLEY**
Langley Chamber of Commerce
220 First St, POB 403, 98260
(206)321-6765

* **OAKHARBOR**
Greater Oak Chamber of
Commerce,5506 SR 20,POB 883,Oak
Harbor,98277,(206)675-3535

WHIDBEY ISLAND
...Located in Island
County, is the second
largest island in the
48 contiguous United
States. It is 50 miles
long, Long Island in
New York is the
largest.

LIBERTY BELL MOUNTAIN
...Is an impressive
7,600 foot jagged
mountain on Highway 20
near Washington Pass in
the North Cascades.

FAIRS AND FESTIVALS

Mystery Weekend
Langley, February
(206)321-6765

Skagit Valley Tulip Festival
Anacortes, Burlington,
LaConner, Mount Vernon,
Sedro Woolley
April (206)428-8547

Ski to Sea
Bellingham, May
(206)384-6452

Loggerodeo
Sedro Woolley, June
(206)855-1841

**Annual Whidbey Island
Regatta**
Oak Harbor, July
(206)675-3535

Arts & Crafts Festival
Anacortes, August
(206)293-3832

Orcas Island Library Fair
Eastbound, August
(206)376-4985

San Juan County Fair
Friday Harbor, August
(206)378-4310

Taste of Edmonds
Edmonds, August
(206)776-6711

**Washington State
International Air Fair**
Everett, August
(206)355-2266

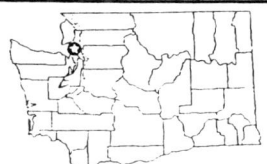

ISLAND COUNTY

island
The name is descriptive.

Created: January 6, 1853

1 NE Seventh Street, Couperville 98239

AREA: 211.6 square miles, State Ranking: 38th

MAJOR ECONOMIC ACTIVITIES:
Manufacturing, Agriculture and Fishing,
Tourism, Wood Products

ASSESSED VALUE: $2,399,207,560

POPULATION: (1989 Estimate): 55,300

Percentage of state: 1.2%
Density: 261.3 persons per square mile

ETHNIC BREAKDOWN: 1988 Estimate
    White   47,838
    Black   952
    Native American   508
    Asian and Pacific Islanders   2,507
    Other   1,595
       Spanish origin (included in above)   2,208

PRIMARY CITIES   Population
    Couperville, county seat   1,295
    Langley   785
    Oak Harbor   14,790

CLIMATE: Couperville – elevation 73 feet

Average	JAN	APR	JUL	OCT
Max Temp (F)	43.3	57.2	71.3	57.9
Min Temp	33.3	40.2	50.5	43.0
Mean Temp	38.5	48.7	60.9	50.5
Precipitation in inches	2.01	1.12	.67	1.73

Average Annual Maximum Temperature: 57.4
Average Annual Minimum Temperature: 41.9
Average Annual Mean Temperature: 49.7
Average Annual Precipitation: 17.73 inches

PUBLIC SCHOOL DISTRICTS

Couperville School District #204
POB 726, Couperville 98239
(206)678-4522
Enrollment: 730

Oak Harbor School District #201
1250 Midway Blvd, Oak Harbor 98277
(206)679-5800, Enrollment: 5,610

South Widbey School District #206
POB 346, Langley 98260, (206)3210-6100
Enrollment: 1,616

HOSPITAL

Whidbey General Hospital
Main St, POB 400
Coupeville 98239
(206)678-5151
Total Beds: 51

THE COURTS

SUPERIOR COURT   Area Code (206)
Sixth & Main, POB 5000, Coupeville 98239
Allan R. Hancock, Judge 679-7361
Richard L. Pitt, Judge 679-7361
County Clerk, 679-7359

JUVENILE COURT
502 N Main, POB 5000, Coupville 98239
Administrator: Elizabeth A. McKay 679-7325

DISTRICT COURT
7006 70th NE, Oak Harbor 98277
Merle E. Wilcox, Judge 675-5988

SITES OF INTEREST:

Historic Coupeville
Whidbey Island
Camano Island

CRISIS

North Whidbey Help
4029 40th,Northwest,Oak Harbor
98277,(206)675-3888, 24 hour
crisis line.

COUNSELING MENTAL/HEALTH

**Catholic Community Service
Northwest,** 5047 50th NW,Oak
Harbor,(206)679-1502, Mental
health counseling, all persons
sliding fee.

Island Mental Health Center
904 N.Main,Copeville,98239
(206)678-5555, POB 160,Coupe-
ville,(206)321-4868, Out-
patient treatment, family
therapy, assessment,
individual & group counseling
child abuse programs;
8:30-5 M-F, residents of
city, sliding fee.

EMPLOYMENT & TRAINING

Northwest Washington Private Industry Council, POB 2009 Bellingham,(206)671-1660, JTPA, job search assistance, counseling, OJT, GED, supplemental services, economically disadvantaged persons, fee.

FAMILY PLANNING

Planned Parenthood POB 125,Oak Harbor,98277,(206) 679-3404, Family planning, pregnancy.

Pregnancy Aid, (206)321-4767, Pregnancy counseling for those in need of services.

FOOD/CLOTHING/HOUSING

Good Cheer, (206)321-6451, Thrift store & food bank.

Helphouse, (206)675-0681, Food bank.

Island County Housing Authority, 7 NW 6th St Coupeville,98239,(206)678-4181 Housing referrals for low income persons.

SUBSTANCE ABUSE

Camano-Whidbey Addiction Services, 2134 200th,Ave.W Suite 1,Oak Harbor,98277 (206)679-4525, Certified alcohol & drug outpatient treatment, information school, DWI client assessment; 8:30-4:30 M-F, sliding fee.

Herbert Johnson Clinic 2090 300th SW,Oak Harbor,98277 (206)675-7984, Certified alcohol & drug information school, DWI client assessment, alcohol outpatient treatment, mental health care; 24 hour line, sliding fee.

TRANSPORTATION

Inland Transit, 1180 S.Highway 20,POB 1097,Caupeville,98239 (206)678-7771, Free system.

VICTIMS

Citizens Against Domestic Violence, POB 796, Langley 98260 (206)321-4181, POB 190,Oak Harbor,98277 (206)321-2232, Domestic violence advocacy, support groups & referrals, safehomes resources available with family law issues, sexual assault programs; 24 hours, free.

For additional information see also Skagit County

SAN JUAN COUNTY

Named for Juan Francisco de Eliza, a lieutenant
in the Spanish Army and governor of the
short-lived Spanish settlement at Nootka Sound.

Created: October 31, 1873

350 Court Street, Friday Harbor 98250

AREA: 179.3 square miles, State Ranking: 39th

MAJOR ECONOMIC ACTIVITIES:
Agriculture and Fishing,
Tourism

ASSESSED VALUE: $1,153,750,306

POPULATION: (1989 Estimate): 9,700

Percentage of state: 0.2%
Density: 54.1 persons per square mile

ETHNIC BREAKDOWN:	1988 Estimate
White	9,307
Black	12
Native American	73
Asian and Pacific Islanders	70
Other	138
Spanish origin (included in above)	105

PRIMARY CITIES	Population
Friday Harbor, county seat	1,540

CLIMATE: Olga - elevation 80 feet

Average	JAN	APR	JUL	OCT
Max Temp (F)	43.6	57.0	70.0	58.0
Min Temp	33.6	40.2	48.9	43.7
Mean Temp	38.6	48.6	59.6	50.9
Precipitation in inches	4.04	1.65	.88	3.04

Average Annual Maximum Temperature: 57.2
Average Annual Minimum Temperature: 41.7
Average Annual Mean Temperature: 49.5
Average Annual Precipitation: 28.78 inches

PUBLIC SCHOOL DISTRICTS

Lopez School District #144

Route 1, Box 1190, Lopez 98261
(206)468-2201   Enrollment: 205

Orcas Island School District #137
POB 167, Eastsound 98245
(206)376-2284   Enrollment: 385

San Juan Island School District #149
85 Blair St., POB 458
Friday Harbor 98250
(206)378-4133   Enrollment: 702

Shaw Island School District #10
Shaw Island 98286, (206)468-2570
Enrollment: 12

THE COURTS

SUPERIOR COURT   Area Code (206)
350 Court St, POB 1249, Friday Harbor,
WA 98250
Allan R. Hancock, Judge   378-2399
Richard L. Pitt, Judge   378-2399
Mary Jean Cahail,   County Clerk:
                              378-2163
JUVENILE COURT
135-A Rhone St, POB 1055, Friday Harbor,
WA 98250, Administrator: Tom Kearney
                              378-4620
DISTRICT COURT
Second & Court Sts, POB 127, Friday Harbor,
WA 98250
John O. Linde, Judge   378-4017
Marion Melville, Chief Clerk 378-4017

SITES OF INTEREST:

American Camp, English Camp

CRISIS

**Emergency Number Dial "0"
ask for Zenith 8750.**

msc

**Department of Social & Health
Services**
355A Spring St, POB 1215, Friday
Harbor, 98250, (206)241-2255.

Friday Harbor Fire Department
60 2nd St, Friday Harbor, 98250
(206)378-4117, 378-4183
Community services, those in
need of services.

COUNSELING MENTAL/HEALTH

**North Island Counseling &
Psychotherapy**
820 Guard, Friday Harbor, (206)
378-2669, Orcas Island, (206)
376-2272, Mental health
outpatient individual & group
counseling, information,
assessment, referral; sliding
fee.

EMPLOYMENT & TRAINING

**Northwest Washington Private
Industry Council**
POB 2009, Bellingham, (206)671-

1660, JTPA, job search assistance, counseling, OJT, GED, supportive services; economically disadvantaged persons, free.

Vocational Services Northwest 611 W. Division,Mount Vernon 98273,(206)336-3136, 2215 Elm St,Bellingham,98225,(206) 676-1660, Resume preparation, employment counseling, placement & job referral; 9-5 M-F, ex-offenders, free.

FOOD/CLOTHING/HOUSING

Orcas Food Bank Orcas,98280,(206)367-2677

San Juan Food Bank, County Fairgrounds,Friday Harbor 98250,(206)378-4820

MEDICAL/DENTAL

San Juan County Health Department, 145 Rhone, POB 607 Friday Harbor,98250,(206)378-4474, Health information, limited care & services, immunizations, food handler testing, AIDS testing, WIC program, maternal & child health; sliding fee.

SUBSTANCE ABUSE

Community Alcohol Center 5047 S NW,Oak Harbor,98377 (206)679-1502, Information referral, detoxification, outpatient counseling, alcohol information school, involuntary commitment; sliding fee.

San Juan Community Alcoholism Center, 842 Guard St,Friday Harbor,(206)378-4994, Certified alcohol & drug outpatient treatment, information school, DWI client assessment, ADATSA; sliding fee.

VICTIMS

Volunteers Against Violence Star Route Box 115,Eastsound 98245,(206)562-6025, POB 325

Friday Harbor,98250, Route 1 Box 1813,Lopez,98261, Domestic violence advocacy, safehome.

For additional information see also Island and Skagit Counties

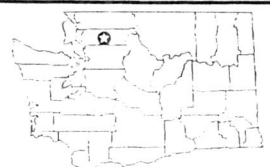

SKAGIT COUNTY

Named for the Skagit Indians.

Created: November 28, 1883

205 Kincaid Street, Mount Vernon 98273

AREA: 1,734.6 square miles, State Ranking: 25th

MAJOR ECONOMIC ACTIVITIES:
Wood Products, Agriculture,
Petroleum and Coal Processing
Food Processing

ASSESSED VALUE: $2,897,836,943

POPULATION: (1989 Estimate): 72,400

Percentage of state: 1.6%
Density: 41.7 persons per square mile

ETHNIC BREAKDOWN:	1988 Estimate
White	66,145
Black	110
Native American	1,328
Asian and Pacific Islanders	522
Other	2,695
Spanish origin (included in above)	2,905

PRIMARY CITIES	Population
Anacortes	10,600
Burlington	3,830
Mount Vernon, county seat	14,790
Sedro Woolley	6,430

CLIMATE: Mount Vernon – elevation 29 feet

Average	JAN	APR	JUL	OCT
Max Temp (F)	45.1	58.2	75.1	60.3
Min Temp	32.5	39.4	49.3	42.3
Mean Temp	38.8	48.8	62.2	51.3
Precipitation in inches	4.22	2.40	.81	3.60

Average Annual Maximum Temperature: 59.5
Average Annual Minimum Temperature: 41.0
Average Annual Mean Temperature: 50.3
Average Annual Precipitation: 32.15 inches

PUBLIC SCHOOL DISTRICTS

Anacortes School District #103
2200 M Ave., Anacortes 98221
(206)293-1200   Enrollment: 2,276

Burlington-Edison School District #100
927 E. Fairhaven Ave., Burlington 98233
(206)757-3311   Enrollment: 2,591

Concrete School District #11
Box 386, Concrete 98237
Enrollment: 650

Conway School District #317
1798 E. Conway Hill Ln.
Mount Vernon 98273   (206)445-5785
Enrollment: 350

La Conner School District #311
Box D, La Conner 98257
(206)466-3171   Enrollment: 470

Mount Vernon School District #320
124 E Lawrence St, Mount Vernon 98273
(206)428-6110   Enrollment: 3,950

Sedro-Woolley School District #101
2079 Cook Rd, Sedro-Woolley 98284
(206)856-0831   Enrollment: 3,047

HOSPITALS

Island Hospital
1211 24th St, Anacortes
98221 (206)293-3181
Total Beds: 43

**Skagit Valley Hospital And
Health Center**
1415 Kincaid St, Mt Vernon
98273 (206)424-4111
Total Beds: 137

United General Hospital
POB 410, Sedro Woolley
98284 (206)856-6021
Total Beds: 97

THE COURTS

SUPERIOR COURT Area Code (206)
202 Courthouse, Mount Vernor, WA 98273
Stan K. Bruhn,   Judge   336-9320
Gilbert E. Mullen, Judge   336-9320
Phyllis Coole-McKeehen, County Clerk
                         336-9440

JUVENILE COURT
Courthouse Annex, Mount Vernon, WA 98273, Administrator: Terry Rousseau
336-9360

DISTRICT COURT
Public Safety Bldg, 600 S. Third, Mount Vernon, WA 98273
Eugene C. Anderson, Judge   336-9319
Larry E. Moller, Judge   336-9319
Pamela K. Terwilliger, Court Administrator:
336-9319

SITES OF INTEREST

Upper and Lower Baker Dam
David Douglas Marker
Mount Logan

MULTIPLE SERVICE CENTERS

Department of Social & Health Services, 1800 Continental Pl Mount Vernon,98273,(206)428-1400

Housing Authority of Skagit County
2405 Austin Ln,Mount Vernon,(206)428-1959, Energy assistance, referrals, dental, alcohol & drug referral, shelter, pre-school assistance, daycare, commodities distributor; 8-5 M-F; sliding fee.

Skagit County Community Action Agency, POB 1507, Mount Vernon (206)339-9200, Energy assistance, referrals, dental, alcohol & drug referral, shelter, pre-school assistance, daycare, commodities distributor; 8-5 M-F; sliding fee.

COUNSELING MENTAL/HEALTH

Bethesda-Cascade
1155 N State,Rm 323,Bellingham 98225,(206)676-9535, Individual alcohol, marriage and family counseling; sliding fee.

Catholic Community Services Northwest, 1517 S 2nd St,Mount Vernon,98273,(206)336-6686, Mental health counseling; sliding fee.

Skagit County Mental Health Center, 208 Kincaid,Mount Vernon,(206)336-3193, Emergency services, substance abuse outpatient treatment; sliding fee.

EMPLOYMENT & TRAINING

Job Service Center, 320 Pacific Pl,POB 160,Mount Vernon,(206) 428-1300

Northwest Intertribal Council POB 115,Neah Bay,98257,(206) 645-2201, Vocational counseling assessment training, employment assistance, headstart program; native americans, free.

Northwest Washington Private Industry Council, POB 2009 Bellingham,(206)671-1660, JTPA, job search assistance, counseling, OJT, GED, supplemental services; economically disadvantaged persons, free.

Skagit Valley College, 2405 E College Way,Mount Vernon 98273,(206)428-1261, Academic & vocational courses, GED testing; adults 16+ years of age.

Vocational Services Northwest 611 W Division,Mount Vernon 98273,(206)336-3136, 2215 Elm St,Bellingham,98225,(206) 676-1660, Resume preparation,

employment counseling, placement & job referrals.

Washington Human Development
1615 S 2nd St,Mount Vernon
(206)336-6507, Immigration
services, ESL, ABE, GED, job
development, placement,
vocational counseling; migrant
seasonal farm workers.

FOOD/CLOTHING/HOUSING

Anacortes 100, 512 4th
S,Anacortes,98221,(206)293-
6885, Food and shelter.

Friendship House, 1008 S 3rd
Mount Vernon,98273,(206)336-
5533, Shelter; those in need
of services.

Neighbor in Need, 209 Milwaukee
St,Mount Vernon,98273,(206)
424-6829, Food bank.

**Stagit Valley Displaced
Homemaker Program**
2405 College Way,Mount Vernon
98273,(206)428-1261, Array
of services for displaced
homemakers.

V.R.O.-FLP Mount Vernon
330 Pacific Point, Mount
Vernon,98273,(206)428-1405,
1800 Continental Pl,Mount
Vernon,(206)428-1542, Helps
displaced state residents obtain employment; disabled,
physical & mental persons,
free.

MEDICAL/DENTAL

Skagit County Health Department
Courthouse Administration
Building, Mount Vernon,98273
(206)336-9380, Health information, limited care & services
immunizations, food handler
testing.

SUBSTANCE ABUSE

Pioneer Center North, 2268 Hus
Dr,Sedro Woolly,98284,(206)
856-3186, Certified alcohol
long term residential; sliding
fee.

Skagit County on Alcoholism
1905 Continental Plaza,Mount
Vernon,98273,(206)428-7835,
Certified alcohol & drug outpatient treatment, information
school, DWI client assessment,
alcohol recovery program,
family awareness; 8-5 M-F;
fee.

Skagit Community Mental Health
208 Kincaid,Mount Vernon,98273
(206)856-3186, Certified drug
outpatient treatment.

VICTIMS

**Skagit Rape Relief/Battered
Women Services,** POB 301,Mount
Vernon,98273,(206)336-9593,
Domestic violence, sexual
assault advocacy, counseling
& support groups, resources
available with family law
issues, emergency shelter,
food, clothing.

For additional information see also
Island and San Juan Counties

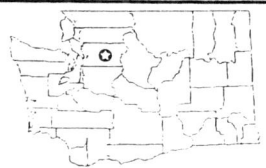

SNOHOMISH COUNTY

Named for the Snohomish Indians.

Created: January 14, 1896
3000 Rockefeller Avenue, Everett 98201

AREA: 2,098.2 square miles, State Ranking: 13th

MAJOR ECONOMIC ACTIVITIES:
Wood Products, Food Processing,
Transportation Equipment Manufacturing
Electronic and Electrical Equipment

ASSESSED VALUE: $16,610,429,447

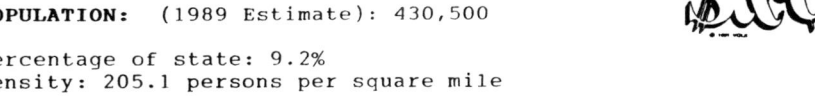

POPULATION: (1989 Estimate): 430,500

Percentage of state: 9.2%
Density: 205.1 persons per square mile

ETHNIC BREAKDOWN:	1988 Estimate
White	381,805
Black	3,172
Native American	5,695
Asian and Pacific Islanders	10,166
Other	8,662
Spanish origin (included in above)	10,830

PRIMARY CITIES	Population
Edmonds	29,720
Everett, county seat	64,170
Lynnwood	26,280
Marysville	8,150
Mill Creek	5,920
Mountlake Terrace	17,590
Mukilteo	6,130
Snohomish	5,860

CLIMATE: Everett – elevation 36 feet

Average	JAN	APR	JUL	OCT
Max Temp (F)	44.6	58.8	72.4	59.8
Min Temp	32.6	40.4	52.3	43.8
Mean Temp	38.6	49.6	62.4	51.8
Precipitation in inches	4.45	2.39	.93	3.54

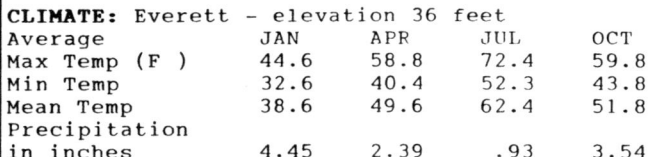

Average Annual Maximum Temperature: 58.8
Average Annual Minimum Temperature: 42.4
Average Annual Mean Temperature: 50.6
Average Annual Precipitation: 35.24 inches

PUBLIC SCHOOL DISTRICTS

Arlington School District #16
600 E First St.,POB 309
Arlington 98223,   (206)435-2156
Enrollment: 3,375

Darrington School District #330
Box 27, Darrington 98241
(206)436-1323   Enrollment: 530

Edmonds School District #15
3800 196th SW, Lynnwood 98036
(206)670-7000   Enrollment: 17,837

Everett School District #2
4730 Colby Ave.,POB 2098
Everett 98203 (206)339-4200
Enrollment: 14,377

Granite Falls School District #332
Box H, Granite Falls 98252
(206)691-7717   Enrollment: 1,124

Index School District #63
436 Index Ave., Index 98256
(206)793-1330   Enrollment: 40

Lake Stevens School District #4
12708 20th St NE, Lake Stevens 98258
(206)335-1500   Enrollment: 3,839

Lakewood School District #306
17110 16th Dr, NE, POB 220
Lakewood 98259,   (206)652-7519
Enrollment: 1,506

Marysville School District #25
4220 80th St NE, Marysville 98270
(206)653-7058   Enrollment: 7,826

Monroe School District #6
Ferry & Fremont, Monroe 98272
(206)794-7777   Enrollment: 3,565

Mukilteo School District #6
9401 Sharon Dr., Everett 98204
(206)356-1220   Enrollment: 9,091

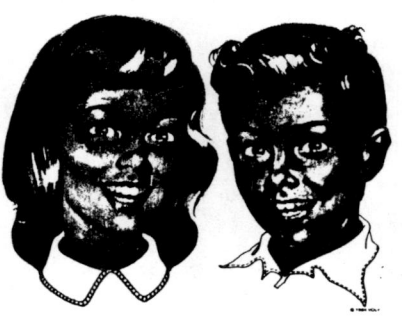

Snohomish School District #201
301 Union Ave., Snohomish 98290
(206)568-3151   Enrollment: 7,270

Stanwood School District #401
POB 430, Stanwood 98292
(206)629-9575   Enrollment: 2,507

Sultan School District #311
Box 399, Sultan 98294
(206)793-0111   Enrollment: 1,400

HOSPITALS

Cascade Valley Hospital
330 S Stillaguamish, Box 370
Arlington 98223
(206)435-2133
Total Beds: 48

**General Hospital Medical
Center,** POB 1147, Everett
98206 (206)258-6300
Total Beds: 257

Providence Hospital
POB 1067, 916 Pacific Ave
Everett 98201 (206)258-7123
Total Beds: 218

Stevens Memorial Hospital
21600 76th Ave W
Edmonds 98020 (206)774-0555
Total Beds: 217

Valley General Hospital
14701 179th SE
Monroe 98272 (206)794-7497
Total Beds: 72

THE COURTS

SUPERIOR COURT   Area Code (206)
3000 Rockefeller Ave, Everett, WA 98201
Robert C. Bibb, Judge   388-3608
Stuart C. French, Judge   388-3418
Paul D. Hansen, Judge   388-3607
Daniel T. Kershner, Judge   388-3356
Gerald L. Knight, Judge   388-3571
James H. Allendoefer, Judge 388-3408
Joseph A. Thibodeau, Judge 388-3421
Richard Thorpe, Judge   388-3532
John F. Wilson, Judge   388-3449
Kathryn E. Trumbull, Judge 388-3607
Kay D. Anderson, County Clerk:
                              388-3543

JUVENILE COURT
2801 Tenth St, Everett, WA 98201
Administrator: Michael F. Sullivan
                              259-0031

DISTRICT COURT
Cascade
415 E. Burke, Arlington, WA 98223
Jay F. Wisman, Judge   652-9552
Jill Koepp, Court Administrator:
                              652-9552

Everett
3000 Rockefeller Ave, Everett, WA 98201
Thomas Kelly, Judge   388-3533
Donald E. Priest, Judge   388-3580
Lois A. Eaden, Court Administrator:
                              388-3590

Evergreen
14414 179th St, POB 625, Monroe, WA 98272
Steven M. Clough, Judge   794-8033 or 568-8572
Karen A. Wick, Court Administrator: 794-8033
South
20520 68th Ave West, Lynnwood, WA 98036
Robert E. Schillberg, Judge   774-8803
W. Laurence Wilson, Judge   774-8803
Thomas J. Wynne, Judge   774-8803
Carol J. Wilson, Court Administrator:
                                   774-8803

SITES OF INTEREST

Wallace Falls, Glacier Peak
Sunset Falls, Culmback Dam

CRISIS

Care Crisis Lone
POB 839,Everett,98206,(206)
258-4357, Crisis assessment,
information & referral, phone
only.

MULTIPLE SERVICE CENTERS

**Department of Social & Health
Services,** 840 N Broadway,Bldg
A,Everett,98201,(206)339-4000,
21309 44th Ave W,Mountlake
Terrace,98043,(206)775-5555,
3310 Smokey Point Dr,POB
3099,Arlington,98223,(206)
653-0500.

Northshore Multi Service Center
18220 96th Ave NE,Bothell,98011
(206)485-6521, Referrals to
other community agencies; disadvantaged & unemployed persons, free.

Prison Fellowship USA, POB 2426
Everett,98203,(206)353-9079,
Counseling, educational training & job training; ex-offenders.

**Snohomish County Human Services
Department,** 1316 Wall,Everett
98201,(206)339-9200, Energy
assistance, referrals, dental,
alcohol & drug referral,
shelter, pre-school assistance,
daycare, commodities dis-
tributor; 8-5 M-F; sliding
fee.

COUNSELING MENTAL/HEALTH

Counterpoint, 6520 212th St
SW,Lynnwood,98036,(206)778-2644
Emergency services, substance
abuse, outpatient treatment;
sliding fee.

Family Counseling Services
111 SE Everett Mall Way,Suite
1,Everett,(206)348-5989, Emergency services, substance abuse
outpatient treatment; sliding
fee.

Luther Child Center, POB 2097
Everett,98203,(206)258-2371,
Emergency services, substance
abuse, outpatient treatment;
sliding fee.

**Mental Health Services of
Snohomish County,**   4526 Federal
Ave,Everett,(206)252-7154,
Mental health services; sliding
fee.

Mental Health Services
1712 Pacific Ave,Everett,98201
(206)258-1504, Therapy to
children & adult survivors of
domestic violence, sexual
assault child abuse; those
in need of services, $50.00
per hour.

EMPLOYMENT & TRAINING

Division of Vocational

Rehabilitation, 840 N Broadway
Everett,(206)339-4800,
Vocational rehabilitation
training, job placement,
counseling; 8-5 M-F, free.

Edmonds Community College
20000 68th Ave W,Lynnwood
(206)771-8385, Academic &
vocational courses, GED
testing; adults.

Everett Community College
801 Eastmore Ave,Everett,98201
(206)259-7151, Academic &
vocational courses, GED
testing; adults.

Everett Public Library
2702 Hoyt Ave,Everett,98201
(206)259-8790, Educational &
job information, GED testing,
SAT & Civil Service testing,
financial aid information.

Interaction, 1148 NW Leary
Way,Seattle,98107,(206)784-7744
Resume preparation, job readiness & job assistance; physically & developmentally
disabled persons, free.

Job Service Center
840 Broadway N, POB 870,Everett
98206,(206)339-4901.

M-2 Job Therapy, 205 Ave C
Snohomish,98290,(206)468-3268,
Counseling, job placement,
referrals for supportive services; ex-offenders and substance abusers, free.

**North Puget Sound Operation
Improvement Foundation**
2932 Hoyt,Everett,(206)258-1122
Placement, employment, OJT.

Pre-Prosecution Diversion
Snohomish County Courthouse
Everett,98201,(206)259-9456,
Referral to employment &
training, placement programs;
8-5 M-F, eligible for per-trail
diversion, free.

**Private Industry Council of
Snohomish County,** 917 134th Ave
SW,Everett,98204,(206)743-9669,

JTPA, job search assistance,
counseling, OJT, GED, supplemental services; 8-5 M-F,
economically disadvantaged,
free.

V.R.O., 840 N Broadway,Bldg
B,Everett,98201,(206)339-4868
1309 44th Ave W,Montlake
Terrace,98042,(206)672-2363,
3310 Smokey Point Dr,Arlington
98223,(206)653-0525, Helps
disabled state residents obtain
employment & training; 8-5
M-F, disabled, physical and
mental persons, free.

FAMILY PLANNING

Planned Parenthood, POB 1051
Everett,98206,(206)339-3389,
Help with planned parenthood;
8-5 M-F, free.

**Snohomish County Family
Counseling Services**
111 SE Everett Mall Way
Everett,98208,(206)348-5989
Family counseling, marriage
counseling; sliding fee.

FOOD/CLOTHING/HOUSING

**Community Action Council
Service Outlet,** 9624 Darrington
Darrington,(206)436-1833, Food
& clothing for indigent people
and low income persons, free.

**Community Housing Improvement
Program,** 3002 Wetmore Ave
Everett,(206)259-8735, Low
income help in-home improvements, rental rehabilitation.

Goodwill Industries, 2309 State
St,Everett,98201,(206)252-6163,
3002 Hoyt,Everett,98201, Low
cost clothing & furniture;
8-5 M-F.

Salvation Army, 2525 Rucker
Ave,Everett,98206,(206)259-8129
Low cost clothing and other
needs; 9-4 M-F; fee.

World for Women, 20000 68th Ave W,Lynnwood,98046,(206)774-9843, Resource services for family issues; 9-4:30, free.

MISCELLANEOUS

Bureau of Indian Affairs of Puget Sound, 3006 Colby Ave Everett,(206)258-2651, Services for people of Indian descent; Indians, free.

Energy Assistance Center 2915 Lombard Ave,Everett,98201 (206)259-5185, Energy assistance; those in need of service.

Everett Gospel Mission 3007 Hewitt Ave,Everett,98202 (206)552-4776, Homeless facility for men; bed capacity 30+, can stay 5 days.

Treatment Alternative to Crime (TASC) Referral Service 9201 Rucker,Everett,98201,(206) 259-7142, 19324 40th Ave W,Lynnwood,98036,(206)771-8385, Evaluation & assessment, referral service, urinalysis testing, alternatives to crime; ex-offenders, drug abusers; sliding fee.

SUBSTANCE ABUSE

Alcoholics Anonymous 1721 Hewett,POB 1387,Everett 98206,(206)252-2525, Support group for recovering alcoholics.

Catholic Community Services - Snohomish County, 1918 Everett 98201,(206)259-9188, Certified alcohol & drug outpatient treatment, DWI client assessment, counseling, foster care, pregnancy out-reach, anger management.

Community Alcohol & Drug Services, City Hall,Arlington 98223,(206)435-4463, 19920 Hwy 99,Lynnwood,(206)775-4686

2812 Hoyt Ave,Everett,98201 (206)258-2662, Certified alcohol & drug outpatient treatment, information school, DWI client assessment; ADATSA, alcohol & drug counseling; 8-5 M-F; sliding fee.

Conquest Center, 8021 230th SW Edmonds,98020,(206)774-9551, Certified drug intensive in-patient treatment, residential facility; those in need of services & offenders court committment; sliding fee.

Cosby Enterprises, Inc., 19707 44th W,Lynnwood,98036 (206)774-2955, Certified alcohol & drug outpatient treatment, information school, DWI client assessment, AL-Anon & ACOA, anger management; sliding fee.

Drug Abuse Council of Snohomish County, 2720 Rucker Everett,98201,(206)259-7142, 19324 40th W,Suite,Lynnwood (206)771-8385, Certified alcohol & drug outpatient treatment, information school, DWI client assessment, ADATSA, cocaine project, outpatient therapy assessment and referral services; 8-5 M-F; sliding fee.

Evergreen Outpatient Services 2617 Summit Ave,Everett,98201 (206)253-2407, Certified alcohol & drug outpatient treatment, information school, DWI client assessment; sliding fee.

Focus, 909 SE Everett Mall Way Everett,98201,(206)355-1250, Certified alcohol & drug out-patient treatment, information school, DWI client assessment; sliding fee.

Norcross Clinic, Inc., 209 Dayton,Edmonds,98020,(206) 771-1194, 16000 Bothell-Everett Hwy,Mill Creek,98020,(206)742-5233, Certified alcohol & drug outpatient treatment, information school, DWI client assessment, 2 year deferred, counseling & mental health counseling; fee.

Options, Pacific & Nassau Lynnwood,98206,(206)258-7300, Certified alcohol & drug outpatient treatment; free.

Snohomish County Alcohol Detoxification Center
County Court House,Everett 98201,(206)258-3255, Certified alcohol detoxification, non-violent ex-offenders; sliding fee.

Solberg Recovery Center
3209 Colby Ave,Everett,98201 (206)258-2255, Certified alcohol & drug outpatient treatment, information school, DWI client assessment, family and youth programs; sliding fee.

South Snohomish County District Court, 2020 68th Ave W,Lynnwood,98036,(206)771-4417 Certified alcohol & drug outpatient treatment, DWI client assessment; free.

Tulalip Tribal Alcoholism Program, 7624 40th Dr NW Marysville,(206)771-4417, Certified alcohol & drug outpatient treatment, DWI client assessment; free.

Valley General Hospital & Alcohol Treatment Center
14701 179th Ave SE,Monroe,98272 (800)533-3046, Certified alcohol & drug inpatient & outpatient treatment, DWI client assessment, alcohol detoxification; 24 hours; flat rate.

Walnut Recovery House
1409 Walnut Ave,Everett,98201 (206)258-2407, 2601 Summit POB 7386,Everett,98201, Certified alcohol & drug recovery house, detoxification & outpatient treatment; flat rate & sliding fee.

TRANSPORTATION

Community Transit
8905 Airport Rd,Everett,98204 (206)348-7100, (800)562-1375, South county area, 60¢.

VICTIMS

Providence Sexual Assult Center
POB 1067,Everett,98206,(206) 252-2882, Resource services for family law issues, sexual assault programs; 8-5 M-F; sliding fee.

Stop Abuse, 2731 10th St Everett,98201,(206)258-3543, Domestic violence & sexual assault advocacy, counseling, support, resource services for family law issues.

WHATCOM COUNTY

Named for Indian Chief Whatcom.

Created: March 9, 1854

311 Grand Avenue, Bellingham 98225

AREA: 2,126.2 square miles, State Ranking: 12th

MAJOR ECONOMIC ACTIVITIES:
Wood Products, Agriculture,
Petroleum Refining, Manufacturing,
Food Processing

ASSESSED VALUE: $4,527,210575

POPULATION: (1989 Estimate): 122,200

Percentage of state: 2.6%
Density: 57.5 persons per square mile

ETHNIC BREAKDOWN:

	1988 Estimate
White	110,721
Black	406
Native American	3,898
Asian and Pacific Islanders	1,350
Other	2,725
Spanish origin (included in above)	3,157

PRIMARY CITIES

	Population
Bellingham, county seat	47,290
Blaine	2,470
Everson	1,230
Ferndale	4,810
Lynden	4,840
Nooksack	520
Sumas	785

CLIMATE: Bellingham - elevation 50 feet

	JAN	APR	JUL	OCT
Average				
Max Temp (F)	43.2	56.9	72.9	59.3
Min Temp	31.3	39.7	52.8	42.2
Mean Temp	37.3	48.4	62.9	58.8
Precipitation				
in inches	4.28	2.56	.93	4.09

Average Annual Maximum Temperature: 57.9
Average Annual Minimum Temperature: 41.6
Average Annual Mean Temperature: 49.8
Average Annual Precipitation: 35.12 inches

PUBLIC SCHOOL DISTRICTS

Bellingham School District #501
Box 878, Bellingham 98227
(206)676-6404   Enrollment: 10,496

Blaine School District #503
Box S, Blaine 98230, (206)332-5881
Enrollment: 1,258

Ferndale School District #502
Box 698, Ferndale   98248
(206)384-9200   Enrollment: 3,605

Lynden School District #504
1203 Bradley Rd., Lynden 98264
(206)354-4443   Enrollment: 1,655

Meridian School District #505
214 W. Laurel Rd., Bellingham
99226,   (206)398-7111
Enrollment: 1,275

Mount Baker School District #507
Deming 98244,   (206)592-5153
Enrollment: 1,577

Nooksack Valley School District #506
POB 307, Nooksack 98276
(206)988-4754   Enrollment: 1,200

HOSPITALS

St. Joseph's Hospital
Main Campus, 2901 Squalicum
Parkway, Bellingham 98225
(206)734-5400
South Campus
809 E Chestnut St,
Bellingham 98225
(206)734-8300
Total Beds: 253

THE COURTS

SUPERIOR COURT   Area Code (206)
311 Grand Ave, Bellingham, WA 98225
Michael F. Moynihan, Judge 676-6725
David A. Nichols, Judge   676-6795
Bryon L. Swedberg, Judge   676-6793
N.F. Jackson, County Clerk 676-6777

JUVENILE COURT
311 Grand Ave, Bellingham, WA 98225
Administrator: Gerald K. Wood 676-6780

DISTRICT COURT
311 Grand Ave, Bellingham, WA 98225

David E. Rhea, Jr, Judge   676-6770
Edward B. Ross, Judge   676-6770
Linda Gill, Administrator   676-6770

SITES OF INTEREST:

Mount Baker
Fort Bellingham
Ross Lake

CRISIS

Bellingham Crisis Clinic
24 hour crisis line
(206)734- 7271

The Crisis Center, 124 E Holly
Rm 201,Bellingham,98225,(206)
671-5714, 24 hour crisis line
(206)384-3748

MULTIPLE SERVICE CENTERS

Community Information Center
314 E Holly,2nd Fl,Bellingham
(206)384-1470, Information &
referrals; 8-5 M-F, free.

**Department of Social & Health
Services,** 4101 Meridian St
Bellingham,98227,(206)676-2570

The Opportunity Council
POB 159,Bellingham,98227
(206)734-5121, Energy assistance, referral, dental,
alcohol & drug referral,
shelter, pre-school assistance
daycare, commodities dis-
tributor; 8-5 M-F; sliding fee.

Whatcom Opportunity Council
314 E Hooly,2nd Fl,POB 159
Bellingham,98227,(206)734-5121
Education workshop & child
nutrition.

COUNSELING MENTAL/HEALTH

Bethesda-Cascade, 1333 King St
#B,Bellingham,98225,(206)676-
9535, Individual alcohol counseling, family counseling,
marital counseling; 8-5 M-F;
sliding fee.

**Catholic Community Services
Northwest,** POB 5704,Bellingham

98225,(206)733-5800, Mental
health counseling; sliding
fee.

**Whatcom Counseling &
Psychiatric Clinic**
1135 Mount Baker Hwy
Bellingham,(206)676-8455,
Emergency services, substance
abuse, outpatient treatment;
sliding fee.

EMPLOYMENT & TRAINING

**Bellingham Vocational
Technical Institute**
3028 Lindberg Ave,Bellingham
(206)676-6490, Vocational &
continued education, GED
testing, adults in need of
services.

Job Service Center, 216 Grand
Ave,POB 938,Bellingham,98227
(206)676-2060

**Northwest Washington Private
Industry Council,** POB 2009
Bellingham,(206)671-1660, Job
search, economically dis-
advantages persons, free.

Vocational Services Northwest
2115 Elm St,Bellingham,98225
(206)676-1600, Job placement;
sliding fee.

FAMILY PLANNING

Family Planning, 500 Grant St
Bellingham,98225,(206)734-9095,
Parenting, adoption counseling,
prenatal care, pregnancy
prevention.

FOOD/CLOTHING/HOUSING

Alternatives to Hunger
1919 Franklin St,POB 6056
Bellingham,(206)676-0392, Food
bank.

Blaine Food Bank, 545 Peace
Portal Dr,Blaine,98230,(206)
332-6675, 332-8030

Deming Foothills Food Bank
6206 Mount Baker Hwy,Deming
98224,(206)592-5950

Ferndale Project Concern
2034 Washington Ave,Ferndale
98248,(206)384-1506,
Food bank.

Noosack Valley Food Bank
204 N Washington,Everson,98247
(206)966-3748

V.R.O., Bellingham
4101 Meridian CS 9706
Bellingham,98227,(206)676-2125
Helps disabled state residents
obtain employment, training,
disabled, physical & mental
persons, free.

Women's Care Shelter
Bellingham,98225,(206)734-3438,
Shelter for women of domestic
violence.

MEDICAL DENTAL

Bellingham-Whatcom County
509 Girard St,Bellingham,98225
(206)676-6720, Health information, limited care & services, immunizations, food
handler testing; fee.

MISCELLANEOUS

Lighthouse Rescue Mission
POB 548,Bellingham,98225
(206)733-5120, Homeless
facility for men.

SUBSTANCE ABUSE

**Catholic Community Services
Northwest,** 1700 Iowa St
Bellingham,(206)733-5840,
Certified alcohol & drug
treatment, DWI client assess-
ment; sliding fee.

Community Alcohol & Drug Center
1728 Iowa,Bellingham,98225
(206)733-1400, Certified
alcohol & drug outpatient
treatment, information school,
support groups, individuals
counseling; sliding fee.

Contact Counseling
1229 Cornwall Ave,Bellingham
98225,(206)671-3277, Certified
alcohol & drug information
school, DWI client assessment
family counseling & intervention, 24 hour phone;
sliding fee.

Human Services Association
215 Flora St,Bellingham,98225
(206)671-9797, Certified
alcohol & drug information
school, family counseling;
sliding fee.

Lummi Tribal, 2616 Kwina Rd
Bellingham,98225,(206)647-6226,
Certified alcohol outpatient
treatment, family counseling;
sliding fee.

Meridian Center, 776 "H" St
Lynden,98264,(206)354-4050,
Certified alcohol & drug intensive treatment, 24 hour
phone; sliding fee.

**Noosack Tribal Chemical
Dependency,** 6750 Mission Rd
Everson,98247,(206)966-7704,
Certified alcohol & drug out-
patient treatment, information
school, DWI client assessment.

Olympia Center, 1603 E Illinois
Bellingham,98225,(206)733-9111,
Certified alcohol & drug in &
out patient treatment, youth
treatment, 24 hour phone,
detoxification.

**Recovery Center for Alcoholism
& Addictions,** 2901 Squalicum
Parkway,Bellingham,98225,(206)
734-5400, Certified alcohol &
drug treatment.

TRANSPORTATION

Whatcom County Trans Authority
2200 Nevada St,Bellingham,98226
(206)676-RIDE, 25¢ per ride,
tokens 25 for $5.00.

VETERANS SERVICES

Dr. Hayyim Grossman
2505 Cedarwood,Bellingham,98225
(206)647-1674, Delayed stress
counseling.

VICTIMS

Domestic Violence Program
124 E Holly,Bellingham,98225
(206)671-5714, Domestic violence
advocacy, support for women,
rape referral, anger
management; 8:30-4:30 M-F,
24 hour phone.

Rape Relief, 124 E Holly
Bellingham,98225,(206)671-5714
Resource services for family
law issues, sexual assault
programs; free.

**For additional information see also Skagit
County**

SEATTLE
KING

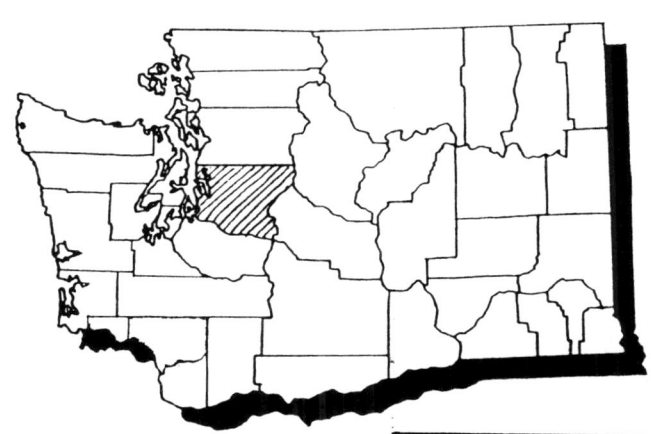

KING

Seattle/
King County

SEATTLE-KING COUNTY
TOURISM DEVELOPMENT
COUNCIL
520 Pike St, Suite 1300
Seattle 98101
(206)461-5840

King

HISTORICAL APPEAL

Bellevue Art Museum, Bellevue

Black Diamond Historical Museum, Black Diamond

Snoqualmie Valley Historical Museum, North Bend

Marymoor Museum, Redmond

Renton Historical Museum, Renton

SEATTLE

Children's Museum

Coast Guard Museum.Northwest

Klondike Gold Rush National Historic Park

Nordic Heritage Museum

Seattle Art Museum

Thomas Burke Memorial Museum

Wing Luke Memorial Museum

CITIES

AUBURN
Auburn Chamber of Commerce, 24 B St NE,Auburn,98002,(206) 833-0700

Auburn is the 16th largest city in Washington, with a population of 32,500. It is located in northwestern Washington in King County, 15 miles north of Tacoma. It is a railroad division point and service center. Founded in 1887, Auburn was named Slaughter for a hero of the Indian wars. Its present name, adopted in 1893, is derived from Oliver Goldsmith's line: "Sweet Auburn! loveliest village of the plain."

BLACK DIAMOND BREAD... Comes in 26 different delicious varieties. It is baked in an 1900s type wood-fired brick oven which gives the bread it uniqueness. The bakery is located in Black Diamond, King County.

DEEPEST PORT... Grays Harbor, discovered in 1792 is the largest deep water harbor on the west coast of the United States.

BELLEVUE
Bellevue Chamber of Commerce,
110 110th Ave NE #300,Bellevue
98004, (206)454-2464

Bellevue is a city in King
County. It is a residential
suburb of Seattle. With a
population of 86,400, it is
the fourth largest city in
Washington. Bellevue is
located 2 miles east of
Seattle, on the eastern
shore of Lake Washington.

It manufactures electrical
and electronic components,
control systems, and
prefabricated homes. A
floating bridge across Lake
Washington provides easy
access to Seattle.

BOTHELL
The Chamber of Commerce serving
Bothell, Kenmore, Mill Creek &
The North Shore Region,18120
Bothell Way NE,Suite A5, Bothell
98011, (206)486-1245

DES MOINES
Des Moines Chamber of
Commerce,21630 11th Ave S, Des
Moines,98198,(206)878-7000

ENUMCLAW
Enumclaw Area Chamber of
Commerce,1237 Griffin
Ave,Enumclaw,98022,(206)825-
7666

FEDERAL WAY
Federal Way Chamber of Commerce
POB 3440,Federal Way,98063,
(206)838-2605

Federal Way is the sixth
largest city in Washington,
with a population of 58,000.
It is located eight miles
north of Tacoma, in King
County. It is considered a
"white collar" area.
Thirty-seven percent of the
adults earn over $40,000 per
year, and thirty-nine
percent are between the ages

**THE RHODODENDRON
SPECIES FOUNDATION
GARDEN**...Was founded in
1964 at Federal Way,
King County. It has 24
acres of gardens with
over 2200 different
varieties of
rhododendrons.

of 25 and 44 years of age.

Federal Way's Enchanted Village is a unique family entertainment park, which offers three acres of family fun. One price for all day includes admission, unlimited use of 14 rides, parking, zoo, aviary, wax museum, doll and toy museums, 13-hole Krogolf, picknicking, and wading ponds.

KENT
Kent Area Chamber of Commerce
POB 128,841 Central Ave N
#105,Kent,98035,(206)854-1770

Kent is the 14th largest city in Washington, with a population of 35,000. It is located in King County, near Puget Sound, 18 miles south of Seattle. It is a residential community with small industries. Saltwater State Park on Puget Sound is nearby, and the Cascade and Olympic mountains are easily accessible.

KIRKLAND
Greater Kirkland Chamber of Commerce,301 Kirkland,98033, (206)822-7066

MAPLE VALLEY
Greater Maple Valley Chamber of Commerce,POB 302,Maple Valley,98038,(206)432-0222

MERCER ISLAND
Mercer Island Chamber of Commerce,POB 111,Mercer Island,98040,(206)232-3404

NORTH BEND
North Bend Chamber of Commerce POB 357,North Bend,(206)888-1678

REDMOND
Greater Redmond Chamber of Commerce,POB 791,16210 NE 80th,Redmond,98052

THE LONGEST RAILROAD TUNNEL...The Burlington Northern Railroad Tunnel near the summit of Stevens Pass, King County, is 7.79 miles long. It is the longest RR tunnel in North America.

©

RENTON

Greater Renton Chamber of
Commerce,300 Rainier Ave N,
Renton 98055,(206)226-4560

Renton is the 10th largest
city in Washington, with a
population of 38,500. It is
located in King County, 11
miles southeast of Seattle.
The manufacture of aircraft
is the major industry.
Points of interest include
the Will Rogers Memorial
(the last leg of his
ill-fated flight around the
world originated in Renton);
Longacres Racetrack, which
provides a summer
horse-racing program; and
the Renton Historical
Museum.

SEATTLE

Ballard Chamber of Commerce,
2208 NW Market #312,Ballard
98107, (206)784-9705

Central Area Chamber of
Commerce,2108 E
Madison,Seattle,98112,(206)325-2864

Greater Greenwood Chamber of
Commerce,208 N 85th,Seattle
98103,(206)789-1148

Greater University Chamber of
Commerce,4710 University Way
NE,Suite 214,Seattle,98103,
(206)527-2567

Lake City Chamber of Commerce
2611 NE 125th St,Suite 102,Lake
City,98125,(206)363-3287

Seattle King County Convention &
Visitors Bureau,666 Stewart,
Seattle,98101,(206)447-4240

Shoreline Chamber of Commerce
17077 Meridian Ave N,Seattle
98133, (206)546-6698

Wedgewood Chamber of Commerce
2707 NE103rd,Seattle,98115,
(206)525-0766

PIKE PLACE MARKET...
Is located downtown
Settle, King County.
Established in 1907.
With over 200 small
businesses, Pike Place
Market is the oldest
continually active open
air markets in the
nation. They sell
everything from
antiques, arts and
crafts, produce, and
fresh sea food.

Seattle is the largest city in Washington with a population of 497,200. It is the county seat of **King County**. Seattle is located in western Washington on hilly land between Lake Washington and Puget Sound. Across the Sound are the majestic snowcapped peaks of the Olympic Mountains. To the southeast is Mount Rainier with its breathtaking snowcapped peak looming 14,410 feet in the air.

Downtown Seattle faces Elliott Bay, a superb natural harbor and the cities principal port area. A short distance from the business district stands the 607-foot Space Needle build for the 1962 World's Fair.

SEATTLE'S ECONOMY

Seattle is the largest city in the Pacific Northwest. Although nearly 150 miles from the open sea, it is still an important port and gateway to Alaska and Asia. Infact, it is closer to Asia than any other major port on the United States West Coast. Grain, lumber, and wood products make up the majority of the cargo shipped. Aircraft manufacture is a major industry; the Boeing Aircraft plants in Seattle and suburban Renton and Everett, produce commercial and military aircraft, as well as missile and satellite parts. Commercial fishing and associated canning and freezing, shipbuilding and repair, and the manufacture of machinery and paper are other important activities. The computer software business is also a new and growing industry of the Seattle area.

Seattle is served by all principal means of transportation. It has a network of

HOW BIG IS THE SEATTLE KINGDOME?...The home of the Seahawks and Mariners is 250 feet high and 720 feet in diameter, it consists of 52,800 cubic yards of cement and 443 tons of steel. It has the largest self-supporting concrete roof in the world.

toucHdown

292

railroads and highways, including two Interstate routes (Interstates 5 and 90) that provide service to all parts of the country and Canada. Seattle-Tacoma (SEA-TAC) International Airport is a major terminal for overseas flights. The Port of Seattle includes the Lake Washington Ship Canal, linking Puget Sound, Lake Union, and Lake Washington; locks in the canal rise ships 26 feet to the lakes. Ferries cross Puget Sound to Bremerton and other cities; two floating bridges carry highway traffic over Lake Washington.

ATTRACTIONS

With water bording much of Seattle, outdoor activities like boating and fishing are extremely popular. Some of Seattle's residents make their permanent home on houseboats on Lake Union. Beaches, parks, and other recreation areas dot the shores of Seattle and much of the Puget Sound region.

On a hill near the central business stands the **Seattle Center**, on the site of the 1962 World's Fair. Some of the Center's attractions include the Space Needle, science and art exhibits, shops, and restaurants. Major sporting events are held in the Seattle Center Arena and in the Kingdome. Seattle's cultural institutions rank among the finest in the Western United States.

AIRPORT

SEATTLE-TACOMA INTERNATIONAL AIRPORT, POB 1209, Seattle 98111,(206)728-3406

SNOQUALMIE
Snoqualmie Chamber of Commerce

POB 356,301 River St,Snoqualmie
98065, (206)888-2233

TUKWILA
Greater Burien,Sea/Tac, Tukwila
Chamber of Commerce,POB
58591,Kukwila,98138,(206)244-
3160

VASHON ISLAND
Vashon Business Association,POB
1035,Vashon,98070,(206)567-4179

WOODINVILLE
Woodinville Chamber of
Commerce,13110 NE 177th Pl,Sp
B104,Woodinville,98072,(206)481-
8300

FAIRS AND FESTIVALS

Folklife Festival
Settle, May (206)684-7300

Marymoor Heritage Festival
Redmond, June
(206)885-2216

Jazz Festival
Bellevue, July
(206)451-4106

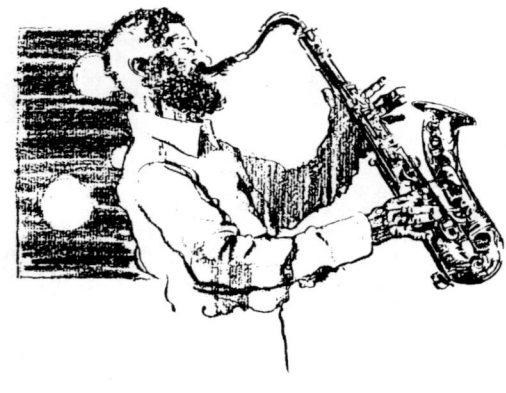

Strawberry Festival
Vashon, July
(206)463-3304

Seafair
Seattle, July
(206)728-0123

King County Fair
Enumclaw, July
(206)825-7777

Waterland Festival
Des Moines, July
(206)878-7000

**Pacific Northwest Arts &
Crafts Fair**
Bellevue, July
(206)454-3322

Bumbershoot Arts Festival
Seattle, August
(206)684-7337

Salmon Days
Issaquah, October
(206)392-0661

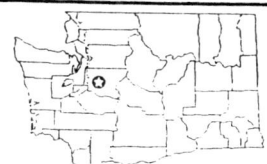

KING COUNTY

Named for civil rights leader Martin Luther King, Jr., in 1986. It had been originally named for William Rufus Devane King vice president of the U.S. under Franklin Pierce.

Created: December 21, 1852

Courthouse, 516 Third Avenue,
Seattle, 98104
County Administration Bldg, 500 Fourth Avenue,
Seattle 98104

AREA: 2,130.9 square miles, State Ranking: 11th

MAJOR ECONOMIC ACTIVITIES:
Manufacturing, Shipping and Trade, Agriculture, Business Services, Shipbuilding, Fishing, Tourism, Wood Products

ASSESSED VALUE: $72,742,545,375

POPULATION: (1989 Estimate): 1,446,000

Percentage of state: 31.0%
Density: 678.6 persons per square mile

ETHNIC BREAKDOWN:	1988 Estimate
White	1,213,798
Black	67,052
Native American	14,450
Asian and Pacific Islanders	83,039
Other	31,561
Spanish origin (included in above)	39,763

PRIMARY CITIES	Population
Auburn	32,460
Bellevue	86,350
Federal Way	58,000
Kent	34,860
Kirkland	36,620
Mercer Island	20,380
Redmond	33,400
Renton	38,480
Sea-Tac	24,200
Seattle, county seat	497,200

```
CLIMATE: Seattle - elevation 14 feet
Average            JAN      APR      JUL      OCT
Max Temp (F )      45.6     59.4     75.1     60.4
Min Temp           36.8     44.1     56.1     48.3
Mean Temp          41.2     51.8     65.6     54.4
Precipitation
in inches          5.19     1.97     .63      3.28
Average Annual Maximum Temperature:    60.0
Average Annual Minimum Temperature:    46.4
Average Annual Mean Temperature:       53.2
Average Annual Precipitation:  34.10 inches
```

PUBLIC SCHOOL DISTRICTS

Auburn School District #408
915 Fourth St NE, Auburn 98002
(206)931-4900,   Enrollment: 9,980

Bellevue School District #405
12111 NE First St.,POB 90010
Bellevue, 98009 (206)455-6015
Enrollment: 14,718

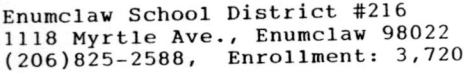

Enumclaw School District #216
1118 Myrtle Ave., Enumclaw 98022
(206)825-2588,   Enrollment: 3,720

Federal Way School District #210
31405 18th Ave, Federal Way 98003
(206)941-0100,   Enrollment: 16,250

Highline School District #401
15675 Ambaum Blvd SW, Box 66100
Seattle 98166, (206)433-0111
Enrollment: 15,992

Issaquah School District #411
565 NW Holly St., Issaquah 98027
(206)392-0700,   Enrollment: 8,082

Kent School District #415
12033 SE 256th, Kent 98031
(206)852-9550,   Enrollment: 19,977

Lake Washington School District #414
10903 NE 53rd, POB 2909, (206)828-3200
Kirkland 98083,   Enrollment: 22,171

Mercer Island School District #400
4160 86th Ave SE, Mercer Island, 98040
(206)236-3300,   Enrollment: 3,299

Northshore School District #417
18315 Bothell Way NE, Bothell 98011
(206)485-0417,   Enrollment: 17,155

Renton School District #403
435 Main Ave S., Renton 98055
(206)235-2200,   Enrollment: 11,628

Riverview School District #407
32240 NE 50th St., Carnation 98014
(206)333-4115,   Enrollment: 2,132

Seatle School District #1
815 Fourth Ave N., Seattle 98109
(206)281-6000,   Enrollment: 40,567

Shoreline School District #412
17077 Meridian Ave N., Seattle 98133
(206)367-6111,   Enrollment: 9,137

Skykomish School District #404
Skykomish 98288, (206)677-2318
Enrollment: 93

Snoqualmie Valley School District #410
POB 400, Snoqualmie 98065
(206)888-2334,   Enrollment: 3,559

South Central School District #406
4640 S. 144th St., Seattle 98168
(206)244-2100,   Enrollment: 1,688

Tahoma School District #409
23015 SE 216th Way, Maple Valley 98038
(206)432-4481,   Enrollment: 3,601

Vashon Island School District #402
Route 3, Box 358, Vashon 98070
(206)463-2121,   Enrollment: 1,540

HOSPITALS

**CareUnit Hospital of
Kirkland (Alcoholism Hosp.)**
POB 480, 10322 NE 132nd
Kirkland 98033 (206)821-1122
Total Beds: 83

Auburn General Hospital
20 Second St NE, Auburn
90002 (206)833-7711
Total Beds: 149

Ballard Community Hospital
POB C-70707, NW Market and
Barnes, Seattle 98107
(206)782-2700
Total Beds: 163

**Children's Hospital and
Medical Center,** 4800 Sand
Point Way NE, Seattle 98105
(206)526-2000
Total Beds: 208

Group Health Cooperative
Central Hospital, 201 16th
Ave E, Seattle 98112
(206)326-3322
Total Beds: 346

Group Health Eastside
Hospital, 2700 152nd Ave NE
Redmond 98052 (206)883-5183
Total Beds: 179

Harborview Medical Center
325 Ninth Ave, Seattle 98104
(206)223-3036 223-3000
Total Beds: 413

Highline Community Hospital
Main Campus, 16251 Sylvester
Rd SW, Seattle 98166
(206)244-9970
Riverton Campus
12844 Military Rd S, Seattle
98168 (206)431-5235
Total Beds: 296

Northwest Hospital
1550 No 115th, Seattle 98133
120 Northgate Plaza, Seattle
98125 (206)364-0500
Total Beds: 281

Overlake Hospital Medical
Center, 1035 116th NE,
Bellevue 98004 (206)454-4011
(206)454-4011
Total Beds: 235

Providence Medical Center
500 17th Ave, C-34008
Seattle 98122 (206)326-5555
Total Beds: 376

St. Francis Xavier Cabrina
Hospital, 920 Terry Ave
Seattle 98104 (206)682-0500
Total Beds: 189

St. Francis Community
Hospital, 34515 9th Ave S,
Federal Way 98003
(206)838-9700
Total Beds: 110

Schick Shadel Hospital
(Alcoholism Hospital)
12101 Ambaum Blvd SW
Seattle 98146
(206)244-8100
Total Beds: 63

Swedish Hospital Medical
Center, 747 Summit Ave,
Seattle 98104 (206)386-6000
Total Beds: 697

University of Washington
Medical Center, 1959 NE
Pacific St, Seattle 98195
(206)548-3300
Total Beds: 450

Valley Medical Center
400 S 43rd St, Renton 98055
(206)228-3450
Total Beds: 303

Virginia Mason Hospital
925 Seneca, Seattle 98111
(206)624-1144
Total Beds: 336

West Seattle Community
Hospital, 2600 SW Holden,
Seattle 98126 (206)938-6000
Total Beds: 198

Snoqualmie Valley Hospital
1505 Ethan Wade SE,
Snoqualmie 98065
(206)888-1438
Total Beds: 28

Community Memorial Hospital
2125 "C" Street, Enumclaw
98022 (206)825-2505
Total Beds: 38

Evergreen Hospital Medical
Center, 12040 NE 128th St
Kirkland 98033 (206)821-1111
Total Beds: 134

Fairfax Hospital
(Psychiatric Hospital)
10200 NE 132nd St, Kirkland
98034 (206)821-2000
Total Beds: 133

Fifth Avenue Medical Center
POB C, 10560 5th Ave NE
Seattle 98125 (206)364-2050
Total Beds: 80

THE COURTS

SUPERIOR COURT   Area Code (206)
C-903 King County Courthouse
516 Third Ave., Seattle 98104

Robert H. Alsdorf, Judge   296-9203
Patricia H. Aitken, Judge   343-2662
Sharon S. Armstrong, Judge 296-9130
James W. Bates, Judge   296-9115
Lloyd W. Bever, Judge   296-9120
Bobbe J. Bridge, Judge   296-9250
Mary Wicks Brucker, Judge   296-9285
Jerome M. Johnson, Judge   296-9215
Terrence A. Carroll, Judge   296-9290
Warren Chan, Judge   296-9125
John M. Darrah, Judge   296-9160
Robert E. Dixon, Judge   296-9135
James J. Dore, Judge   296-9145
William L. Downing, Judge   296-9362
Joan DuBuque, Judge   296-9255
Anne L. Ellington, Judge   296-9095
Faith Enyeart, Judge   296-9140
George A. Finkle, Judge   296-9235
Michael J. Fox, Judge   296-9180
Donald D. Haley, Judge   296-9165

©

Edward Heavey, Judge   296-9170
Nancy Ann Holman, Judge   296-9175
Norma Smith Huggins, Judge   296-9096
Richard M. Ishikawa, Judge   296-9185
Charles V. Johnson, Judge   296-9190
Robert S. Laskin, Judge   296-9113
J. Kathleen Learned, Judge   296-9205
George T. Mattson, Judge   343-2662
LeRoy McCullough, Judge   296-9245
James D. McCutcheon, Jr Judge 296-9210
James A. Noe, Judge   296-9220
Carmen Otero, Judge   296-9275
Marsha J. Pechman, Judge   296-9103
Arthur E. Piehler, Judge   296-9225
Norman W. Quinn, Judge   296-9230
Dale B. Ramerman, Judge   296-9235
Carol Schapira, Judge   296-9150
Steven G. Scott, Judge   296-9111
Peter K. Steere, Judge   296-9251
Frank L. Sulivan, Judge   296-9260
Liem E. Tuai, Judge   296-9265
Anthony P. Wartnik, Judge   296-9270
R. Joseph Wesley, Judge   296-9280

Larry A. Jordon, Judge   296-9105
Ricardo S. Martinez, Judge   296-9295
Sally Pasette, Judge   296-9213
Joseph R. Wesley, Judge   296-9280
Mark Hatcher   Administrator 296-9305

JUVENILE COURT
1211 E. Alder, POB C22314, Seattle
98122, Director: Bruce Knultson   296-1132

DISTRICT COURTS
King County District Courts Administrator
Office of the Presiding Judge, E-340
King Co. Courthouse, Seattle 98104

AUKEEN
1210 South Central, Kent 98031
Donald A. Eide, Judge   296-7740
Darrell E. Phillipson, Judge 296-7740
Stephen M. Sward, Judge 296-7740
Le Sanchez, Administrator 296-7749

BELLEVUE
585 112th Ave SE, Bellevue 98004
Brian D. Gain, Judge   296-3650
Joel A.C. Rindal, Judge 296-3650
Frederick L. Yeatts, Judge 296-3650
Lorraine Nelson, Administrator 296-3650

FEDERAL WAY
33506 10th Pl S., Federal Way 98003
Carolyn J. Hayek, Judge   838-6970
E.T. Leverette, Judge   838-6970
Janet McCrary, Administrator 838-6970

ISSAQUAH
640 NW Gilman Blvd, Issaquah 98027
Peter D. Jarvis, Judge   296-7688
Jackie Roberts, Administrator 296-7688

MERCER ISLAND
8525 SE 68th, Mercer Island 98040
Suzanne Biggs Stables, Judge   232-7760
Neva R. Ely, Administrator 232-7760

NORTHEAST
15920 NE 85th, POB 425, Redmond 98073
David S. Admire, Judge   296-3667
Rosemary P. Bordlemay, Judge 296-3667
Will Roarty, Judge   296-3667
J. Wesley Sain Claire, Magistrate
                          296-3667

RENTON
3407 NE Second St., Renton 98056
Charles J. Delaurenti, Judge 296-3532
Robert E. McBeth, Judge   296-3532
Melanie M. Gain, Admin.   296-3532

SEATTLE
E-327 King County Courthouse
516 Third Ave., Seattle 98104
Darcy C. Goodman, Judge   296-3610
Laura C. Inveen, Judge   296-3630
Philip Y. Killien, Judge   296-3630
Mark Chow, Judge   296-3620
John G. Ritchie, Judge   296-3625
James B. Gorham, Magistrate
                           296-3589
Cathleen M. Grindle, Admin. 296-3617

SHORELINE
18110 Midvale Ave., N, POB 7056
Seattle 98133
Douglas J. Smith, Judge   296-3679
Robert A. Wacker, Judge 296-3679
Donna K. Brunner, Administrator

                          296-3679

SOUTHWEST
601 SW 149th St., Seattle 98166
Vicki M. Seitz, Judge   296-0133
Richard P. Thompson, Judge296-0133
Gary N. Utigard, Judge 296-0144
Neri Zenk, Administrator 296-0133

VASHON ISLAND DEPT
(Southwest District Court)
99th SW and SW 192nd, POB 111
Vashon Island 98070
Susan Wolfenbarger, Clerk 296-3664

SITES OF INTEREST:

Snoqualmie Falls
Seattle Area

CRISIS

**Abused Deaf Women's Advocacy
Services,** POB 15114,Seattle
98115,(206)522-9475, POB 5125
Seattle,98125, Sexual assault
programs, crisis line and 24
hour shelter, free.

**Alcohol & Drug 24 hour Help
Line,** POB 18317,Seattle,98118
(206)722-3700, Emergency
crisis counseling, phone referral to appropriate agency;
24 hour answering, alcohol &
drug abusers & their families
free.

**Alcohol & Drug 24 hour Help
Line,** 3700 Rainier Ave.S
Seattle,98144,(206)722-3703,
Certified alcohol & drug
crisis intervention; 24 hour
sliding fee.

Crisis Clinic, 1515 Dexter Ave
N,Seattle,98102,(206)461-3222,
Crisis & community information
line, daycare referral, survivors of suicide referral to
self help agency; all persons.

**National Gay & Lesbian Crisis-
line,** (800)221-7044, Advocacy
services for those harassed
because of sexual abuse;
8-10 AM M-F, Gays & Lesbians.

**Washington State Shelter Net-
work,** HCR 78 Box 336,Naselle
98638,(800)562-6025, Hotline,
domestic violence, counseling,
referral service, children &
men; 24 hours, abuse women &
men of domestic violence,
free.

MULTIPLE SERVICE CENTERS

Broadway Emergency Shelter
POB 31151,Seattle,98103
(206)662-4933, Emergency
housing, information and
referral, crisis counseling,
3 month transitional housing,
domestic violence & sexual
assault advocacy and
counseling, self support
groups; 9-5 M-F, sliding
fee.

Catholic Community Services
100 23rd Ave,S,Seattle,98144
(206)325-6890, Legal assistance, mental health counseling & outpatient care, family planning, pregnancy, certified alcohol & drug treatment, all persons, free.

Central Area Motivation Program, 722 18th Ave,Seattle 98122,(206)329-411, Energy assistance, referrals, dental alcohol & drug referral, shelter, pre-school assistance, daycare, commodities distributor; 8-5 M-F, sliding fee.

City of Seattle DHR
400 Yesler Bldg,Seattle 98104,(206)625-5445, Energy assistance, referrals, dental, alcohol & drug referral, shelter, pre-school assistance, daycare, commodities distributor; 8-5 M-F, sliding fee.

Correctional Specialities
201 116th NE,Bellevue,98004 (206)453-1234, Sexual deviancy evaluations(adult&juvenile), comprehensive sexual deviancy treatment, polygraph examinations, victim-spouse therapy & support, adult & juvenile psychological evaluations, competency evaluations, training, expert testimony and professional consultation services, presentations to professionals; ex-offenders, sliding fee.

Department of Social & Health Services, 2809 26th,Ave S Seattle (206)721-4334, 2106 2d Ave,Seattle,(206)464-7060, 15811 Ambaum Blvd,SW,Seattle 98166, (206)433-1336, 6330 35th SW,Seattle,98126,(206) 464-6156 1700 E.Cherry,Seattle 98122, (206)464-6958 15821 NE,8th,St,Bellevue,98008 (206)455-7148 907 NW Ballard Way,Seattle,98107,(206)789-5200, 25620 74th Ave,S,POB 848

Kent,98032,(206)872-2145, 1717 S 324th,POB 4629,Federal Way,98003,(206)872-2263, 3600 S.Graham,Seattle,98118,(206) 721-4676

El Centro de la Raza, 2524 16th Ave S,Seattle,98144 (206)329- 9442, Employment referrals, housing, educational counseling daycare free lunches, food & nutrition; 8-5:30 M-F, all persons, free.

Federal Way Emergency Services
31623 Pacific Highway S,Federal Way,(206)941-2881, Emergency shelter for women, families and children, food bank; 10-2 M-F, free.

Freemont Public Association
3601 Freemont Ave N,Seattle 98103,(206)632-1285, Employment services, job listing, food bank, legal clinic, daycare & re-employment advocacy, housing counseling, welfare right advocates; 8-5 M-F, unemployed and disadvantaged persons, free.

Friends of Youth, 414 Front St N,Issaquah,98027,(206)392-KIDS, Emergency shelter for women, families & children, alcohol & drug programs, employment counseling, 8:30-4:30, all persons, sliding fee.

Group Health Cooperative
1600 E. John,Seattle,98122 (206)325-7057, Outpatient alcohol & drug treatment, information referral, domestic violence counseling & support groups; 9-5 M-F, members of Group Health, fee.

Lutheran Social Services
19230 Forest Park Dr,NE,Seattle 98155,(206)365-2700, Pregnancy mental health counseling, life enrichment, adoption services, lifeline; 8:30-6 M-F, all persons.

Metro Center YMCA, 909 4th Ave Seattle,98104,(206)382-5013, Energy assistance, referrals, dental, alcohol & drug referral shelter, pre-school assistance, daycare, commodities distributor; 8-5 M-F, sliding fee.

Millionair Club Clinic
2515 Western Ave,Seattle,98104 (206)223-5915 Medical treatment, referrals, employment, low cost clothing & meals; 8-12 M-F, all persons, sliding fee.

Neighborhood House, 905 Spruce Seattle,98104,(206)447-8430, Energy assistance, referrals, dental, alcohol & drug referral, shelter, pre-school assistance, daycare, commodities distributor; 8-5 M-F, sliding fee.

Northeast King County Multiple Service Center, 18220 96th Ave NE,Bothell, Energy assistance, referrals, dental, alcohol & drug referral, shelter, preschool assistance, daycare, commodities distributor; 8-5 M-F, sliding fee.

Ryther Child Center
2400 NE 95th St,Seattle,98115 (206)525-5050, Child abuse services, adolescent alcohol & substance abuse programs, parenting; all persons, sliding fee.

Seattle King County Public Health Department Assessment Clinic & Resource Center
1116 Summit Ave,Seattle,(206) 296-4999

Auburn Public Health Center
20 Auburn Ave,Auburn,98002 (206)852-8400

Central Environmental Health Center, 172 20th Ave,Seattle 98122,(206)296-4632

Columbia Health Center, 3722 S Hudson St,Seattle,98122 (206)587-4650

Downtown Public Health Center
610 3rd Ave,Seattle,98104 (206)296-4761

East Public Health Center, 2424 156th Ave NE,Bellevue,98007 (206)344-6882

North Seattle Public Health Center, 10501 Meridian Ave N,Seattle,(206)296-4765

Renton Public Health Center
3001 NE 4th St,Renton,98055 (206)232-3590

Sexually Transmitted Disease Clinic, 325 9th Ave,Seattle 98104,(206)232-3590

Southwest Public Health Center
10821 8th Ave SW,Seattle,98146 (206)296-4646 Dental care and referrals, family planning, pregnancy, child health clinic, all persons, sliding fee.

Seattle Veterans Action Center
2024 E Union,Seattle,98122 (206)625-4656, Energy assistance, referrals, dental, alcohol & drug referral, shelter, pre-school assistance, daycare, commodities distributor; 8-5 M-F, sliding fee.

South King County Multi-Service Center, 1505 S 356th,Federal Way,(206)838-6810, Transportation, food, clothing, employment, daycare, alcohol services, information, referral to resources for abused women, assistance with shelters & literacy program; 8:30-5 M-F, those in need of services, sliding fee.

World for Women, POB 5627 Lynnwood,98046,(206)774-9843, Help for abused women, shelter, counseling, classes, employment assistance, shared housing; women in need of services.

COUNSELING MENTAL/HEALTH

Asian Counseling & Referral
409 Maynard S,Seattle,98104 (206)461-3606, Individual, marital, family, child abuse counseling, employment

orientation, supportive services; all persons.

Atlantic Street Center, 2103 S.Atlantic St,Seattle,98144 (206)329-2050, Counseling & mental health, case management; 9-5 M-F, all persons, free.

Cancer Lifeline, 107 Cherry St,Seattle,98104,(206)447-4542, (800)255-5505, Mental health counseling; 24 hours, 7 days, all persons.

Central Area Mental Health Center, 4900 Rainier Ave S Seattle,98118,(206)723-1980, Specialized services for ex-offender, treatment for black offenders with a history of institutionalization; blacks & low income, sliding fee.

Community House, 431 Boylston Ave E,Seattle,98102,(206)322-2387, Mental health counseling, outpatient, cronic mental illness and assault rapes; 11-5 M-F, all persons, medical coupons, sliding fee.

Community Psychiatric Clinic 4319 Stone Way N,Seattle,98103 (206)447-3614, Emergency services, substance abuse, outpatient treatment, all persons, sliding fee.

CPC Fairfax Hospital, 10200 NE 132nd St,Kirkland,98034 (206)821-2000, Mental health inpatient hospital, adolescent care; 24 hours, persons needing mental help, insurance payment.

Divorce Lifeline, 1013 8th Ave Seattle,98104,(206)624-2959, Mental health counseling, outpatient treatment, support group for divorced families; 9-4:30 M-F, all persons, sliding fee.

Eastside Mental Health 1605 116th NE,Bellevue,98004 (206)455-4357, 2840 Northrup Way,Bellevue,(206)827-9100, Mental health counseling; 8-4 M-F, all persons, sliding fee.

Harborview Community Mental Health Center, 326 9th Ave Seattle,98104,(206)223-3000, Mental health counseling, outpatient treatment, all persons, medical coupons.

Highline West Mental Health Center, 10015 28th Ave SW Seattle,98146,(206)932-8328, Mental health counseling outpatient treatment; 9-5 M-F, all persons, free.

Jewish Family Service, 1214 Boylston,Seattle,98101 (206)447-3240 Mental health counseling & outpatient treatment; 9-5 M-F, those of the Jewish faith.

Lutheran Counseling Network 17404 8th NE,Seattle,98155 (206)364-1046, Mental health counseling, outpatient treatment, answering service, all persons.

Mental Health North 10501 Meridian Ave N,Seattle 98133,(206)365-5550, Mental health counseling; 8-5 M-F, all persons, sliding fee.

Montlake Institute, 2200 24th Ave E,Seattle,98112,(206) 328-0910, Mental health counseling, outpatient treatment; 8-6 M-F, all persons, private practice.

Parent Place, 15064 15th NE Seattle,98115,(206)364-9963, Mental health counseling, outpatient, parenting; all persons.

Presbyterian Counseling Service 564 NE Ravena,Seattle,98115 (206)527-2266, Outpatient mental health counseling, marital counseling; 9-9 M-F, all persons, sliding fee.

Puget Counseling Center, 1111
Harvard Ave,Seattle,98122
(206)329-5050, 113 1st Ave N
Seattle,98109 (206)286-8656,
Outpatient mental health
counseling; 9-5 M-F, all
persons, sliding fee.

Redmond Counseling Service
12025 Willow Rd,Redmond,98073
(206)895-1480, Mental health
counseling, 9-8 M-F, all
persons, sliding fee.

Resource Center for the
Handicapped, 20150 45th Ave
NE,Seattle,98155,(206)362-CARE
Outpatient mental health
counseling, vocational training
for the handicapped; 8-4:30
M-F, all persons handicapped,
sliding fee.

Sea-Dru-Nar, 200 W.Comstock
Seattle,98188,(206)284-2010,
Residential 9-12 month program,
nursery services available,
counseling, group therapy;
9-5 M-F, drug abuser 17+ years
of age, sliding fee.

Seattle Counseling Services
1505 Broadway,Seattle,98122
(206)329-8707, Outpatient
mental health counseling,
all persons.

Seattle Mental Health, 1600
E.Oliver St,Seattle,98122
(206)281-4300, Outpatient services, counseling, consulting
staff services, referrals,
acute care & older adult
services; sliding fee.

Southwest Community Center
9407 16th Ave SW,Seattle
(206)625-4261,Counseling
help, women needing help.

Treat Alternatives to Street
Crime(TASC), 817 S.3rd,St
Renton,(206)228-2122,
Counseling, alternatives
to crime; adults felons with
substance abuse problems,
sliding fee.

University Hospital, 1959 NE

Pacific,Seattle,98109,(206)
548-4455,Outpatient & inpatient
mental health counseling; all
persons, sliding fee.

Valley Cities Mental Center
2704 I St.NE,Auburn,98002
(206)833-7444, Mental health
counseling and outpatient care;
8:30-5 M-F, all persons,
sliding fee.

Washington Advocates for the
Mentally Ill, 225 N.70th
Seattle,98103,(206)783-9264,
Outpatient mental health re-
ferral and self help; 9-5 M-F,
24 hours, all persons, free.

Well Mind Clinic, 557 Roy
Seattle,98104,(206)285-1289,
Mental health counseling;
9-5 M-F, sliding fee.

Western State Hospital-Tacoma
Fort Steilacoom,98494,(206)
756-2656, Mental health
counseling, inpatient
hospital; all persons, fee.

YWCA of Seattle, 1118 5th
Ave,Seattle,98101,(206)447-
4855, Outpatient mental counseling; women only, no fee.

EDUCATION TRAINING

ANEW (Women in Trades),
Seattle,(206)523-6613, Employment services to help train
for jobs, classes; single women
only.

Association of Women Con-
tractors, Suppliers & Design
217 9th Ave N,Seattle,98109
(206)623-8632, Promotes growth
for women in business in
non-traditional industries;
8-5:30 M-F, all persons.

Bellevue Community
College-Displaced Homemakers
3000 Landerholm Cir.S,Bellevue
98009,(206)641-2279, Employment
services for displaced homemaker, 5 week course for single
women, referral services;
displaced homemakers.

Bellevue Community College
3000 Landerholm Cir S,Bellevue
98009,POB 92700,Bellevue,98009
(206)641-0111, Academic &
vocational counseling, GED
testing, career counseling,
displaced homemakers; adults
16+ years of age.

Center for Career Alternatives
3700 Rainier Ave S,Seattle
98144,(206)723-2286, Career
counseling, information on
referrals, financial aid
preparation, job market
analysis; women, students,
minorities.

Center for Displaced Homemakers
1701 Broadway,Seattle,(206)
587-3855, Educational development, individual counseling,
free.
**Division of Vocational
Rehabilitation,** 1030 Greenwood
Blvd,Issaquah,98027,(206)453-
6250, Vocational rehabilitation
program, OASVS; 9-4:30 M-F,
all persons, sliding fee.

Donham-Weyant, Inc,
Seattle,(206)523-4964,
Vocational rehabilitation
program, OASVS, counseling;
8-4 M-F, all persons.

Edmonds Community College
2000 68th Ave W,Lynnwood
98036,(206)771-1500, Academic
& vocational counseling,
GED testing, development,
education, job placement;
8-8 M-F, adults 16+,
sliding fee.

Employment Opportunities Center
4726 Rainier Ave S,Seattle
98118,(206)725-8200, Career
counseling, assessment, skills
& resume bank, bilingual
counseling; 8-5 M-F, unemployed
& disadvantaged persons, free.

Federal Job Information Center
915 Seneca Ave,Seattle,98174
(206)442-4365, Employment
services and help; all persons
free.

**Federal Women's Program/
National Marine Fisheries,**
7600 Sand Point Way NE,Seattle
98115,(206)526-6107, Promotes
employment for women in federal
work; 9-5 M-F, women only,
free.

FOCUS, 509 10th Ave E,Seattle
98102,(206)329-7918, Job referral, 750 members; 9-2:30
M-F, women, free.

Goodwill Industries, 1400 S
Lane St,Seattle,98144,(206)
329-1000, Employment pre-
paration, orientation in 9
months program, on site career
planning, on the job training
(OJT); 8:30-12:30, vocational
& economically disadvantaged,
fee.

Green River Community College
12401 SE 320th,Auburn,98002
(206)833-9111, Academic &
vocational courses, GED testing & high school completion,
registration 9AM-8PM, hours
8-5 M-F, adults 16+ years of
age, sliding fee.

Highline Community College
POB 98000,Des Moines,98198
(206)878-3710, Academic &
vocational courses, GED
testing, high school com-
pletion; 8-8 M-Thur, adults
16+ years of age, grant.

Interaction, 1148 NW Leary Way
Seattle,98107,(206)784-7744,
Resume preparation, interview
techniques, job readiness,
goal setting; physically &
disadvantaged persons.

Job Service Center
2707 I St NE,POB 547,Auburn
98002,(206)931-3912, 13133
Bel-Red Rd,POB 91313,Bellevue
98009,(206)455-7100 12550
Aurora Ave N,POB 33820,Seattle
98133,(206)545-6526 1000 Index
Ave NE,POB 3055,Renton,98056
(206)764-4346 2106 2nd Ave
Seattle,98121,(206)464-6449

Lake Washington Vocational Technical Institute, 11605 132nd Ave NE,Kirkland,98034 (206)828-5600, Vocational & continued education, GED testing, ESL, displaced homemakers; 8-4 M-F, adults 16+, sliding fee.

National Alliance of Business 1236 5th Ave,Seattle,98101 (206)622-2531,Liaison with business, industry, labor education & community groups to assist in development; 8-4:30 M-F, employers & agencies who train, sliding fee.

North Seattle Community College 9600 College Way N,Seattle 98103,(206)527-3600, Academic & vocational courses, GED testing, ABE, daycare & early childhood; all persons.

Operation Improvement Foundation, 3201 Rainier Ave S Seattle,98144,(206)721-5101 Placement in vocational skills training program at public & private training institutions; economically disadvantaged.

Operation Emergency Center – Ex-Offender Work Orientation 3800 S.Othello,Seattle,98118 (206)725-2100, Employment counseling, job referral & placement assistance, emergency services, career development; ex-offenders & disadvantaged persons, free.

PHS – Pioneer Industries, 7000 Highland Parkway SW,Seattle 98106,(206)762-7737, Temporary employment, work experience in sheltered workshop setting, 18 month training program.

PHS – Central Food Services 220 11th Ave,Seattle,98122 (206)343-0552, Kitchen employment operation; adults.

Renton Vocational Technical Institute, 3000 NE 4th St Renton,98056,(206)235-2352,

Vocational & continued education, GED testing, adults 16+ years of age, sliding fee.

Salvation Army, 416 2nd Ave Seattle,98104,(206)223-9180, Employment services, sliding fee.

Seattle Central Community College, 1701 Broadway,Seattle 98122,(206)537-3855, Job search & employee assistance, career information, counseling, womens educational career goals referral to help women return to school; 8-4:30, women in need.

Seattle Community College 1701 Broadway,Seattle,98122 (206)324-8500, Academic & vocational courses, GED testing, employment services for displaced homemakers, work activities, educational & career goals, signal parents; 8:30-4:30 M-F, displaced homemakers, free.

Seattle Indian Center,Inc. 611 12th Ave S,#300,Seattle 98144,(206)329-8700, Vocational counseling & assessment, training & employment assistance, clothing & food banks, sliding fee.

Seattle Urban League, 105 14th Ave,Seattle,98104,(206)625-7999, Employment services; all persons.

Seattle City Personnel Department, 710 2nd Ave,Seattle 98104,(206)625-7999, Employment services; all persons.

Seattle King County Private Industry Council, 2001 Western Ave,Market Pl One #250,Seattle 98121,(206)684-7390, JTPA, job search assistance, counseling, OJT, GED, supplement services; economically disadvantaged persons, free.

Seattle-King County Public Defenders Association, 810 3rd Ave,Seattle,98104,(206)447-3900 Vocational counseling, assessment, training & supportive services, job referral; economically disadvantaged persons, sliding fee.

Self Placement Program, 1601 2nd Ave,Seattle,98101,(206) 464-6865, Employment help, referral service, resume, coping & mailing; 9-5 M-F, all persons, free.

Shoreline Community College 16101 Greenwood Ave N,Seattle 98133,(206)546-4101, Academic & vocational courses, GED testing; 9-4 M-F, adults 16+ years of age, sliding fee.

South Seattle Community College 6000 16th Ave SW,Seattle,98106 (206)764-5300, Academic & vocational courses, GED testing, adults 16+, sliding fee.

University of Washington – Staff Employment Office, 1320 NE Campus Parkway,Seattle 98195,(206)634-3460, Employment opportunities with the University of Washington; those enrolled at the U of W.

United Indians of All Tribes Foundation, 1945 Vale Pl E Seattle,98102,(206)325-6381, Employment counseling, job referral, placement assistance, GED & test center, social service planning department; 8-5 M-F, ex-offender with GED only.

University YWCA (Job Finding) Seattle,(206)632-4747, Employment services; women in need of services.

V.R.O –Ballard: 907 NE Ballard Way,Seattle,98107,(206)545-7730 Bellevue:15831 NE 8th St,Bellevue,98008,(206)453-6520 Burien: 15811 Ambaum Blvd

Seattle,98166,(206)433-1319 Green River Community College, A.R.A. Bldg,Rm SU-8,Auburn (206)464-6133 Northgate: 9620 Stone Ave N,#202,Seattle 98103,(206)545-6679 Seattle Community College: Seattle,98122,(206)464-7647, Helps disabled state residents obtain employment; 8-5 M-F, disabled, physical & mental persons, free.

Washington Human Development 4636 E.Marginal Way S,Suite 108,Seattle,(206)762-5192, Immigration services, ESL, ABE, GED, job development & placement, vocational counseling, training clerical, word processing, auto, custodial skills; 8-5 M-F, migrant seasonal farm workers; free.

Washington Women's Employment & Education, 1525 4th Ave,#510 Seattle,98101(206)447-9786 Helps women break the poverty line with training, search, placement; 8-5 M-F, low income women, free.

WEN(Women Employment Network), South Seattle Community College 6000 16th Ave SW,Seattle,98106, Employment services, placement assistance, computer training; 8:30-4:30 M-F, women in need of services, free.

YWCA(Job Finding), 1118 5th Ave 2nd Fl,Seattle,98101,(206)447-4862, Employment services; women in need of services, free.

YWCA-North Area Job Bank 12531 28th NE,Seattle,98125 (206)364-6810, Employment services, all persons, free.

FAMILY PLANNING

Abortion, Pregnancy Referral Service, 701 NE Northlake Way,Seattle,98105,(206)634-3460, Family planning, pregnancy, referral for counseling, birth control, pregnancy information, health care & social services; all persons, sliding fee.

Adoption Services of WACAP
543 Industry Dr,Tykwila,98188 (206)575-4550, Family planning, pregnancy, adoption counseling; 9-12 & 1-4, all persons, free.

Apple Parenting Program
1102 J St,SE,Auburn,98022 (206)939-0870, Parenting classes for prenatal care; 8:30-5 M-F, all persons, low income.

Children's Home Society of Washington, 3300 NE 65th Seattle,98115,(206)524-6020, Family support services; all persons.

Children's Hospital & Medical Center, 4800 Sand Point Way NE,Seattle,98105,(206)526-2500 Parenting, counseling for prenatal care, Lamaze classes; all persons.

Community Obstetrics Referral Program, 200 Broadway,Seattle 98122,(206)467-1771, Family planning, pregnancy, referral for prenatal care and delivery; 8-4 M-F, low income.

Crisis Pregnancy Center of King County, 3229 NE 125th,Seattle 98125,(206)367-2222, Family planning, pregnancy; all persons.

Department of Human Resources, City of Seattle, 105 Union Seattle,98101,(206)386-1001, Child care cost assistance, home daycare, food service, youth services; 8-5 M-F,free.

Family Services, 107 Cherry St Seattle,98104,(206)447-3883, 461-3883, Renton,Kent & Seattle area. Anger management classes, widowed information, facing aging, child guidance, consultation services;

8-5 M-F, widows, families, abused women, sliding fee.

Harborview Medical Center-Women's Clinic, 325 9th Ave Seattle,98104,(206)223-3000, Family planning, pregnancy; 24 hours, all persons, medical coupons.

Medina Children's Service
123 16th Ave,Seattle,98122 (206)324-9470, Family planning, pregnancy; 9-5 M-F.

New Hope of Washington, 2611 NE 125th,Suite 146,Seattle 98125.(206)363-1800, Pregnancy, adoption & foster care services, 8-4 M-F, all persons, free.

Options of Pregnancy, POB 88007 Seattle,98188,(206)732-1887, Family planning, pregnancy, all persons.

Planned Parenthood, 2211 E. Madison,Seattle,98112,(206) 328-7700, Family planning & pregnancy, training & education adoption referral, STD checks; 11:30, all persons, sliding fee.

Pregnancy Aid, 509 Olive Way, #1507,Seattle,98101,(206)621-1721, Family planning & pregnancy; 11:30, all persons, sliding fee.

Seattle Head Start, 105 Union St,Seattle,98101,(206)447-3660, Daycare; all persons.

Sex Information Line, (206)328-7711, Planned parenthood, sexually transmitted disease, birth control; 2-8 M-Thur; all persons, free.

Supervision Services, Inc, (206)771-9402, Facilitators for parent-child visitations; those in need of services.

The Rubber Tree, 4426 Burk Ave N,Seattle, Non-prescription contraceptives, reasonable prices, family planning; all persons.

University Hospital-Medical Clinic, 1959 NE Pacific,Seattle 98195,(206)543-4030, Family planning, pregnancy; all persons, sliding fee.

FOOD CLOTHING HOUSING

Auburn Community Fund, POB 464 Auburn,98002,(206)833-8925, Food, clothing, emergency aid, emergency housing; 9-1:30, free.

American Hotel, 520 South King Seattle,(206)223-9282, Shelter, women's program, women & children, $5.00 per night.

Bethlehem House, 7132 35th SW Seattle,98126,(206)937-7521, Emergency shelter for women; those in need of services, free.

Bread of Life Mission, 97 S Main,Seattle,98104,(206)682-3579, Emergency shelter of men with breakfast & dinner, beds & showers; 9:30-11:30 M-W-F, men in need, free.

Camp, Seattle,(206)329-4111, Family shelters, emergency housing, food bank, energy & unemployment programs, inner city self help & youth; food bank open Thur & Fri, 8:30-12, regular hours 8:30-5, economically disadvantaged.

Chabad House, Seattle (206)527-1411, Emergency shelter for men, $10.00 each night, $5.00 for children, food, bed, showers; 8-4 M-F, jewish men in need, free.

Friendly Inn, 522 S.King Seattle,Shelter for women; $5.00 per night.

Georgetown Service Center 733 S. Findlay St,Seattle 98108, 6200 13th Ave S,Seattle 98108, (206)767-7888, Emergency food, clothing & housing

furnishing; those in need of services; free.

Inn Between, 6205 222nd SW Montlake Terrace,Seattle,98043 (206)774-9843, Emergency help for women & children, housing counseling for misplaced homemakers, sliding fee.

International District Housing Alliance, 6205 222nd SW Montlake Terrace,Seattle,98104 (206)623-5132, Assistance in finding low cost housing & emergency shelter; low income persons.

Lutheran Compass Center, 77 S Washington,Seattle,98104, (206)623-6326, Emergency shelter for men & women with some counseling available, set fee.

Multi-Service Centers of North & East King County, 18220 96th NE,Bothell,98011, Emergency shelter for women, families & children, 8:30-4:30 M-F, all persons, .free.

Neighborhood House, 905 Spruce St,Seattle,98104,(206)447-8430, Emergency services, information & referrals, advocacy; 8:30-5 M-F, low income families in public housing, free.

Northshore Multi Service Center 18220 98th NE,Seattle,98011 (206)485-6521, Referrals to community agencies for support services, food, clothing; 8:30-4:30 M-F, disadvantaged & unemployed persons, free.

Peniel Mission, Seattle,(206) 682-7423, Emergency shelter for men in need.

PHS Bishop Lewis House-Work Release, 703 8th Ave,Seattle 98104,(206)464-7000

Dalton House: 4510 2nd Ave.NE Seattle,19805(206)545-8512

Fellowship House-Work Release
220 11th Ave,Seattle,(206)
642-5472

Madison Inn-Work Release
102 21st Ave.E,Seattle,(206)
464-5847

Mark Cooper House, 1110 18th
Ave.E.,Seattle,98112,(206)328-
7144

The Bridge, 1102 E.Spruce
Seattle,98122,(206)446-6370

Vantage Point, 5614 17th
NW,Seattle,98107,(206)782-6787
Residential facility; offenders,
state, federal, county, sliding
fee.

Providence Hospitality House
POB 22382,Seattle,98122(206)
322-2107, Emergency shelter
for women & children, meals,
4 family; 9-4 M-F, all
persons, free.

Sacred Heart Shelter
232 Warren Ave N,Seattle
98109,(206)285-7489,
Emergency shelter for women,
families & children, males or
females with families, single
women; 9-5 M-F, free.

**Salvation Army Catherine Boothe
House,** POB 20128,Seattle,98102,
Shelter for abused women,
sliding fee.

Salvation Army Red Shield Lodge
Seattle,(206)621-0145, Emergency shelter for men only.

**Seattle Emergency Housing
Services,** 905 Spruce St
Seattle,98104,(206)447-3660,
Emergency shelter for women,
families & children, sliding
fee.

Second Chance Reynolds House
410 4th Ave,Seattle,98104
(206)464-6320, Residential
facility; offenders referred
by DOC.

**South King County-Federal Way
Bank,** 3163 PHS Freeway,Seattle
98003,(206)941-2881, Emergency
shelter for single women;
10-2 M,W,F, Federal Way
residents only, free.

**St. Martin De Porres
Shelter-Catholic Community
Center,** 1561 Alaskan Way S
Seattle,98134, Emergency
shelter for men, laundry,
health care, alcohol counseling,
mental health counseling, meals;
after 6:30pm, men 50+ years of
age in need, free.

State Shelter Network Hotline:
(800) 562-6025, Shelter
referrals.

Traveler's Aid Society, 909 4th
Ave,Seattle,(206)447-3888,
Assistance in finding housing,
bus fare & travel expenses
provided; 8:30-9 M-F,
ex-offender & new residents,
free.

**U.S. Social Security
Administration,** 720 Olive
Way,Seattle,98101,(800)234-5772
Emergency food, food stamps;
all persons.

Union Gospel Mission, 520 King
St,Seattle,98104,(206)223-9282,
Shelter for women & families in
need of services.

Union Gospel Mission, 318 2nd
Ave,Exit South,Seattle,(206)
622-5177, Emergency shelter
for men, some meals, rehabilitation, clothing, 24 hours,
men in need, $1.00 meals,
$2.00 beds.

World for Women, 6205 222nd SW
POB 5627,Montlake Terrace
98043,(206)774-9843, Counseling,
shelter, housing, displaced
homemakers program, share,
education & children; 24
hours; 9-5 M-F, all persons,
sliding fee.

YWCA - Downtown, 1118th 5th Ave
3rd Floor,Seattle,98101,(206)

461-4882, Emergency shelter for single women; those in need of services, free.

YWCA – South County Branch
1025 So. 3rd,Renton,98055
(206)255-1201
East Cherry Branch, 2820 E. Cherry,Seattle,98122,(206) 322-0186, Emergency shelter for women, families & children; all persons, no fee.

LEGAL

American Civil Liberties Union
1720 Smith Tower,Seattle,98104 506 5th Ave,Seattle,(206) 624-2180, Legal assistance; 9-5 M-F, all persons, free.

Dispute Resolution Center of King County, POB 21148,Seattle 98111,(206)329-3944, Landlord disputes, mediator service, merchant consumer, 8:30-5:30, those in need of services, free.

King County – Family Court Services, Courthouse, W #364,Seattle,98101,(206)583-4690

Office of Public Defense, 2015 Smith Tower,Seattle,98104 (206)344-3452
Prosecuting Attorney, 516 3rd Ave,Seattle,98104,(206)683-2200 Legal assistance; all persons.

Northwest Women's Law Center
119 S.Main St,Seattle,98104 (206)682-9552, Legal assistance information referral over phone 9:30-4 M-F, all persons.

Pacific Family Mediation Institute, 12505 Bel Red Rd Bellevue,98055,(206)451-7940, Legal assistance, answering service, all persons.

Seattle King County Bar Association, 600 Bank of California,900 4th,Seattle (206)624-9365, Legal assistance, lawyer referral, telephone law, neighborhood

legal clinic; 9-5 M-F, all persons, $20.00 first 1/2 hour, otherwise varies.

Seattle Rape Relief, 1825 S. Jackson,Seattle,98144 (206)632-7273, Counseling, family law resources, legal advocacy; abused women & rape victims, free.

Sexual Assault Center
325 Ninth Ave,Seattle,98104 (206)223-3047, Resource services for family law issues; all persons.

MEDICAL/DENTAL

Easter Seal Society of Washington, 521 2nd Ave W,Seattle,98119,(206)281-5700 Dental access program, disable programs, referrals; all persons, free.

Forty Fifth Street Clinic
1629 N 45th St,Seattle,98103 (206)633-3350, Outpatient health care, general medical care, HIV testing; 9-5 M-F, all persons, sliding fee.

Georgetown Dental Clinic
733 S.Findlay,Seattle,98108 (206)762-4070, Dental services general and prothodontics; 9-5 M-F, adults, sliding fee.

International District Emergency Center, POB 14103 Seattle,98114,(206)623-3321, Medical, emotional & other support groups in acute emergencies; 24 hours, must call first and live in area, free.

King District/King County Health, 10501 Meridian Ave N,Seattle,(206)363-4765, Health information, limited care & services, immunizations, food handler testing; 8-4:30 M-F, all persons, sliding fee.

Odessa Brown Children's Clinic
2101 E. Yesler Way,Seattle 98122,(206)329-7870, Dental

care, medical clinic, foster care & WIC; hours 8-5 M-F, all persons, sliding fee.

Optometric Center of Seattle
172 29th Ave,Seattle,(206)325-1100, Eye care; 8-4 M-F, sliding fee.

Rainier Vista Medical Clinic
3006 S.Oregon,Seattle,98108 (206)723-6151, Medical care; all ages, sliding fee.

Regional Division-King County Health, 1200 Public Safety Bldg Seattle(206)587-2752, Health information, limited care & services, immunizations, food handler testing; 8-5 M-F, all persons, sliding fee.

Sea-Mar Community Health Clinic
8720 14th Ave S,Seattle,98101 (206)762-3730, Dental care outpatient, medical, WIC homeless program, home health; 8-6 M-F, all persons, sliding fee.

Seattle King County Dental Services, 720 Oliver Way #913,Seattle,98101,(206)624-4912, Dental care & referral; all persons, free.

Seattle Poison Center
4800 Sand Point Way NE,Seattle 98105,(206)526-2121, Emergency information; 9-5 M-F, all persons, free.

Seattle King County Department of Public Health
110 Prefontaine Pl S,Seattle 98104,(206)587-2720, Health information, limited care & services, immunizations, food handler testing; 8-4 M-F, all persons, sliding fee.

Southeast Seattle Community Dental Clinic, 3800 S. Myrtle St,Seattle,(206)723-0922, Dental care; all persons, sliding fee.

Sydney Miller Community Service Center, 169 19th Ave,Seattle

98144,(206)322-1038, Sickle cell testing, transportation to prisons, medicine; those in need of services, sliding fee.

University of Washington School of Dentistry, 1959 NE Pacific Seattle,98195,(206)543-5830, Dental care; all persons, sliding fee.

Yesler Terrace Health Clinic
102 Broadway,Seattle,98122 (206)625-9260, Dental services, general and root canals, medical; all ages, sliding fee.

MISCELLANEOUS

Bread of Life Mission
97 S Main St,Seattle,98104 (206)682-3579, Homeless facility for men; bed capacity 40+, can stay 14 days.

Child Look Out, POB 231,Seattle 98043,(206)771-7335, Operation lookout for missing children, legal, searching, parenting; all persons, free.

Community Correction 420 E Main,MS NA-48,Auburn,98002 (206)931-3965, 23 148th SE, MS NB-69,Belevue,98007,(206)455-7180, 15111 8th Ave SW,POB 66768,Seattle,(206)246-2039, 1601 2nd Ave,Suite 905,MS TB-12,Seattle,(206)464-7387, 9620 Stone Ave N, #102,MS TB-07,Seattle,(206)545-6651, 110 Prefontaine Pl S,MS TB-11 Seattle,(206)464-7950, 817 S 3rd St,MS NR-62,Renton,98055 (206)764-4225, Information & referrals limited to felony offenders sentenced under the Sentencing Reform Act (SRA) who are not receiving supervision within one year after release.

Concilio for the Spanish Speaking, 157 Yesler,Seattle 98104,(206)774-9551, 8021 230 SW,Edmonds,98020,(206)774-9551 Employment referrals, hispanic news magazine & bilingual re-

ferrals, alcohol, drug &
cocaine addiction.

**Downtown Emergency Service
Center,** 210 Jefferson,Seattle
98102,(206)464-1570, Homeless
facility foe men.

Highline High Point Branch
1010 S 146th,Seattle,(206)
932-3266,241-0990, Anger
management classes; all persons, sliding fee.

Interaction Transition
935 16th Ave,Seattle,98122
(206)329-4408,328-1860,
Aid in transition from
incarceration to society,
employment counseling, job
referral & placement assistance, help for transition to
community; ex-offenders.

Lutheran Compass Center
77 S Washington,Seattle,98104
(206)623-6326, Homeless
facility for men; bed capacity
20, fee for staying.

Salvation Army Shelter
811 Maynard,Seattle,98104
(206)621-0145, Homeless
facility for men; bed capacity
50+, can stay 14 days, no
meals provided.

**Seattle Counseling Service for
Sexual Minorities**
1505 Broadway,Seattle,98122
(206)329-8707, Anger control
support group for lesbians;
12-9, lesbians.

Seattle Indian Alcohol Program
611 12th Ave S,Seattle,98144
(206)324-9360, Jail/prison
outreach, assessment, counseling, resource coordination,
referral services; those in
need of services; sliding fee.

Union Gospel Mission, 318 2nd
Ave,Seattle,98104,(206)622-5177
Homeless facility for men; bed
capacity 220+, can stay 2 days.

SUBSTANCE ABUSE

Adult Children of Alcoholics
POB 23067,Seattle,98102,(206)
722-6117, Alcohol & drug
support groups and counseling;
24 hours, 7 days, all persons,
free.

Advantages, 14042 NE 8th
Bellevue,98007,(206)643-5028,
Certified alcohol & drug
information school, DWI client
assessment, alcohol outpatient
treatment.

Al-Anon Family Groups, 1402 3rd
Ave #921,Seattle,98101,(206)
625-0000, Support groups, referral to agency; all persons,
free.

Alcoholics Anonymous
1507 Queen Anne Ave N,Seattle
98109,(206)282-4441, Regular
AA meetings and support
groups; All persons, free.

Alternative, 1818 Westlake N
Seattle,98109,(206)282-4161,
Certified alcohol & drug
treatment, DWI client assessment, alcohol outpatient
treatment; 8-6 Tue-F, fee.

Alburn Youth Resources
816 F St SE, Auburn,98002
(206)939-2202, Certified drug
outpatient treatment, youth
family counseling, teen
therapy for run aways; 9-5
M-F, by appointment, pri-
marily youths.

**Ballard Community Hospital
Care Unit,** Box C-70707,Seattle
98107,5300 Tallman Ave NW
Seattle,98107, Certified
alcohol detoxification and
inpatient treatment and after
care, chemical outpatient.

Bellevue Probation Division
655 120th Ave SE,Bellevue
98009,(206)6956, Certified
alcohol & drug treatment,
DWI client assessment;
8:30-5 M-F, Bellevue District
Court only, free.

Calm-Justice Associates, Inc,
1207 N 200th St,Seattle,98133
(206)542-1136, Certified
alcohol & drug outpatient
treatment, information school,
DWI client assessment, custody
assessments, family marital
court; 8-4:30 M-S; free.

Care Unit Hospital
10322 NE 132nd St,Kirkland
98034,(206)821-1122, Certified
alcohol & drug inpatient
treatment, alcohol detoxification, free assessment,
public lectures, chemical
inpatient treatment; 24
hours, sliding fee.

Cedar Hill Treatment Center
15900 227th Ave SE,Maple
Valley,98038,(206)392-9159,
296-8700, Chemical alcohol
inpatient treatment, after
care, certified alcohol & drug
intensive in patient treatment
alcohol extended care recovery
housing; 8-4, all persons.

Center for Human Services
17011 Meridian Ave N,Seattle
(206)546-2411, Outpatient
treatment, counseling, general
counseling, assessment, certified alcohol & drug treatment,
DWI client assessment, drug
outpatient treatment;
9-5 Wed, sliding fee.

Chemical Dependency Program
1945 Yale Pl E,Seattle,98102
(206)325-0070, 682-4695,
Certified alcohol outpatient
treatment, night classes,
inpatient treatment; 8-5,
sliding fee.

Chinook Center, 550 Mercer St
Seattle,98109,(206)282-9991,
Certified alcohol & drug outpatient treatment, information
school, DWI client assessment,
intensive outpatient treatment;
24 hours, sliding fee.

Cocaine Anonymous
45310,Seattle,98145
(206)722-6114, Support groups,
12 step group; 24 hours, all

persons, free.

Comprehensive Alcohol Services
23830 Pacific Highway S,Kent
(206)824-5565, Certified
alcohol & drug information
school, DWI client assessment,
alcohol outpatient treatment.

Consejo Counseling Referral
3808 S. Angeline,Seattle,98118
(206)721-0800, 2524 16th Ave S
Seattle, 762-5665, Certified
alcohol & drug outpatient
treatment, information school,
DWI client assessment, outpatient treatment & counseling
sliding fee.

Cornerstone Treatment Centers
610 NW 4th,Seattle,98107,(206)
784-9947, Certified alcohol &
drug information school, DWI
client assessment, alcohol
outpatient treatment, anger
management, family counseling;
24 hours.

Crosby Enterprises, 13751 Lack
City Way NE,Seattle,98125
(206)362-0062, Certified
alcohol & drug outpatient
treatment, DWI client
assessment.

Dell Craig Therapist, Inc,
22030 7th Ave S,Des Moines
98188,(206)824-9273, Certified
alcohol & drug information
school, DWI client assessment,
alcohol outpatient treatment;
8-8 M-F, insurance payment.

Eastside Alcohol Center
606 120th Ave NE,Bellevue,98005
(206)454-1505,722-3700,
Certified alcohol & drug outpatient treatment, information
school, DWI client assessment,
counseling, free.

Evergreen Treatment Services
1250 1st Ave S,Seattle,98134
(206)223-2644, Certified drug
outpatient treatment, methadone
treatment, detoxification &
urinalysis testing, 7-4 M-F,
free.

Federal Way Counseling Services
32700 Pacific Highway S,Federal
Way,(206)874-874-4443, Certified alcohol & drug, DWI
client assessment, alcohol
outpatient treatment, 9-5 M-F,
free.

Federal Way Youth Services
1411 SW Dash Point Rd,Federal
Way,(206)839-6555, Certified
drug outpatient, intensive
outpatient treatment, sliding
fee.

First Step, 14400 NE Bel-Red
Rd,Bellevue,98007,(206)746-3888
25608 74th Ave S,Kent,98032
(206)859-0951, 12063 15th Ave
NE,Seattle,98125,(206)363-0081
Alcohol & drug information
school, counseling, inpatient
& outpatient treatment,
assessment; 9-6 M-F, adults
and children; sliding fee.

Genesis House, 621 34th Ave
Seattle,98108,(206)328-0881,
Certified drug long term
residential, after care,
inpatient drug treatment;
sliding fee.

Group Health Cooperative
Adaption, 2661 Bel Red Rd
Bellevue,98005,(206)885-9492,
2700 152nd Ave NE,Redmond
(206)883-5151, Certified
alcohol & drug outpatient
treatment & detoxification,
information school,
Intensive impatient treatment
sliding fee.

Highline Youth Service Bureau
POB 66086,Seattle,98166,(206)
243-5544, Certified alcohol &
drug outpatient treatment,
social skills, teen patient
classes; 9-5 M-F, primarily
youths, sliding fee.

Intercept Associates
30620 Pacific Highway S
Federal Way,98003,(206)941-
7555, Certified alcohol & drug
outpatient treatment, information school, DWI client
assessment, counseling,
answering service, sliding
fee.

King County Alcohol Center,
Eastside: 606 120th Ave NE
Bellevue,(206)454-1505,
King Services, 10501 Meridian
Ave N,Seattle,(206)364-3925
SW Community: 15025 4th SW
Seattle,98166,(206)828-3506,
Central: 1401 E. Jefferson
Seattle,98122,(206)322-2970,
Treatment Facility, 1421 Minor
Ave,Seattle,(206)587-0161,
Outpatient treatment, alcohol
information school & referral,
counseling, urine testing
service, drug abuser treatment
DWI deferred prosecution
evaluations, certified alcohol
& drug detoxification
service, 9-5 M-F, sliding fee.

King County District Court
Probation Service, 516 3rd
Ave,Seattle,(206)344-3897,
Certified alcohol & drug
treatment, DWI client
assessment by court,
7:30-5:30 M-F, sliding fee.

McClure Associates Counseling
1818 Westlake Ave N,Seattle
98109,(206)282-9251, Certified
alcohol & drug outpatient
treatment, information school,
DWI client assessment;
7-5 M-F, sliding fee.

Mercer Island Youth & Family
Services, 8236 SE 24th St
Mercer Island,(206)236-3525,
Certified alcohol & drug out-
patient treatment; 9-5 M-F,
sliding fee.

Milam Counseling Center, Angel
Lake: 9530 Pacific Highway
S,Seattle,(206)824-9780,
Eastlake: 10422 NE 37th
Cir,Kirkland,98033,(206)822-
5095,
Northlake: 17962 Midvale Ave
N,Seattle,(206)542-6106, Cert-
ified alcohol & drug outpatient
treatment, information school,
DWI client assessment;
9-5 M-F, initial interview
is free.

Moss & Associates, 1410 130th NE,Bellevue,98005,(206)453-0550 Certified alcohol & drug treatment, DWI client assessment, alcohol outpatient treatment, set fee.

Moss Bay Comprehensive Treatment Center, 1912 E. Madison,Seattle,98122,(206)325-0459, Certified drug outpatient treatment, alcohol & drug assessment, counseling with treatment, answering service, sliding fee.

Mount Baker Youth Service Bureau Community Associates 1730 Brandner Pl. S,Seattle 98144, Certified drug outpatient treatment; 8-5 M-F, sliding fee.

Muckleshoot Tribal Alcoholism Program, 39015 172nd SE,Auburn 98002,(206)939-3311, Certified alcohol & drug outpatient treatment, information school, DWI client assessment; 8-5 M-F, sliding fee.

Narcotics Anonymous, POB 24192 Seattle,98124,(206)329-1618, Support groups, 24 hours, all persons.

North Seattle Youth Services 9250 14th Ave NW,Seattle,98117 (206)789-3163, Certified drug outpatient treatment, counseling; 8:30-5 M-F, sliding fee.

Northwest Treatment Center 130 Nickerson St,Seattle,98107 (206)283-9101,Alcohol & drug outpatient program, counseling & assessment, 10:30-7:30, adults, sliding fee.

Northwest Teen Challenge 1808 18th St,Seattle,98122 (206)846-0888, Certified drug intensive inpatient treatment, sliding fee.

PHS/St Regis Hotel, 116 Stewart St,Seattle,98108,(206)782-6787, Alcohol & drug free hotel, adults.

Positive Addicts, LTD, 30640 Pacific Highway S,Federal Way 98003,(206)839-5852, Certified drug & alcohol information school, DWI client assessment, sliding fee.

Renaissance Recovery House 1111 4th NE,Auburn,98002 (206)833-4304, Certified alcohol & drug recovery house, mental counseling, inpatient & outpatient treatment; 8-5 M-F, sliding fee.

Renton Area Youth Services 1025 S. Third.Renton,98055 (206)271-5600, Certified drug outpatient treatment, counseling for youth & families; 9-5 M-F, primarily youths, sliding fee.

Renton Vocational Technical Institute, 3000 NE Fourth St,Renton,(206)235-2352, Certified alcohol & drug information school, DWI client asessment; 7:30-8 M-F, sliding fee.

Riverton General Hospital Care Unit, 12844 Military Rd S Seattle,(206)248-4790, Certified alcohol inpatient treatment & detoxification, chemical inpatient treatment, 24 hour line; 8-4:30, sliding fee.

Ryther Child Center, 2400 NE 95th St,Seattle,98115,(206) 525-5050, Certified alcohol & drug inpatient treatment, per school outpatient services, sliding fee.

Saint Cabrini Recovery Program Terry & Madison,Seattle,98104 (206)583-4344, Certified alcohol & treatment school, DWI client assessment, chemical inpatient treatment, recovery program; 8-5 M-F, sliding fee.

The Salvation Army Harborlight Center, 416 2nd Ave,Seattle 98104,(026)621-0145, Certified drug recovery house.

Schick Shadel Hospital, 12101 Ambaum Blvd SW,Seattle,98146 98146,(206)244-8100, Chemical inpatient treatment, certified alcohol & drug intensive inpatient treatment, DWI client assessment, alcohol detoxification, fee.

Seadrunar, Queen Anne,200 W Comstock,Seattle,98119,(206) 284-2431
Phase I – Georgetown 976 S Hamey,Seattle,98108 (206)767-0244
Phase II – Capitol Hill,809 15th E,Seattle,98112 (206)324-8500, Certified drug long term residential, sliding fee.

Seattle Drug & Narcotics Center POB 24344,Seattle,98124 (206)767-0244, Inpatient & outpatient drug treatment, long term 9-5 M-F, sliding fee.

Seattle Indian Alcoholism Program, 611 12th Ave S Seattle,(206)324-9360, Certified alcohol outpatient treatment, sliding fee.

Seattle Indian Health Board 2222 2nd Ave S,Seattle,98144 (206)324-9360, Outpatient treatment & counseling for alcoholics; Indians only.

Shamrock Group, Inc. 8535 Phinney Ave N,Seattle 98103,(206)789-4784, Certified alcohol & drug information school, DWI client assessment, alcohol outpatient treatment.

Social Treatment Opportunity Programs, 620 M St NE,Auburn (206)735-2718, Certified alcohol & drug information school, DWI client assessment, intensive outpatient and anger management classes; 9-9 M-F, sliding fee.

Southeast Community Alcohol & Drug Center, 232 S 2nd Ave Kent,(206)854-6513, Certified alcohol & drug outpatient treatment, information school, DWI client assessment, anger management; 8:30-5 M-F, free.

Southwest Community Recovery Center, 15025 4th Ave SW Seattle,(026)242-3506, Certified alcohol & drug out- patient treatment, information school, DWI client assessment; 9-5 M-F, sliding fee.

Square One, 1275 12th Ave NW POB 1178,Issaquah,98027 (206)392-7815, 7811 159th Pl NE,Redmond,98052, Certified alcohol & drug information school, DWI client assessment information & referrals; 8-5 M-F, sliding fee.

St Frances Xavier, 920 Terry Ave,Seattle,98104,(206)583- 4344, Outpatient programs, detoxification, sliding fee.

TASC of King County 1111 Dexter Horton Bldg Seattle,98104,(206)467-0338, 825 S Third,Renton,98055 (206)228-2122, Certified alcohol & drug outpatient treatment, referrals & evaluations, drug testing; 8-5 M-F, sliding fee.

Theraputic Health Services 11116 Summit,Seattle,98101 (206)323-0930, 17962 Midvale Ave N,Seattle,98133 (206)546-9766, Certified alcohol & drug outpatient treatment, information school, DWI client assessment; serves pregnant women (pre and post) comprehensive treatment drug abuse, methadone, counseling, detoxification 2 year maintenance; 8-4:30, sliding fee.

Thunderbird Treatment Center 9236 Renton Ave S,Seattle,98118 (206)722-7152, Intensive care residential treatment program, group & individual counseling, medical services, recovery house, adolescent program; 8-5 M-F, sliding fee.

Tough Love, (206)523-3862,
Self help group for families
of children who are addicts
& alcoholics.

V.R.O Alcohol Program
1421 Minor Ave,#617,Seattle
98104,(206)464-6304, Helps
disabled state residents
obtain employment, referrals,
alcohol counseling; 8-5 M-F,
disabled, physical & mental,
free.

Vashon Community Alcohol Center
Route 5 Box 41,Vashon,98070
(206)567-4069, Alcohol outpatient treatment & counseling;
9-5 M-F, sliding fee.

Vashon Community Alcohol Center
POB 99,Vashon,98070
(206)463-9492, Certified
alcohol & drug information
school, DWI client assessment;
8-5 M-F, sliding fee.

**Washington Drug Rehabilitation
Center,** 421 30th Ave,Seattle
98144,(206)325-4005, Certified
drug long term residential,
inpatient long term drug
treatment; 9-5 M-F, sliding
fee.

Women in Recovery, 1011 Boren
Ave,POB 805,Seattle,98104
(206)722-6117, Support group
for women in alcohol & recovery; 24 hours, women only,
free.

Youth Eastside Services
16150 NE 8th St,Bellevue,98008
(206)747-4YES Certified alcohol
& drug outpatient treatment,
information school, DWI client
assessment, family & youth
counseling, incest; par-
ticularly youths, sliding fee.

TRANSPORTATION

Metro Transit, 821 2nd
Ave,Seattle,(206)447-4800,
Rider information, all
persons.

VETERANS SERVICES

Agent Orange Hotline, 505 E
Union,Olympia,98502
(206)562-2308, Stress
counseling, claims assistance,
outreach programs; 24 hours,
Veterans, free.

**Alcohol Dependence Treatment
Program,** 4435 Beacon Ave S
Seattle, 1660 S. Columbia
Way,Seattle,(206)762-1010,
Outpatient monitor antibuse
control program, inpatient
program; 9-5 M-F, Veterans,
payment.

American Legion, 915 2nd Ave
Rm 1044,Seattle,98174
(206)442-7043

Disabled American Veterans
915 2nd Ave Rm 1058,Seattle
(206)442-7048

Dr. Emmett Early, 4719
University Way NE,#206,Seattle
98105,(206)527-4684,
Delayed stress counseling.

Paralyzed Veterans of America
901 SW 152nd,Seattle,98166
(206)241-1843, Help identify &
apply benefits, counseling
information; all veterans.

Seattle Veterans Action Center
105 14th Ave #2A,Seattle,98122
(206)684-4708, Employment
counseling, general benefits,
counseling & assistance,
Veteran education & transition
housing for homeless veterans;
8-4 M-F, veterans including
offenders, free.

**U.S. Veterans Administration
Medical Center,** 1660 S Columbian Way,Seattle,98108,
Outpatient mental health
counseling, alcohol & drug
dependence, medical, denta,
inpatient treatment; 8-4:30
M-F, sliding fee.

VICTIMS

Alternatives to Fear, 1605 17th Ave,Seattle,98122,(206) 328-5347, 2811 E. Madison Seattle, Publications & lectures available for sexual assault prevention; M-F, sliding fee.

Catherine Booth House, 200 Wilomas Bldg 425,Seattle 98102,(206)281-4371, POB 20128,Seattle,98102,(206) 325-8101 324-4943, Temporary shelter for battered women & children, support groups, counseling, domestic violence advocacy; 9-5.

Center for Prevention of Sexual & Domestic Violence, 1914 N 34th,Seattle,98103 (206)634-1903, Resource ser- vices for family law issues, sexual assault programs; 9-4:30, free.

City of Seattle, Law Depart- ment (Criminal), 600 4th Ave,Seattle,98104,(206)625- 2119, 1414 Dexter Horton St,Seattle,(206)684-7770, Family violence program; victims only, abused women, free.

Committee for Children, 172 20th Ave,Seattle,98122,(206) 322-5050, Child abuse ser- vices, family law resources, sexual assault programs, prevention of child exploitation; 9-5 M-F, fee.

Center for Prevention of Sexual & Domestic Violence, 1914 N 34th,Suite 105,Seattle 98103,(206)634-1903 Educational materials, re- sources & counseling referral, presentation referrals, dom- estic violence counseling; 9-4 M-F, free.

Dawn, POB 1521,Kent,98032 (206)846-0764, Domestic vio- lence advocacy, support groups, community education,

resource services for family law issues; 9-5 M-F, free.

Downtown Emergency Center, 240 Jefferson,Seattle,98032,(206) 464-1570, Helper for abused women, shelter & housing, 200 people, hot meal program; 12-2:30 & 3:30-9, abused women, free.

Eastside Domestic Violence Program, Seattle,(206)746- 1940, POB 6398,Bellevue,98008 (206)746-1946, Emergency help for battered women & children support group & counseling for domestic violence, safehomes, transition; abused women.

Family Violence Project, 1000 Municipal Bldg,Seattle,98104 (206)684-7770, Domestic violence advocacy & referrals resource services for family law issues sliding fee.

Harborview Medical Center, 325 9th Ave,Seattle,98104 (206)233-3000, Counseling & treatment for sexual assault; 24 hours, medical coupons.

King County Rape Relief, 1025 S 3rd Ave,Renton,98055,(206) 226-RAPE, (800)825-7273, Counseling for rape victims, legal advocacy.

King County Victim Assistance Unit, 516 3rd Ave,Seattle 98104,(206)583-4422, Victim assistance; 8:30-4:30 M-F.

New Beginnings, POB 75125 Seattle,98125,(206)522-9472, Shelter for women, battered children, community support groups; 24 hours; abused women & children, sliding fee.

Overlake Hospital, 1035 116th Ave NE,Bellevue,98004,(206) 462-5130, Treatment of sexual assaults - Eastside; all persons.

Pacific Family Mediation Institute, Seattle,98004 (206) 451-7940, Classes for alternative solutions to family disputes; families in dispute.

Parents Anonymous, POB 15301 Seattle,98115,(206)524-5977, Child abuse services, parenting, training & support services; 8:30-5 M-F, free.

Seattle City Attorneys Family Violence Project, 1710 2nd Ave,#1414,(206)684-7770 Seattle, Battered women, legal services, 8:30-5 M-F, all persons, free.

Seattle Institute for Sexual Therapy, 100 NE 56th,Seattle 98105,(206)522-8588, Counseling & group therapy for recovery from rape & molestation; victims of rape & molestation, sliding fee.

Victim Assistance Unit - King County, Seattle,98104,(206) 583-4442, Information, legal support, advocacy, crisis intervention; 8-5 M-F, free.

YWCA Downtown Emergency Center, 1118 5th Ave,Seattle 98101,(206)461-4882, Domestic violence counseling & shelter free.

SOUTH PUGET SOUND

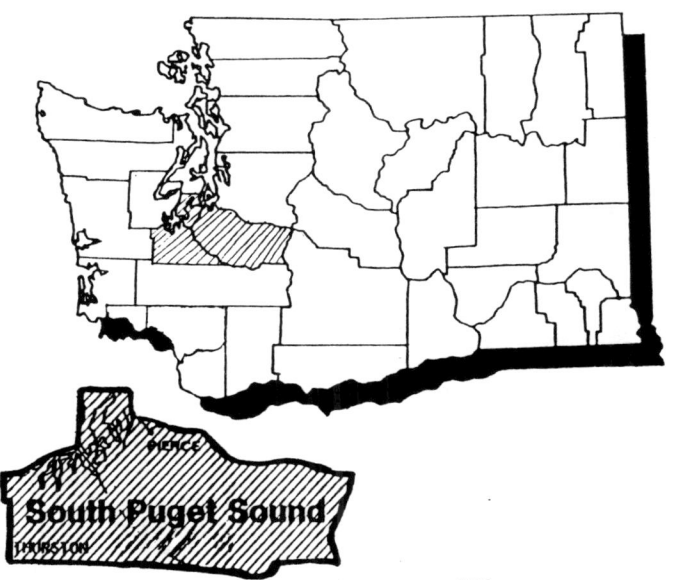

Pierce

Thurston

SOUTH PUGET SOUND
TOURISM ASSOCIATION
POB 1754, Tacoma 98401
(206)627-2836

HISTORICAL APPEAL

Pioneer Farm, Eatonville

Fort Lewis Military Museum,
Fort Lewis

Old State Capitol Building,
Olpympia

State Capital Museum, Olympia

Ezra Meeker Mansion, Puyallup

Steilcoom Historical Society
Museum, Steilcoom

Seymour Conservatory, Tacoma

Fort Nisqually, Tacoma

Tacoma Art Museum, Tacoma

Washington State Historical
Society Museum, Tacoma

Tenino Depot Museum, Tenino

Crosby House, Tumwater
Historical District

CITIES

BUCKLEY
Buckley Chamber of Commerce
POB 168,Buckley,98321,(206)
829-0322

CAPITOL CITIES

*   LACEY
Lacy Area Chamber of Commerce
POB 3206,5602 Pacific Ave
SE,Lacey,98503,(206)491-4141

*   OLYMPIA
Olympia/Thurston County Chamber
of Commerce,POB 1427,1000 Plum
St,Olympia,98501,(206)357-3363

Olympia is the state capitol
of Washington and is the seat
of **Thurston County.** The state
buildings stand on a bluff
overlooking Puget Sound. It
is the 17th largest city
in Washington. Olympia is in

**THE PALACE OF
VERSAILLES...**The
Pantages Theatre in
Tacoma seats 1161
people. It was
patterned after the
Palace of Versailles
and a vaudeville house.

**THE LARGEST CLAMS IN
WASHINGTON...**The
Geoduck (Gooey-duck) is
the largest clam in
North America, they can
weigh as much as 40
pounds. The Pacific
Giant Salamander can
grow longer than a
foot. Also, the largest
octopus in the world
can be found in Puget
Sound, weighing up to
300 pounds.

WESTERN FRONTIER MUSEUM
In Puyallup, Pierce
County, has the largest
collection of Western
artifacts in the World.

the southern tip of Puget
Sound, 47 miles southwest of
Seattle. It is the port of
an area rich in lumber,
agricultural, and mineral
products. The oyster industry,
wood processing, fruit and
vegetable canning, and brewing
are important activities.

EATONVILLE
Eatonville Chamber of Commerce
POB 845,Eatonville,98328,(206)
832-6600

FIFE
City of Fife Visitor Information Center, (206)922-2489

GIG HARBOR
3125 Judson St, Gig Harbor
98335, (206)851-6865

PUYALLUP
Puyallup Area Chamber of
Commerce,POB 1298,Puyallup,
98372,(206)845-6755

TACOMA
Tacoma/Pierce County Chamber
of Commerce,POB 1933,Tacoma
98690, (206)627-2175

Lakewood Area Chamber of
Commerce,11208 Bridgeport
Way,Tacoma,98690,(206)582-9400

Tacoma is the third largest
city in Washington and is
the seat of **Pierce County.**
Tacoma is located on Puget
Sound at the head of
Commencement Bay, and on the
Puyallup River, 25 miles south
of Seattle. The manufacture of
forest products, such as
lumber, furniture, doors,
plywood, and paper, is
Tacoma's chief industrial
activities.

Tacoma has an excellent
natural harbor and seaport;
shipping and shipbuilding are
important activities. It is
served by major airlines from
Seattle-Tacoma (SEA-TAC)

CHENEY DISCOVERY CENTER
...Located at North
West Trek near
Eatonville, Pierce
County, is a special
exhibit for youngsters.
It has a 12 foot high
live butterfly atrium,
a beehive, a 150 gallon
fish tank, and a
reptile touch tank.

**THE GROVE OF THE
PATRIARCHES**...This is a
breathtaking rainforest
located at Steven's
Canyon Entrance to Mt
Rainier National Park
on Route 123.

© 1984 VOLK

**THE LARGEST FLORAL
PARADE IN WASH**...Is The
Daffodil Festival in
Puyallup, Pierce
County. It is the
third largest floral
parade in the nation.

**THE FIRST INCORPORATED
TOWN IN WASHINGTON**...
was Steilcoom in 1854,
Pierce County.

International Airport, several transcontental railroads, and Interstate Highway 5.

FAIRS AND FESTIVALS

Old Time Music Festival
Tenino, March
(206)264-5075

Daffodil Festival
Orting, Puyallup, Sumner, Tacoma
April, (206)627-6176

Sound to Narrows Race
Tacoma, June
(206)597-8560

Jazz

Taste of Tacoma
Tacoma, July
(206)627-2175

HOW BIG IS THE TACOMA DOME?...It is 150 feet high and 530 feet in diameter. It is the largest wooden roof in the world, it will seat 26,000. The acoustics are fantastic!

Capitol Lakefair
Olympia, July
(206)943-7344

Prairie Days
Yelm, July
(206)458-7447

Pierce County Fair
Graham, August
(206)627-2836

Jazz Festival
Gig Harbor, August
(206)627-1504

Harbor Days
Olympia, September
(206)357-3370

Western Washington Fair
Puyallup, September
(206)845-1771

WOLVES...Can be seen at Wolf Haven located about 10 miles south of Olympia, Thurston County, off exit 99 from I-5. It was established in 1982 as a preserve to help protect this endangered species.

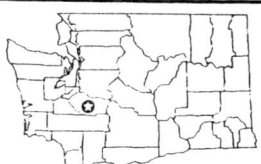

PIERCE COUNTY

Named for Franklin Pierce, who at the time of the country's creation was president-elect of the U.S.

Created: December 22, 1852

930 South Tacoma Avenue, Tacoma 98402
County Public Service Building
  South 35th Street, Tacoma 98409

AREA: 1,675.9 square miles, State Ranking: 23rd

MAJOR ECONOMIC ACTIVITIES:
Wood and Paper Products, Agriculture,
Metal Industries, Manufacturing, Shipbuiding,
Chemical and Allied Products, Apparel and Textiles,
Tourism

ASSESSED VALUE: $15,709,464,246

POPULATION: (1989 Estimate): 560,900

Percentage of state: 12.0%
Density: 334.7 persons per square mile

ETHNIC BREAKDOWN: 1988 Estimate
  White   464,861
  Black   36,484
  Native American   7,006
  Asian and Pacific Islanders   22,314
  Other   17,035
    Spanish origin (included in above)   20,052

PRIMARY CITIES   Population
  Bonney Lake   6,810
  Fircrest   5,440
  Puyallup   21,290
  Steilacoom   5,420
  Sumner   5,750
  Tacoma, county seat   161,100

CLIMATE: Tacoma - elevation 150 feet

Average	JAN	APR	JUL	OCT
Max Temp (F)	44.2	57.8	74.3	59.8
Min Temp	34.3	41.4	54.3	45.9
Mean Temp	39.9	50.8	64.4	53.0

```
Precipitation
in inches          5.34      2.37      .74      3.81
Average Annual Maximum Temperature:    59.1
Average Annual Minimum Temperature:    44.3
Average Annual Mean Temperature:       52.1
Average Annual Precipitation:  37.06 inches
```

PUBLIC SCHOOL DISTRICTS

Bethel School District #403
516 East 176th, Spanaway 98387
(206)536-7272   Enrollment: 11,121

Carbonado School District #406
POB 131, Carbonado 98323,
(206)829-0121   Enrollment: 122

Clover Park School District #400
10020 Gravelly Lake Dr., SW
Tacoma 98499,   (206)584-9411
Enrollment: 12,392

Dieringer School District #343
1320 178th Ave E., Sumner 98390
(206)862-2537   Enrollment: 862

Eatonville School District #404
POB 698, Eatonville 98328
(206)832-4766   Enrollment: 1,592

Fife School District #417
5602 20th St E., Tacoma 98424
(206)922-6697   Enrollment: 2,000

Franklin Pierce School District #402
315 South 129th St., Tacoma 98444
(206)537-0211   Enrollment: 5,989

Orting School District #344
Box 460, Orting 98360,   (206)893-6500
Enrollment: 1,200

Peninsula School District #401
14015 62nd Ave., NW, Gib Harbor 98335
(206)857--6171   Enrollment: 7,100

Puyallup School District #3
109 East Pioneer, POB 370
Puyallup 98371,   (206)841-1301
Enrollment: 14,000

Steilacoom Historical School Dist. #1
510 Chambers, Steilacoom 98388
(206)588-1772   Enrollment: 1,640

Sumner School District #320
1202 Wood Ave., Sumner 98390
(206)863-2201   Enrollment: 4,705

```
Tacoma School District #10
Box 1357, Tacoma 98401
(206)593-1000  Enrollment: 29,511

University Place School District #83
8805 40th St W., Tacoma 98466
(206)564-1400  Enrollment: 4,060

White River School District #416
Box G, Buckley 98321,  (206)829-0600
Enrollment: 2,925
```

HOSPITALS

Allenmore Hospital
POB 11414, Tacoma 98411
S 19th and Union, Tacoma
98405 (206)572-2323
Total Beds: 130

**Good Samaritan Hospital And
Rehabilitation Center**
POB 1247, 407 14th Ave SE,
Puyallup 98371 (206)848-6661
Total Beds: 225

St. Clare Hospital
11315 Bridgeport Way SW
Tacoma 98499 (206)588-6422
Total Beds: 86

**Mary Bridge Children's
Health Center**
317 S K St, Tacoma 98405
(206)594-1400
Total Beds: 56

Puget Sound Hospital
215 S 36th St, Tacoma 98408
(206)474-0561
Total Beds: 160

**St. Joseph Hospital And
Health Care Center**
1718 S I St, Tacoma 98405
(206)627-4101
Total Beds: 340

Tacoma General Hospital
POB 5299, 315 S K St
Tacoma 98405
(206)594-1000
Total Beds: 415

THE COURTS

SUPERIOR COURT Area Code (206)
930 Tacoma Ave, S. Tacoma, WA 98402
J. Kelley Arnold, Judge	591-3655
Nile E. Aubrey, Judge	591-7564
Rosanne Buckner, Judge	591-7502
Bruce W. Cohoe, Judge	591-3646
James P. Healy, Judge	591-7566
E. Albert Morrison, Judge	591-7568
Robert H. Peterson, Judge	591-7562
Thomas R. Sauriol, Judge	591-7571
Karen G. Seinfeld, Judge	591-3651
D. Gary Steiner, Judge	591-7572
Waldo F. Stone, Judge	591-7573
Thomas A. Swayze Jr, Judge	591-7574
Donald H. Thompson, Judge	591-7576
Brian M. Tollefson, Judge	591-7565
Arthur W. Verharen, Judge	591-7578
Frederick B. Hayes, Judge	596-6630
Terry D. Sebring, Judge	596-6640
Karen L. Strombom, Judge	596-6650
Ted Rutt, County Clerk	591-7464

JUVENILE COURT
5501 Sixth Ave. S, #601, Tacoma, WA
98406, Administrator: Steve E. Johnson
756-0606

DISTRICT COURTS
Pierce County #1
930 Tacoma Ave, S, #601, Tacoma, WA
98402
James R. Heller, Judge	591-7485
Thomas P. Larkin, Judge	591-7488
Filis L. Otto, Judge	591-7483
Rudolph J. Tollefson, Judge	591-7483
Michael A. Kilborn, Court Administrator:	
	591-7788

Pierce County #2
6659 Kimball Dr, NW, Bldg "D", Gig Harbor, WA
98335
Thomas Farrow, Judge   851-5131
Barbara J. Smith, Court Administrator:
                           851-5131

Pierce County #3
201 Center St. W, POB 105, Eatonville, WA
98328
A'Lan S. Hutchinson, Judge 832-6000
Rosemarie Van Cleve, County Clerk:
                           832-6000

Pierce County #4
811 Main St, POB 110, Buckley, WA 98321
Richard F. DeJean, Judge   863-6047
Shirley Wytko, Chief Clerk 829-0411

SITES OF INTEREST:

Mount Rainier National Park
Fort Lewis
La Grande Dam

CRISIS

Child Find, Inc.
7 Innis Ave,POB 277,New Paltz, NJ,125561,(800)426-5678, Reporting agency for parents to call if child is missing, free.

Tacoma Crisis Clinic,
(206)759-6700, 24 hour crisis line.

Washington Coalition of Sexual Assault Programs, HCR 78, Box 336,Tacoma,98638,(800)562-6025, Hotline aiding victims of domestic violence, free.

Washington State Shelter Network - Hotline,
Battered women hotline statewide,(800)562-6025 24 hours, 9-5 M-F, free.

MULTIPLE SERVICE CENTERS

Consumer Credit Counseling
11306 Bridgeport Way SW,Tacoma 98499,(206)588-1858, Financial counseling, education budget, money management, debt management program; 8:30 - 5:30, sliding fee.

Department of Social & Health Services, 1949 S State,Tacoma 98405,(206)593-2950 9201 Pacific Ave,Tacoma,98444,(206) 593-2840 1004 E Main St Puyallup,98372,(206)593-8600

Lutheran Social Services of Washington, 223 N Yakima Tacoma,(206)272-8433, Food bank, meals on wheels, marriage & family therapy, divorce counseling, home helpers, life line; sliding fee.

Metropolitan Development Council, 622 Tacoma Ave S,Suite 6,Tacoma,(206)383-3921, Energy assistance, referrals, dental, alcohol & drug referral, shelter, pre-school assistance, daycare, commodities distributor; 8-5 M-F; sliding fee.

Pierce County Community Action Agency, 2401 S 35th Ave,Tacoma (206)591-7240, Energy assistance, referrals, dental, alcohol & drug referral, shelter, pre-school assistance,daycare, commodities distributor; 8-5 M-F; sliding fee.

Small Tribes of Western Washington, 13616 Valley Ave E,Sumner,98390,(206)593-2894, Alcohol programs, food vouchers, certified alcohol & drug outpatient treatment, alcohol & drug information school, DWI client assessment; sliding fee.

YWCA,
405 Broadway,Tacoma 98402,(206) 272-4181, Blue collar training program for women, emergency housing, support shelter, classes, information, assertiveness, self-esteem, domestic violence, resource center, women in transition, job search, employment readiness, safe place for children after school from 4 to 6, free and ability to pay.

COUNSELING MENTAL/HEALTH

Aids Hotline - Tacoma Pierce County Health Department
3629 "D" St,Tacoma,98408,(800) 432-2437, Aids information, confidential counseling & antibody testing, free.

Allenmore Psychiatric - Family Anger Management
1530 Union Ave,Tacoma,98405 (206)752-7320 Constructive nonviolence expression of anger management; 8:30-7 M-Thur; fee.

Bayside Counseling, 2201 N 30th St,Suite C,Tacoma,98403,(206) 627-7207, Counseling & therapy, custody evaluation, divorce mediation; sliding fee.

**Behavioral Sciences Services -
Mary Bridge,** 311 S "L" St
Tacoma,(206)594-1465, Evaluation
& treatment of medically related
mental health needs; 8-4:30 M-F,
by physician referral; fee.

Bipolor Support Group, 6315 S
19th St,Tacoma,98466,(206)272-
2234, Support group for manic
depression, mailing list; 9-5
M,Tue,W.

Catholic Community Services
5410 N 44th St,Tacoma,98407
(206)752-2455, Individual,
couple & child counseling;
sliding fee.

Christian Counseling Service
704 S "J" St,Tacoma,98405
(206)272-2279, All types of
counseling; sliding fee.

**Comprehensive Mental Health
Center,** 1201 S Proctor,Tacoma
98405,(206)756-9960, Child
family counseling, crisis
intervention, adolescent day
treatment; 8-5 M-F; sliding
fee.

**Good Samaritan Mental Health
Center,** 407 14th Ave SE
Puyallup,(206)848-5571,
Counseling, outpatient counseling with psychology assessment, minority affairs programs; 8-8 M-Thur, residents
of area.

**Greater Lakes Mental Health
Center,** 9307 Bridgeport Way
Tacoma,98404,(206)535-6484,
Therapy, marital, individual
& group therapy, medication
evaluation, child & family
therapy; Piece County Residents, sliding fee.

**Puyallup Tribal Authority -
Kwawachee Center,** 2209 E 32nd
St,Tacoma,98404,(206)593-0291,
Crisis intervention, individual
family counseling, group
therapy, outreach services,
native americans, sliding fee.

EMPLOYMENT & TRAINING

**Catholic Community Services -
Centro Latino,** 1304 S Yakima
Ave,Tacoma,98405,(206)383-3698,
ESL, OJT, job assistance,
translation & interpretation
services; hispanics with low
income, sliding fee.

**City of Tacoma Comprehensive
Employment Service,**
(206)756-5671

**Clover Park Vocational Technical
Institute,** 4500 Steilacoom Blvd
SW,Tacoma,98499(206)756-5671,
Vocational & continuing ed-
ucation, GED testing; adults
16+ years of age, sliding fee.

**Education Opportunity &
Resource Center,** 622 Tacoma Ave
S,Tacoma,98402,(206)572-5960,
Career counseling, assessment,
resource information on training
& financial programs; 8-4:30 M-F
county residents free.

Goodwill Industries of Tacoma
714 S 27th St,Tacoma,98409
(206)272-5166, Vocational rehabilitation program. OASVS,
JTPA; 8-4:30; sliding fee.

Green River Community College
12401 SE 320th,Auburn,98002
(206)924-0182, Education &
vocational training, GED
testing.

Job Service Center
1313 Tacoma Ave S,Tacoma,98402
(206)593-2607, 4908 112th St
SW,Tacoma,(206)581-3030, 330
3rd St SW,Puyallup,98371,(206)
840-8561.

Manpower Temporary Services
1148 Broadway,Suite 230,Tacoma
98402,(206)383-4338, Placement
for a large variety of
temporary jobs; adults, no fee.

**MDC Education Opportunity
Resource,** Tacoma,(206)383-3921,
Employment information; low
income, no fee.

Metropolitan Development Council
622 Tacoma Ave S,Tacoma,(206)
383-3921, Help for minority
employment, minorities, sliding
fee.

Salvation Army Casual Labor
1501 6th Ave,Tacoma,98405
(206) 627-1364, Matches men
& women with temporary jobs,
no fee.

Tacoma Community College
5900 S 12th St,Tacoma,98465
(206)566-5027, Educational &
vocational training, academic
& vocational courses, GED
testing, tuition help, waiver
for certain unemployment to
return to school; adults 16+
years of age, full tuition.

Tacoma Community House
1314 E "L" St,Tacoma,98405
(206)383-3951, 9112 Lakewood
Dr SW,Tacoma,98499,(206)582-
6521, Help for minority employment, JTPA adult literacy,
limited English only;
minorities.

**Tacoma - Pierce County
Employment & Training
Consortium,** 7407 Market,Tacoma
98402, JTPA, job search assistance, counseling, OJT, GED,
supplemental Services; low
income, economically
disadvantaged,free.

Tacoma Urban League
2550 S Yakima Ave,Tacoma,98405
(206)572-5005, OJT, secretarial
improvement program, job counseling, vocational training,
job referrals; unemployment
& disadvantaged persons.

Total Vocational Services, Inc
309 S "G",Tacoma,98405,(206)
383-3714, Vocational rehabilitation program, medical problems; $50.00 per hour.

**University of Puget Sound -
Counselor Education,** 1500 N
Warner,Tacoma,98416,(206)756-
3344, Counseling with UPS

students getting practical experience; prefer non-chronic
persons, $1,000

V.O.T.E - Pierce College
9401 Far West Sr SW,Tacoma
98498,(206)964-6603, Vocational
testing, analysis, placement
assistance; low income &
ADATSA clients, no fee.

V.R.O.
2817 Wheaton Way,#20,Bremerton
98310,(206)478-4732, 1115 Main
St,Sumner,98390, (206)840-8704,
1949 S State St,Tacoma,98405
(206)593-2350, Helps disabled
state residents obtain employment; disabled physical &
mental persons, sliding fee.

**Washington Women's Employment
& Education,** 1517 Fawcett S
Tacoma,98402,(206)627-0527,
Women's employment & education,
single head of household women;
very low income, free.

**Western Washington Individual
Employment & Training**
4505 Pacific Hwy E,Tacoma,98424
(206)593-2656, Training education programs; native
americans, free.

FAMILY PLANNING

Cooperative Nursery School
1101 S Yakima,Tacoma,98405
(206)597-7240, Cooperative
nursery school, parenting
classes, Lamaze classes.

Day Care Parents Association
Tacoma,(206)752-1817, Referral
for daycare; free.

Eastside Day Care Center
4420 Portland Ave,Tacoma,98404
(206)473-0202, Child daycare
& pre-school; sliding fee.

Hilltop Day Care Center,
Tacoma,(206)627-7554, Child
daycare, sliding fee.

Pacific Care Center,
Tacoma,(206)47505717,
Educational daycare.

Parent Warm Line
POB 7458,Tacoma,98409,(206)
756-0744, Phone line to discuss
child problems, family concerns;
anyone via phone, free.

Puyallup Playcare Center
120 McElroy Pl,Puyallup,98371
(206)848-4232, Child daycare
for low income families &
parents in job training;
6:30-6, sliding fee.

**Salvation Army Child Care
Cente,** 1110 S Puget Sound
Tacoma,98401,(206)752-1661,
Child daycare & family ser-
vices; children 18 months to
6 years; sliding fee.

Tacoma Day Nursery, 1113 S "I"
St,Tacoma,98405,(206)627-5671,
Child daycare, developmental
daycare center for ages K-2;
both parents working; sliding
fee.

Valley Child Development Center
Tacoma,(206)863-8800,
Educational daycare.

**Vasectomy Clinic - Family
Planning Clinic,** 3629 S "D" St
Tacoma,(206)591-6404, Vasectomy
counseling, information & referral, physical for birth
control, pregnancy; ment 21+
years of age; sliding fee.

FOOD/CLOTHING/HOUSING

**Christmas House Tacoma - Pierce
County,** South 43rd&Junett
Tacoma,(206)272-8036, Provides
free Christmas gifts, 1 toy & 1
clothing item per child;
interview during December;
free.

**Emergency Food Network -
Associated Ministries**
2560 6th Ave,Tacoma,(206)383-
2144, Distribution center for
food donations, major feeding
program; free.

F.I.S.H, Fife, Milton,
Edgewood, NE Tacoma, Fife
Presbyterian Church, 6112 20th

St E,(206)383-1811, Food bank;
open M,W & F by appointment,
9-1 M,W & F phone is answered.
Graham, Thrift Community Hall,
13202 224th St E,(206)383-1986,
Food bank.
Lakes Area, Little Church on
the Prairie, 6310 Motor Ave SW
(206)383-1812, Food bank.
Northwest Tacoma: 6th Avenue
Baptist,(206)383-1813
Bethany Presbyterian,4420 N
41st. Fircrest Presbyterian
1250 Emerson. Grace Baptist
2507 N Vassault. Mason
Methodist,2710 N Madison.
Redeemer Lutheran,1001
Princeton. St Lukes Episcopal
3615 N Grove. Skyline
Presbyterian,6301 Westgate.
University Methodist,8108
27th W. Food banks; phone
answered from 9-4:30 M-F.
Oldtown Hilltop, 1224 S "I" St
(206)383-1810 Food bank.
Puyallup Valley, 900 E Main
St,(206)383-1814, Food bank,
Roy, 315 Water St,State Hwy
507 & 280th St,(206)383-1976,
Food bank.
South Tacoma, Unitarian Church,
S 56th & "L" St,(206)383-1816,
Food bank.

Southeast Tacoma, 1704 E 85th
(206)383-1815, Food bank.
Spanaway, Lutheran Church,16001
"A" St,(206)383-1817, Food
bank.
Sumner, next to Methodist
Church, 913 Wood Ave,(206)383-
1817, Food bank.
Francis House, 2502 McKinley
Ave,Tacoma,98404,(206)272-3381,
Adult & children's clothing,
some bedding & household items,
first come, first serve;
11-2:30 W&F, low income &
unemployed persons, free.

Goodwill Industries
714 S 27th St,Tacoma,98409
(206)272-7030, Clothing &
necessities.
Hope Guest Home, 915 7th St
Tacoma,98372,(206)627-3620,
Emergency housing; women , DSHS
referrals only.

Operational Emergency Center
3800 S Othello,Seattle,98118
(206)725-2100, Provides for
emergency needs, food, clothing, household items, no fee.

Puyallup Housing Authority
212 W Pioneer,Puyallup,98371
(206)845-1758, Help with rent
if qualify, section 8 program,
62 older, disabled or family;
low income in Puyallup, no fee.

**Salishan House-Eastside Lutheran
Mission,** 1720 E 44th,Tacoma
98404,(206)475-3352, Clothing,
food & some furniture by
donation, free feeding program;
Pierce County resident, not fee.

**St Leo's Church-The Food
Connection,** 710 S 13th St
Tacoma,(206)383-5048, Surplus &
donated food given to those in
need once a week, no fee.

St Vincent de Paul's
4009 S 56th St,Tacoma,98409
(206)472-1783, Clothing &
necessities, rent; free
with voucher, Catholic Church,
all persons.

WIC-Food Program, 316 N "L"
St,Tacoma,98403,(206)572-5757,
Food, nutrition programs for
pregnant women, infants &
children; low income persons,
free.

LEGAL

Chapter 13
POB 1255,Tacoma,98401,(206)
572-6600, Financial counseling,
financial counseling after
filing Chapter 13 Bankruptcy;
flat rate.

Equal Defense Alliance
POB 1018,Tacoma,98401,(206)474-
7260, Legal advice, counseling
for women who need to defend
themselves.

Legal Assistance, 813 S "K"
St,Tacoma,(206)572-4343,
Landlord/tenant programs,
divorce & custody; low income
families, no fee.

**Puget Sound Legal Assistance
Foundation,** 813 S "K" St,Tacoma
(206)572-4343. Legal assistance
to low income clients, civil
law only; Pierce County, low
income residents, sliding fee.

**Tacoma-Pierce County Bar
Association**
930 Tacoma Ave S,Tacoma,98402
(206)383-3432, Lawyer referral
service, $15 for 1½ hours.

Tel-Law, 930 Tacoma Ave S
Tacoma.98402,(206)383-3624,
Information casette tapes on
legal problems; call for
brochure list, free.

MEDICAL/DENTAL

**Blood Bank-Tacoma Pierce
County,** 220 S "I" St,
Tacoma 98405,(206)383-
2553, Receives blood
donations; 10-5:30 M-F
& 9-1 Sat.

**Clover Park Vocational
Technical Institute,**
4500 Stelacoom Blvd SW
Tacoma 98499, (206)756-
5742, Complete dental work,
children & adults with
marginal income, set fees.

**Dr Pavillon-Financial
Assistance Program,**
315 S "K" St, Tacoma 98405
(206)594-1319, Financial
aid programs for hospital
bills at multicare fac-
ilities, Tue & Fri, free.

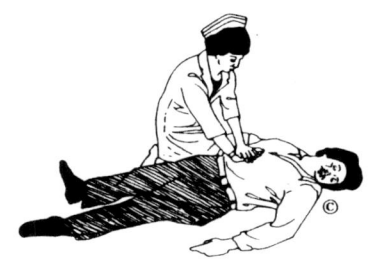

Eastside Health Care
1720 E 44th St,Tacoma,98404
(206)472-9647, Adult & child
primary health care; low income
families, sliding fee.

**Medical Society of Pierce
County,** 705 S 9th, Suite 203
Tacoma 98405, (206)572-3666
Public referral services for
physicians, arrange medical
speakers, no fee.

St Joseph's Hosptial Pharmacy
1718 S "I" St,Tacoma,98405
(206)591-6684, 24 hour
pharmacy; anyone needin
prescriptions filled.

Sumner Health Clinic
1110 Fryer Rd,Sumner,98390
(206)863-0406, Primary health
care, immunizations, pap test,
birth control; sliding fee.

**Tacoma-Pierce County Health
Department,** 3629 "D" St,Tacoma
98408,(206)591- 6500, Health
information, limited care &
services, immunizations,
food handler testing, child
guidance clinic, family
planning, well child clinic,
testing for sexually transmitted diseases, AIDS testing,
certified methadone treatment;
sliding fee.

Tacoma Rescue Mission
1509 Commerce St,Tacoma,98401
(206)383-7493, Medical and
dental services; those who
qualify, free.

Tel-Med, 114 Broadway Plaza
Tacoma,98402,(206)627-6181,
Informational cassette tapes on
certain medical problems; call
for free brochure & list.

MISCELLANEOUS

**Department of Public Utilities
Budget Payment Plan**
POB 11007,Tacoma,98411,(206)
383-9600, Customer service for
budget billing for utilities;
free.

**Metropolitan Development Council
Energy,** 1950 Pacific Ave,Tacoma
(206)272-5557, Provides
applications for energy
assistance programs; low income
families within city limits,
no fee.

National Organization for Women,
POB 1030,Tacoma,98401,(206)473-
7667, Equality issues in main-
stream of society, sliding fee.

Nativity House, 1517 Commerce
Tacoma,98402,(206)272-5266,
Drop in center for street people
with coffee & sandwiches
available; free.

**Neighborhood Preservation
Program,** 447 Market St,Tacoma
98402,(206)591-5230, Provides
rehabilitation loans to owner
occupants single family homes;
property owners in Tacoma
area, no fee.

Over Eaters Anonymous, POB 789,
Tacoma,98401,(206)472-5356,
Support group for those desiring
to stop over eating, no fee.

Pierce County Alliance (PAC)
710 S Fawcett,Tacoma,98402,
(206) 756-0757, Current
alliance programs.

**Puyallup Tribal Health
Authority,** 2209 E 32nd St
Tacoma,98404,(206)593-0232,
Medical clinic, pharmacy,
dental, community health counseling; native americans,
sliding fee.

**Treatment Alternatives to
Street Crime (TASC)**
710 S Fawcett,Tacoma,(206)572-
4750, Counseling, alternatives
to crime, outpatient treatment;
adult felons, sliding fee.

Human/Women's Rights Department
747 Market St,Tacoma,98402
(206)591-5161, Investigations
due to discrimination, sex,
marital status, age, religion;
no fee.

SUBSTANCE ABUSE

A.C.O.A. South Sound Intergroup
POB 42101,Tacoma,98442,(206)
927-1781, Support group for
those raised in alcohol or
other addiction environment,
refer to AA meetings only;
adults, free.

Acacia Counseling, 3019 Judson
Gig Harbor,98335,(206)851-7880,
Certified alcohol & drug outpatient treatment, DWI client
assessment.

ADATSA Assessment Center, 710 S
Fawcett,Tacoma,98402,(206)572-
4750, Assessment, referral,
treatment coordination, monitoring all clients in alcohol
& drug assessment, 8:30-5 M-F,
referrals from DSHS public
assistance.

Al-Anon/Al-Teen, Various
location,Tacoma,(206)272-3081,
Support group for families &
friends of alcoholics & teenage
alcoholics; 24 hours, no fee.

**Alcohol & Drug Abuse Prevention
& Control Program,** HQ I Corps,
Fort Lewis,(206)967-4351,
Certified alcohol & drug information school, DWI client
assessment, alcohol outpatient
treatment; 8-5 M-F, free to
active duty military members
and their family members.

**Alcohol Involuntary Treatment
Program,** 633 N Mildren,Tacoma
(206)572-3212, Services to
individuals making rational
decisions needing treatment
for alcohol abuse; sliding fee.

Alcoholics Anonymous, 622 Tacoma
Ave SW,Tacoma,98401,(206)584-
5873, Support groups, no fee.

Alcoholism Assessment Center
3629 S "D" St,Tacoma,98408
(206)591-6402, Certified alcohol
& drug treatment, client
assessment; 8-4 M-F; flat fee.

Allied Counseling Services
1222 46th Ave E,Fife,98424
(206)922-6738, Certified
alcohol & drug information
school, DWI client assessment,
alcohol outpatient program,
intensive outpatient treatment, all types of alcohol &
drug assessment; 9-9 M-Sat;
flat fee.

Alpha House/F.O.R.C.E.
4214 Portland Ave,Tacoma
98404,(206)472-4418, Certified
alcohol & drug outpatient
treatment, alcohol & drug
information school; adolescents
only; sliding fee.

C.A.R.E., 1502 Tacoma Ave S
Tacoma,98402,(206)572-2273,
Certified crisis intervention
for alcohol & drug, telephone
information & referral; no fee.

Catholic Community Services
14824 S "C" St,Tacoma,98444
(206)537-8467, Certified
alcohol & drug outpatient
treatment, information school,
DWI client assessment.

Community Alcohol Center
4112 Lakewood Dr SW,Tacoma
98402,(206)582-5600, Alcohol
information & referral
treatment; sliding fee.

**Community Alcohol Receiving &
Treatment Detoxification**
622 6th Ave,Tacoma,(206)572-
5333, Alcohol detoxification,
72 hour program, alcohol only;
24 hours; sliding fee.

Counselor, 315 39th Ave SW
Puyallup,98373,(206)848-2242,
Certified alcohol inpatient &
outpatient treatment, alcohol &
drug information school, DWI
client assessment; 8-5:30 M-F;
flat fee.

Crossroads Treatment Center
5909 Orchard W,Tacoma,98467
(206)473-7474, Certified
alcohol outpatient treatment,
information school, DWI client

assessment, court evaluations, intensive outpatient treatment; flat fee.

Dotter's Counseling Service, Inc., 205 15th Ave SW,Suite C,Puyallup,(206)841-4284 Certified alcohol outpatient treatment, alcohol & drug information school, DWI client assessment, anger management course, free consultations flat fee.

First Step, 3640 S Cedar St Tacoma,98409,(206)474-8777, Certified alcohol & drug inpatient treatment, information school, DWI client assessment; flat fee.

Gig Harbor Alcohol Counseling Service, 8803 State Hwy 17,Gig Harbor,(206)851-2552, Certified alcohol outpatient treatment, information school, DWI client assessment; sliding fee.

Group Health Adaption 4301 S Pine St,Tacoma,98409 (206)472-3200, (800)228-0407 Certified alcohol & drug inpatient & outpatient treatment, client assessment family therapy, individual counseling; 24 hours.

Narcotics Anonymous, 36th St & Pacific Ave,Tacoma,98403,(206) 531-8792, Support group for those using & abusing drugs; free.

New Beginnings, 5702 100th St SW,Tacoma,98499,(206)582-4357, Certified intensive inpatient alcohol & drug detoxification; youth only 11-19 years of age.

Olalla Guest Lodge, 12851 SE Lala Cove Ln,Olalla,98359 (206)857-6201, Non-medical treatment for alcohol & drugs, 21-28 day program.

Olympia Counseling Service 233 N Yakima,Tacoma,98403 (206)564-0220, Certified alcohol & drug outpatient treatment, DWI client assess-

ment, adult and children; $75.00.

Passages Professional Counseling & Education Services 10209 Bridgport Way SW,Tacoma 98499,(206)581-5556, Certified alcohol outpatient; set fee.

Puget Sound Treatment Center 215 S 36th St,Tacoma,98408 (206)756-9548, Detoxification program, includes pregnant women 3 week inpatient treatment; 24 hours; flat fee.

Puyallup Tribal Treatment Center 2209 E 32nd St,Tacoma,98404 (206)593-0291, Certified alcohol & drug inpatient & outpatient treatment, information school, DWI client assessment, native americans; sliding fee.

Salvation Army, 409 Puyallup Ave,Tacoma,98421,(206)627-8118 90 day inpatient treatment & counseling for alcohol & drugs; no fee.

Serenity Counseling Service 1103 "A" St,Tacoma,98402 (206)383-4077, Certified alcohol & drug outpatient treatment, DWI client assessment; sliding fee.

Shared Health Services - Alcohol Center, 9112 Lakewood Dr SW Tacoma,98499,(206)582-5600, 1920 64th Ave W,Tacoma,98466,(206) 564-2526, 12812 101st Ave Ct E,Puyallup,(206)848-5598, Alcohol & drug information, counseling, intensive outpatient treatment, aftercare, alcohol information school; sliding fee.

Tacoma Detoxification Center 745 Court "D",Tacoma,98402 (206)572-5333, Certified alcohol detoxification center and referrals, receiving center for intoxicated persons, 3 to 5 day program; sliding fee.

The Center-M.D.C., 815B S 28th St, Tacoma, 98409, (206)572-8200, 6209 21st NE, Tacoma, 98422 (206)927-1806, Certified alcohol & drug inpatient treatment, information school, DWI client assessment; certified recovery house of alcohol, long-term residential program, drug anyone 18+ years of age; sliding fee.

Western Washington Alcoholism Center, 3049 S 36th St, Tacoma 98409, (206)473-7122, Certified alcohol outpatient treatment, information school, DWI client assessment; free.

VETERANS SERVICES

American Veterans Service Office
3820 S Union, Tacoma, 98409 (206)472-1966, Counseling, claim work, education, appeal hearings; 9-4 M-F, veterans & family, free.

Lev Bakker & Associates
10116 36th Ave SW #7, Tacoma 98499, (206)584-2637, Rehabilitation, counseling, family & career counseling, Rap group; veterans.

Veterans Administration Med Center, American Lake, Tacoma 98493, (206)582-2440, IO medic, alcohol services, drug programs, veterans, sliding fee.

Veterans Bureau of Pierce County, 930 Tacoma Ave S Tacoma, 98402, (206)591-7449, Counseling, information & referral on limited service basis; wartime veterans & indigent.

Veterans Job Information
1313 Tacoma Ave, Tacoma, 98401 (206)593-2490, Veterans information, free.

Vietnam Veterans Outreach Cen
4801 Pacific Ave, Tacoma, 98408 (206)473-0731, Counseling, rap groups, outreach & support, active duty during Vietnam.

Washington Soldiers Home
POB 500, Ortig, 98360, (206) 893-2156.

VICTIMS

Catholic Community Services – Counseling & Humanity
5410 N 44th St, Tacoma, 98407, Counseling for sexually abused children & survivors of sexual assault & abuse; sliding fee.

Chrestos Counseling Center
8818 Pacific Ave S, Tacoma, 98444 (206)531-6599, Specializes in treating child sexual abuse victims, general counseling, program for adolescent sex offenders, victims counseling; sliding fee.

Center for Child Abuse Prevention Services
949 Market St, Suite 411, Tacoma 98402, Resource services for family law issues, sexual assault program, parenting plus, CSAPA/project safe place for youth in crisis, resource library and referral service; free.

Domestic Violence – Police Department
930 Tacoma Ave S, Tacoma, (206) 591-5508, Information for domestic violence victims, help in court orders, those who qualify, free.

Evergreen Human Services
POB 8004, Tacoma, 98408, (206) 474-2294, Resource services for family law issues, battered women support group, domestic violence advocacy & support groups, safehome.

Family Counseling Community Services, 1008 S Yakima, Tacoma 98405, (206)627-6105, 9112 Lakewood Dr SW, Tacoma (206)627-6105, 601 2nd SW Puyallup, 98371, (206)848-7217, Family centered counseling, sexual abuse counseling, stress support; live/work Pierce County; sliding fee.

Family Renewal Shelter
POB 98318,Tacoma,(206)584-8998
Shelter, education & other
services to battered women &
children,counseling, Christian
women; sliding fee.

**Fort Lewis Family Advocacy
Program,** Fort Lewis Army Base,
Ft Lewis,(206)967-716, Resources available with family
law issues, domestic violence
& sexual assault advocacy,
counseling & support; active
duty, retired & their
dependents, free.

Outreach, 15 Orgeon Ave,Tacoma
98409,(206)474-7500, Counseling
of abused women & children,
sexual assault, women's issues;
sliding fee.

**Women Survivors of Childhood
Sexual Abuse,** 5410 N 44th St
Tacoma,98407,(206)752-2455,
Safe environment to explore
feelings with sexual abuse;
women of childhood, $15.00 fee.

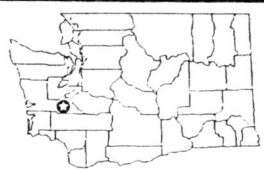

THURSTON COUNTY

Named for Samuel R. Thurston, The Territory of
Oregon's first non-voting delegate to the United
States House of Representatives.

Created: January 12, 1851

2000 Lakeridge Drive SW, Olympia 98502

AREA: 714.0 square miles, State Ranking: 32nd

MAJOR ECONOMIC ACTIVITIES:
State Government, Wood Products,
Agriculture, Food Processing

ASSESSED VALUE: $4,946,063,657

POPULATION: (1989 Estimate): 155,100
Percentage of state: 3.3%
Density: 217.2 persons per square mile

ETHNIC BREAKDOWN: 1988 Estimate

White	136,634
Black	1,428
Native American	2,309
Asian and Pacific Islanders	5,205
Other	3,724
Spanish origin (included in above)	4,971

PRIMARY CITIES Population

Lacey	16,940
Olympia, county seat	31,070
Rainier	1,020
Tenino	1,290
Tumwater	8,200
Yelm	1,425

CLIMATE: Olympia - elevation 114 feet

Average	JAN	APR	JUL	OCT
Max Temp (F)	43.1	59.2	77.5	60.8
Min Temp	30.0	36.4	49.0	40.7
Mean Temp	38.1	50.5	63.9	51.4
Precipitation in inches	7.85	2.96	.76	5.28

Average Annual Maximum Temperature: 60.0
Average Annual Minimum Temperature: 39.4
Average Annual Mean Temperature: 50.8
Average Annual Precipitation: 52.37 inches

PUBLIC SCHOOL DISTRICTS

Griffin School District #324
6530 33rd Ave NW, Olympia 98502
(206)866-2515 Enrollment: 425

North Thurston School District #3
305 College St., NE, Lacey 98506
(206)491-4300 Enrollment: 8,989

Olympia School District #111
1113 Legion Way SE, Olympia 98501
(206)753-8850 Enrollment: 7,055

Rainier School District #307
Rainier 98576, (206)446-2207
Enrollment: 570

Rochester School District #401
Box 457, Rochester 98579
(206)273-5536 Enrollment: 1,603

Tenino School District #402
Tenino 98589, (206)264-4123
Enrollment: 1,335

Tumwater Schol District #33
419 Linwood Ave., SW
Tumwater 98502, (206)786-6400
Enrollment: 4,500

Yelm Community Schools #2
404 Yelm Ave., W., Box 476
Yelm 98597, (206)458-1900
Enrollment: 3,060

HOSPITALS

**Black Hills Community
Hospital,** 3900 Capital Mall
Dr, SW, Olympia 98502
(206)754-5858
Total Beds: 110

**St. Peter Chemical
Dependency Program
(Psychiatric and Alcoholism
Hospital)**
4800 College St, Lacey
98503 (206)459-8811
Total Beds: 40

St. Peter Hospital
413 N Lilly Rd, Olympia
98506 (206)491-9480
Total Beds: 340

THE COURTS

SUPERIOR COURT   Area Code (206)
2000 Lakeridge Dr SW, Bldg 2
Mailstop GQ-11, Olympia, WA 98502

Daniel J. Berschauer, Judge	786-5562
Paul Cassey, Judge	786-5562
Robert J. Doran, Judge	786-5561
Carol A. Fuller, Judge	786-5563
Richard A. Strophy, Judge	786-5565
Thomas Wm. McPhee, Judge	786-5574
Carolyn Failing, Admin.	786-5559

JUVENILE COURT
1520 Irving St, SW, Tumwater, WA 98502
Administrator: Corinne Newman 786-5575

DISTRICT COURT
2000 Lakeridge Dr. SW, Bldg 3
Olympia, WA 98502

Susan A. Dubsisson, Judge	786-5450
Clifford L. Stilz Jr, Judge	786-5450
Judy Lawrence, Court Admin:	786-5450

SITES OF INTEREST:

State Capitol Campus
Olympia Brewery
State Capital Museum

CRISIS

Crisis Clinic of Thurston & Mason Counties
POB 2463,Olympia,(206)352-2211
Crisis intervention, information & referrals, phone only, volunteer intervention services, certified alcohol & drug crisis intervention; 24 hours; sliding fee.

MULTIPLE SERVICE CENTERS

Community Mental Health Center
4422 6th Ave,Lacey,98503,(206) 433-1900, Counseling, emergency services, crisis outpatient services, alcohol & drug treatment; sliding fee.

Department of Social & Health Services, 5000 Capitol Blvd,POB 1908,Olympia,98504,(206)753-5983.

South Sound Advocacy – Disabled Citizens, 111 N Columbia Olympia,(206)754-7576,
Advocacy, legal services & ADATSA assessment center, disabled persons.

COUNSELING MENTAL/HEALTH

Thurston-Mason County Mental Health Center, POB 592,Olympia (206)438-1900, Emergency services, substance abuse, outpatient treatment; sliding fee.

EMPLOYMENT & TRAINING

Friendship, Inc., 1800 11th Ave SW,POB 2481,Olympia,(206)357-8021, Employment counseling, job referral & placement, 8-5 M-F, ex-offenders & those in need of services; sliding fee.

Job Search Network Resource Center, 216 East 10th,Olympia 98501,(206)786-5416, Job search assistance, OJT, support services; 9-2 M-F, unemployed persons.

Job Service Center
5000 Capitol Blvd,POB 9848
Olympia,(206)753-7285

Lacey Timberland Library
4516 Lacey Blvd,Lacey,98503
(206)491-3860, Education & job
information in print, computer
& video format, referral to
crisis & non-crisis support
services, free.

**South Puget Sound Community
College,** 2011 Mottman Rd
SW,Olympia,(206)754-7711,
Vocational & academic courses,
GED testing, adults 16+ years
of age & older.

**Thurston County Employment &
Training,** 921 Lakeridge Dr
#202,Olympia,98502,(206)786-
5586, JTPA program to place
entry level positions with
private industry, job search
assistance activities;
economically disadvantaged
persons, dislocated workers,
free.

**Thurston County Job Search
Network,** 216 E 10th Ave
Olympia,98501,(206)786-5416,
Resource center for persons
seeking employment, telephone
and message service, em-
ployment bulletins, type-
writers, newspapers, hidden
job market information, employment counseling;
9-2 M-Thur, free.

**Thurston County Pacific
Mountain Job Development &
Training,** 2617A 12th Ct SW
Olympia,98502,(206)754-4113,
OJT, GED, supplement services;
economically disadvantaged
persons.

V.R.O. Olympia, 5000 Capitol
Blvd.,Olympia,98504,(206)753-
2762, Helps disabled state residents obtain employment,
free.

FOOD/CLOTHING/HOUSING

American Red Cross
POB 1547,Olympia,98507,(206)
352-8575, Emergency shelter.

**Seventh Day Adventist Community
Service Center,** 1029 N Puget
St,Olympia,98506,(206)943-1518,
Clothing and food bank.

Thurston County Food Bank, 413
N Franklin, Olympia,98501,(206)
352-8597, Three day supply of
food; those in need of service, free.

**United Citizens Betterment
Organization,** 502 Yelm Ave
Yelm.98597,(206)458-2841, Food
bank, clothing bank, surplus
commodities.

MEDICAL/DENTAL

**Thurston County Health
Department,** 529 SW 4th
Olympia,98501,(206)786-5581,
Health information, limited
care & services, immunizations
food handler testing, pregnancy
prevention & detection; sliding
fee.

MISCELLANEOUS

Salvation Army, 418 Plum
Olympia,98501,(206)352-8598,
Homeless facility for men; bed
capacity 10+, can stay until
work is found.

**Small Business Development
Center,** 919 Lakeridge SW
Olympia,98502,(206)753-5614,
In depth assistance to
individual owners & small
businesses, free.

SUBSTANCE ABUSE

Alcoholics Anonymous
203 E 4th,Rm 313,Olympia,(206)
352-7344, Medical advice,
books, treatment center;
9-4 M-F, free.

Alpine Clinical Services, Inc.
931 Poplar St,Lacey,98502,(206)

459-7122, Certified alcohol &
drug outpatient treatment,
information school, DWI client
assessment; sliding fee.

C.G. Campbell Association
1220 E 4th Ave,Olympia,98506
(206)754-2102, Certified
alcohol & drug outpatient
treatment, DWI client assessment, 24 hour answer service;
flat & reduced rates.

Cascade Oaks, 4800 College St
SE,Lacey,98503,(206)459-8811,
Certified alcohol & drug
treatment.

**Social Treatment Opportunity
Program,** 1107 W Harrison
Olympia,(206)754-3861, POB
988,Yelm,98597,(206)458-3656,
Certified alcohol & drug outpatient treatment, information
school; sliding fee.

**St Peter Hospital Chemical
Dependency Program,** 413 N Lilly
Rd,Olympia,98506,(206)456-7575,
Certified alcohol & drug in
and out patient treatment,
detoxification; sliding fee.

TAMARC, POB 5080,Lacey,98503
(206)943-8510, 1012 Holmann
SE,Lacey,98503,(206)438-1866,
Residential outpatient counseling; alcohol & drug
abusers; sliding fee.

**Thurston & Mason County/
Alcoholism Recovery Council**
1625 Mottman Rd SW,Olympia
98507,(206)943-6849, Certified
alcohol & drug outpatient
treatment, information school,
recovery house; sliding fee.

VETERANS SERVICES

Mr. Mark Fischer
7735 Mirimichi Dr NW,Rt 1
Olympia,98502,(206)866-7994,
Delayed stress counseling.

Mr. Larry Moore
9011 Old Highway 88 SE
#161,Olympia 98501
(206)330-2832, Delayed
stress counseling.

VICTIMS

**Feminists in Self Defense
Training,** POB 1883,Olympia
98501,(206)438-0288, Sexual
assault programs, information
& referrals; sliding fee.

Heatsparkle Players, POB 1883
Olympia,98507,(206)843-6772,
Sexual assault programs.

**Safeplace Rape Relief & Women's
Shelter Services,** POB 1605
Olympia,(206)754-6300,
Domestic violence & sexual
assault advocacy, counseling
& support groups, resource
services for family law issues,
women's shelter service, free.

For additional information see also
Mason County

111

SOUTHWEST

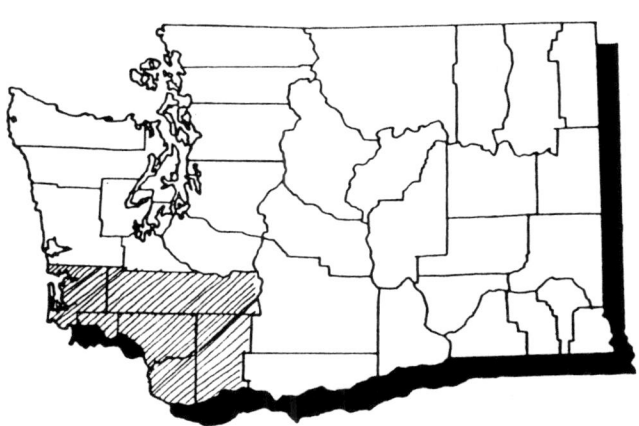

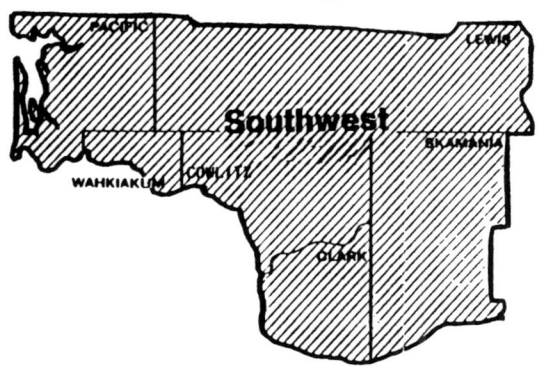

Clark

Cowlitz

Lewis

Pacific

Skamania

Wahkiakum

REGIONAL TOURISM
INFORMATION PROGRAM OF
SOUTHWEST WASHINGTON
POB 876, Longview 98632
(206)423-8400

HISTORICAL APPEAL

Grays Harbor Historical Seaport
Aberdeen

Camas-Washougal Historical
Museum, Camas

Wahkiakum County Historical
Museum, Cathlamet

Fort Borst Black House,
Centralia

Lewis County Historical
Museum, Chehalis

Fort Columbia, Chinook

Lewis and Clark Interpretive
Center, Fort Canby State Park,
Ilwaco

Cowlitz County Historical
Museum, Kelso

East Lewis County Historical
Museum, Morton

Skamokawa Historic District,
Skamokawa

Pacific County Courthouse,
South Bend

Skamania County Museum,
Stevenson

Clark County Historical
Museum, Vancouver

Fort Vancouver, National
Historic Site, Vancouver

SKAMANIA COUNTY MUSEUM
Has the largest collection of antique coffee grinders in the United States.

CITIES

BATTLE GROUND
Battle Ground Chamber of
Commerce,110 E Main,POB 366
Battle Ground,98604,(206)
687-1510

CAMAS
Camas-Washougal Chamber of
Commerce,422 NE 4th Ave,POB
915,Camas,98607,(206)834-2472

CASTLE ROCK

Castle Rock Visitor Information
Center,POB 721,113 N Huntington
Ave,Castle Rock,98611,(206)
274-6603

CATHLAMET
Cathlamet Commercial Club
Chamber of Commerce,POB 52
Cathlamet

COUGAR
Cougar - Yale Chamber of
Commerce,230 Hwy #503
Ariel,Cougar,98603,(206)231-
4333

ILWACO
(See Long Beach Merchants
Assn)

KALAMA
Kalama Tourist Center,5055 N
Meeker,Kalama,98625,(206)673-
2456

KALSO
Kalso Chamber of Commerce
105 Minor Rd,Kelso.98626

LONG BEACH PENNINSULA
Long Beach Penn. Association
POB 310,Long Beach,98631,(206)
642-4421

LONGVIEW
Longview Chamber of Commerce
1563 Olympia Way,Longview
98632, (206)423-8400

Longview, a city in Cowlitz
County, is the 18th largest
city in Washington with a
population of 30,320. The

Columbia and Cowlitz rivers
meet at Longview, 45 miles
north of Portland, Oregon.
The Columbia is crossed here
by a cantilever bridge with
a 1,200 foot center span.
Fishing, lumbering, and
manufacture of pulp and

THE LARGEST TOTEM POLE
...Kalama, Cowlitz
County, has the largest
single tree totem pole
in the world. It was
carved by Chief
LaLooska, and stand 140
feet.

paper are the main
occupations. Longview was
founded as a planned city by
the Long-Bell Lumber Company
in 1922.

MORTON
Morton Chamber of Commerce,POB
10,Morton,98356,(206)496-6086

MOOSYROCK
Mossyrock Chamber of Commerce
POB 55,Mossyrock,98564,(206)
983-3712

OCEAN PARK
Ocean Park Chamber of Commerce
POB 403,Ocean Park,98640,(206)
665-5011

SKAMANIA
Skamania County Chamber of
Commerce, POB 1037, Stevenson
98648, (509)427-4449

SOUTH BEND
South Bend Chamber of Commerce
POB 335,801 Broadway,South
Bend,98586,(206)875-5533

STEVENSON
Skamania County Chamber of
Commerce,POB 1037,Stevenson
98648,(509)427-8911

TOKELAND
Tokeland N Cove Chamber of
Commerce,POB 603,Tokeland,98509
(206)267-2625

TOLEDO
South Lewis County Chamber of
Commerce,205 Cowlitz St,POB
815,Toledo,98591,(206)864-2076

TWIN CITIES
Twin Cities Chamber of Commerce
I-5 at National Ave,POB 1263
Chehalis,98532,(206)748-8885

*   **CENTRALIA**

*   **CHEHALIS**

Centralia and Chehalis
located in Lewis County are
known as the Twin-Cities of

**THE OLDEST HOUSE IN
WASHINGTON**...The John
R. Jackson House was
build in 1845 at Mary's
Corner near Centralia,
Lewis County:

Washington. They are quiet, working-class cities situated between Seattle and Portland, Oregon.

Centralia is the only city in Washington founded by a black man. George Washington was the slave of James C. Cochran, a Missouri man who, in 1850 filed claim on the land where Centralia is now located. Washington was set free and adopted by Cochran, he later bought the land for $6,000 and established the city.

VANCOUVER

Greater Vancouver Chamber of Commerce,404 E 15th St,Suite 11 Vancouver,98663,(206)694-2588

Vancouver is the ninth largest city in Washington with a population of 44,450. It is the seat of **Clark County.** It lies on the Columbia River, just north of Portland, Oregon, and 140 miles south of Seattle. Vancouver is a deepwater port, handling mainly lumber and wheat, and has industries producing paper and wood products, aluminum, and processed foods. Within the city is Fort Vancouver Historic Site. The fort, which has been partly reconstructed, was the Pacific headquarters of the Hudson's Bay Company, 1824-46.

Vancouver, the oldest settlement in the state, was founded by the Hudson's Bay Company in 1824 and was the economic and political center of the Pacific Northwest for two decades. It became part of the United States with the signing of the Oregon Treaty in 1846 and was incorporated in 1857.

| OLDEST PUBLIC SQUARE |
...The oldest public square in Washington is located in Ester Short Park in Vancouver at 8th and Columbia. It was built in 1853, Clark County.

| THE OLDEST APPLE TREE...In the Northwest is in Vancouver, Clark County. It was planted by Dr John Mcloughlin of the Hudson Bay Company in 1826.

FIREWORKS...The largest 4th Of July Fireworks display west of the Mississippi is held at Fort Vancouver, Vancouver, Clark County.

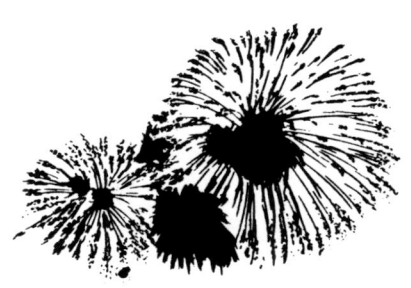

WOODLAND
Woodland Chamber of Commerce
Tourist Information Center,POB
1012,1225 Lewis River Dr
Woodland,98674,(206)225-9552

THE HULDA KLAGER LICAC
GARDENS...Located in
Woodland, Cowlitz
County, is the most
pleasant scented four
and a half acres on
Earth. More than 50
varieties of lilacs are
grown here.

FAIRS AND FESTIVALS

Lilac Week
Woodland, April or May
(206)225-8996

Mount St. Helens Anniversary
May 18th, (206)423-8400

Summerfest
Centralia, Chehalis
July, (206)736-5954

Bald Eagle Days
Cathlamet, July
(206)795-8705

**Columbia Gorge Bluegrass
Country Festival**
Stevenson, July
(509)427-8911

Fort Vancouver Days
Vancouver, July
(206)693-1313

**Thunder Mountain
Rodeo/Cowlitz County Fair**
Longview, July
(206)423-8400

Loggers' Jubilee
Morton, August
(206)496-6086

International Kite Festival
Long Beach, August
(206)642-2400

Cranberry Festival
Ilwaco, October
(206)642-2400

©

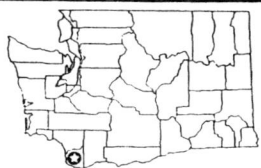

CLARK COUNTY

Named for William Clark, second-in-command of the
Lewis and Clark Expedition.

Created: August 18, 1845

1200 Franklin Street, POB 5000
Vancouver 98668

AREA: 627.1 square miles, State Ranking: 35th

MAJOR ECONOMIC ACTIVITIES:
Wood and Paper Products, Food Processing
Metal Processing, Textiles

ASSESSED VALUE: $7,496,130,204

POPULATION: (1989 Estimate): 220,400

Percentage of state: 4.7%
Density: 351.5 persons per square mile

ETHNIC BREAKDOWN:

	1988 Estimate
White	203,383
Black	2,088
Native American	1,828
Asian and Pacific Islanders	3,720
Other	3,481
Spanish origin (included in above)	4,671

PRIMARY CITIES	Population
Battle Ground	3,550
Camas	6,000
Ridgefield	1,145
Vancouver, county seat	44,450
Washougal	4,090

CLIMATE: Vancouver - elevation 175 feet

Average	JAN	APR	JUL	OCT
Max Temp (F)	44.3	62.8	79.9	64.2
Min Temp	33.2	42.4	55.1	46.1
Mean Temp	38.8	52.6	67.5	55.2
Precipitation in inches	5.63	2.31	.46	3.58

Average Annual Maximum Temperature: 62.7
Average Annual Minimum Temperature: 44.3
Average Annual Mean Temperature: 53.5
Average Annual Precipitation: 39.00 inches

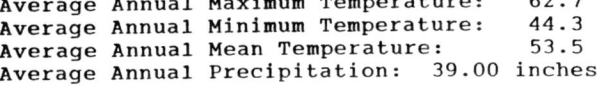

PUBLIC SCHOOL DISTRICTS

Battle Ground School District #119
Battle Ground 98604 (206)687-5171
Enrollment: 7,388

Camas School District #117
2028 NE Garfield, Camas 98607 (206)834-2811
Enrollment: 2,250

Evergreen School District #114
13905 NE 28th St, Vancouver 98682 (206)256-6000
Enrollment: 14,350

Green Mountain School District #103
Route 1, Box 66, Woodland 98674
(206)225-7366   Enrollment: 75

Hockinson School District #98
15916 NE 182nd Ave, Bush Prairie
(206)256-5270   Enrollment: 913

LaCenter School District #101
Box 168, LaCenter 98629 (206)263-2131
Enrollment: 805

Ridgefield School District #122
Box 488, Ridgefield 98624 (206)887-3514
Enrollment: 1,214

Vancouver School District #37
605 N Devine Rd, Vancouver 98661
(206)696-7000   Enrollment: 15,170

Washougal School District #112-6
2349 B St, Washougal 98671 (206)835-2191
Enrollment: 2,046

HOSPITALS

Southwest Washington Hospitals, dba St. Joseph Community Hospital and Vancouver Memorial Hospital:

Southwest Washington Medical Center, POB 1600, 600 NE 92nd Ave, Vancouver 98664 (206)256-2082
Memorial Campus, POB 1600, 3400 Main St, Vancouver 98663 (206)696-5000

THE COURTS

SUPERIOR COURT   Area Code (206)
1200 Franklin St, POB 5000, Vancouver
98668,   Robert L. Harris, Judge   699-2017

Barbara D. Johnson Judge 699-2005
James D. Ladley, Judge   699-2248
Thomas L. Lodqe, Judge   699-2260
Roger A. Bennett, Judge 699-2315
John N. Skimas, Judge 699-2354

JUVENILE COURT
500 West 11th St, POB 5000
Vancouver 98668 Administrator: Gary Ripley
699-2201

DISTRICT COURT
1200 Franklin St, POB 5000, Vancouver 98668
Kenneth R. Eiesland, Judge   699-2414
Randal B. Fritzler, Judge   699-2414
Robert D. Moilanen, Judge   699-2414
Fred J. Stoker, Judge   699-2414
Darvin J. Zimmerman, Judge 699-2414
Vernon L. Schreiber, Magistrate 699-2414

SITES OF INTEREST:

Fort Vancouver, Vancouver Barracks, Merwin Lake

Old Minning Arrastra

CRISIS

Crisis Line East Clark County
Vancouver,98663,(206)834-5890,
Crisis line for sex abuse &
neglect, emergency counseling;
all persons.

Crisis Line Vancouver
(206)696-9500, Crisis line for
sex & neglect, emergency counseling; all persons.

MULTIPLE SERVICE CENTERS

**Clark County Community
Services Department**
POB 5000, Vancouver,(206)
253-4790, Energy assistance,
referrals, dental, alcohol &
drug referral, shelter,
pre-school assistance, daycare,
commodities distributor; 8-5
M-F, sliding fee.

COUNSELING MENTAL/HEALTH

**Elahan Center for Mental
Health & Family Living**
1950 Fort Vancouver Way,
Vancouver,98663,(206)695-3416
Counseling and outpatient services and referrals; all
persons, sliding fee.

**Treat Alternatives to Street
Crimes(TASC),** 1209 Jefferson
St,Vancouver,98660,(206)693-
2243 Counseling, alternatives
to crime, drug & alcohol;
adult felons with substance
abuse, sliding fee.

EMPLOYMENT & TRAINING

Clark College
1800 E. McLoughlin,Vancouver
98663,(206)694-6521, Academic
and vocational courses, GED
testing; 9-5 M-F, adults 16 +,
sliding fee.

Clark County Corrections
707 W. 13th St,Vancouver,98668
(206)699-2484, Vocational
counseling and assessment,
training & referrals, employment assistance and placement
ex offender, sliding fee.

**Vocational Rehabilitation
Office,** 613 W. Evergreen Blvd
Vancouver 98660,(206)696-6611,
Helps disabled state residents

PUBLIC SCHOOL DISTRICTS

Castle Rock School District #401
Box 220, Castle Rock, 98611 (206)274-8311
Enrollment: 1,315

Kalama School District #402
548 China Garden Road, Kalama 98625
(206)673-5225, Enrollment: 730

Kelso School District #458
601 Crawford St, Kelso 98626
(206)577-2400, Enrollment: 4,391

Longview School District #122
28th & Lilac Sts, Longview 98632
(206)577-2700, Enrollment: 7,017

Toutle Lake School District #130
5050 Sprit Lake Memorial Highway
Toutle 98649 (206)274-6182
Enrollment: 550

Woodland School District #404
Box 370, Woodland 98674, (206)225-9451
Enrollment: 1,282

HOSPITALS

Hospice Care Center Hospital
1035 11th Ave, Longview
98632 (206)425-8510
Total Beds: 4

St. John's Medical Center
POB 3002, 1614 E. Kessler
Campus, Longview 98632
(206)423-1530
Total Beds: 346

THE COURTS

SUPERIOR COURT   Area Code (206)
312 SW First Street, Kelso 98626
Milton R. Cox, Judge   577-3086
Alan R. Hallowell, Judge   577-3085
Don L. McCulloch, Judge   577-3143

JUVENILE COURT
906 Croy Street, Kelso 98626
Administrator: C. Mel Jewell   577-3100

DISTRICT COURT
312 SW First Street, Kelso 98626
Robert R. Altenhof, Judge   577-3073
Randolph Furman, Judge   577-3073
Kathy A. Lohmeyer, Admin.   577-3072

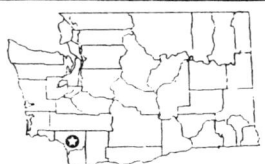

COWLITZ COUNTY

Named for the Cowlitz River, which Lewis and Clark named during their exposition in 1805.

Created: April 21, 1854

County Administration Building
207 Fourth Avenue North, Kelso 98626

AREA: 1,143.9 square miles, State Ranking: 28th

MAJOR ECONOMIC ACTIVITIES:
Metal Producting, Shipping, Wood & Paper Products

ASSESSED VALUE: $3,289,205,319

POPULATION: (1989 Estimate): 82,100

Percentage of state: 1.8%
Density: 71.8 persons per square mile

ETHNIC BREAKDOWN: 1988 Estimate

	1988 Estimate
White	77,868
Black	195
Native American	979
Asian and Pacific Islanders	865
Other	593
Spanish origin (included in above)	1,095

PRIMARY CITIES | Population
	Population
Castle Rock	2,100
Kalama	1,125
Kelso, county seat	11,270
Longview	30,320
Woodland (part)	2,530

CLIMATE: Dayton – elevation 1,612 feet

Average	JAN	APR	JUL	OCT
Max Temp (F)	44.5	61.4	77.8	63.2
Min Temp	31.8	38.6	50.4	43.0
Mean Temp	38.1	50.0	64.1	53.1
Precipitation in inches	5.81	2.72	.75	4.40

Average Annual Maximum Temperature: 61.6
Average Annual Minimum Temperature: 41.0
Average Annual Mean Temperature: 53.3
Average Annual Precipitation: 40.10 inches

obtain employment; disabled,
physical-mental.

FOOD/CLOTHING/HOUSING

Clark County Emergency Housing
1115 W. 13th,Vancouver,98668
(206)695-7658, Share housing,
those in need of services.

FISH, 10401 4th Place Blvd
Vancouver,98668,(206)256-2400,
Food bank, free.

St. Lutheran Church, 14th &
Franklin,Vancouver,98668
(206)695-4903, Food bank;
those in need of service,
free.

**Seventh Day Adventist Service
Center,** 2007 E,12th,Vancouver
98668,(206)695-8632,
Food bank, free.

MEDICAL/DENTAL

**Vancouver Clark County Health
Center,** 2000 Fort Vancouver
Way,Vancouver,98663,(206)695-
9215, Health information,
limited care & services,
immunizations, food handler
testing, aids testing, water,
sewer, food, child birth,
lab services, all persons,
sliding fee.

MISCELLANEOUS

Share House, 1115 W.13th
Vancouver,98660,(206)695-7658
Homeless facility for men; bed
capacity 20+, can stay 3 days.

SUBSTANCE ABUSE

Brighten Center, 306 E.16th
Vancouver,98668,(206)696-2283,
Certified alcohol & drug out-
patient treatment, information
school, DWI client assessment,
anger management, sliding fee.
**Clark County Council on
Alcoholism Vancouver**
Alcohol & drug outpatient
treatment, information school,
DWI client assessment, re-
covery house, sliding fee.

Recovery Northwest
1514 Broadway,Vancouver,98663
(206)963-4975

TRANSPORTATION

C-Tran, POB 2529,Vancouver
98668,(206)696-4494, 1 zone
$18.00, 4 zone $40.00, 60¢.

VICTIMS

**Clark County Sexual Assault
Program,** 1115 E.Esther St
Vancouver,98660,(206)695-0617
Resource services for family
law issues, sexual assault
programs; 8-12 & 1-5 M-F,
all persons.

Safechoice, 1115 E.Esther
Vancouver,98660,(206)695-0501
Domestic violence & sexual
assault advocacy, counseling
and support assistance.

Mount St. Helens Volcano Viewpoint, Silver Lake,
Ariel Dam, Merwin Lake

CRISIS

**Emergency Support Shelter &
Crisis Line,** 309 S,1st West
Kelso,98626,(206)636-8471,
Emergency support shelter,
crisis line, family law resources; those in need of
services.

Longview Crisis Line,
(206)425-5453, 24 hour crisis
line.

MULTIPLE SERVICE CENTERS

**Department of Social & Health
Services,** 711 Vine,POB 330
Kelso,98626,(206)577-2001

Drug Abuse Prevention Center
2112 S.Kelso Dr,Kelso,98626
(206)636-1050, Certified
alcohol & drug outpatient
treatment & long term
residential outpatient
information school, women's
groups and standard assistance
counselor, evaluation; drug &
alcohol abusers, sliding fee.

**Lower Columbia Community Action
Counsel,** POB 2129,Longview,
206)425-3430, Energy assistance,
referrals, dental, alcohol &
drug referral, shelter,
pre-school assistance, daycare,
commodities distributor; 8-5
M-F, sliding fee.

COUNSELING MENTAL/HEALTH

Child Protective Services
POB 330, 771 Vine St,Kelso
98626,(206)577-2152, Mental
health counseling, child
protective services.

EMPLOYMENT & TRAINING

**Longview Education & Job
Information Center**
1600 Louisiana St,Longview

98632, Education & job
information, test guides,
financial aid, resume &
interview help, counseling;
general public.

FAMILY PLANNING

WIC Program
729 Vandercook Way,Longview
98632,(206)425-8679 Family
planning, pregnancy testing,
nutrition program.

FOOD/CLOTHING/HOUSING

Community House on Broadway
1105 Broadway,Longview,98632
(206)636-1100, Food and
shelter, free.

Kelso Housing Authority
1415 S.10th,Kelso,98626,(206)
423-3490, Housing needs,
sliding fee.

Longview Housing Authority
1312 Hemlock St,Longview,98632
(206)423-0140,Housing needs,
low income, sliding fee.

Salvation Army
703 Grant,Kelso,98626,(206)
423-3990, Food, clothing &
shelter, 24 hours, free.

MEDICAL/DENTAL

**Cowlitz-Wahkiakum Health
District,** 1516 Hudson,Longview
98632,(206)425-7400, Health
information, limited care &
services, immunizations, food
handler testing, all persons,
sliding fee.

SUBSTANCE ABUSE

Care Unit, 10322 NE 132 St
Kirkland,98034,(206)821-1122,
Abuse, alcohol & drug treatment

Lower Columbia Council on Substance Abuse, 1260 Commerce Longview,98632,(206)5477-2216, Certified alcohol & drug out-patient treatment, information school, DWI client assessment, ADATSA; those in need of services, sliding fee.

TRANSPORTATION

Community Urban Bus Service POB 128,Longview,98632,(206) 577-3399, 50¢ daily, $10.00 monthly.

For additional information see Wahkiakum County

VICTIMS

Emergency Support Shelter POB 877,Kelso,98626, Domestic violence advocacy, support, counseling groups and shelter; those in need of services.

LEWIS COUNTY

Named for Meriwether Lewis, leader of the Lewis and Clark Expedition.

Created: December 21, 1845
Courthouse, 351 NW North Street,
Chehalis 985432
Annex, 345 West Main Street, Chehalis

AREA: 2,449.1 square miles, State Ranking: 6th

MAJOR ECONOMIC ACTIVITIES:
Wood Products, Agriculture, Publishing
Metal Industries, Manufacturing, Food Processing

ASSESSED VALUE: $1,950,745,436

POPULATION: (1989 Estimate): 58,000

Percentage of state: 1.2%
Density: 23.7 persons per square mile

ETHNIC BREAKDOWN:	1988 Estimate
White	56,077
Black	86
Native American	516
Asian and Pacific Islanders	413
Other	308
Spanish origin (included in above)	754

PRIMARY CITIES	Population
Centralia	11,840
Chehalis, county seat	6,320
Morton	1,175
Napavine	755
Pe Ell	585
Toledo	560
Winlock	1,045

CLIMATE: Centralia – elevation 185 feet

Average	JAN	APR	JUL	OCT
Max Temp (F)	45.6	62.8	79.1	62.8
Min Temp	32.7	39.2	51.0	43.1
Mean Temp	39.2	51.0	65.1	53.0
Precipitation				
in inches	6.36	2.68	.73	4.50

Average Annual Maximum Temperature: 62.5
Average Annual Minimum Temperature: 41.5
Average Annual Mean Temperature: 52.0
Average Annual Precipitation: 45.53 inches

PUBLIC SCHOOL DISTRICTS

Adna School District #226
POB 118, Adna 98522, (206)748-0362
Enrollment: 460

Bolstfort School District #234
983 Bolstford Rd, (206)245-3343
Curtis,   Enrollment: 135

Centralia School District #401
POB 610, Centralia 98531
(206)736-9387, Enrollment: 3,394

Chehalis School District #302
16th & Wilson, Chehalis 98532
(206)748-8681, Enrollment: 2,416

Evaline School District #323
111 Schoolhouse Rd, Winlock 98596
(206)785-3460, Enrollment: 54

Morton School District #214
Box H, Morton 98356, (206)496-5300
Enrollment: 538

Mossyrock School District #206
POB 478, Mossyrock 98564
(206)983-3182, Enrollment: 497

Napavine School District #14
Napavine 98565,   (206)262-3303
Enrollment: 471

Onalaska School District #300
540 Carlisle, Onalaska 98570
(206)978-4111, Enrollment: 785

Pe Ell School District #301
POB 368, Pe Ell 98572
(206)291-3244, Enrollment: 310

Toledo School District #237
Toledo 98591, (206)864-6325
Enrollment: 829

Valder School District #18
Box 149, Vader 98593
(206)295-3351, Enrollment: 130

White Pass School District #303
Randle 98377, (206)497-3791
Enrollment: 900

Winlock School District #232
311 NW Fir St, Winlock 98596
(206)785-3582, Enrollment: 650

HOSPITALS

**Providence Hospital –
Centralia: Centralia Campus**
1820 Cooks Hill Rd,
Centralia 98531
(206)736-2803
Chehalis Campus
500 SE Washington Ave,
Chehalis 98532 (206)748-4445
Total Beds: 191

Morton General Hospital
POB C, Morton 98356
(206)496-5112
Total Beds: 20

THE COURTS

SUPERIOR COURT   Area Code (206)
351 NW North St, POB 357
Chehalis 98532
David R. Draper, Judge   748-9121
John H. Hall, Judge   748-9121
Louise M. Amell, Administrator
748-9121

JUVENILE COURT
1255 SW Pacific, POB 923, Chehalis
98532, Administrator: Richard A. DeVany
748-9121

DISTRICT COURT
345 West Main, POB 336, Chehalis 98532
Michael P. Roewe, Judge   748-9121
James S. Turner, Judge   748-9121
Pamela Zimmerman, Admin. 748-9121

SITES OF INTEREST:

Borst Blockhouse, Claquato Church,
Palisades Rock, Cowlitz Mission
Cowlitz Landing

CRISIS

Crisis Hotline, POB 337
Chehalis,98532,(800)458-3080
(206)748-6601, 24 hour crisis
line.

MULTIPLE SERVICE CENTERS

C.A.R.E. Service
POB 337 Chehalis,98532,(206)
748-6601, (800)458-3080, Domestic violence advocacy,
counseling, safehomes, Spanish
interpreter, resource services
for family law issues, sexual
assault programs, 24 hours,
free.

**Department of Social & Health
Services**
2025 NE Kresky Rd,POB 359
Chehalis,98532,(206)748-0041

**Lewis County Mental-Mental
Retardation Program**
135 W Main,(206)748-6696,
Family planning, alcohol &

drug crisis intervention;
7-5 M-F, 24 hour phone line,
sliding fee.

COUNSELING MENTAL/HEALTH

Lewis County Mental Health Center
135 W Main, POB 1445,Chehalis
(206)748-6696, Emergency services, substance abuse, outpatient treatment, sliding fee.

EMPLOYMENT & TRAINING

Centralia Community College
600 W Locust,Centralia,98531
(206)753-3433, Academic &
vocational courses, GED testing
high school completion; adults
16+ years of age, set fee.

**Educational Service District
#113,** 125 N Market Blvd
Chehalis,98532 (206)748-6671,
JTPA, job search and basic
remediation assistance;
8-5 M-F, those who qualify,
sliding fee.

Friendship, Inc, 1800 11th SW
Olympia,98507,(206)357-8021,
Employment counseling, self
orientation, job referrals, job
placement & supportive services;
8-5 M-F, ex-offender, free.

Job Service Center
2015 NE Kresky Rd,POB 1187
Chehalis,98532,(206)748-8653,
job search and basic remediation
assistance; 8-5 M-F, those who
qualify, sliding fee.

**Thurston County-Pacific
Mountain Job Development &
Training**
2617A 12th Court,Olympia,98502
(206)754-4133, JTPA, job search
assistance, counseling, OJT,
GED, supplement services,
economically disadvantaged
persons.

V.R.O. Chehalis
2025 NE Kresky Rd,Chehalis
98532,(206)748-4429, Helps
disables state residents
obtain employment; 8-5 M-F,

disabled, physical & mental
persons, free.

FOOD/CLOTHING/HOUSING

Centralia Food Bank
113 E 1st,Centralia,98531
(206)736-4339, Food bank,
clothing, shelter.

Chehalis Food Bank
1914 S Market Blvd,Chehalis
98532,(206)748-8628, Food bank
clothing, shelter.

Freedom Center
1511 S Gold,Centralia,98531
(206)736-6172, Emergency shelter.

Morton Food Bank
154th St,Morton,98356,(206)496-
5438, Food bank, clothing,
shelter.

MEDICAL/DENTAL

Lewis County District
360 NW North St,Chehalis,98532
(206)748-9121, Health information, limited care & services, immunizations, food
handler testing, family planning; 8-5 M-F, sliding fee.

SUBSTANCE ABUSE

Addictions Recovery Center
1820 Cooks Hill Rd,Centralia
98531,(206)736-4357, Certified
alcohol & drug intensive
inpatient treatment,
detoxification; 24 hours,
sliding fee.

Recovery Northwest-Chehalis
129 NW Chehalis,98531,(206)
748-9204, Certified alcohol &
drug outpatient treatment,
information school, DWI client
assessment, ADATSA, anger
management; 8-5 M-F, medical
coupons, sliding fee.

Starting Point
118 Market Blvd,Chehalis,98532
(206)748-7268, Certified
alcohol & drug outpatient, DWI

client assessment, alcohol
information; 9-5 M-F, sliding
fee.

TRANSPORTATION

Twin Transit
POB 418,Chehalis,98532,(206)
330-2072, 30¢ per trip, 60¢ all
day, $9.00 monthly.

VICTIMS

Care Services
POB 337,Chehalis,98532,(206)
748- 6601, Legal, shelter,
clothing, counseling,
advocacy.

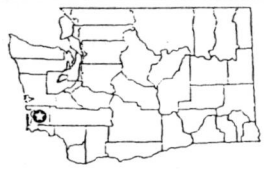

PACIFIC COUNTY

Named for the Pacific Ocean which forms its western border.

Created: February 4, 1851

300 Memorial Avenue, South Bend 98586

AREA: 908.2 square miles, State Ranking: 30th

MAJOR ECONOMIC ACTIVITIES:
Wood Products, Agriculture,
Seafood Processing

ASSESSED VALUE: $559,617,181

POPULATION: (1989 Estimate): 17,700

Percentage of state: 0.4%
Density: 19.5 persons per square mile

ETHNIC BREAKDOWN:	1988 Estimate
White	16,930
Black	36
Native American	386
Asian and Pacific Islanders	130
Other	136
Spanish origin (included in above)	184

PRIMARY CITIES	Population
Ilwaco	812
Long Beach	1,310
Raymond	2,870
South Bend, county seat	1,625

CLIMATE: Long Beach – elevation 10 feet

Average	JAN	APR	JUL	OCT
Max Temp (F)	48.5	56.0	65.5	61.8
Min Temp	35.5	40.3	50.3	43.9
Mean Temp	41.8	48.0	58.4	52.8
Precipitation in inches	12.62	6.10	1.09	7.91

Average Annual Maximum Temperature: 58.2
Average Annual Minimum Temperature: 42.4
Average Annual Mean Temperature: 50.2
Average Annual Precipitation: 8.79 inches

PUBLIC SCHOOL DISTRICTS

Naselle-Grays River Valley
School District #155
HCR78, Box 471-S, Naselle 98638
(206)484-7121   Enrollment: 495

North River School District #200
HCR 77, Box 395, Cosmoplis 98537
(206)532-3078   Enrollment: 50

Ocean Beach School District #101
POB 860, Ilwaco 98624, (206)642-3739
Enrollment: 1,083

Raymond School District #116
1016 Commercial St, Raymond 98577
(206)942-3415   Enrollment: 700

South Bend School District #118
POB 437, South Bend 98586
(206)875-5421   Enrollment: 451

Willapa Valley School District #160
Menlo 98561, (206)942-5855
Enrollment: 475

HOSPITALS

Ocean Beach Hospital
First and Fir
Drawer H, Ilwaco 98624
(206)642-3181
Total Beds: 25

Willapa Harbor Hospital
POB 438, South Bend 98586
(206)875-5526
Total Beds: 36

THE COURTS

SUPERIOR COURT   Area Code (206)
County Court House, POB 67, South Bend   98586
Joel Penoyar, Judge   875-6541
Marilyn Stakicka, Admin.   875-9327

JUVENILE COURT
County Court House, POB 93, South Bend   98586
Administrator: James Briganti   875-9350

DISTRICT COURTS
County Court House, POB 134, South Bend 98586
Andrew L. Monson, Judge   875-9354
Jan Wilson, Clerk,   875-9354

SOUTH DISTRICT COURT
N. Second, POB 445, Long Beach 98631
Douglas Goetz, Judge 642-9417
Tamara Fluharty, Clerk 642-9417

SITES OF INTEREST:

Willapa Bay, Fort Canby,
Willie Keil's Grave
Willapa National Wildlife Refuge

MULTIPLE SERVICE CENTERS

American Red Cross
316 6th St Raymond,98577
(206)942-2007, Clothing bank,
domestic violence counseling.

**Coastal Community Action
Program** 117 E 3rd St,Aberdeen
98520 (206)533-5100
(800)828-4885, Senior programs
in home care, children &
family services, advocacy
outreach emergency shelter,
food, clothing, information
& referrals.

**Department of Social & Health
Services**
724 W Robert Bush Dr,POB 87
South Bend,98586,(206)875-6501,
603 S Oregon,POB 1170,Long
Beach,98631,(206)642-3791.

**Pacific County Community
Services**
County Court House,South
Bend,98586,(206)875-6541, Mental health counseling, alcohol
& drug abuse services, food
assistance for pregnant women.

**Twin Harbors Community
Coalition**
2724 Simpson Ave,POB 569
Aberdeen,(206)532-2497, 507
Duryea St,Raymond,98577,(206)
942-3465, Alcohol & drug abuse
counseling, family & children
needs, employment counseling,
community needs & education,
mental health counseling, employment information, food
bank, health services,
emergency housing, physical &
mental disabilities, legal
assistance, advocacy for

unemployment insurance, minority information, senior services, credit counseling;
8:30-4:40 M-F.

COUNSELING MENTAL/HEALTH

Evergreen Counseling Service
215 Becker Bldg.,Aberdeen,98520
(206)532-8629, Mental health
counseling & referrals,
sliding fee.

Willapa Counseling Center
POB 65,South Bend,98586,(206)
875-6541, Mental health counseling; sliding fee.

EMPLOYMENT & TRAINING

Grays Harbor Community College
Edward Smith Dr,Aberdeen,(206)
532-9020, Academic & vocational
courses, GED testing, adult
schooling, small business
courses; adults 16+ years of
age, fee.

Job Service Center, 601 South
Oregon,POB 876,Long Beach,98631
(206)642-3117.

**Older Workers Employment
Network**
515 N 3rd,Raymond,(206)942-2486
Help find work for adults 49 and
older.

**Thurston County-Pacific Mountain
Job Development & Training
Department**
2617-A-12th Court SW,FQ-11
Olympia,98502,(206)754-4113.

FOOD/CLOTHING/HOUSING

FISH Peninsula Emergency Service
Long Beach,98631,(206)777-8294
Food, lodging, gas.

Pace Nutrition and Chores Services
Old Ilwaco Hospital,Ilwaco
98624,(206)642-3378,
Emergency food bank and
shelter.

Pacific County Crisis Support Network
POB 189,Naselle,98638,(206)484-7191, Emergency food bank and
shelter.

Salvation Army Extension
Penny Wise,Park Ave,Raymond
98577,(206)942-3442, Clothing
bank.

South Park County, POB 146,Ocean
park,98640,(206)665-5445, Food
bank.

Union Gospel Mission, 405 E
Heron,Aberdeen,98520,(206)533-1064, 24 hour shelter for men.

Willapa Harbor Food Bank
Park Ave,Raymond,98577,(206)
942-2208, Food bank - once a
month.

Women & Children's Shelter
700 N "F" St,Aberdeen,98520
(206)533-1064, 24 hour shelter
for women & children,free.

MEDICAL/DENTAL

Pacific County Health Department
POB 26,South Bend,98586,(206)
875-6541, Health information.
limited care & services,
immunizations, food handler
testing; sliding fee.

SUBSTANCE ABUSE

Kairos Center - Grays Harbor Community Alcoholism
100 S "I" St,Aberdeen,98520

Intensive outpatient program,
information & referrals,
individual & group counseling;
alcohol information school;
alcohol & drug abusers, sliding
fee.

TRANSPORTATION

Pacific Transist, 216 N 2nd
St,Raymond,98577,(206)875-9418,
35¢ to 50¢, $20.00 monthly.

VICTIMS

Harbor Shelter Service
POB 1825,Aberdeen,98520,(206)
538-3733, Victims of domestic
violence, anger management,
survivors of incent.

Pacific County Crisis Support Network, HCR 78,POB 336
Naselle,98638,(206)484-7191,
Resources available with family
law issues, sexual assault
programs, safehome, shelter,
anger management, free.

SKAMANIA COUNTY

Named is derivation of the Indian word meaning "swift water."

Created: March 9, 1854

240 NW Vancouver, PO Box 790, Stevenson
  98648

AREA: 1,672.3 square miles, State Ranking: 24th

MAJOR ECONOMIC ACTIVITIES:
Wood Products, Agriculture,
Tourism

ASSESSED VALUE: $292,159,099

POPULATION: (1989 Estimate): 8,100

Percentage of state: 0.2%
Density: 4.8 persons per square mile

ETHNIC BREAKDOWN: 1988 Estimate

White	7,833
Black	7
Native American	96
Asian and Pacific Islanders	26
Other	38
Spanish origin (included in above)	81

PRIMARY CITIES   Population

North Bonneville	440
Stevenson, county seat	1,104

CLIMATE: Wind River – elevation 1,150 feet

Average	JAN	APR	JUL	OCT
Max Temp (F)	38.4	59.7	80.0	61.4
Min Temp	25.6	33.6	46.9	37.4
Mean Temp	32.0	46.6	63.5	49.4
Precipitation				
in inches	16.05	6.26	1.01	8.74

Average Annual Maximum Temperature: 59.5
Average Annual Minimum Temperature: 36.2
Average Annual Mean Temperature: 47.8
Average Annual Precipitation: 99.61 inches

PUBLIC SCHOOL DISTRICTS

Mill A School District #31

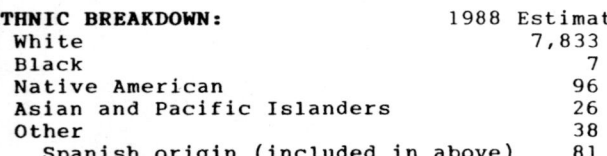

MP 1.11 R Jessup Rd, Cook 98605
(509)538-2700   Enrollment: 60

Mount Pleasant School District #29-93
MPO 15R Marble Rd, Washougal 98648
(206)835-3371   Enrollment: 55

Skamania School District #2
MPO 12R Butler Loop, Skamania 98648
(509)427-8239   Enrollment: 112

Stevenson-Carson School District #303
POB 850, Stevenson 98648
(509)427-5674   Enrollment: 1,051

THE COURTS

SUPERIOR COURT   Area Code (509)
Second & Russell, POB 790, Stevenson,
WA 98648
Ted Kolbaba, Judge   427-5141
Christine Jaekel, Admin.   773-5755

JUVENILE COURT
Second & Russell, POB 790, Stevenson,
WA 98648, Administrator: Thomas McDonnell
                        427-5141

DISTRICT COURT
Second & Russell, POB 790, Stevenson,
WA 98648
Ronald Reynier, Judge   427-5141
Karen S. Wyninger, Court Administrator:
                        427-5141

SITES OF INTEREST

Mount St Helens
Ice Caves
Government Mineral Springs
Bonneville Dam

MULTIPLE SERVICE CENTERS

Counseling and Resource Center
POB 420,White Salmon,98672
(509)493-3400, Provides alcohol
& drug information & referral
mental health, geriatric,
marriage & family counseling,
24 hour crisis line.

**Department of Social & Health
Services**
200 2nd St,POB 817,Stevenson
98648,(509)427-5611.

**Klickitat-Skamania Community
Action Council**
POB 1580,White Salmon,(509)

493-2662, Energy assistance,
referral, dental, alcohol &
drug referral, shelter, pre-
school assistance, daycare,
commodities distributor; 8-5
M-F; sliding fee.

COUNSELING MENTAL/HEALTH

Skamania Counseling Center
POB 790, Stevenson,98648,(509)
427-5636, Emergency services,
substance abuse, outpatient
treatment; sliding fee.

EMPLOYMENT & TRAINING

Network, POB 5000, Vancouver

98668,(206)696-8417, JTPA,
job search assistance, counseling, OJT, GED testing,
supplemental services;
economically disadvantaged
persons, free.

**Southwest Washington
Consortium-Clark County Network**
POB 5000 Vancouver,98668,(206)
696-8417.

FOOD/CLOTHING/HOUSING

**Klickitat-Skamania Community
Development Council**
1003 Jewett,POB 1580,(509)
493-2662, Emergency food bank
and shelter.

MEDICAL/DENTAL

**Stevenson/Skamania County Health
Center,** POB 162,Stevenson 98648
(509)427-5136, Health information limited care & services,
immunizations, food handler
testing.

SUBSTANCE ABUSE

**Skamania County Counseling
Center,** POB 790,Stevenson
98648,(509)427-5636, Certified
alcohol & drug outpatient
treatment, information school,
DWI client assessment, ADATSA.

VICTIMS

**Skamania County Council on
Domestic Violence**
POB 477,Stevenson,(509)427-
5636 Domestic violence &
sexual assault advocacy,
counseling, support, resources
services for family law
issues; free.

**For additional information see also Klickitat
County**

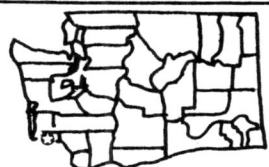

WAHKIAKUM COUNTY

Name is derivation of the Indian name meaning "tall Timber."

Created: April 24, 1854

64 Main Street, PO Box 543, Cathlamet 98612

AREA: 260.7 square miles, State Ranking: 37th

MAJOR ECONOMIC ACTIVITIES:
Wood Products, Agriculture

ASSESSED VALUE: $80,769,688

POPULATION: (1989 Estimate): 3,500
Percentage of state: 0.1%
Density: 13.4 persons per square mile

ETHNIC BREAKDOWN: 1988 Estimate
  White   3,425
  Black   0
  Native American   47
  Asian and Pacific Islanders   11
  Other   17
    Spanish origin (included in above)   54

PRIMARY CITIES   Population
  Cathlamet, county seat   615

CLIMATE: Grays River - elevation 50 feet

Average	JAN	APR	JUL	OCT
Max Temp (F)	45.0	57.0	73.0	62.0
Min Temp	33.0	38.0	49.0	42.0
Mean Temp	39.0	48.0	61.0	52.0
Precipitation in inches	20.54	7.22	1.77	10.50

Average Annual Maximum Temperature: 60.0
Average Annual Minimum Temperature: 41.0
Average Annual Mean Temperature: 51.0
Average Annual Precipitation: 111.32 inches

PUBLIC SCHOOL DISTRICTS

Wahkiakum School District #200
Box 398, Cathlamet 98612
(206)795-3971   Enrollment: 477

THE COURTS

SUPERIOR COURT Area Code (206)
64 Main St, POB 116, Cathlamet, WA 98612
Joel Penoyar, Judge   795-3558
Phyllis Wika, County Clerk 795-3558

JUVENILE COURT
County Court House, POB 93, South Bend, WA
98586, Administrator: James Briganti 875-9350

DISTRICT COURT
64 Main St, POB 144, Cathlamet, WA 98612
William J. Faubion, Judge   795-3461
Diana Nichols Chief Clerk   795-3461

SITES OF INTEREST

Columbia River
Puget Island

CRISIS

Emergency Support Shelter And Crisis Line
309 S 1st West,Kelso,98626
(206)636-8471, Emergency
support shelter, crisis line.

Wahkiakum County Mental Health Services, POB 293,Cathlamet
98612,(206)795-8630, Individual
counseling, group therapy, 24
hour crisis line; sliding fee.

MULTIPLE SERVICE CENTERS

Community Information & Referral Center, POB 293,Cathlamet,98612
(206)795-3917, Information,
community services, applications, Evergreen Legal Services, drug & alcohol referrals,
free.

Department of Social & Health Services, POB 38,Cathlamet
98612,(206)795-3226.

Drug Abuse Prevention Center
2112 S Kelso Dr,Kelso,98626
(206)636-1050, Certified
alcohol & drug outpatient
treatment & long term residential, eduction help, job
search, career planning.

COUNSELING MENTAL/HEALTH

Child Protective Services
711 Vine,Kelso,98626,(206)
577-2152, Child protective
services, parent, teenage
counseling, free.

Lower Columbia Mental Health Center, 811 17th Ave,Longview
98632,(206)425-5380, Mental
health counseling, emergency
number 425-6064, sliding fee.

EMPLOYMENT & TRAINING

Longview Public Library
1600 Louisiana Ave,Longview
98632,(206)577-3380, GED, SAT,
Civil Service testing, financial aid information,
counseling & referrals.

Network, 1950 Fort Vancouver
Way #B, POB 5000,Vancouver
98665,(206)696-8417, Job search
assistance, counseling, OJT,
GED, supplemental services,
youth workers; economically
disadvantaged persons.

Southwest Washington Consortium-Clark County Network
POB 5000,Vancouver,98668,(206)
696-8417

FOOD/CLOTHING/HOUSING

Community House on Broadway, Longview,98632,(206)425-8679, Food, clothing & shelter; sliding fee.

F.I.S.H., Box 135,Longview 98632,(206)636-1100, Food, clothing, shelter; free.

Kelso Housing Authority 1415 S 10th,Kelso,98626,(206) 423-3490, Housing needs.

Longview Housing Authority 1312 Hemlock,Longview,98532 (206)423-0140, Housing needs.

Salvation Army, 703 Grant,Kelso 98626,(206)423-3990, Food, clothing, shelter, energy assistance, prescriptions, hot lunches; 8-3:30 M-F; free.

SUBSTANCE ABUSE

Lower Columbia County on Substance Abuse, 1260 Commerce #313,Longview,98632,(206)577-2216, Certified alcohol & drug outpatient treatment, information school, DWI client assessment, youth programs, shoplifting classes; sliding fee.

Recovery Northwest Inpatient Center, 600 Broadway,Longview 98632,(206)636-4859, 1415 15th St,Longview,98632,(206)423-6020 Certified alcohol & drug intensive inpatient treatment, detoxification, information school, DWI client assessment.

Southwest Washington Alcoholism Recovery Foundation 600 Broadway,POB 1487,Kelso 98626,(206)425-1914, 1614 E Kessler Blvd,Longview,98632 (206)636-4859, Drug treatment, counseling & prevention, in and out patient treatment; sliding fee.

The Phoenix Center, 1417 15th St,Longview,98632,(206)423-6020 Certified alcohol & drug out-patient treatment, information school, DWI client assessment; sliding fee.

VETERANS SERVICES

Veterans Hospital 4th Plain & St John's Blvd Rm 11,Vancouver,98661,(206) 696-4061

VICTIMS

Emergency Support Shelter POB 877,Kelso,98626,(206) 636-8454, Domestic violence advocacy, support, counseling groups, shelter, sexual assault, medical & legal advice; minimal fee.

For additional information see also Cowlitz County

OLYMPIA PENINSULA

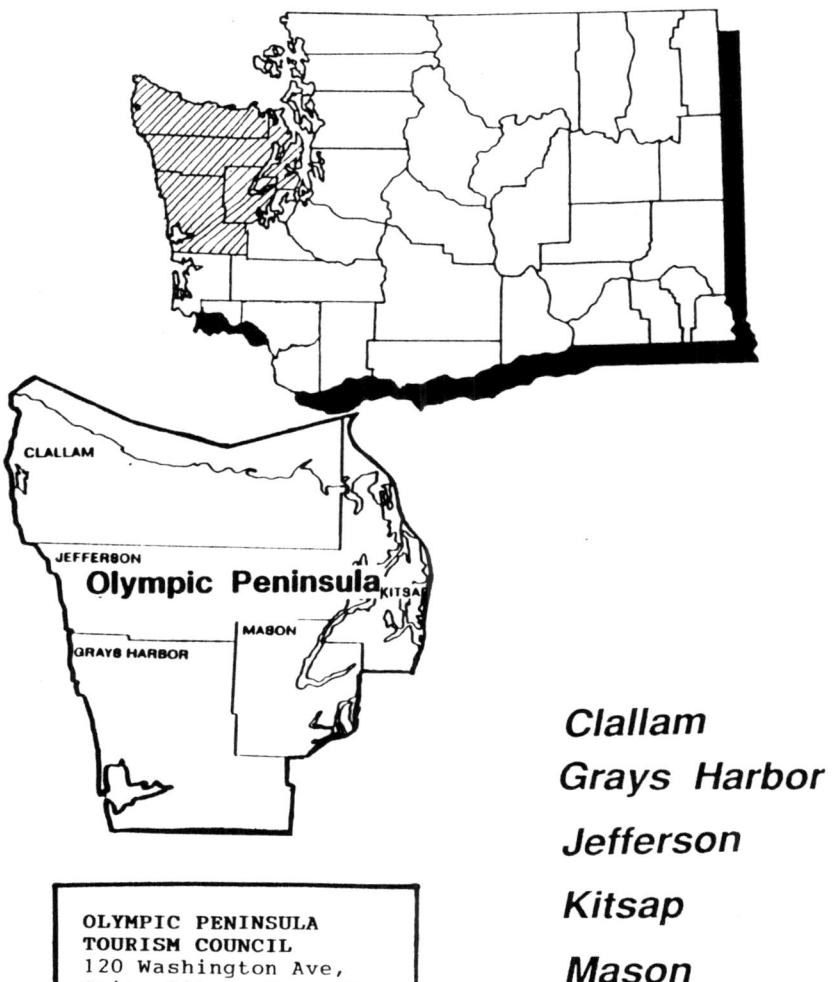

CLALLAM

JEFFERSON

Olympic Peninsula

KITSAP

MASON

GRAYS HARBOR

Clallam

Grays Harbor

Jefferson

Kitsap

Mason

OLYMPIC PENINSULA
TOURISM COUNCIL
120 Washington Ave,
Suite 101-A, Bremerton
98310 (206)479-3599

HISTORICAL APPEAL

Navy Shipyard Museum, Bremerton

Forks Timber Museum, Folks

Polson Park and Museum, Hoquiam

Hoquiam Castle, Hoquim

Makah Cultural and Research Center/Museum, Neah Bay

Calallam County Museum, Port Angeles

Of Sea and Shore Museum, Port Gamble

Pope and Talbot Historical Museum, Port Gamble

Fort Worden National Landmark, Port Townsend

Jefferson County Historical Museum, Port Townsend

Sequim-Dungeness National Historic Museum, Sequim

Kitsap County Historical Museum, Silverdale

Suquamish Museum, Suquamish

Maritime Museum, Westport

CITIES

ABERDEEN
Aberdeen Chamber of Commerce
POB 450,2704 Sumner Ave
Aberdeen,98520, (206)532-1924

Aberdeen is the 31st largest city in Washington, with a population of 17,200. Located in Grays Harbor County, it is the largest urban center and principal seaport in southwest Washington, and is important as a trading center and as a gateway to the 890,000-acre Olympic National Park. Aberdeen is situated at the confluence of the Wishkah

SEA OTTERS...Can be seen in the kelp beds around Destruction Island, Cape Johnson, Sand Point, and Cape Alava in the northwest corner of the Olympic Peninsula.

© 1981 VOLK

THE BEST FISHING IN WASHINGTON...Excellent Deep-Sea fishing can be found in Westport and Ocean Shores in Grays Harbor County, and Long Beach and Ilwaco in Pacific County. Grant County is known for excellent fishing. Okanogan County is known for great trout fishing. The Cowlitz River in Cowlitz County has excellent steelhead fishing. Wahkiakun County is said to have the largest population of White Sturgeon in the World.

and Chehalis rivers, 18 mile
east of the Pacific Ocean.
The city is adjacent to
Hoquiam to the west and lies
46 miles west of Olympia.
The city's Community Center
contains an art gallery, and
the Grays Harbor Historical
Association has a museum
with local historical items.

AMANDA PARK
Washington Coast Chamber of
Commerce,POB 430,Ocean
Shores,98569,(206)289-4552

BAINBRIDGE ISLAND
Brainbridge Island Chamber of
Commerce,153 Madrone Lane
N,Brainbridge Island,98110,
(206)842-3700

BREMERTON
Bremerton Area Chamber of
Commerce,POB 229,837 Fourth
St,Bremerton,98310,(206)479-
3588

Bremerton is the eleventh
largest city in Washington
with a population of 37,080.
It is located in Kitsap
County across Puget Sound
from Seattle. Economically,
the city is largely
dependent on the giant U.S
navy shipyard and other
naval installations located
there. The USS Missouri, the
battleship on which the
Japanese signed the
surrender documents at the
end of World War II, is a
tourist attraction.

CLALLAM BAY
Clallam Bay/Sekiu Chamber of
Commerce, POB 355, Clallam Bay
98381, (206)963-2402

COPALIS BEACH
Washington Coast Chamber of
Commerce,POB 430,Ocean
Shores,98569,(206)289-4552

COPALIS CROSSING
Washington Coast Chamber of
Commerce,POB 430,Ocean
Shores,98569,(206)289-4552

THE LOOP... The Olympic
Highway (Highway 101)
takes a complete
circuit of the Olympic
Peninsula. It is one of
the most beautiful
scenic highways in
America.

**GRAYS HARBOR NATIONAL
WILDLIFE REFUGE...**Lo-
cated in the area of
Bowerman Basin has the
largest concentration
of shorebirds on the
west coast south of
Alaska.

ELMA
Elma Chamber of Commerce,POB
8,Elma,98541,(206)482-2212

FOLKS
Folks Visitor Information
Center,Hwy 101 S,POB
1249,Folks,98331,(206)374-2531

HANSVILLE
Hansville Chamber of Commerce
POB 272,Hansville,98340,(206)
638-2214

HOQUIAM
Hoquiam Chamber of Commerce
(206)532-1924

HUMPTULIPS
Washington Coast Chamber of
Commerce,POB 430,Ocean
Shores,98569,(206)289-4552

KALALOCH
Washington Coast Chamber of
Commerce,POB 430,Ocean
Shores,98569,(206)289-4552

KINGSTON
Kingston Chamber of Commerce
POB 78,Kingston,98346,(206)
297-3813

McCLEARY
McCleary Chamber of Commerce
POB 66,McCleary,98557,(206)
495-3265

MOCLIPS
Washington Coast Chamber of
Commerce,POB 430,Ocean Shores
98569,(206)289-4552

MONTESANO
Montesano Chamber of Commerce
POB 688,107 Broadway,Montesano
98563,(206)249-3414

OCEAN CITY
Washington Coast Chamber of
Commerce,POB 430,Ocean
Shores,98569,(206)289-4552

OCEAN SHORES
Ocean Shores Chamber of
Commerce,POB 389,Ocean
Shores,98569,(206)289-2451

PROTECTION ISLAND...In
Clallam County is home
to most of the nesting
birds in Puget Sound.

GRIZZLY BEAR...The
largest population of
Grizzly Bear in the
state outside of the
national parks and
forests, of which there
is only about 50 is
probably in Ollala,
Kitsap County.

PACIFIC BEACH
Washington Coast Chamber of
Commerce,POB 430,Ocean
Shores,98569,(209)289-4552

PORT ANGELES
Port Angeles Chamber of
Commerce,121 E Railroad,Port
Angeles,98362,(206)452-2363

Port Angeles, the seat of
Clallam County, is the 30th
largest city in Washington,
with a population of 17,500.
It is located in
northwestern Washington on
the Strait of Juan de Fuca,
17 miles south of Victoria,
British Columbia, and 65
miles northwest of Seattle.
Nearby is Hurricane Ridge,
one of the most magnificent
mountain settings in the
Western United States. The
city has a commercial fish
terminal and boat haven. The
economy centers on the
lumber industry, and
manufacturing includes wood
and paper products. Fishing
is also important, with
salmon the main catch. The
region has dairy and beef
cattle, and hay, seed and
fruit are grown. With hot
springs and the Olympic
National Park in the area,
Port Angeles is a popular
tourist resort. It was
designated by Abraham
Lincoln in 1862 as a federal
city, sharing this
distinction only with
Washington, D.C., and was
organized in 1890.

PORT ORCHARD
South Kitsap Chamber of
Commerce,727 Bay St,Port
Orchard,98366,(206)876-3505

PORT TOWNSEND
Port Townsend Visitor Center
2437 Sims Way,Port Townsend
98368, (206)385-2722

POULSBO
Poulsbo Chamber of Commerce

> **OLYMPIC GAME FARM...**
> Is near Sequim in
> Clallam County. It
> covers over 90 acres
> and has about 60
> different kinds of
> animals including
> rhinoceros, coyotes,
> cougars, grizzly bear,
> and timber wolf.

19044 Jensen Way NE,Poulsbo
98370, (206)779-4848

QUINAULT
Washington Coast Chamber of
Commerce,POB 430,Ocean
Shores,98569,(206)289-4552

SEQUIM
Sequim-Dungeness Valley
Chamber of Commerce, 1210 E,
Washington, Sequim 98382
(206)683-6197

SHELTON
Shelton/Mason County Chamber
of Commerce,POB 666,3rd &
Railroad,Shelton,98584,(206)
426-2021

SILVERDALE
Silverdale Chamber of Commerce
POB 1218,9191 Bayshore Dr
Silverdale, 98383,(206)692-
6800

WESTPORT
Westport/Grayland Chamber of
Commerce,POB 306,Westport,98595,
(800)345-6223

THE CHRISTMAS TREE
CAPITOL OF THE WORLD...
Shelton, Mason County
is known as the
Christmas Tree Capitol
of the World. It is
also called Christmas
Town USA.

FAIRS AND FESTIVALS

Irrigation Festival
Sequim, May
(206)683-6197

Poulsbo Viking Fest
Poulsbo, May
(206)779-4848

Rhododendron Festival
Port Townsend, May
(206)385-2722

Forest Festival
Shelton, June
(206)426-2021

Grays Harbor County Fair
Elma, August
(206)532-1924

Salmon Derby Days
Port Angeles, September
(206)452-2363

**West Coast Oyster Shucking
Championship**
Shelton, October
(206)426-2021

Historic Homes Tours
Port Townsend, May
(206)385-2722

Festival of Lights
Montesano, December
(206)249-3414

CLALLAM COUNTY

Named for the Clallam Indians, whose tribal name means "strong people."

Created: April 26, 1854

223 East Fourth, Port Angeles 98362

AREA: 1,725.5 square miles, State Ranking: 20th

MAJOR ECONOMIC ACTIVITIES:
Wood Products, Agriculture, Tourism

ASSESSED VALUE: $1,936,883,375

POPULATION: (1989 Estimate): 55,200

Percentage of state: 1.2%
Density: 31.5 persons per square mile

ETHNIC BREAKDOWN:

	1988 Estimate
White	50,995
Black	126
Native American	2,306
Asian and Pacific Islanders	530
Other	443
Spanish origin (included in above)	794

PRIMARY CITIES

	Population
Folks	2,930
Port Angeles, county seat	17,490
Sequim	3,400

CLIMATE: Port Angeles – elevation 36 feet

Average	JAN	APR	JUL	OCT
Max Temp (F)	43.7	54.4	66.6	56.6
Min Temp	33.5	40.1	51.0	43.6
Mean Temp	38.6	47.2	58.8	43.6
Precipitation in inches	2.87	1.08	.48	2.48

Average Annual Maximum Temperature: 55.3
Average Annual Minimum Temperature: 42.1
Average Annual Mean Temperature: 48.7
Average Annual Precipitation:

PUBLIC SCHOOL DISTRICTS

Cape Flattery School District #401

Box 109, Sekiu 98381, (206)963-2329
Enrollment: 525

Crescent School District #313
POB 2, Joyce 98343, (206)928-3126
Enrollment: 330

Port Angeles School District #121
216 East Fourth
Port Angeles 98362, (206)457-8575
Enrollment: 4,770

Quillayute Valley School District #402
POB 60, Forks 98331, (206)374-6262
Enrollment: 1,500

Sequim School District #323
503 N Sequim Ave
Sequim 98382, (206)683-3336
Enrollment: 2,120

HOSPITALS

Forks Community Hospital
RR 3, Box 3575, Forks 98331
(206)374-6275
Total Beds: 37

Olympia Memorial Hospital
939 Caroline St, Port
Angeles 98362 (206)457-8513
Total Beds: 126

THE COURTS

SUPERIOR COURT   Area Code (206)
223 E Fourth St, Port Angeles 98362
Grant S. Meiner, Judge   452-7831
Gary W. Velie, Judge   452-7831

JUVENILE COURT
18th & M Sts, Box 357, Port Angeles
98362, Peter A. Peterson   452-7831

DISTRICT COURTS
Clallam County One
223 E Fourth St, Port Angeles 98362
Richard A. Headrick, Judge   452-7831

Clallam County Two
Fifth & Division, POB 1937, Folks 98331
Susan J. Owens, Judge   374-6383

Sites of Interest:

Olympic National Park, Cape Flattery,
Hurricane Ridge, Crescent Lake

CRISIS

Umbrella, POB 1858, Port Angeles,98362, (206)452-HELP, 452-3188, Sexual assault, emergency family housing, child abuse, family reconciliation, sliding fee.

MULTIPLE SERVICE CENTERS

Calallam-Jefferson Community Action Council, 540 E. 8th, Port Angeles,98632, (206)452-4727, Information and referral food, shelter & housing, free.

Clallam-Jefferson Community Action Council, 802 Sheridan, 1st Fl, Port Townsend,98368, (206)385-2571 Energy assistance, referrals, dental alcohol & drug referral, shelter, pre-school assistance, daycare, commodities distributor; 8-5 M-F, sliding fee.

Department of Social Health Services, Bayview Ave, Community Building, POB 153, Neah Bay, (206)645-2569, 516 5th Ave, SW, Rt 3, Box 3570, Forks,98331, (206)374-2257, 1016 E. 1st St, Port Angeles 98362, (206)452-3381, Works to prevent and control the causes of disease, injury, disability and premature death.

COUNSELING MENTAL/HEALTH

Lev Bakker & Associates 2631 12th Cwt,SW,Olympia 98502, (206)943-8000, 584-2637, Rehabilitation counseling, family and career counseling, Rap group; veterans.

Penninsula Counseling Center 603 E,18th,St,Port Angeles 98362, (206)457-0431, Family & mental health services, evaluation & treatment, certified drug treatment program, day treatment kids; 24 hours

a day, all persons, sliding fee.

West End Outreach Services RR 3, Box 3575,Forks,98331, (206)374-6177 Emergency services, substance abuse, out patient treatment; all persons sliding fee.

EMPLOYMENT & TRAINING

Job Service Center 1601 E,Front St,POB 992,Port Angeles, (206)457-9407, 516 15th Ave,SW,POB 420,Forks,98331 (206)374-6186, Screens job seekers, offer employment counseling, job search assistance.

FOOD/CLOTHING/HOUSING

Clallam County Emergency Housing, 2602 1/2 W,18th,Port Angeles, (206)452-3811, Clothing, food; all persons, free.

Salvation Army, POB 778,Port Angeles,98362,(206)452-7679, Food bank, emergency lodging, clothing; all persons, free.

MEDICAL/DENTAL

Clallam County Health Department, 223 E. 4th St,Port Angeles, (206)452-7831, Health information, limited care & services, immunizations, food handlers test; 8-6 M-F, all persons, sliding fee.

SUBSTANCE ABUSE

Clark's Counseling, 934 1/2 Caroline,Port Angeles,98362, (206)452-7831, Certified alcohol & drug out patient treatment, DWI client assessment.

North Olympia Alcohol & Drug Center, 315 E,8th,St,Port Angeles,98362, (206)452-2381, Certified alcohol & drug out patient treatment, information

school, DWI client assessment,
ADATSA.

West End Outreach Services
Rt 3,Box 3575,Forks,98331,
(206)374-6177, Certified
alcohol & drug out patient
treatment, information
school.

TRANSPORTATION

Clallam Transit System
2417 W,19th,Airport Industrial
Park,Port Angeles,
(206)452-4511, 50¢ in
zone, additional 25¢ out of
zone, monthly $18.00 for one
zone, $25.00 for all zones.

VICTIMS

**Domestic Violence/Sexual
Assault Program,** POB 743,Port
Townsend, (206)385-5291,
Domestic violence & sexual
assault advocacy, counseling
and support services; 9-5
M-F.

Forks Abuse Program, POB 1775
Forks,98331, (206)374-2273,
Resources available with family
law issues, domestic violence
& sexual assault advocacy,
counseling and support
services, **women only;** 24
hours a day, free.

**For additional information see also Jefferson
County**

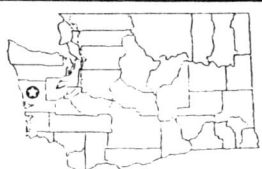

GRAYS HARBOR COUNTY

Named for nearby Grays Harbor and its discoverer Captain Robert Gray.

Created: April 14, 1854

100 West Broadway, Montesano 98563

AREA: 1,909.8 square miles, State Ranking: 14th

MAJOR ECONOMIC ACTIVITIES:
Wood and Paper Products, Seafood Processing, Food Processing, Manufacturing

ASSESSED VALUE: $1,798,590,926

POPULATION: (1989 Estimate): 63,600

Percentage of state: 1.4%
Density: 33.3 persons per square mile

ETHNIC BREAKDOWN: 1988 Estimate

White	60,677
Black	69
Native American	2,099
Asian and Pacific Islanders	379
Other	176
Spanish origin (included in above)	673

PRIMARY CITIES	Population
Aberdeen	17,140
Cosmopolis	1,545
Elma	2,420
Hoquiam	9,100
McCleary	1,460
Montesano, county seat	3,140
Ocean Shores	2,210
Westport	1,910

CLIMATE: Aberdeen- elevation 12 feet

Average	JAN	APR	JUL	OCT
Max Temp (F)	45.3	58.0	69.7	61.9
Min Temp	34.0	39.5	50.4	43.5
Mean Temp	39.7	48.7	60.1	52.7
Precipitation in inches	12.70	5.56	1.51	8.13

```
Average Annual Maximum Temperature:      58.7
Average Annual Minimum Temperature:      41.9
Average Annual Mean Temperature:         50.3
Average Annual Precipitation:       84.54 inches
```

PUBLIC SCHOOL DISTRICTS

Aberdeen School District #5
216 North G St, Aberdeen 98520
(206)532-7690
Enrollment: 3,582

Cosmopolis School District #99
Box 479, Cosmopolis 98537
(206)532-7181, Enrollment: 199

Elma School District #68
30 Elma-Monte Rd, Elma 98541
(206)482-2822, Enrollment: 1,615

Hoquiam School District #28
312 Simpson Ave, Hoquiam 98550
(206)532-6543, Enrollment: 2,230

McCleary School District #65
Box 8, McCleary 98557
(206)495-2305, Enrollment: 305

Montesano School District #66
108 Marcy West, Montesano 98563
(206)249-3942, Enrollment: 1,440

North Beach School District #64
POB 159, Ocean Shores 98569
(206)289-2447, Enrollment: 640

Oakville School District #400
Box H, Oakville 98568
(206)273-8229, Enrollment: 380

Ocosta School District #172
Westport 98595, (206)268-9125
Enrollment: 800

Quinault Lake School District #97
Box 38, Amanda Park 98526
(206)288-2260, Enrollment: 310

Satsop School District #104
POB 96, Satsop 98583
(206)482-5330, Enrollment: 35

Taholah School District #77
POB 249, Taholah 98587
(206)276-4729, Enrollment: 155

Wishkah Valley School District #117
Route 1, Box 308
Aberdeen 98520, (206)532-3120
Enrollment: 206

HOSPITALS

Grays Harbor Community Hospital
915 Anderson Dr
Aberdeen 98520 (206)532-8330
Total Beds: 96

Grays Harbor Community Hospital East
1006 N. H St, Aberdeen 98520
(206)883-5151
Total Beds: 163

Mark Reed Hospital
322 S. Birch St, McCleary
98557 (206)495-3244
Total Beds: 24

THE COURTS

SUPERIOR COURT   Area Code (506)
100 W Broadway, POB 590, Montesano
98563
David E. Foscue, Judge   249-3812
Michael G. Spencer, Judge,   249-5140
Jackie Busse, County Clerk   249-3842

JUVENILE COURT
103 Junction City Rd, Aberdeen 98520
Administrator: Rod Herling   533-3919

DISTRICT COURTS
Grays Harbor #1, 100 W Broadway #202,
POB 647, Montesano 98541
Stephen E. Brown, Judge   249-3441

Grays Harbor #2
2109 Sumner Ave, #201, POB 142
Aberdeen 98520
L. Thomas Parker, Judge   532-7061

SITES OF INTEREST:

Grays Harbor
Fort Chehalis
Quinault Indian Reservation

CRISIS

Grays Harbor Rape Crisis Services, 215 Becker Bldg
Aberdeen,98520,(206)532-4357,
Sexual assault program,
referrals, medical coupons,
sliding fee.

MULTIPLE SERVICE CENTERS

Coastal Community Action Program, 117 E.3rd St,Aberdeen
98520,(206)533-5100, Senior
programs, in home care, children & family services, advocacy, outreach emergency
shelter, food clothing, infor-

mation & referrals; those in
need of services.

**Department of Social & Health
Services,** 405 W.Wishkah,POB
189,Aberdeen,98520,(206)533-
9222,   575 E.Main,Suites
A,B,&C, Box 799,Elma,98541
(206)482-2777

**Twin Harbors Community
Coalition,** 2724 Simpson Ave
POB 569,Aberdeen,(206)532-2497
507 Duryea St,Raymond,98577
(206)942-3465 Alcohol & drug
abuse counseling, family &
children needs, employment
counseling, community needs &
education, mental health
counseling, employment information, food bank, health
services, emergency housing,
physical and mental disa-
bilities, legal assistance,
advocacy for unemployment
insurance, minority information, senior services,
credit counseling;
8:30-4:30 M-F.

Union Gospel Mission
405 E.Heron St,Aberdeen,98520
(206)533-1064, 24 hour shelter
for men, women & children,
food, referrals, counseling.

COUNSELING MENTAL/HEALTH

Evergreen Counseling Center
215 Becker Bldg,Aberdeen,98520
(206)532-8629, Family and
individual counseling, mental
health counseling and referral;
all persons, ability to pay and
sliding fee.

EMPLOYMENT & TRAINING

Aberdeen Job Service Center
2700 Simpson Ave,Aberdeen,98520
(206)532-2347, JTPA, job search
and basic remediation assistance; 8-5 M-F, those who
qualify.

Grays Harbor College
Edward Rice Dr,Aberdeen,98520
(206)532-9020, Academic &
vocational courses, GED

testing; adults 16+ years of
age, sliding fee.

**Vocational Rehabilitation
Office,** 405 W.Wishkah,Aberdeen
98520,(206)533-9274, Helps
disabled state resident obtain
employment; disabled physical
& mental.

W.H Able Memorial Library
125 Main St,S.Montesano,98563
(206)249-4211, Education and
job information in print,
computer and video format,
referral to crisis and
non-crisis support services,
free.

FAMILY PLANNING

Family Planning Clinic
2109 Summer Ave,Aberdeen,98520
(206)532-8631, Teenage
pregnancy counseling, food
and nutrition; those in need of
services.

FOOD/CLOTHING/HOUSING

Aberdeen Clothing Bank
401 E.3rd Ave,Aberdeen,98520
(206)533-5100, Clothing bank.

Aberdeen Community Food Bank
117 E.3rd,Aberdeen,98520
(206)482-2609, Food bank.

Elma Food Bank, 515 N.3rd St
Elma,98541,(206)482-2609, Food
bank.

Galilean Chapel, Ocean Shores
Blvd.98551,(206)289-3319,
Shelter, clothing & food, all
persons.

Humtpulips Grange, POB 100
Humptulip,98552,(206)987-2448,
Food bank.

Peoples Food Bank, H & Wishkah
St,Aberdeen,98520,(206)533-5767,
Food bank, low income families.

MEDICAL DENTAL

Community Health Representative Program, POB 189,Taholah (206)276-8211, Maternal child health care, better health care and support for our elders, transportation for health reason, dental & health education, rehabilitation activities; 8-4 M-F, those in need of services, free.

Grays Harbor County Health Department, 2109 Sumner Ave Aberdeen,(206)532-8631, Immunizations, TB clinic, WIC clinic, family planning, food handlers testing, health information, limited care & services; all persons, sliding fee.

Harbors Home Health
117 N.Broadway,Aberdeen,98520 (206)532-5454, In home nursing care, MSW,OT,SP; those in need of services, set fee.

SUBSTANCE ABUSE

Grays Harbor Community Alcoholism Center, 100 S.I St Aberdeen,(206)533-4940, Certified alcohol & drug out-patient treatment, information school, DWI client assessment, ADATSA; those in need of services, sliding fee.

Kairos Detoxification & Recovery House, 611 8th,St Hoquiam,98550,(206)533-2529, Certified detoxification & re-covery house, those in need of service, sliding fee.

Quinault Indian Nation
POB 189,Taholah,98587 (206)276-8211, Certified alcohol & drug information school, DWI client assessment, alcohol outpatient treatment.

TRANSPORTATION

Grays Harbor Transportation Authority
3000 Bay Ave,Hoquiam,98550 (800)526-9730, 25¢, $1.00 to Olympia, $10.00 monthly.

VICTIMS

Harbor Shelter Services
2306 Summer Ave,Hoquiam,98550 (206)538-0733, Domestic violence advocacy, counseling support groups, outreach pro-grams, counseling & shelter for victims of domestic violence, family law issues and sexual issues; those in need of services, free.

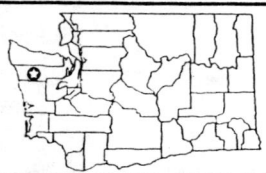

JEFFERSON COUNTY

Named for Thomas Jefferson, the 3rd president of the U.S.

Created: December 22, 1852

1820 Jefferson Street, Port Townsend 98368

AREA: 1,850.2 square miles, State Ranking: 18th

MAJOR ECONOMIC ACTIVITIES:
Wood Products, Agriculture and Fishing, Tourism

ASSESSED VALUE: $981,912,937

POPULATION: (1989 Estimate): 6,940

Percentage of state: 0.4%
Density: 10.6 persons per square mile

ETHNIC BREAKDOWN:

	1988 Estimate
White	17,536
Black	55
Native American	573
Asian and Pacific Islanders	176
Other	260
Spanish origin (included in above)	362

PRIMARY CITIES

	Population
Port Townsend, county seat	6,940

CLIMATE: Port Townsend - elevation 10 feet

Average	JAN	APR	JUL	OCT
Max Temp (F)	44.0	57.3	71.4	58.6
Min Temp	34.9	41.4	51.2	44.7
Mean Temp	36.4	49.4	61.3	51.6
Precipitation in inches	2.20	1.12	.68	1.68

Average Annual Maximum Temperature: 57.9
Average Annual Minimum Temperature: 43.2
Average Annual Mean Temperature: 50.5
Average Annual Precipitation: 18.34 inches

PUBLIC SCHOOL DISTRICTS

Brinnon School District #46
46 Schoolhouse Road (206)796-4646
Brinnon 98320, Enrollment: 75

```
Chimacum School District #49
Box 278, Chimacum 98325 (206)385-3922
Enrollment: 1,606

Port Townsend School District #50
1610 Blaine St., Port Townsend 98368
(206)385-3614    Enrollment: 1,404

Queets-Clearwater School District #20
HC80, Box 1750, Forks 98331
(206)962-2395, Enrollment: 34

Quilcene School District #48
POB 40, Quilcene 98376
(206)765-3363,   Enrollment: 270
```

HOSPITAL

Jefferson General Hospital
834 Sheridan
Port Townsend 98368
(206)385-2200
Total Beds: 42

THE COURTS

SUPERIOR COURT   Area Code (206)
Jefferson & Cass Sts, POB 1220
Port Townsend, 98368
William E. Howard Judge 385-9130
Marianne Waters, County Clerk 385-9125

JUVENILE COURT
1820 Jefferson St.,POB 1220
Poet Townsend, 98368
Administrator: Lois M. Smith 385-9190

DISTRICT COURT
1820 Jefferson St., POB 1220
Port Townsend, 98368
Thomas J. Majhan, Judge 385-9135
Sue K. Dillingham, Clerk 385-9137

SITES OF INTEREST:

Olympic National Park,
Historic Port Townsend

CRISIS

Community Counseling
802 Sheridan,MS 113,Port
Townsend,98368,(206)385-0321,
24 hour crisis counseling.

MULTIPLE SERVICE CENTERS

**Department of Social & Health
Services,** 623 Sheridan, POB
554,Port Townsend,98368,(206)
385-0200

Mekah County Services, Neah Bay
98357,(206)645-2200, Health,
education & welfare referral
for Makah Indians, free.

COUNSELING MENTAL/HEALTH

**Jefferson County Mental Health
Services,** 802 Sheridan,Port
Townsend,(206)385-0321, Outpatient counseling & contact
with local relief services;
all persons, sliding fee.

EMPLOYMENT & TRAINING

Job Service Center
1002 Lawrence St,Port Townsend
(206)385-5564.

Peninsula College
1502 E.Lauridsen Blvd.Port
Angeles,98362,(206)385-4605,
Limited program of college
transfer courses, GED testing;
adults 16 years or older,
grants.

FOOD/CLOTHING/HOUSING

Hoodsport Christian Pantry
N.19591 Highway 101,Shelton
98584, Food for all who are in
need; 1st & 3rd Mondays from
1-3 PM, free.

LEGAL

Safehome/Rape Relief
POB 1858,Port Angeles,98362
(206)385-5291, Resource services
for family law issues; all
persons.

MEDICAL/DENTAL

**Jefferson County Health
Department,** 802 Sheridan,Port
Townsend,98368 (206)385-0722,
Health information, limited
care & services, immunizations,
food handlers testing; all
persons.

SUBSTANCE ABUSE

**Community Alcoholism & Drug
Abuse Center,** 802 Sheridan,Port
Townsend,(206)385-0650, Certified alcohol & drug outpatient
treatment, information school,
DWI client assessment, ADATSA;
9-5 M-F, sliding fee.

TRANSPORTATION

Jefferson Transit Authority
1615 W.Slims Way,Port Townsend
98368,(206)385-4777, 50¢,
$18.00 monthly.

VICTIMS

**Domestic Violence & Sexual
Assault Program,** POB 743,Port
Townsend,(206)385-5291,
Individual short term counseling, support groups,
victims of domestic violence,
sexual abuse, child support
services, resources available
with family law issues; victims
of domestic violence, free.

Safehome & Rape Relief
POB 1858,Port Angeles,98362
(206)452-3811, 452-HELP, Sexual
assault, emergency family
housing, child abuse, family
reconciliation services.

**For additional information see also
Clallam County**

KITSAP COUNTY

Name means "brave chief."

Created: January 16, 1857

614 Division Street, Port Orchard 98366

AREA: 392.7 square miles, State Ranking: 36th

MAJOR ECONOMIC ACTIVITIES:
Fishing, Forest Products, Agriculture,
US Government

ASSESSED VALUE: $5,964,000,805

POPULATION: (1989 Estimate): 181,500

Percentage of state: 3.9%
Density: 462.2 persons per square mile

ETHNIC BREAKDOWN: 1988 Estimate
  White   157,750
  Black   3,744
  Native American   2,679
  Asian and Pacific Islanders   7,958
  Other   5,169
    Spanish origin (included in above) 7,212

PRIMARY CITIES   Population
  Bremerton   37,080
  Port Orchard, county seat   4,860
  Poulsbo   4,270
  Winslow   2,822

CLIMATE: Bremerton - elevation 30 feet

Average	JAN	APR	JUL	OCT
Max Temp (F)	44.3	58.8	76.3	61.0
Min Temp	33.4	40.8	53.2	44.6
Mean Temp	38.9	49.8	64.7	52.8
Precipitation in inches	8.46	3.10	.50	4.48

Average Annual Maximum Temperature: 59.8
Average Annual Minimum Temperature: 42.9
Average Annual Mean Temperature: 51.4
Average Annual Precipitation: 49.36 inches

PUBLIC SCHOOL DISTRICTS

Bainbridge School District #303
8489 Madison Ave NE, (206)842-4714
Bainbridge Island 98110
Enrollment: 2,754

Bremerton School District #100-C
300 N Montgomery, (206)478-5151
Bremerton 98312, Enrollment: 6,085

Central Kitsap School District #400
18360 Caldart Ave NE, (206)779-3971
Poulsbo 98370, Enrollment: 4,150

South Kitsap School District #402
1962 Hoover Ave SE, (206)876-7300
Port Orchard 98366, Enrollment: 9,978

HOSPITAL

Harrison Memorial Hospital
2320 Cherry Ave, Bremerton
98310 (206)377-3911
Total Beds: 297

THE COURTS

SUPERIOR COURT   Area Code (206)
614 Division St, Port Orchard 98366
Karen B. Conoley,   Judge   876-7140
Terence Hanley,   Judge   876-7140
Leonard W. Kruse,   Judge   876-7140
James I. Maddock,   Judge   876-7140
James D. Roper,   Judge   876-7140
William J. Kamps, Judge   876-7140
Madelyn Botta Mays, Admin. 876-7140

JUVENILE COURT
1338 SW Old Clifton Rd, Port Orchard
98366
Administrator: J. Edward Friswold
                       876-7055

DISTRICT COURTS
Kitsap County North
19050 Jensen Way NE, POB 910
Poulsbo 98370
Stephen E. Alexander, Judge   876-7066
                    or   779-5600
Kitsap County South
614 Division St, Port Orchard 98366
W. Daniel Phillips,   Judge   895-3769
James M. Riehl,   Judge   895-3786

SITES OF INTEREST:

Hood Canal,
Hood Canal Floating Bridge

CRISIS

Help Line, 282 Knechtel, Brainbridge Island,98110,(206)842-7621, Information & referral, crisis intervention, temporary employment, career & mental health counseling, food bank free.

Crisis Clinic – Kitsap Mental Health, 4060 Wheaton Way Bremerton,98310,(206)479-3033 Information, counseling, referrals; 24 hour phone, free.

MULTIPLE SERVICE CENTERS

Department of Social & Health Services, 4810 Auto Center Way,Bremerton,98312,(206)478-4995

Kitsap Community Action Program 1200 Elizabeth Ave,Bremerton (206)377-0053, Supportave services, medical programs, energy program, ADATSA programs; 8-4:30 M-F, unemployed, disadvantaged & low income persons, free.

Navy Alcohol & Drug Safety Action Program, Puget South Naval Shipyard,Bremerton,98314 (206)476-2594, Education referral services, alcohol school, screening limited outpatient; Active Duty Navy personnel & dependents, free.

COUNSELING MENTAL/HEALTH

Kitap Mental Health, 500 Union,Bremerton,98310,(206) 373-5031, Mental health outpatient counseling & referrals mentally ill.

EMPLOYMENT & TRAINING

Job Service Center, 4980 Auto Center Way,POB 519,Bremerton (206)478-4941

Kitsap County Personnel & Human Resources Department 614 Division St,Port Orchard 98366 (206)876-7185

Olympia Community College 16th & Chester,Bremerton 98310,(206)478 -4506, Academic & vocitional courses, GED testing; 8-4:30 M-F, all persons, set fee.

V.R.O. Bremerton, 2817 Wheaton Way,Bremerton,98310,(206)478-4732, Helps disabled state residents obtain employment; disabled, physical & mental persons, some free services.

FOOD/CLOTHING/HOUSING

Helpline/Fishline, 282 Knectel Way,Bainbridge Island,98110 (206)842-7621, Emergency food bank & shelter.

Bremerton Food Line, 5204 1/2 1st,St,Bremerton,98310 (206)479 -6188, Emergency food bank & shelter.

Kitsap Community Action Program 1200 Elizabeth Ave,Bremerton 98310,(206)377-0053, Emergency food bank & shelter.

North Kitsap Fishline, POB 1517 Poulsbo,98370,(206)799-5180, Emergency food bank & shelter.

LEGAL

Kitap County Rape Response POB 1327,Bremerton,98310,(206) 479-1788, Resource services for family law issues; all persons.

MEDICAL/DENTAL

Bremerton/Kitsap City Health Department, 109 Austin Dr Bremerton,98310,(206)478-5235, Health information, limited care & services, immunizations, food handler testing, STD, Aids counseling, TB testing; 8-4:30 M-F, sliding fee.

SUBSTANCE ABUSE

AGAPE, 5464 Kitap Way
Bremerton,98312,(206)373-1529,
Certified alcohol & drug outpatient treatment, information
school, DWI client assessment;
sliding fee.

Awareness Express, 614 Division
St,Port Orchard,98366,
(206)876- 9430, certified
alcohol & drug outpatient
treatment, information school,
DWI client assessment, free.

Bennett Counseling Services
19045 Highway 3, Poulsbo,98370
(206)842-1028, Certified
alcohol & drug treatment,
information school, DWI client
assessment, outpatient
treatment.

**Bremerton Municipal County
Probation Department,** 239 4th
St,Bremerton,(206)478-5268,
Certified alcohol & drug
treatment, Must be in Bremerton
Court System, $75.00.

**Kitsap Community Alcoholism
Recovery Program,** 2051 Pottery
Ave,Port Orchard,98366(206)876
-5577 Certified alcohol intensive inpatient treatment, 21
days.

**Kitsap County Council on
Alcoholism,** 532 5th St
Bremerton,98310,(206)377-0051,
Certified alcohol & drug
treatment, residential detoxi-
fication, referral, alcohol.

**Kitsap County Council on
Alcoholism,** 122 Moe St,Poulsbo
98370,98370,(206)779-2900,
Certified alcohol & drug
treatment, court referrals,
sliding fee.

Madrona House or Apple House
500 Union,Bremerton,98312,(206)
478-4994, Certified intensive
outpatient drug treatment; all
children, sliding fee.

Olalla Guest Lodge, 12851 Lala
Cove Ln S,Olalla,98359,(206)
857-6201, Certified alcohol &
drug intensive inpatient
treatment program; 24 hours,
adults only, set fee.

Tara Counseling Center
509 4th St #7,Bremerton,98310
(206)373-8645, Certified
alcohol & drug outpatient
treatment, information school;
9-8 M-F, set fee.

TRANSPORTATION

Kitsap Transit, 234 S Wycoff
Bremerton,98310,(206)479-6969,
377-2877, 50¢ daily, $18.00
monthly.

VICTIMS

Alive, 611 Highland Ave
Bremerton,98310,(206)479-1980,
Resource services for family
law issues, shelter, domestic
violence, advocacy, support,
counseling; 24 hours, free.

Kitsap Sexual Assult Center
POB 1327,Bremerton,98310,(206)
479-1788, Sexual assault programs.

**N Kitsap Advocates for
Sexually Assulted Persons**
POB 11678,Bainbridge Island
98110,(206)842-1930, Resource
services for family law issues,
sexual assault programs,
all persons.

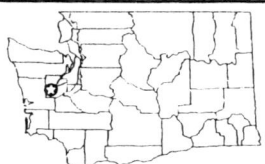

MASON COUNTY

Named for Charles H. Mason, the first secretary of the Territory of Washington.

Created: March 13, 1854

Fourth and Alder, Shelton 98584

AREA: 962.3 square miles, State Ranking: 29th

MAJOR ECONOMIC ACTIVITIES:
Wood Products, Food Processing, Agriculture Manufacturing

ASSESSED VALUE: $1,446,264,413

POPULATION: (1989 Estimate): 37,500

Percentage of state: 0.8%
Density: 3.8 persons per square mile

ETHNIC BREAKDOWN: 1988 Estimate
  White   34,158
  Black   175
  Native American   1,330
  Asian and Pacific Islanders   453
  Other   684
    Spanish origin (included in above)   799

PRIMARY CITIES   Population
  Shelton, county seat   7,620

CLIMATE: Shelton – elevation 12 feet

Average	JAN	APR	JUL	OCT
Max Temp (F)	44.9	61.2	77.6	61.6
Min Temp	31.7	38.0	50.8	42.1
Mean Temp	38.4	49.7	64.7	51.9
Precipitation in inches	10.37	3.89	.80	6.09

Average Annual Maximum Temperature: 61.2
Average Annual Minimum Temperature: 40.9
Average Annual Mean Temperature: 51.1
Average Annual Precipitation: 64.29 inches

PUBLIC SCHOOL DISTRICTS

Grapeview School District #54
E. 822 Mason-Benson Road
Grapeview 98546,   (206)426-4921
Enrollment: 139

Hood Canal School District #404
N. 111 Highway 106
Shelton 98584,   (206)877-9700
Enrollment: 345

Mary M. Knight School District #311
Rt 1, Box 134, Elma 98541 or
POB 113, Matlock 98560
(206)426-6767 Enrollment: 230

North Mason School District #403
POB 167, Belfair 98528,
(206)2750-2881 Enrollment: 1,670

Pioneer School District #402
E. 611 Agate Road, Shelton 98584
(206)426-8291   Enrollment: 650

Shelton School District #309
811 W. Pine St, Shelton 98584
(206)426-1687 Enrollment: 3,198

Southside School District #42
SE 161 Collier Rd, Shelton 98584
(206)426-9970 Enrollment: 194

HOSPITAL

Mason General Hospital
2100 Sherwood Ln, Shelton
98584 (206)426-1611
Total Beds: 68

THE COURTS

SUPERIOR COURT   Area Code (206)
Fourth & Alder Sts, POB 340 Shelton 98584
James B. Sawyer, II, Judge   427-9670
Pat Swartos, County Clerk   427-9670

JUVENILE COURT
Fourth & Alder Sts, POB 368, Shelton 98584
Administrator:Catherine F. Wilson 427-9670

DISTRICT COURT
Fourth & Alder Sts, POB "O", Shelton 98584
Larry J. King, Judge   427-9670
Shirley J. Rogers, Clerk   427-9670

SITES OF INTEREST:

Hood Canal,
Lake Cushman

CRISIS

Crisis Clinic of Thurston & Mason Counties POB 2463
Olympia,98507 (206)426-3311
24 hour crisis intervention;
all persons, free.

MULTIPLE SERVICE CENTERS

Department of Social & Health Services
110 West K St,POB 1127,Shelton
98584,(206)427-0165

Mason-Thurston Community Action Council
1408 E State St,Olympia
(206)352-9910 Energy assistance
referrals, dental, alcohol &
drug referral, shelter,
pre-school assistance, daycare,
commodities distributor; 8-5 M-F,
sliding fee.

South Sound Advocates for Disabled Citizens
111 N Columbia,Olympia
(206)754-7576, Advocacy,
individual assistance,
information & referral services
legal services, ADATSA, housing
assistance; 8-5 M-F, disabled
persons, sliding fee.

Thurston-Mason Community Mental Health Center, 1800 Olympia
Highway S. POB A,Shelton,98584,
Medical services, mental health
outpatient services, family
programs, disability program,
drug treatment programs;
8-5 M-F, sliding fee.

COUNSELING MENTAL/HEALTH

Community Mental Health Center
1800 Olympia Highway S,Shelton
(206)426-1696, Individual
& group family counseling,
emergency services, crisis
intervention, alcohol referrals;
all persons, sliding fee.

EMPLOYMENT & TRAINING

Friendship, Inc., 1800 SW
11th,Olympia,98507

(206)357-8021, Employment
counseling & orientation,
job referral, job referral,
job placement & support
services; 8-5 M-F,
ex-offenders free.

Job Service Center
256 West K St,Shelton,98584
(206)426-5900

Mason County JTPA
256 West K St,Unit#6,Shelton
98584,(206) 426-5900 Job
search & basic remediation
assistance; 8-5 M-F, those who
qualify, sliding fee.

Olympia College, 16th &
Chester,Bremerton,98310
(206)478-4798 Academic &
vocational courses, GED
testing, fee.

Thurston County Job Search Network, 216 E 10th Ave
Olympia,(206)786-5416, Re-
source center for persons
seeking employment, including
telephone & message information service, employment
bulletins, typewriters,
newspapers, hidden job market
information, employment
counseling; 9-2 M-Thur, free.

Thurston County-Pacific Mountain Job Development & Training Department
2671 A 12th Court SW,FQ-11,
Olympia,(206)754-4113

V.R.O. Shelton, 110 West K
St,Shelton,98584,(206)426-0163
Helps disabled state resident
obtain employment.

FOOD/CLOTHING/HOUSING

American Red Cross
POB 1547,Olympia,98507
(206)352-8575, (800)562-6025
Emergency shelter.

Natural Food Co-op
Shelton,(206)426-3516

MEDICAL/DENTAL

Mason County Health Department
411 N 5th,Shelton,98584
(206)426-4407, Health information, limited care & services,
immunizations, food handler
testing; all persons.

SUBSTANCE ABUSE

Alcoholics Anonymous
310 E 4th,Shelton,98584
(206)426-8446 Support group &
counseling; 9-4 M-F, free.

**Mason County District Court
Probation Services**
County Courthouse, Shelton
(206)426-2878 Certified
alcohol & drug treatment, DWI
client assessment, sliding fee.

Narcotics Anonymous
Shelton,98584,(206)754-4433,
Support group, narcotics
counseling.

**Social Treatment Opportunity
Program**
1107 W harrison, POB 10238
(206)754-3861 Olympia, Alcohol
& drug education and
treatment, sliding fee.

**St Peter Hospital-Chemical
Dependency Program**
413 N Lilly Rd,(206)456-7575,
Olympia Pre-admission
assessment interviews,
detoxification, short term
inpatient (2 weeks) with 3
weeks intensive out-patient
treatment, family and senior
programs, continuing care
support groups AA-NA meetings,
community education,
individualized treatment;
24 hours, sliding fee.

Tamarc, 1625 Mottman Rd SW
Olympia,98503 (206)943-8510,
1012 Holman Dr,Lacey 98503
(206)438-1866, 615 W Adler
Shelton 98503,(206)426-9190,
Residential & outpatient
counseling, ADATSA; 8-5 M-F,
alcohol & drug abusers, youth

only in Lacey branch, set
fee, some sliding.

VICTIMS

Recovery, POB 1132,Shelton
98584,(206) 426-5878, Aid for
victims of sexual & domestic
violence abuse, resources
available with family law
issues, sexual assault
programs; 10-5 M-F, all
persons free.

**For additional information see also
Thurston County**

City-County

CITY-COUNTY REFERENCE LIST

Aberdeen--Grays Harbor
Airway Heights--Spokane
Albion--Whitman
Algona--King
Almira--Lincoln
Anacortes--Skagit
Arlington--Snohomish
*Asotin--Asotin
Auburn--King

Battle Ground--Clark
Beaux Arts Village--King
Bellevue--King
*Bellingham--Whatcom
Benton City--Benton
Bingen--Klickitat
Black Diamond--King
Blaine--Whatcom
Bonney Lake--Pierce
Bothell--King
Bremerton--Kitsap
Brewster--Okanogan
Bridgeport--Douglas
Brier--Snohomish
Buckley--Pierce
Bucoda-Thurston
Burlington--Skagit

Camano Island--Island
Camas--Clark
Carbonado--Pierce
Carnation--King
Cascade--Snohomish
Cashmere--Chelan
Castle Rock--Cowlitz
*Cathlamet--Wahkiakum
Centralia--Lewis
*Chehalis--Lewis
Chelan--Chelan
Chaney--Spokane
Chewelah--Stevens
Clarkston--Asotin
Clearwater--Jefferson
Cle Elum--Kittitas
Clyde Hill--King
*Colfax--Whitman
College Place--Walla Walla
Colton--Whitman
*Colville--Stevens
Concrete--Skagit
Connell--Franklin

Cosmopolis--Grays Harbor
Coulee City--Grant
Coulee Dam--Okanogan
*Coupeville--Island
Creston--Lincoln
Cusick--Pend Oreille

Darrington--Snohomish
*Davenport--Lincoln
*Dayton--Columbia
Deer Park--Spokane
Des Moines--King
DuPont--Pierce
Duvall--King

East Wenatchee-Douglas
Eastonville--Pierce
Edmonds--Snohomish
Electric City--Grant
*Ellensburg--Kittitas
Elma--Grays Harbor
Endicott--Whitman
Entiat--Chelan
Enumclaw--King
*Ephrata-Grant
*Everett--Snohomish
Everson--Whatcom

Federal Way--King
Ferndale--Whitcom
Fife--Pierce
Fircrest--Pierce
Forks--Clallam
*Friday Harbor--San Juan

Garfield--Whitman
George--Grant
Gig Harbor--Pierce
Gold Bar--Snohomish
*Goldendale--Klickitat
Grand Coulee--Grant
Grandview--Yakima
Granger--Yakima
Granite Falls--Snohomish

Harrah--Yakima
Harrington--Lincoln
Hoquiam--Grays Harbor
Hunts Point--King

---

*County Seat

Ilwaco--Pacific
Inchelium--Ferry
Index--Snohomish
Ione--Pend Oreille
Issaquah--King

Kahlotus--Franklin
Kalama--Cowlitz
*Kelso--Cowlitz
Kennewick--Benton
Kent--King
Kettle Falls--Stevens
Kirkland--King
Kittitas--Kittitas

LaCenter--Clark
Lacey--Thurston
LaConner--Skagit
LaCrosse--Whitman
Lake Forest Park--King
Lake Stevens--Snohomish
Langley--Island
Leavenworth--Chelan
Lind--Adams
Long Beach--Pacific
Longview--Cowlitz
Lynden--Whatcom
Lynnwood--Snohomish

Mabton--Yakima
Mansfield--Douglas
Marcus--Stevens
Marysville--Snohomish
Mattawa--Grant
McCleary--Grays Harbor
Medicine Lake--Spokane
Medina--King
Mercer Island--King
Mesa--Franklin
Metaline--Pend Oreille
Metaline Falls-Pend Oreille
Milwood--Spokane
Milton--Pierce
Monroe--Snohomish
*Montesano--Grays Harbor
Morton--Lewis
Moses Lake--Grant
Mossyrock--Lewis
Mountainlake Terrace--
                 Snohomish
*Mount Vernon--Skagit
Moxee City--Yakima
Mukiltoe--Snohomish

Napavine--Lewis
Nespelem--Okanogan
*Newport--Pend Oreille
Nooksack--Whatcom

Normany Park--King
North Bend--King
North Bonneville--Skamania
Northport--Stevens

Oak Harbor--Island
Oaksdale--Whitman
Oakville--Grays Harbor
Ocean Shores--Grays Harbor
Odessa--Lincoln
*Okanogan--Okanogan
*Olympia--Thurston
Omak--Okanogan
Oroville--Okanogan
Orting--Pierce
Othello--Adams

Pacific--King
Palouse--Whitman
*Paco--Franklin
Pateros--Okanogan
Pe Ell--Lewis
*Pomeroy--Garfield
*Port Angeles--Clallam
*Port Orchard--Kitsap
*Port Townsend--Jefferson
Poulsbo--Kitsap
Prescott--Walla Walla
*Prosser--Benton
Pullman--Whitman
Puyallup--Pierce

Quilcene--Jefferson
Quincy--Grant

Rainier--Thurston
Raymond--Pacific
Reardan--Lincoln
Redmond--King
Renton--King
*Republic--Ferry
Richland--=Benton
Ridgefield--Clark
*Ritzville--Adams
Riverside--Okanogan
Rockford--Spokan
Rock Island--Douglas
Rosalia--Whitman
Roslyn--Kittitas
Roy--Pierce
Royal City--Grant
Ruston--Pierce

St. John--Whitman
*Seattle--King
Sedro Woolley--Skagit
Selah--Yakima

* County Seat

404

Sequim--Clallam
*Shelton--Mason
Skykomish--King
Snohomish--Snohomish
Snoqualmie--King
Soap Lake--Grant
*South Bend--Pacific
South Cle Elum--Kittatas
South Prairie--Pierce
*Spokane--Spokane
Sprague--Lincoln
Springdale--Stevens
Stanwood--Snohomish
Starbuck--Columbia
Steilacoom--Pierce
*Stevenson--Skamania
Sultan--Snohomish
Sumas--Whitcom
Sumner--Pierce
Sunnyside--Yakima

*Tacoma--Pierce
Tekoa--Whitman
Tenino--Thurston
Toledo--Lewis
Tonasket--Okanogan
Toppenish--Yakima
Tukwila--King
Tumwater--Thurston
Twisp--Okanogan

Union Gap--Yakima

Vader--Lewis
*Vancouver--Clark
Vashon Island--King

Waitsburg--Walla Walla
*Walla Walla--Walla Walla
Wapato--Yakima
Warden--Grant
Washougal--Clark
Washtucna--Adams
*Waterville--Douglas
*Wenatchee--Chelan
Westport--Grays Harbor
West Richland--Benton
White Salmon--Klickitat
Wilbur--Lincoln
Winlock--Lewis
Winslow--Kitsap
Winthrop--Okanogan
Woodland--Cowlitz
Woodway--Snohomish

Yacolt--Clark
*Yakima--Yakima
Yarrow Point--King
Yelm--Thurston

Zillah--Yakima

---

*County Seat

Books

ABOUT WASHINGTON

TRAVEL AND DESCRIPTION

Seattle Best Places,
1984. Brewster, David.
Sasquatch, Seattle. Food,
accommodations, things to
see and do in and around
Seattle.

Northwest Best Places,
1985. Sasquatch, Seattle
Food, accommodations, things
to see and do in Washington,
Oregon, and British Columbia.

**Exploring Washington's
Smaller Cities,** 1984.
Burke, Clifford. Quartzite
Books, Nicely covers 11 of
Washington's smaller cities

Washington Free, 1984.
Canniff, Kiki. Ki2
Enterprises, Portland. Lists
free attractions such as
parks, dams, museums, etc.

Water Trails of Washington,
1979. Furrer, Werner.
Signpost Books, Edmonds, WA.
Lists Washington area rivers
for canoes and kayaks.

**Bed and Breakfast
Washington,** 1984. Green,
Lewis. New Horizons,
Seattle. Lists Bed and
Breakfast throughout
Washington State.

**Touring the Wine Country of
Washington,** 1983. Holden,
Ronald and Glenda. Holden
Pacific, Inc. Covers
Washington wineries.

**Cross Country Ski Trails of
Washington's Cascades and
Olympics,** 1983. Kirdendall,
Tom amd Vicky Spring. The
Mountaineers, Seattle.
Covers over 80 ski trails.

Exploring Puget Sound by Car,
1984. Krenmayr, Janice. The
Writing Works, Seattle.
Tours, shops, parks, and
other attractions around the
Puget Sound area.

Northwest Wine, 1983.
Meredith, Ted, Nexus Press,
Kirkland, WA. A guide to
wineries in Washington,
Oregon, and Idaho.

**Cruising the Columbia and
Snake Rivers,** Nelson,
Sharlene P. and LeMieux,
Joan. Pacific Search Press,
Seattle. Covers cruises in
the inland waterway.

**The Sierra Club Guide to the
National Areas of Oregon and
Washington,** 1983. Perry,
John and Perry, Jane
Greverus. Sierra Club Books,
San Francisco. Covers
activities, boating, and
camping in national parks,
beaches, etc.

**Our Superlative Pacific
Northwest,** 1984. Saling,
Ann. Ansal Press, Edmonds,
WA. Trivia and facts about
the Pacific Northwest.

The Seattle Guidebook, 1986. Satterfield, Archie. Pacific Search Press, Seattle. Sights of Seattle, tours, parks, tours, activities, etc.

Wildlife Areas of Washington, 1976. Schwatz, Susan. Superior Publishing Co, Seattle. Covers flora and fauna of the national recreation areas.

The Wet Side of the Mountains, 1981. Speidel, Bill. Nettle Creek Publishing Co, Seattle. Tours and highlights of western Washington, lots of historical facts.

Trips and Tours 2, 1972. Sterling, E.M. Nettle Creek The Mountaineers, Seattle. Covers hikes, campgrounds, and view roads of the South Cascades and Mt Rainier.

Sunset Washington Travel Guide, 1987. Lane Publishing Co, Menlo Park, CA. A beautifully photographed book of Washington's highlights.

Kayak Trips in Puget Sound and the San Juan Islands, 1986. Washburn, Randel. Pacific Search Press, Seattle. Covers launching information, and routes of kayak trips.

Places to Go With Children Around Puget Sound, 1986. Welke, Elton. Chronicle Books, San Francisco, CA. Covers attractions that appeal to all age groups.

Bicycling The Backroads, Woods, Erin and Woods, Bill. The Mountaineers, Seattle. Three volumes--**Around Puget Sound, Of Southwest Washington, and Of Northwest Washington,** Nicely done, in-depth book on bike routes, terrain, and points of interest.

CLIMBING AND HIKING

Cascade Alpine Guide: Climbing and High Routes, 1987. Beckey, Fred. The Mountaineers, Seattle. Covers Cascade climbing routes, three detailed volumes.

Hiking the North Cascades, 1982. Darvill, Fred T. Sierra Club Books, San Francisco, CA. A pocket-sized guide to trails of the North Cascade Range.

100 Hikes in the Inland Northwest, 1987. Landers, Rich and Dolphin, Ida Rowe. The Mountaineers, Seattle. Descriptions, and maps of hikes in eastern Washington, parts of Idaho, Montana, and Oregon.

Footsore 1,2,3,4: Walks and Hikes Around Puget Sound. Manning, Harvey. The Mountaineers, Seattle. Covers hikes from Bellingham around the Sound to the Olympic Peninsula.

Guide to Trails of Cougar Mountain and Squak Mountain, 1982. Issaquah Alps Trail Club, Issaquah, WA. Maps and trail descriptions.

50 Hikes in Mount Rainier National Park, 1978. Spring, Ira and Manning, Harvey. The Mountaineers, Seattle. Covers 50 hikes, includes maps and photos.

100 Hikes in the Alpine Lakes, South Cascades, and Olympics. 1978. The Mountaineers, Seattle.

101 Hikes in the North Cascades, 1979. The Mountaineers, Seattle.

100 Hikes in the South Cascades and Olympics, 1985. The Mountaineers, Seattle.

Teanaway County: A Hiking and Scrambling Guide to Washington's Central Cascades, 1980. Sutliff, Mary. Signpost Books, Seattle. Covers hikes from Lake Kachess to Blewett Pass.

Olympic Mountains Trail Guide, 1984. Wood, Robert L. The Mountaineer, Seattle. Covers in detail the national parks and forest trails.

HISTORY

Dryden's History of Washington, 1968. Dryden, Cecil. Binfords and Mort, Portland, OR. A easy reading history of Washington.

The Story of Soap Lake, 1976. Fiege, Bennye. Soap Lake Chamber of Commerce, Soap Lake.

The Pacific Northwest: Past, Present, and Future, 1986. Lambert, Dale A. Directed Media, Inc, Wenatchee, WA. A easy reading, nicely illustrated textbook.

Centralia: Tragedy and Trail, 1920. Lampman, Ben Hur. Reproduced by The Shorey Book Store, Seattle. The American Legion's story of the Centralia Massacre.

Washington State, 1986. LeWarne, Charles P. University of Washington Press, Seattle. Washington history textbook, covering pre-history through modern times.

Washington Times and Trails, 1970. Olson, Joan and Olson, Gene. Windridge Press, Grants Pass, OR. A easy reading history.

Sons of the Profits, 1967. Speidel, William C. Nettle Creek Publishing Co, Seattle. Covers Seattle between 1851-1901.

The Great Seattle Fire, 1965. Reproduced by The Shorey Book Store, Seattle. An outstanding collection of original artifacts describing the Seattle fire of 1889.

Peter Puget, 1979. Wing, Robert C. Newell, Gorden. Gray Beard Publishers,

Seattle. Coffee-table book of history of Peter Puget's travels around the Northwest.

NATURAL SCIENCES

Marine Birds and Mammals of Puget Sound, 1984. Angell, Tony and Balcomb Kenneth C III. University of Washington Press, Seattle. Habits and habitats of western Washington birds and marine mammals.

Grzimek's Animal Life Encyclopedia, 1974. Van Norstrand Reinhold Co, New York. Has an extensive listing of all kinds of animals, thirteen volumes.

Northwest Beginning Birding, 1984. Hanners, Al. North Cascades Audubon Society, Bellingham, WA. Where types of birds are located in western Washington.

The Oxford Encyclopedia of Trees of the World, 1981. Hora, Bayard. The Oxford University Press.

The Olympic Seashore, 1962. Kirk, Ruth. The Olympic Natural History Association. Covers in detail Washington's beautiful coastline.

Common Seashore Life of the Pacific Northwest, 1962. Smith, Lynwood. Naturegraph Co, Healdsburg, CA. Covers starfish, crabs, clams, and other seas animals.

A Pictorial History of Sea Monsters and Other Dangerous Marine Life, 1972. Sweeney, James B. Crown Publishers, New York.

MISCELLANEOUS

Climates of The States, 1974. Water Information Center, Inc, New York. Everything you ever wanted to know about weather, two volumes.

Backpacking One Step At A Time, 1980. Manning, Harvey. Vintage Books, New York. A basic guide to backpacking.

The Freedom of The Hills, 1982. Peters, Ed. The Mountaineers, Seattle. Tips and techniques on snow travel, rock climbing, first aid, etc.

Washington Almanac, 1988. Evergreen Publishing, Seattle. Facts, recipes, and folklore about Washington.

Washington Handbook, 1989. Moon Publications, Chino, CA. Covers in detail Washingtons sights, sounds, and attractions.

Washington State Yearbook: A Guide to Government in the Evergreen State, 1990. The Information Press, Eugene, OR. Covers in detail everything you ever wanted to know about government in Washington State. Published yearly.

Almanac of Washington, 1990. The Information Press, Eugene, OR. Covers the economic and demographics of Washington State. Has many excellent charts and graphs.

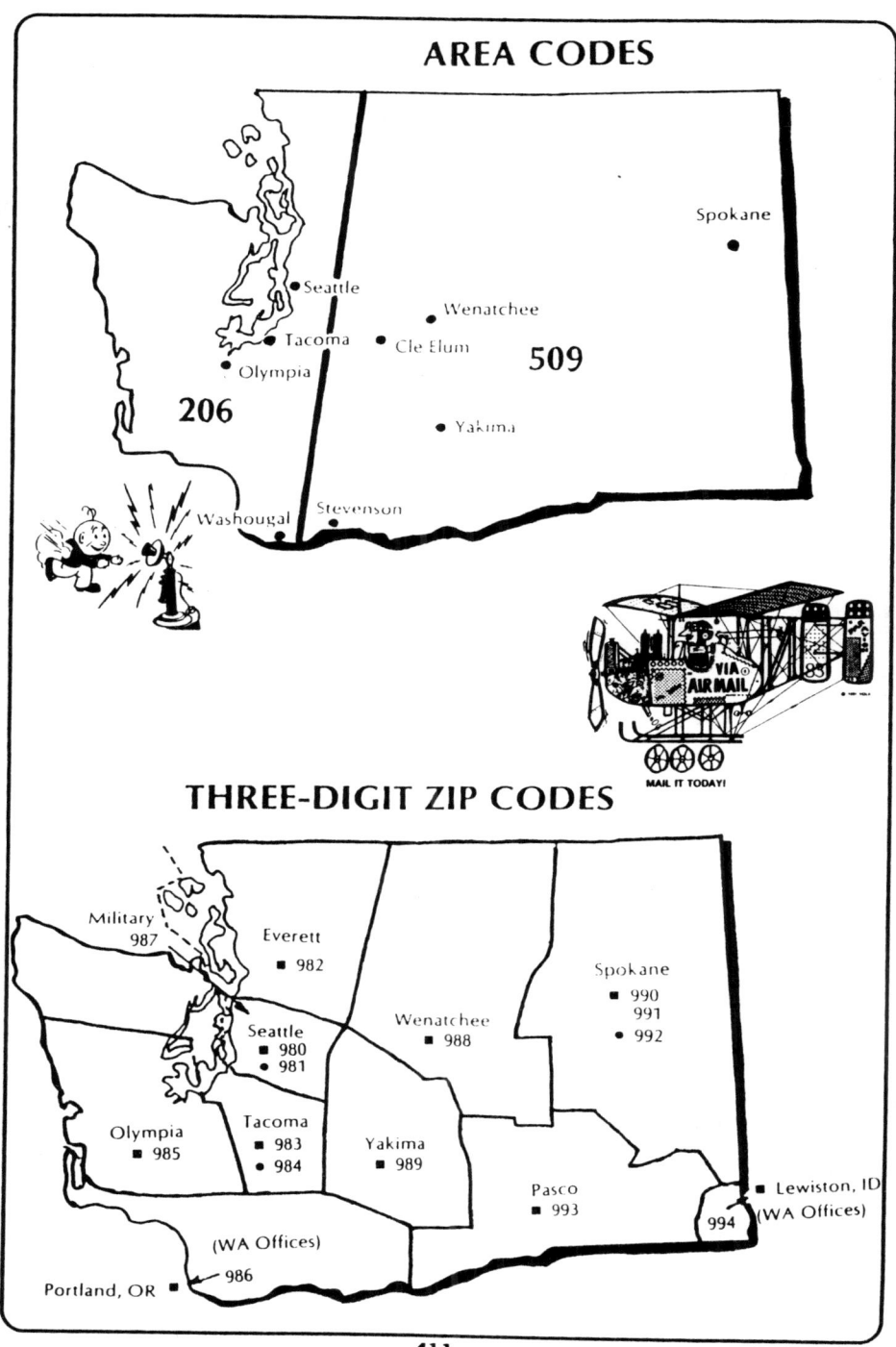

AREA CODES

206

509

THREE-DIGIT ZIP CODES

AIRPORTS

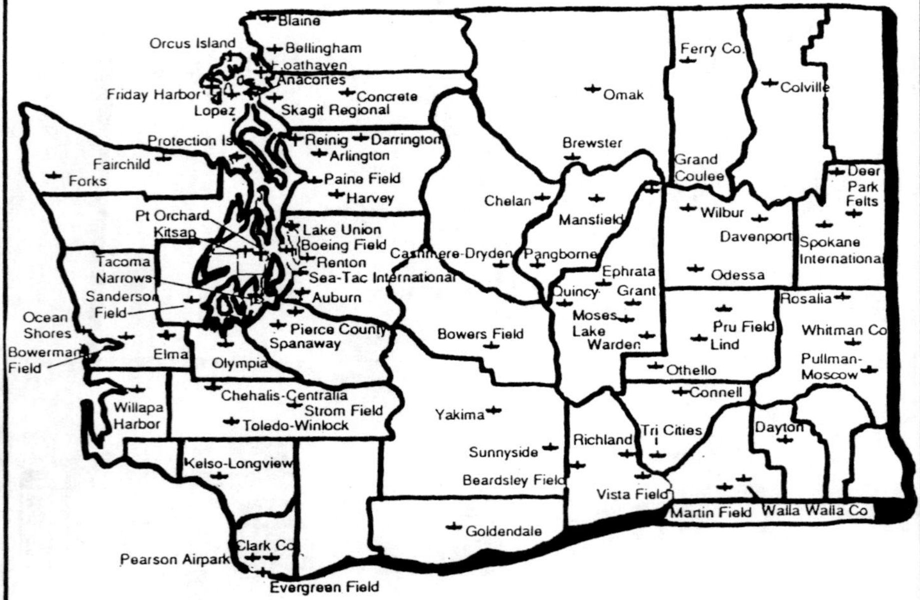

Blaine
Orcus Island
Bellingham
Loathaven
Friday Harbor
Anacortes
Lopez
Concrete
Skagit Regional
Protection Is
Reinig Darrington
Arlington
Fairchild
Forks
Paine Field
Harvey
Pt Orchard
Kitsap
Lake Union
Boeing Field
Tacoma
Narrows
Renton
Sea-Tac International
Sanderson
Field
Auburn
Ocean
Shores
Pierce County
Spanaway
Bowerman
Field
Elma
Olympia
Chehalis-Centralia
Strom Field
Willapa
Harbor
Toledo-Winlock
Kelso-Longview
Clark Co
Pearson Airpark
Evergreen Field

Omak
Colville
Ferry Co.
Brewster
Grand
Coulee
Deer
Park
Felts
Chelan
Mansfield
Wilbur
Cashmere-Dryden Pangborne
Davenport
Spokane
International
Ephrata
Grant
Odessa
Quincy
Moses
Lake
Warden
Rosalia
Bowers Field
Pru Field
Lind
Whitman Co
Othello
Pullman-
Moscow
Connell
Yakima
Tri Cities
Dayton
Sunnyside
Richland
Beardsley Field
Vista Field
Martin Field Walla Walla Co
Goldendale

SEATTLE–TACOMA
INTERNATIONAL AIRPORT

Located 13 miles from downtown Seattle off of Interstate 5.
Following is a listing of some of the carriers that serve
SEA-TAC

Alaska	1-800-426-0333	Markair	1-800-426-6784
American West	1-800-247-5692	Mexicana	1-800-531-7921
American	1-800-223-5436	Northwest	1-800-225-2525
Canadian	1-800-426-7000	Pan American	1-800-221-1111
Delta	1-800-221-1212	Scandinavian	1-800-221-2350
Eastern	1-800-EASTERN	Thai	1-800-426-5204
Finnair	1-800-950-5000	TWA	1-800-221-2000
Hawaiian Air	1-800-367-5320	United	1-800-241-6522
Horizon	1-800-547-9308	United Exp.	1-800-241-6522
Japan Air	1-800-525-3663	US Air	1-800-428-4322

HIGHWAY DISTANCES

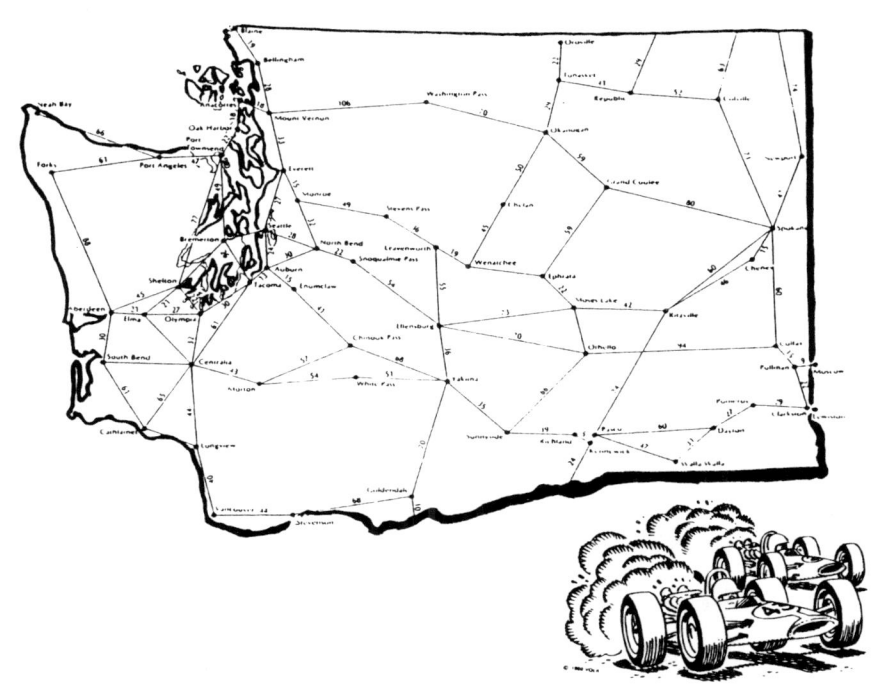

Driving Distances

(in miles)

Aberdeen																							
197	Bellingham																						
81	89	Bremerton																					
396	395	306	Clarkston																				
197	182	107	199	Ellensburg																			
137	60	29	335	122	Everett																		
245	288	212	240	106	228	Goldendale																	
316	277	227	189	120	217	219	Grand Coolee																
95	214	120	375	203	154	149	323	Kelso															
267	253	177	154	69	192	171	73	268	Moses Lake														
170	27	62	368	155	35	261	250	187	224	Mount Vernon													
416	392	326	158	218	332	294	132	405	153	360	Newport												
327	267	222	247	156	207	260	58	337	111	240	190	Okanogan											
49	148	56	347	147	88	215	267	66	218	121	365	271	Olympia										
290	289	214	127	107	229	113	143	247	65	262	182	181	261	Pasco									
125	115	76	380	181	82	286	295	183	251	91	395	281	120	288	Port Angeles								
376	359	284	35	177	299	242	154	356	133	332	123	212	327	129	358	Pullman							
108	89	Ferry	306	107	29	212	227	125	177	62	326	222	59	214	74	284	Seattle						
389	345	278	111	171	285	247	85	353	105	318	47	143	318	134	352	76	278	Spokane					
77	120	33	319	119	60	225	239	96	189	93	339	243	28	228	109	300	31	292	Tacoma				
134	252	160	337	217	192	111	330	38	282	225	389	371	104	209	224	338	163	342	132	Vancouver			
335	335	260	98	153	275	159	188	293	115	308	205	227	307	46	334	114	260	158	276	255	Walla Walla		
237	182	135	220	71	122	175	95	255	66	153	210	91	187	135	197	159	138	165	159	288	181	Wenatchee	
204	219	144	212	37	155	69	150	166	102	192	239	191	175	86	220	190	144	192	156	180	132	106	Yakima

413

WASHINGTON FERRY SYSTEM

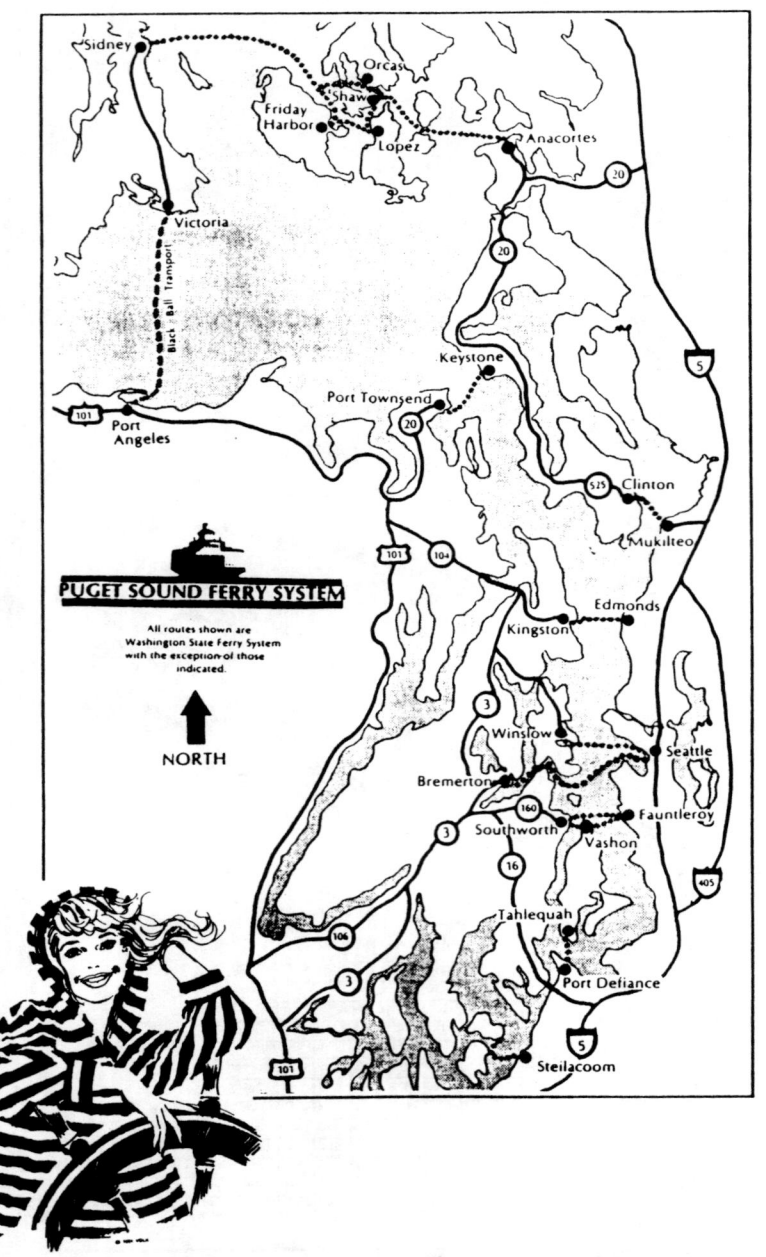

SKI AND SNOW REPORTS

SKI-PAK INTERNATIONAL
13400 Northup Way, Bellevue
98005 (206)644-8888

MT BAKER SKI REPORT
2009 Iron, Bellingham 98225
(206)671-0211

SKI REPORT
Centralia 98531
(206)736-7141

BLUEWOOD SKI LINE
116 N 3rd, Dayton 99328
(509)382-2877

SKI REPORT
Longview 98632
(206)423-2754

ALPENTAL-SKI ACRES
Mercer Island 98040
(206)236-1600

SKI REPORT
Mt Vernon 98273
(206)336-3542

LOOP LOOP SKI BOWL
POB 1686, Omak 98841
(509)826-2720

BLUEWOOD SKI LINE
Pasco 99301
(509)545-6651

KONA AM-FM RADIO
2823 W Lewis, Pasco 99301
(509)547-1123

CASCADE SKI REPORT
4556 University Way NE
Seattle 98105 (206)634-0200

CROSS COUNTRY SKI REPORT
903 NE 45th, Seattle 98105
(206)632-7787

MT HOOD SKI REPORT
903 NE 45th, Seattle 98105
(206)632-7799

NORTHWEST SKI REPORT
903 NE 45th, Seattle 98105
(206)634-0071

SUN VALLEY SKI REPORT
903 NE 45th, Seattle 98105
(206)633-4005

WHISTLER/BLACKCOMB SKI
903 NE 45th, Seattle 98105
(206)634-2226

SCHWEITZER SKI
W 216 Park Pl, Spokane 99205
(509)328-5632

SKI BC
N 9304 Newport Hwy
Sopkane 99218 (509)483-1150

CASCADE SKI REPORT
823 Pacific Ave, Tacoma
98402 (206)572-4300

BLUEWOOD SKI LINE
Walla Walla 99362
(509)529-9685

CASCADE SKI REPORT
Pasco Hwy, Walla Walla 99362
(509)529-7500

SKI REPORT
Walla Walla 99362
(509)525-8651

CASCADE SKI REPORT
Riverside Rd, Yakima 98901
(509)248-6966

skiing centers and resorts

BEAR MOUNTAIN MGMT, INC.
808 106th NE, Bellevue 98004
(206)453-5785

MINI MOUNTAIN SKI CENTER
1900 132nd NE, Bellevue
98005 (206)746-7547

SNO PAK
13400 Northup Way
Bellevue 98005 (206)747-9903

MT BAKER RECREATION CENTER
1017 Iowa, Bellingham 98226
(206)734-8771

SALMON RIDGE CROSS-COUNTRY
SKI, 1515 Cornwall Ave,
Bellingham 98225
(206)671-4615

INDEX

A

Aberdeen, 378
Abuse, substance (see indiv county)
Accupuncture, 57
Accupuncturists, 58
Adams County, 158
Aerospace, 7
Age, 4
Agriculture, 7,8
AIDS, (see indiv county)
AIDS Hotline, 205
Airports, 412
Alcohol, treatment, (see indiv county)
Amanda Park, 379
Anacortes, 260
Apartment, finding service, 30-33
Apples, 243
Apprenticeship, trng, 74
Area codes, 411
Arlington, 260
Arts, performing, 5
Asotin, city, 154, county 162
Auburn, city, 288
Auctions, 22, 105

B

Bainbridge Island, 379
Banks, 103
Barter, 102
Battle Ground, 348
Bears, grizzly 380
Bed and Breakfasts, 115-121
Bellevue, 289
Bellingham, 260
Benton, city, 154, county 165
Big Bend, 155
Bingen, 242
Birch Bay, 261
Blaine, 261
Boats, 5
Boeing, 261
Books, 407
Bothell, 289
Bread, 288
Bremerton, 379
Bridgeport, 218
Brewster, 218

Buckley, 324
Business, development centers, 55-56
Business, home, 51
Burlington, 261
Burlington Northern RR Tunnel, 290

C

Camano Island, 261
Camas, 349
Cascade mountains, 3
Cashmere, 218
Castle Rock, 349
Cathlamet, 349
Centralia, 350
Chataugua, 191
Cheese, The Wash Co, 261
Chehalis, 350
Chelan, city 218, county, 222, lake 218,
Cheney, 188, Discovery Center 325
Chewelah, 188
Children services, 143
Christmas tree capitol, 382
Churches, Wash Assoc Of 75
City-county reference list, 403-405
Clallam Bay, 379
Clallam county, 383
Clams, 324
Clark county, 353
Clarkston, 154
Cle Elum, 242
Clinton, 264
Climate, 3, (see indiv county)
Clothing, (see indiv county)
Cochran, James C., 351
Coffee grinders, 348
Colleges, 68-71
Colfax, 154
Columbia Center, 261 county 169, river 155, 156
Colville, 188
Commencement Bay, 325
Conconully, 219
Concrete, 261

Congressional reps, 13-15
Connell, 154
Copalis Bay, 379,
Cost of living, 9
Corrections, Dept Of, 99
Cougar, 349
Coulee City, 219
Counties, map, 150

Couperville, 264
Court, district,
juvenile, superior, (see
indiv county), small
claims, 91
Cowlitz, county 357
Creston, 188
Crime, 97
Crisis, (see indiv
county)
Crossing 379

D
Darrington, 261
Davenport, 189
Daycare, (see indiv
county)
Dayton, 154
Deer Park, 189
Dental (see indiv
county)
Des Monies, 289
Divorce, 95
Douglas county, 227

E
East Wenatchee, 219
Eastonville, 325
Economic Development,
Dept Of, 54
Economy, 7,8
Edmonds, 261
Education, 5,65, aid 66
Elk, 243
Ellensburg, 242
Elma, 380
Employment, 8,35,66
Employers, largest by
county, 40-50
Employment, Security
Dept, 139
Employment, training (see
indiv county)
Enchanted Village, 290
Enumclaw, 289
Ephrata, 219
Everett, 261

F
Fairs, (see festivals)
Fantasy Land, 6
Fairfield, 189
Family planning, (see
indiv county)
Farmland, 18
Federal Way, 289
Ferndale, 262
Ferry county, 192
Ferry System, 414
Festivals:
Air Fair, Wash State
Int'l, 264
Antique Show, 244
Apple Blossom Festival,
221
Arts and Crafts Festival,
264
Bald Eagle Days, 352
Benton-Franklin County
Fair, 157
Bluegrass County
Festival, Columbia Gorge,
352
Bloomsday Run, 191
Bumbershoot Arts
Festival, 294
Capitol Lakefair, 326
Columbia Cup for
unlimited Hydroplanes,
157
Community Days, 244
Cranberry Festival, 352
Daffodil Festival, 326
Dayton, Days, 157
Deutsches Fest, 191
Festival of Lights, 382
Festival at the Depot,
157
Folklife Festival, 294
Forest Festival, 382
Fort Vancouver Days, 352
Fort Walla Walla Museum
Mountain Man Rendezvous,
157
Freeze Ye Buns Race,
Twisp, 221
Grays Harbor County Fair,
382
Harbor Days, 326
Historic Homes Tours, 382
Hot Air Balloon Stampede,
157
Interstate Fair, 191
Irrigation Festival, 382
Jazz Festival, 294
Jazz Festival, Gig Harbor
326

King County Fair, 294
Kite Festival Int'l, 352
Kittitas County Fair, 244
Library Fair, Orcas
Island, 264
Lilac Festival, 191
Lilac Week, 352
Loggerodeo, 264
Logger's Jubilee, 352
Loon's Day Walk, 191
Maifest, 221
Marymoor Festival, 294
Mayfest, 244
Memorial Day Festival,
221
Moses Lake Spring
Festival, 221
Mount St. Helens
Anniversary, 352
Mystery Weekend, 264
National Lentil Festival,
157
Okanogan Hot Air Balloon
Rendezvous, 221
Old Time Music Festival,
326
Omak Stampede and Suicide
Race, 221
Pacific Northwest Arts
and Crafts Fair, 294
Pierce County Fair, 326
Pioneer Days, 191
Poker Paddle, 191
Poulsbo Viking Fest, 382
Prairie Days, 326
Prospectors Days,
Republic, 191
Quincy Farmer Consumer
Awareness Day, 221
Regatta, Annual Whidbey
Island, 264
Rendezvous Days,
Colville, 191
Rhododendron Festival,
382
Run to Roslyn Antique Car
Show, 244
Sage N' Sunfest, 221
Salmon Days, 294
Salmon Derby Days, 382
San Juan County Fair, 264
Seafair, 294
Ski to Sea, 264
Sound to Narrows Race,
326
Speelyi-Mi Arts and Crafts
Trade Fair, 244
Strawberry Festival, 294
Summerfest, 352

Sunfest Downriver
Bluegrass Festival, 157
Taste of Edmonds, 264
Taste of Tacoma, 326
Thunder Mountain Rodeo,
352
Tri-Cities Int'l Air
Show, 157
Tulip Festival, Skagit
Valley, 264
Waterland Festival, 294
West Coast Oyster
Shucking Championship,
382
Western Art Show and
Auction, 244
Western Wash Fair, 326
Wine and Food Fair, 157
Wine and Food Fest, 244
Yakima Valley Air Fair,
244

Fife, 325
Fishing, 378
Fireworks, 351
Folks, 380
Food, (see indiv county)
Franklin county, 172
Freeland, 264
Friday Harbor, 263
Frontier Western Museum,
324

G
Garfield, 154
Garfield county, 176
GED testing, (see indiv
county)
General Services Admin,
(GSA), 22,23

Geoduck clams, 324
Geography, 3
Gig Harbor, 325
Glacier, 262
Glenwood, 242
Gold, 7
Goldendale Observatory,
243
Goldendale/Status Pass,
242
Grand Coulee Dam Area,
219
Grandview, 243
Grant county, 231
Grays Harbor county, 387
Greenbank, 264

H

Hahnemann, Samuel, 57
Hanford, 156
Hansville, 380
Harrington, 189
Hart's Pass, 221
Health, Dept Of Social
and Health Services, 142
plan of Washington, 63
(see indiv county)
Highway, 101,379,
distances 413
Homesteading, urban 21-22
Homoeopathy, 57
Hospitals (see indiv
county)
Housing, 4, state money
for 21, (see indiv
county)
Hoquiam, 380
HUD, 21
Humptulips, 380
Husum, 243
Hutterities, The, 188

I

Ilwaco, 349
Immunizations, (see indiv
county)
Improvement trng, 73-74
Income, personal 7, by
county 17-18
Indians, 133, tribes
134-135, reservations
map, 135
Inland Empire, 190
Ione, 189
Island county, 265

J

Jackson, John R, 350
Jefferson county, 392
Job, finding 35, service
centers 39, Training
Partnership Act 144
Judges, (see indiv
county)

K

Kalalock, 380
Kalama, 349
Kalso, 349
Kennewick, 155
Kent, 290
Kettle Falls, 189
King county, 295
Kingdome, 292
Kingston, 380
Kitsap county, 395

Kittitas county, 245
Klickitat county, 248
Klondike, 7, Gold Rush
National Park 288

L

Lacey, 324
La Conner, 262
Lake Stevens, 261
Landlord, Tenant Act
23-30
Langley, 264
Laser, light show 219
Leavenworth, 219
Legal, 91
Legal (see indiv county)
Lewis county, 361
Liberty Bell Mountain,
264
Licensing, Dept Of, 54
Lincoln, Abraham, 381,
county 195
Long Beach Peninsula, 349
Longview, 349
Loop, The 379
Lopez Island, 263
Lyle, 243
Lynden, 262
Lynnwood, 262

M

Marblemount, 262
Marriage, 94
Maple Valley, 290
Marysville, 262
Mason county, 399
Mattawa, 219
Media, 77
Medicine, holistic, 57
practitioners, 61
services, 143
Mental, counseling, (see
indiv county)
Mercer Island, 290
Metaline, 189
Military, 137
Moclips, 380
Monroe, 263
Moosyrock, 350
Montesano, 380
Moses Lake, 219
Mount Vernon, 263
Mountain passes, 260
Morton, 350
Museums, 123-129
(see indiv regions)
McCleary, 380

N

Never, Never Land, 6,326
Newspapers, dailies, 86
Newport, 189
North Bend, 290
North Central Region, 217
Northeast Region, 187
Northwest Region, 259

O

Oakharbor, 264
Oaksdale, 154
Odessa, 189
Ocean City, 380
Ocean Park, 350
Ocean Shores, 380
Officials, elected, 11
Okanogan, 219, county 236
Olympia, 1,324
Olympia Peninsula Region 377
Orcas Island, 263
Oroville, 219
Othello, 154

P

Pacific Beach, 381
Pacific County, 366
Pacific Rim, 7,8
Palouse,154
Palouse, The, 190
Panorama, the land, 189
Pantages Theatre, 324

Paralegals, 93
Parks, 131
Partnership, general, limited, 52
Pasco, 156
Passes, mountain 260
Pateros, 219
Patriarches, The Grove Of, 325
Pend Oreille county, 198
Phone numbers, toll-free, 147-148
Pierce county, 327
Pike Place Market, 291
Point Defiance Park, 326
Point Roberts, 263
Political parties, 16
Pomeroy, 154
Population, 1,8,(also see indiv county)
Port Angeles, 381
Port Orchard, 381
Producers, Motion Picture 88-90

Property, unclaimed, 106
values 19
Proprietorship, sole 52
Prosser, 154
Protection Island, 380
Psychotherapy, (see indiv county)
Pullman, 154, George 155
Puyallup, 325

Q

Quinault, 382
Quincy, 219

R

Radio stations, 78-86
Rainbow Bridge, 262
Rape, relief (see indiv county)
Redmond, 290
Refexology, 58
Reflexologists, 62
Religious denominations, 75-76
Renton, 291
Republic, 189
Resume, 36-38
Retirement, 9
Rhododendron, Species Foundation Garden, 289
Richland, 156
Ritzville, 155
Roche Harbor, 263
Rockefeller, John D., 261
Rodeo, Ellensburg, 242
Rosalia, 155
Royal City, 220

S

San Juan county, 268, Island 263
Scholarships, 66-67
School, proprietary 71, public (see indiv county)
Sea otters, 378
Sealed bid, 22
Seattle, 291-293, Center 293, King Region 287
Seattle-Tacoma Int'l Airport (SEATAC), 293,412
Sedro Woolley, 263
Selah, 243
Senators, US 12
Senior citizens, 9
Separation, marriage 94
Service Centers (see indiv county)
social, 139
Sequim, 382

Sheep, big horn, 189
Shelton, 382
Shopping, 101
Sightseeing tours, 111-114
Silverdale, 382
Skagit county, 271, Eagle Reserve 262
Skamania, 350, county 370
Ski reports, 415
Smith, Hiram F., 218
Smokey Point, 263
Snohomish, 263, county 275
Snoqualmie, 293
Snow reports, 415
Soap Lake, 220
South Bend, 350
South Central Region, 241
South Puget Sound Region, 323
Southeast Region, 153
Southwest Region, 347
Spokane, 189, county 201
Sports, 4
Sprague, 190
Standwood, 263
Steilcoom, 325
Stevens county, 213
Stevenson, 350
Studio, motion pictures, 88-90
Sultan, 263
Sunnyside, 243

T

Tacoma, 325, Dome 326
Tax, advantages 53, recordkeeping 54, property exemption 9, retail, property, business, occupation 10, per catita 19
Teapot, 244
Telegrams, singing 104
Telescope, 243
Television stations, 77-78
Tenancies, types 23
Tenant, 23-30
Thurston county, 341
Tokeland, 350
Toledo, 350
Tonasket, 220
Toppenish, 243
Totem Pole, 349
Tours, 111-114
Transportation, (see indiv county)

Travel, 111-114
Trend College, 256
Tri-Cities, 155
Trout Lake, 243
Tuition, 66-68
Tukwila, 294
Tutoring, 72
Twin Cities, 350
Twisp, 220

U

Unemployment, 7, by county 17
Union Gap, 243
Universities, 68-71

V

Vancouver, 351
Veterans, 9, Affairs Dept Of 144, services (see indiv county)
Victims, (see indiv county)

W

Waitsburg, 156
Wahkiakum county, 373
Walla Walla, 156, county 182
Wapato, 243
Waterslides, 6
Waterville, 220
Wenatchee, 220
Westport, 382
Whales, killer 263
Whatcom county, 283
Whidbey Island, 264

Whitman county, 179, Marcus 157
White Salmon, 243
Wilber, 190
Wildlife refuge, 219, Grays Harbor 379
Wine, wineries 107-109
Winthrop, 221
Wolves, 326
Wonderland Trail, 262
Woodland, 352
Worship, 75

Y

Yakima, 244, county 252

Z

Zillah, 244
Zip codes, 411

NOTES

ORDER FORM

Did You Borrow This Book?

There is nothing like owning your own personal copy of **The Unique Inside Guide To Washington State.** Then you can make notes in it and refer to it whenever you need to. To order your personal copy, simply complete the form below, or phone us at (509) 962-3078 to place purchase on your order.

_____ Yes, I'd like_____ copies of The Inside Guide To Washington State.

NAME_____

SIGNATURE_____PHONE (   )_____

ADDRESS_____

CITY/STATE/ZIP_____

The cost is: $19.95 per book. Please add $2.00 for the first book, and 75¢ for each additional book for postage and handling. Washington State residents include $1.10 per book for state sales tax. Note: Canadian orders must be accompanied by a postal money order in U.S. funds.

_____Check or money order enclosed

BULK ORDERS INVITED

For bulk quantity discounts or special handing, please phone (509) 962-3078.

Make your check or money order payable to:

**THE EVERGREEN PRESS
Post Office Box 83
Ellensburg, WA 98926-0083**